NO TIDES TO STEM

VOLUME 3

A HISTORY
OF THE
MANCHESTER PILOT SERVICE
1894 - 1994

by
DEREK A CLULOW

The painting on the front cover, entitled
"PASSING WESTON POINT LOCKS OUTWARD BOUND"
was by the late Mr. W. (Bill) Yates, Pilot First Class and
reproduced by kind permission of his wife Mrs. D. Yates

First published 2001 by Countyvise Limited, 14 Appin Road, Birkenhead, Wirral, Merseyside CH41 9HH in conjunction with the author Derek A. Clulow

British Library Cataloguing in Publication Data.
A catalogue record for this book is available from the British Library.

ISBN 1 901231 23 2

TO

My very dear wife, "Tulip", who for 35 years has suffered silently the unsocial hours of my profession, listened patiently to my endless Accident Reports, mended willingly my broken body from football, helped unfailingly to "dry" me out from time to time and yet through all this, never stopped loving me.

The Author
Manchester Ship Canal Pilot Service
1954 - 1988

Acknowledgements

The longer the task of writing the history of the MANCHESTER SHIP CANAL PILOT SERVICE has been put off, the greater the work of the historian, who will find records get destroyed, the older generation passes on, memories fade and facts blend into legends. In writing this history I found no exception to this rule.

First and foremost, in writing this acknowledgement I must express my deep sense of gratitude to Mrs Jean Capper whose unstinting offer to give up her much loved leisure time to transfer my - at times illegible writings in longhand - words to paper by way of the typewriter. Without Jean's help and happy disposition through these long years - five in all - I could not have ever finished this history of the Pilot Service. With no less a sense of gratitude I sincerely thank Adrian Wood and Graeham and Fran Hulbert for their invaluable contribution in editing and correcting the manuscripts, a task of no mean feat and gratefully appreciated. A special thank you to Mrs Yates for her patience and forbearance with me whilst lending me her late husband's (Mr W (Bill) Yates, Pilot First Class) voluminous photographic and work records which he so painstakingly collected and kept for posterity and for her kind permission for me to use the superb paintings by her late husband of scenes on the Canal especially the one that adorns the jacket of this book.

I shall always be grateful to Miss M Patch and her staff at the Greater Manchester Council County Records Office for their unfailing courtesy and assistance so readily given to me during my researching at that establishment. To Mr David Thornley, ex PRO of the old Manchester Ship Canal Company, very many thanks for allowing me to browse through the hundreds of photographs in the archives thus preserving an era that has gone for ever. To all the Pilots' widows who so kindly lent me their treasured photographs of their loved ones so that they may be ever remembered in the pages of this book, my thanks to you all.

Finally, if I have forgotten to acknowledge anyone from the list below please forgive me, there have been so many and some are bound to be overlooked.

Mr H G Pringle)	
Mr M E Warren)	
Mr J H Warren,)	Manchester Ship Canal Pilots
Mr A E Cooke)	
Mr P K Rali)	
Mr G Collins	
Mr J Southwood,	River Dee Pilot
Mr H Thelwell,	Ex Pilots Clerk
Mr Gib Jackson,	Engineering Department, Manchester Ship Canal
Mrs D Marten)	
Mrs Jan Lemon,)	Pilots National Pension Fund
Mrs Sweet)	
Mr Alan Green,	Liverpool Pilot
Mr Peter Lamey	
Mr H Milsom,	Editor, "Sea Breezes"
Mr A Potts,	Privy Council Office, Whitehall
Mr J Pepper,	Department of Transport
Mr B K Phillips,	Public Record Office, Richmond, Surrey
Mr J Allan,	General Council of British Shipping
Mr S K Conacher,	General Council of British Shipping
Mr P Dunbavand,	Captain, Manchester Ship Canal Tug Servvice
Captain D W Jones, Inspector, Board of Trade	"Dalmor", Nefyn, Gwynedd.
Captain R Kilby-Lennon,	ex Master "Hemsley 1"
Captain G Cubbins,	T & J Harrisons, Liverpool
F Armitt & Son,	Shipping Agents, Liverpool
HM Tax Inspectors,	Head Office, London
British Rail,	National Railway Museum, York
Whitbreads Brewery	
Maritime Musuem,	Albert Dock, Liverpool
Mr E Morrison,	ex Pilot Clerk
Arthur Guinness, Son & Co (Dublin) Ltd	
Mr R A Jamieson,	Archives Assistant, British Waterways, Gloucester
Central Library, Manchester	
Mrs J J Pierpoint	
Mrs J Lang,	Currie (Business Equipment) Ltd, Birkenhead
Merseyside Transport Ltd	
Mrs G Cartwright	
Mr C Parsons,	World Ship Society
John Mills Photography Ltd., Liverpool	
Mr John Young and family	
Bernard Watson Photography, Wirral	

Contents

Contents

All that mankind has done, thought, gained or been: it is lying as in magic preservation in the pages of books.

Thomas Carlyle

The beginning is the most important part of the work.

Plato

1

CANAL PILOT STATIONS

No-one can deny the construction of the Manchester Ship Canal and creation of the first major inland port was indeed the most futuristic idea ever devised in the United Kingdom. But in all the building that went into this project, locks, bridges, docks, quays, lock masters' houses, custom houses, etc, no-one at any time had thought of the need to build accommodation for a future Pilot Service. One must assume the planners of that day thought the River Pilots would be the future pilot service and therefore there was no need to provide pilot station accommodation. However, this was not so, a Manchester Pilot Service was formed in 1894, unaffiliated to the River Pilots. Pilot Stations were proposed and accepted at Dukes Dock (Liverpool), Eastham Locks, Runcorn, Partington and Manchester, without a building of any shape or size, provided for the exclusive use of the Manchester Pilot Service.

The very first reference of any Ship Canal Pilots' accommodation was made at the Pilotage Committee held in May 1896 when it was agreed that they should pay to the Bridgewater Department a sum of 5s 0d (25p) per annum as an acknowledgement for the privilege of the Canal Pilots being allowed to use a shelter on Dukes Dock - this was south of the Canning Dock Entrance, Liverpool, for the purpose of going to or landing from a vessel piloted by them. In those days it was not an uncommon practice for Canal Pilots to join or leave vessels in the River.

In the year 1896 the only road leading down to Eastham Locks (Ferry Road) was a hive of activity, for not only did it lead to Eastham Locks but more importantly to Eastham Ferry Pier. From there frequent sailings were made

1896

Courtesy of Mr G (Gib) Jackson

The busy Eastham Ferry Road. The Pilots first accommodation on the left. "The Regent Rooms" or "Hankinsons Cafe"

by elegant Ferry boats to Liverpool via Rock Ferry and Birkenhead, Woodside. The last quarter of a mile of Ferry Road was the trading area where numerous shops had become well established including a butchers, greengrocer, sweet and tobacconist, a large covered bicycle stand 2d (1p) per day or part thereof, a cobbler and various tea rooms. One of these tea rooms was owned by Mr W G Pearson who boasted a private field for sports and where he catered for day school and Sunday school treats.

At the end of these shops stood the magnificent Eastham Ferry Hotel with its marvellous botanical and zoological gardens and priding itself as having the finest oak sprung floor ballroom in the whole of the north of England. Three private houses also catered for bed and breakfast for those travellers who could not afford the luxury of the Eastham Ferry Hotel, whose tariff was 1s 6d (7 ½p) per night, breakfast included. The "Jewel in the Crown" as far as the Canal Pilots was concerned was a large tea room named *Hankinsons*. From 1896 to 1901 it became the unofficial Canal Pilots' accommodation at Eastham. The Canal Pilots had negotiated a tariff with the proprietor of 6d (2 ½p) per night for the privilege of sleeping either on chairs or on the floor of the tea rooms between the hours of 10pm and 6am. Whilst awaiting the arrival of vessels at Eastham Locks the Pilots took advantage of what was then a fairly extensive menu.

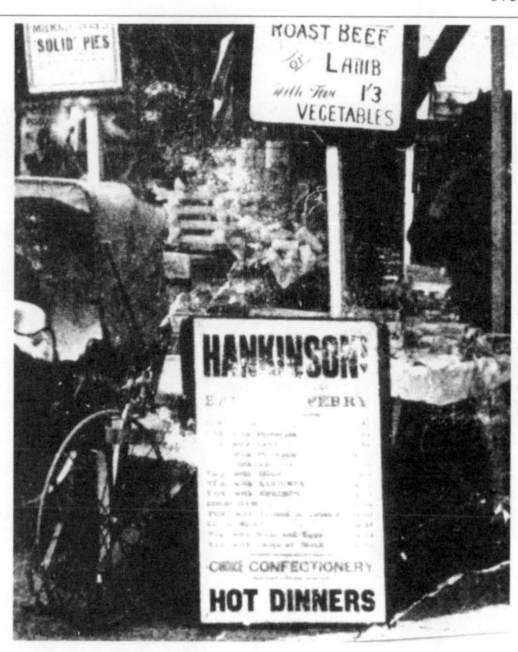

1896

Courtesy of Mr G (Gib) Jackson

Close-up picture of the Menu outside the Regent Rooms. Note the pram and what are "Solid Pies"

Roast Beef or Lamb dinner with two vegetables	1s 3d (6p)
Tea with Eggs	9d (4p)
Tea with Sardines	1s 0d (5p)
Tea with Shrimps	1s 0d (5p)
Tea with Cold Ham	1s 3d (6p)
Tea with Assorted Cold Meats	1s 3d (6p)
Tea with Ham and Eggs	1s 6d (7 ½p)
Tea with Chips and Steak	2s 0d (10p)

All the above meals were accompanied with unlimited fresh bread and butter.

It was not until 3rd October 1901 that any overtures were made by the Canal Pilots to the Pilotage Committee regarding the obtaining of some form of permanent accommodation at Eastham. A letter from Mr P Sinnot (Pilots Representative) was submitted to the Chairman of the Pilotage Committee for him to deal with as he might think desirable.

1900
Courtesy of Mr Gib Jackson
Eastham Ferry Hotel. The second accommodation for Manchester Pilots.

1930
Eastham Ferry Hotel and Gardens Archway at the height of its elegance. All Manchester Pilots were prevented from staying there in 1931
Courtesy of Mr Gib Jackson

"Will you kindly put the following request before your committee for their consideration. The River Pilots have a room at Eastham Locks to shelter in when waiting for their vessels, the Canal Pilots have none. There is a spare room in that building with a fire grate, would you kindly try to grant the Canal Pilots the liberty of using this room as the winter is coming on. Trusting this request will result favourably as it is much needed."

By 8th December 1901 all arrangements had been made for the Canal Pilots to have the use of a room in the Canal Company building known as the Custom House on Eastham Lock, in which building the River Pilots were also provided with a room. The River Pilots and the Canal Pilots entered into an agreement with the Canal Company with regard to the rent payable for such accommodation. This arrangement lasted until 20th February 1904 when at Pilotage Committee the Chairman stated that the room at Eastham which had been set aside for the explicit use of the Canal Pilots had not been made use of. The Canal Company had received notice from Messrs Stuart and Ellis (Pilots' Representatives) who had entered into an agreement with them as to the payment of the rent of the room. They declined to have anything further to do with the matter because the Pilot Association for which they had acted at the time had now been dissolved. Under these circumstances the Chairman decided to cancel the agreement for the use of the room and it would therefore not be available for the use of Canal Pilots.

Some Pilots returned to *Hankinsons* tea room while others negotiated a tariff of 9d (4p) per night, without breakfast, at one of the bed and breakfast houses in Ferry Road. In May 1908 at the Pilotage Committee Meeting the Pilots' representative (Mr H Boxer-Jones) suggested that accommodation should be provided for Canal Pilots on the Canal Company property at Eastham, for at present there was no such accommodation. The Chairman stated that as long ago as December 1901 and again in February 1904 this matter had been discussed at Committee level. He further stated that the provision of such accommodation was not a matter for this Committee but for the Manchester Ship Canal Company who had already provided a room for the River Pilots, such Pilots having undertaken to keep the place clean and in proper order.

Mr Latimer promised that if the Pilots would themselves elect a Committee to take charge of a room at Eastham Locks, look after any furniture which the Canal Company might provide and keep the place clean, paying the expenses thereof, the Canal Company would find a room and fit same out for the Canal Pilots' use. Mr Jones replied that he thought his fellow Pilots would be glad to form a Committee to deal with this matter on the lines suggested and would pursue the question of accommodation.

After divers meetings with the General Superintendent of the Canal Company and with his own Pilots' Association on 1st September 1908, Mr Jones finally obtained accommodation on Eastham Locks. One room was to be provided by the Canal Company on the second floor of a building known as the Old Boiler House for the sole use of Canal Pilots. At the same time the Helmsmen were allocated one room for their sole use on the ground floor in the same building. This was the first time any accommodation had been provided for them by the Canal Company.

The next decade saw the pilots apparently happily ensconced on Eastham Locks, but at the April 1918 Pilotage Committee Meeting the Chairman reported that complaints had been made that the Canal Pilots' room at Eastham was in a very dirty condition. The Pilots' representatives admitted that this was so and said that a number of the Pilots had refused to do their share towards the cleaning of the room with the result it had become very neglected. The Chairman reminded the Pilots' representatives that they were responsible for keeping the room in a proper condition and in that respect he would send a letter to the Secretary of the Pilots' Association reminding him of this obligation. The condition of the accommodation arose from some Pilots refusing to honour their responsibilities on the rota for keeping the accommodation clean. At a Pilots' Association meeting it was clearly agreed that all Pilots using the accommodation would be responsible for its general upkeep. Some Pilots had interpreted the wording "use of room" to mean to have slept in the room and therefore felt they had no obligation to its cleanliness, although they cheerfully utilised the room at all other times.

In December 1920 the Canal Pilots' accommodation was transferred to the Custom House. H M Customs moved into a new purpose built office - a large two storied building with an observation point in the roof. They occupied two rooms on the second floor. The ground floor rooms were divided equally between the River Pilots and the Helmsmen. The rooms were large but extremely sparsely furnished. The Canal Pilots sleeping room was found to be inadequate for their requirements, there being only five berths, one of which was found to be unusable due to draughts. In accordance with the desire of the Canal Pilots for further accommodation to be provided at Eastham, in April 1921 Captain Acraman (Canal Superintendent) had met Mr Hindle (Secretary of the Pilots' Association) along with one of the company's engineers and agreed on the following alterations:

Sleeping Room
Fitting 6 new bunks in position
Fitting 1 electric lamp
Fitting 2 new window blinds
Fitting 1 pane of glass in 9" window

General Room
Fitting 2 new window blinds
Two bunks to be removed to the sleeping room
Skirting boards to be repaired

I hardly think these renovations would have turned the Canal Pilots' accommodation into a suite at a Hilton Hotel - they still did not have an indoor toilet.

Between 1921 and 1935 many renovations and refinements were carried out including the addition of a fully fitted kitchen. An inside toilet was installed at the cost of £110 in June 1926. With the constant drain of these ever-increasing expenditures on the Pilot Fund a further deducation from the Pilots' earnings in 1935 had to be made to stabilise the Pilot Fund. At the Pilotage Committee

Meeting held in February 1944 the Chairman, Mr Leslie Roberts, reported that the Pilots' accommodation at Eastham had been recently examined by a Liverpool architect - Mr Barnish - and he had specially considered the condition of the ventilation and heating systems. The architect submitted certain proposals, which included the addition of accommodation and amenities which it was considered would make the building reasonably comfortable and efficient for its purpose and thus ensure the continued smooth working of the increased wartime shipping using the port.

The estimated cost of effecting these alterations would be £4,500 and the Pilots would be expected to make some contribution, but at the moment it was difficult to say to what extent; it was not intended that the pilots or the Authority should bear the whole cost. The Pilots' representatives said they would like to take this matter back to their Association Meeting. This was agreed upon and it was also arranged for a joint meeting of all parties at the Pilots' accommodation at Eastham to decide whether all the proposed alterations were necessary.

Eastham
Pilots' accommodation on the Canal Bank 1948-1952
Note: Outside toilets and bicycle shed

Eastham
Pilots' purpose-built accommodation 1952-1994

A meeting of all the interested parties was convened on 29th March 1944 at the Canal Pilots' accommodation and reported back to the Pilotage Committee Meeting held in April, stating that if the whole of the architect's plan could not be carried out, no good purpose would be served by attempting to do any portion of it. The Pilots' representatives made it quite clear that the Pilots were not prepared to pay anything towards the cost of the proposed alterations. The Chairman did not like the idea of spending money on a "patched up job" and thought that the erection of Nissan Huts would meet the Pilots' purpose. The Pilots agreed they would be more acceptable than the present unsatisfactory quarters. A compromise was eventually reached between the Pilots' representatives and the Canal Company with regard to the proposed alterations. It fell well short of the estimated expenditure of £4,000 to £5,000 but with all the wartime building restrictions and shortage of materials the original plans never really had any chance of success.

On a happier note in Autust 1944 the Pilots' Association submitted an application for one weeks holiday with pay for Mrs MacKenzie, the caretaker of their accommodation. The Pilotage Committee raised no objection and the application was granted. Mrs MacKenzie had been employed as the caretaker for the Pilots' accommodation since 1937 and this was the first time she had been granted a week's leave with pay or even a week's leave for that matter. "Mrs Mac" - as she was always affectionately known and called - gave 40 years of dedicated and uncomplaining service, seven days a week, to the Manchester Pilot Services comforts, retiring at the age of 76 in 1977. Mrs Mac died in September 1980.

On a humorous note, probably not to the Canal Pilots, the Pilots' representatives drew the attention of the Pilotage Committee in 1944 to the necessity of providing suitable covered bicycle storage accommodation for the Pilots' bicycles at Eastham; the matter was suitably dealt with.

A constant bone of contention with the Pilots was the antiquated heating system. This matter had been passed to the Engineers Department who took readings in what was considered to be the coldest room in the building, the Helmsmen's room on the ground floor - they could never win. The temperatures recorded had never been less than 60°F in the morning and never less than 61°F in the afternoon. This appeared to satisfy the Canal Company that the heating system was adequate to make the accommodation habitable at all times in the winter. The following year the problem of heating the Pilots' accommodation arose again when the firemen employed at the boiler house at Eastham were no longer required. Thus the boiler used for heating the Pilots' accommodation could not be kept going the following winter.
The Pilots had assumed the Canal Company would make the necessary arrangements for heating the rooms, for unless the rooms were properly heated they would become unhabitable. The Canal Company pointed out to the Pilots that their accommodation had been provided by them largely at their own expense, although there was no obligation upon them to do so but they did not think they should provide an official for the purpose of keeping the rooms heated. The Pilots were left to make their own arrangements to heat their accommodation. At the September Pilotage Committee Meeting the Pilots' Representatives announced that they were considering taking over the Pilot House, subject to the introduction of a Station Rate. They proposed that this rate should be at a more reasonable rate than operated in Liverpool as a Pilot Boat rate. They also requested permission to approach the Lockgatemen at Eastham in order to ascertain whether any of them would be prepared to attend to the stoking of the boiler in the Pilot House. This permission was granted.

The Pilots stated that any expense incurred in this respect would be met by their Association and also the Liverpool Pilots and Canal Helmsmen who had accommodation in the building. The problem was solved in November 1945 when arrangements were made for the stoking of the boiler at a cost of £2 per week. The River Pilots paid 10s.0d (50p) per week and the Helmsmen the same whilst the Canal Pilots paid £1 per week. Three years later the Pilot House was demolished, and all thoughts of a station rate with it, when the great reconstruction took place with the building of the Queen Elizabeth II oil dock. For the next four years the Pilots' accommodation was a wooden hut, shared with the Helmsmen, on the bank of the Canal midway between the Crane berth and Eastham Locks. In 1952 the Pilots and Helmsmen moved for the last time into a new purpose-built single storey accommodation with all the latest "mod-cons".

In connection with the Eastham Pilot Station let me finish on a happy note. The Pilots' Association in 1945 requested that Mrs Mac (the caretaker) should receive two weeks' pay for her one week's holiday on the condition she employed a substitute to perform her work during her week's holiday. They also requested that Mrs Mac should receive double pay for VE Day and VJ Day. The Pilotage Committee agreed to implement both these recommendations.

Elsewhere there were problems at the other Pilot stations designated along the Canal. The Runcorn Pilot Station consisted of a stone hut, unlit and heated by an 'asthmatic' coal stove that had been used for nearly 50 years. In July 1944 the Pilots expressed a desire to be given the opportunity of using as sleeping quarters the offices until recently occupied by the Harbour Master's staff at No Man's Land, Runcorn. The Authority agreed to this request and stated they would furnish the building in a similar manner to the accommodation provided at Partington. The cost of providing beds and bedding, cleaning and laundry would have to be borne by the Pilots. The Pilots occupied that accommodation from August 1944 until October 1945 when the Pilots' Association regarded the Runcorn Pilot Station as redundant and it was closed down.

The original Partington Pilot Station was a room at the *George Hotel,* a public house, in Irlam Road, Cadishead, about a mile from the Partington Coaling Basin. The charge for bed and breakfast was 2s 6d (12½p) and 1s 3d (7½p) bed only. In 1925 a wooden hut was provided by the Canal Company on the bank of the Canal on the Cadishead side (north side) for the use of the Pilots. It contained one electric heater, two sleeping berths, one chair and no running water. A water supply was connected to the building in July 1942. Four years later a new block of offices was erected and incorporated within them new accommodation for Pilots and Helmsmen. It was always referred to by the younger Pilots and all Helmsmen as "*The Risley Cell Block Extension*". The whole of the interior decoration, the common brick walls, doors, floors, ceilings were painted with gloss paint called eau-de-nil. The Pilot Station remained unchanged until it was closed down in 1981.

1940-1977
Flying Angel Seamen's Mission, Salford. Opposite the Main Dock Gate. Pilots' accommodation down the side street, first door on left, top floor. Slept 6.

1946-1981
Pilots' accommodation at Partington Coaling Basin. First two small windows Pilots' Bedrooms and Lounge. Slept 4. Window beyond door Helmsmen's accommodation. Slept 4 in bunk beds. Accommodation included bathroom and kitchen.

The accommodation at the Manchester Pilot Station was established in 1898 when permission was granted for the Pilots to use a room in a Canal Company house named *Rose Hill*, situated at the top of what was to be number nine dock. Little is recorded about this accommodation until June 1920 when Mr Beckett (Secretary to the Pilots' Association) reported to the Pilotage Committee that the Pilots had suggested to him the accommodation at *Rose Hill* be closed down, but the Pilots' representatives at that meeting requested that the room should be kept open. The Chairman said that he did not think Mr Beckett had made it clear that all the Pilots were unanimous that the accommodation at *Rose Hill* be closed down and it had been reported to him that use was still being made of the same. Before issuing instructions to close down the accommodation the Committee would like to know that all Pilots were of one mind in respect of closing *Rose Hill.*

It appears the Pilots were in favour of keeping *Rose Hill* open and their request for it to remain available for their use was granted, but in April 1921 a further attempt was made to close it down. At the Pilotage Committee Meeting the Chairman, Mr Browning, reported in the first three months of the year that *Rose Hill* had only been used on nine occasions and five meals had been served. He suggested in view of the little use made of this accommodation, the Pilots may consider to close the room. Mr Hindle said that although little use was made of the accommodation the Pilots still desired to continue with same.

The Chairman explained that *Rose Hill* would be shortly required for other purposes and the accommodation for Pilots would not be available. This was a bluff. The Pilots were still ensconced at *Rose Hill* in August 1925, and they had even added a further two rooms to their quarters. A complaint was lodged in that month by the Pilots' representative, Mr W Langley, saying that he had several complaints to the objectional condition of the Pilots' quarters at *Rose Hill*, especially the bedding. He stated that when the Pilots took over the extra rooms, extra help would be provided to maintain the rooms in a clean condition and he hoped the Committee would endeavour to correct this distressing condition.

The Pilots' accommodation at *Rose Hill* remained at their disposal for another 12 years, until some time in 1937 when the Pilots had to vacate that property. A letter was read at the November Pilotage Committee Meeting from the Secretary of the Pilots' Association:

"You are I think well aware the Pilots are at present without accommodation at Manchester and I am instructed to ask whether the Pilotage Authority is in

a position to offer suitable accommodation for the use of the Pilots when they require to stay in Manchester overnight. I understand that some suggestion has been made in this connection but as the matter is extremely urgent I shall be glad to hear from you as soon as possible if you are able to assist."

Captain Howard, Harbour Master, said there was a room in the Dock Office which might prove suitable if other matters could be arranged, but he was not a present in a position to make any recommendation but would be as expeditious as possible. Six months passed and no agreement had been reached between the Pilotage Committee and the Pilots' Association regarding suitable accommodation for Pilots in Manchester. At the Pilotage Committee Meeting held in May 1938 a letter was read confirming that arrangements had been made by the Pilots to enter into occupation of rooms at 720 Chester Road, Stretford, which could be connected with the company's telephone system. It was suggested that all expenses in connection with this accommodation and that at Eastham were properly charged against the Pilot Fund Account.

HELMSMENS ACCOMMODATION MANCHESTER

1938-1958
150 Langworthy Road, Eccles

This accommodation was not really satisfactory, the main criticism being it was over half a mile from the Docks. In April 1940 the Rev G Wheeler, Port Chaplain to the Mission to Seamen said that he had two bedrooms and a bed sitting room which he could offer to the Pilots on terms to be agreed. On the morning of 24th june 1941, all terms agreed, the Canal Pilots moved for the last time to the Mission to Seamen opposite the Main Dock entrance. There they remained until December 1977 when the Pilot Station was closed down and very shortly after, so did the Mission to Seamen.

The Helmsmen had secured their own accommodation in Manchester as early as 1908 at Mrs Delaneys in Trafford Road, next door-but-one to the infamous *Clowes* public house of world-wide renown - not may I add renowned for its sales of tobacco, ales, wines and spirits. They remained there until Mrs Delaney died in 1938, when they took rooms with Miss Reeves at 150 Langworthy Road, Eccles, a habitation of such Dickensian squalor it is hard to describe and situated two miles from the Main Docks.

The house was so squalid that rats came out at night and gnawed through the sugar bags that had been left on the table for sweetening the tea. The smell of wet rot permeated the whole house, the bedroom containing one double bed and two single beds, was so damp one had to hold the one bar electric fire (the only means of heating in the bedroom) over the sheets and watch the steam rise whilst drying and warming the beds before any attempt was made to sleep in them. The Author was wholly responsible for moving from Langworthy Road when he negotiated a room with four berths in the Seamen's Mission opposite the Main Dock Gate in 1958. They remained there until the Manchester Pilot Station closed down.

There are no records of the Helmsmen's accommodation at Partington until 1946 - presumably because there was none - when they moved into the Pilot block in the new offices. The Eastham accommodation has also limited records, but this has been chronicled earlier in this chapter. The closing of these Piloting Stations was undeniably linked with the decline in shipping transiting the Ship Canal and a new working system.

2

THE PILOTAGE TARIFF 1921-1925

The year 1921 proved to be catastrophic for British Shipping and the Manchester Ship Canal. The icy chill of a great recession in the economy of the country was beginning to be felt, particularly in the north west of England. The annual tonnage using the Ship Canal dropped a record 1,000,000 tons and this in turn was seriously reflected in the Pilots' monthly earnings. Not surprisingly a great deal of concern was evident over the loss of Pilot revenue. Between 1st November 1920 and 4th January 1921, three meetings had been held between a deputation from the Pilots and the Pilotage Committee regarding the proposed new byelaws to incorporate the existing Pilotage Tariff in the general code of the byelaws and a separate byelaw for a temporary increase in the Pilotage Tariff of $33\frac{1}{3}\%$.

The final draft had been forwarded to the Board of Trade on 5th January and returned to the Pilotage Committee on 11th with certain small amendments. Both byelaws were advertised, as required by law in the National press on 18th January. It was reported at the February Pilotage Committee that on 31st January they received the following letter from the Board of Trade:

"With reference to the byelaw proposed for the purpose of increasing the Pilotage rates in the Manchester Pilotage District by $33\frac{1}{2}\%$, I am directed by the Board of Trade to transmit the accompanying copy of a letter in confirmation of a telegram which the Board received from the Manchester Steamship Owners Association objecting to the proposed byelaw."

The letter signed by Mr T Whyman, secretary of the Shipowners' Association read as follows:

"I have the honour to confirm my telegram of this afternoon as follows:

MEETING MANCHESTER STEAMSHIP OWNERS ASSOCIATION TODAY UNAMIMOUSLY RESOLVED THAT THIS MEETING FORMALLY PROTESTS AGAINST THE PROPOSED INCREASE IN PILOTS REMUNERATION ON THE GROUND THAT IT IS UNNECESSARY AND INOPPORTUNE; UNNECESSARY AS REGARDS THE INCREASE COST OF LIVING AND INOPPORTUNE IN THAT WITH THE LACK OF CARGO AND REDUCED FREIGHT RATES THE COST OF OPERATING IS ALREADY OPPRESSIVE. IT IS NOTORIOUS THAT NUMBERS OF STEAMERS ARE ALREADY LAID UP AND ANY INCREASE IN WORKING EXPENSES CAN ONLY LEAD UP AN EXTENSION OF THIS EVIL WITH INCREASED UNEMPLOYMENT TO SEAMEN GENERALLY."

The Shipowners' Association plucked on every heart string they could use in that telegram as they have always done and still continue to do so in this day and age. Mr Hindle, Pilots' representative, intimated he would speak with the other respresentatives, Messrs Cartwright and Lamey, with a view to arranging an interview with the Chairman of the Committee to decide the procedure to be adopted.

On 7th March 1921 the Chairman reported to the Pilotage Committee the result of his interview with the deputation of Pilots. It had been agreed that he, the Chairman, should approach the Steamship Owners with an amended claim as under:

"That for vessels 300 tons and under no change in the present tariff to be made. The 33 1/2% to be reduced to say 25% leaving the exact percentage to him to negotiate if the Steamship Owners objected to the figure of 25% but to try and obtain an amicable settlement at 20%."

The Chairman said he had attended a meeting of the Steamship Owners and had fully explained the circumstances under which the Pilots' Association had made their application. However the Steamship owners had pressed their objection to any increase in the Pilotage Rates and, in addition, to the proposed payment of 10% of the Pilotage Rate by Steamship Owners whose Master or Mates held Pilotage Certificates. He also stated if the Steamship Owners pressed their two objections after the meeting of the sub-committee the following day, he would communicate with the Pilots' representatives appointed to deal with this subject.

The Pilots incensed by the objection to the Byelaw, had instructed their representative, Mr Hindle, to state that the Pilots seeing that the Steamship Owners were objecting to the proposed increase in tariff, they (the Pilots) intended to press for payment for Pilotage services rendered to vessels having deck loads. Manchester was at a disadvantage to Liverpool whose charges for Pilotage services were based on the draught of vessels and not on registered tonnage as in Manchester. The following day the Pilotage Committee received this letter from the Steamship Owners' Association:

"The Manchester Steamship Owners Association regret that they are entirely unable to agree to the proposed increase in Pilotage Rates and the payment of 10% of the Pilotage tariff from officers holding Certificates. They also consider that, the four War Allowances contained in the Pilotage Rates, there should be some provision for reversion to lower rates when conditions change."

During the discussion it was brought out that the general tendency in all directions was towards reductions and not increases.In particular, mention was made of the notice that had already been sent to the National Maritime Board calling for a reduction in the wages of Officers, Engineers and Crews. The Shipowners were going all the way, no holds barred, to cut down on all their expenses and the Maritime branch, which included Pilots were always the first to feel the crunch. A copy of the letter was sent to Mr Hindle and yet another meeting was convened with Mr Latimer to discuss the situation. Mr Hindle opened the meeting by telling the Chairman that having regard to existing circumstances the Pilots did not press for a revision of the tariff put in operation in November 1919 because of the new proposed Byelaw for an increase of 33 ½% which had been promised in the early part of that year. He was also adamant that the percentage on Masters and Mates holding Canal Pilot Certificates should not be dropped.

Mr Latimer told them they would be wise not to pursue this percentage at present as no such scheme was in force in Liverpool. He felt sure there would be opposition from the Steamship Owners many of whom represented Liverpool interests. As an alternative he would recommend to the Canal Company that a sum of £450 in the Pilotage Account should be transferred to commence a Pilotage Superannuation Fund and he would write to the Board of Trade and obtain information as to pilotage Pensions or Benevolent Fund schemes at different ports in the United Kingdom.

1930
Early morning start at the top of No 9 Dock. No Union safety precautions for the docker boarding the SS Cape Ross by rope ladder.
Courtesy of the MSC Company

The Floating Grain Elevator. Note the family narrow barges under the sterm of the "Fabian".
Courtesy of the MSC Company

Mr Hindle then mentioned the question of shelter space used for cargo being included in the ship's registered tonnage upon which pilotage fees should be charged. Mr Latimer again advised caution not to press this point and thus cause delay in the confirmation of the Byelaws. For the year ending 1920 he promised to produce records of space so measured and have a calculation made whereby the Pilots themselves would see how much extra remuneration that system might produce. The meeting was closed.

Once again that wily old fox, Mr Latimer, had succeeded, very cleverly, in circumnavigating the Pilots' proposals by the simple method of proffering the proverbial "carrot" whilst at the same time not committing himself to anything tangible. It showed again what an adept and brilliant man he was in the art of persuasion and negotiation with the Pilots. He had already perceived that the tantalizing "carrot" - the Superannuation and Pension Funds - meant a great deal to Pilots. These Funds should have been and could have been promulgated as early as January 1920. That they had not been earnestly pursued leads one to believe they had been deliberately held in abeyance until such a situation as had now arisen. They then could be used to stave off any further increase in the running costs of the Shipowners using the Canal and therefore maintain their presence in Manchester.

At the April Pilotage Committee the Pilots representatives were still adamant that they did not wish the Byelaws to go forward at that moment, but that they be left over until something transpired definitely as regards rates of pay at Liverpool. Mr Hindle also stated that the Pilots Association were of the opinion that as the Shipowners Association had objected to one clause in the proposed Byelaw the whole would have to be re-considered. At one of the meetings held with the Chairman of Pilotage Committee he gave way on several points to obtain the Committee's sanction to an increase in tariff. This had been objected to by the shipowners, therefore the whole position had changed. The Association failed to see why the shipowners were objecting. Manchester was a non-compulsory Port, therefore shipowners were not compelled to employ Pilots but if they did, they should pay sufficiently well to enable the Pilots to live decently. With increased travelling expenses, coal, house rent, rates, taxes and telephone charges, the Pilots were finding it quite impossible to make ends meet with the present scale of the Pilotage tariff.

The Pilots' Association was in no mood for platitudes, and, incensed by the objections of the Steamship owners, they placed the following letter before the May Pilotage Committee:

"With the object of bringing all Pilotage Byelaws as much as possible into line, the following alterations will be required in the Manchester Pilotage Byelaws sent to London.

1. *Duties, number and pay of Helmsmen should be specified, as Boathands are at Liverpool (see Sec.45 to 58 Liverpool Byelaws).*
2. *Pilots must not be held responsible for any consequences which may arise through their carrying out an order given by an official of the Canal Company (see Sec.76 Liverpool Byelaws).*
3. *Pilots to be provided with reasonable and sufficient food and sleeping accommodation while on board any vessel (see Sec.90 Liverpool Byelaws).*
4. *The Byelaws should specify how the pooled earnings are to be divided (see Sec.107-1 and 2 Liverpool Byelaws).*
5. *Sickness allowance should be specified in the Byelaws (see Sec.110 Liverpool Byelaws).*
6. *Rates for the collection of Pilots' earnings to be specified in the Byelaws, but like Liverpool not to exceed 2% (see Sec.116 Liverpool Byelaws)*
7. *Masters and Mates contributions should be similar to Liverpool not less than £10.10s.0d (£10.50p) (see Sec.131 Liverpool Byelaws).*
8. *Shifting of vessels at Eastham or elsewhere to be paid at the same rate as now in force at Manchester Docks.*
9. *Extra mileage to be paid for vessels over 3,500 tons registered and another 50% for all vessels over 25 feet*
10. *Pilots to be paid on the same tonnage on which canal dues are collected, ie paid for shelter deck space (if occupied) and deck loads."*

Once again a great deal of respect for the Liverpool Pilot Service adminstration was shown by the Manchester Canal Pilots wishing to adopt their style of Byelaws. It is no secret that the Liverpool Pilot Service was frequently used as a model for many Pilotage areas not just in the United Kingdom but throughout the world.

Mr Hindle informed the Chairman that the Association had been in communication with the General Secretary of the United Kingdom Pilots Association requesting advice on their proposed new byelaws which they would press to be implemented should the Steamship Owners persist in their objection to an increase of 33½% and upset the byelaws already sent to London. He also stated that it had been announced in that morning's "Journal of Commerce" that the Liverpool Dock Board had adopted a new Schedule of Rates asked for by the Liverpool Pilots and in some cases those increases were over 150% above pre-war rates and there were many additional charges. Under those circumstances the Association would be glad if the Chairman would expedite the Manchester Byelaw for an increase of 33½%.

The month of April had seen the recession bite deeply into the monthly earnings of the Pilots and to such an extent the figures necessary to provide for the usual payment of £39 and £30 to First Class and Second Class Pilots respectively had not been reached, nor did it look likely to be achieved in May. Such was the sad state into which, in 1921, the financial affairs of the Ship Canal Pilots had fallen. One dare not consider for one moment what the situation would have been if the "catch-as-catch-can" or the "Gang of Four" farming out system had still been in operation. Many Pilots would have undoubtedly been unable to maintain any sort of living from the shipping in the Canal and would certainly have been forced to seek alternative employment. One begs the question "What alternative employment could have been found for Pilots in 1921?". Quite simply - Nothing!

If there is such a thing as divine providence, the introduction of the Rotary and Pooling system, just one short year previous, was just such an intervention. It saved the Manchester Pilot Service from complete disintegration in 1921, a situation from which they would never have been able to recover.

By September 1921 no further progress had been made towards an increase in the Pilotage Tariff. On 10th August the Board of Trade again contacted the Pilotage Committee pressing that early consideration should be given to the outstanding points in connection with the Pilotage Byelaw before them. An attempt was made to arrange an early meeting with the Pilots' representatives to try and settle the outstanding points but unfortunately Mr Hindle, the senior representative, was away on leave.

During all these prolonged discussions the Pilots' Association, which hitherto had been a non-contributory Association, requested that the Ship Canal deduct each quarter £1 from each of the Pilot's earnings who were members of the Association, and such deductions to be deposited into an account opened at Lloyds Bank, Brunswick Street, Liverpool to be called *The Manchester Ship Canal Pilots Association Fund.* There was no objection raised to this request from the Ship Canal Company and the account is still in operation, but the individual contribution in 1988 was £15 per month.

The negotiations came to an abrupt halt in November as no side was willing to concede any point or points. The Board of Trade confirmed they could not proceed with the publishing of the Byelaws until all parties were in complete agreement and this effectively squashed any further meetings on Pilotage Tariff for the next four years. In 1922 shipping returned to the Canal and an annual increase of nearly 1,000,000 tons was recorded and continued to increase by over 500,000 tons per year. This influx of shipping into the Canal did much to relieve the pressure on the Pilots' financial problems, but it did not deter them from pressing at every available and suitable opportunity for an increase in the Pilotage Tariff.

Their persistence was eventually rewarded when in 1925 negotiations were re-opened on the contentious subject of the Byelaws and Tariff. At the July 1925 Pilotage Committee an agreement was at last reached between all parties and it was resolved that an increase of 15% should be granted to the Pilotage Tariff, **but** for a trial period of one year only. This was at the insistence of the Manchester Steamship Owners Association. It had been a long, weary and often bitter set of negotiations for the Pilots' representatives, especially for Mr Hindle, who was now 66 years old and had been piloting for over 21 years. At the final meeting in July 1925 the Steamship Owners and the Pilotage Committee had been unmoving and totally adamant that any increase in the Pilotage Tariff must not exceed 15%. They had also insisted, equally dogmatically, that the new Byelaws (see earlier in this Chapter) to be sent to the Board of Trade should contain the following amendments and deletions.

Para 6. Rate of Collection of Pilots earnings be specified in the Byelaws at 2½%.

Para 7. Masters and Mates contribution will be £3.3s.0 (£3.15p) per annum.

Paras 8, 9, 10 delete.

The Manchester Steamship Owners also stated all these points must be accepted in their entirety.
They were inextricably linked together, there being no choice of accepting one part and rejecting another. Hard times breed hard men and shipowners did not come any harder. The Pilots' representatives fearing another stalemate and consequently a collapse once again of these over-protracted negotiations, had no real alternative but to concede to these stringent demands, no doubt reasoning *"Half a cake is better than none"*. In their case, on that day, sixty-five years ago, it would have been more appropriate to have said *"Quarter of a cake is better than none"*. On 5th August 1925 the Byelaws were confirmed by the Board of Trade and came into force on the 12th August nearly five years after they were first proposed by the Pilotage Association.

Eastham Locks 1925

The small hut on the port side of the big lock, beneath the vessel's funnel is the Pilot Clerk's office. Ashore, top right, end house the Custom House. In the four semi-detached houses, two lock masters and two assistant lock masters lived. The long building was the offices of the civil and mechanical engineers, stores, and blacksmiths. The tall chimney and buildings surrounding it was the hydraulic pumping station to operate the lock gates and sluices. The small house behind was the old Custom House which was never used. As such, it became accommodation downstairs for the Liverpool Pilots and Manchester Helsmen and on the first floor for the Manchester Pilots. The small flat roofed building in front of the pumpting station was a Post Office with its own franking "Eastham Locks". The small hut on the starboard side of the lock by the head tug was the Toll Clerk's Office and main switch board for the telephone system. The roofed huts in the sluice way contained the Custom Launch and the Canal Divers boat.

1934
TS "Danmark" (Gr 10,517, L 491' B 68') leaving
Eastham for Stanlow Oil Dock
Note: Ship's funnel astern of paddle tug had been removed at the sheerlegs crane and placed on a raft to await the return of the vessel from Manchester

3

THE PILOT WORKING SYSTEM 1920-1935

The next two decades were going to prove just as problematical for the Pilot service as the past decades, the working of the rotary system was to be beset with many difficulties, never envisaged at its inception. For such a new and revolutionary system to have been able to operate smoothly, efficiently and fairly, the co-operation of every Pilot to apply himself conscientiously towards the success of the rota system would have been needed. Alas, as always, such an application had never been, nor ever would be, something some Manchester Pilots would excel in. Abuses to the Rota proliferated.

At the Pilotage Committee meeting held on the 5th January 1920, Mr R Bennion, the newly appointed Pilot Clerk, presented to the meeting the first report on the Pilots' Rotary and Pooling system:
"The work performed in the first month (December) of the Rotary system has been 244 separate services. Of these 144 were under 1,000 tons net reg and 104 over 1,000. This works out to 10.5 vessels for each Pilot for a month and it gives an average of approximately 8 Pilots working each day. The total number of vessels which have been moved at Eastham during December - from Locks to Dolphins or vice versa - has been 73 representing about 3.5 for each of the 23 Pilots".

Mr Bennion stated that although all pilotage work in the first month of the new system was satisfactorily performed, he felt sure that when all the Pilots are connected by telephone that the pilotage work would be got through with much less difficulty. The pressure of vessels on some days is greater than others and when pilots 'on turn' are not on the telephone they are apt to think they are not wanted and are difficult to get in touch with. [*Author's Note: There were many other reasons for Pilots not wanting to be connected to a telephone, see the Chapter on the abuses of the Rotary system.*]

The Chairman of the Pilotage Committee (Mr W Browning) thanked Mr Bennion for his very concise report but he did express his deep concern that when Choice Pilots were on leave, under this new system, there was a danger of a shorgage of Pilots and thereby vessels might be delayed in their transits up or down the Canal, awaiting the services of a Pilot. Mr Browning thought this probability should be carefully considered between the Pilots themselves but suggested that a possible solution was that the Choice Pilots, during their leave period, should continue to attend to their "Choice" work. This suggestion was totally rejected by the Pilots' Association on the grounds that the leave system was introduced as a rest period for all Pilots. Should any Pilot be recalled during that rest period all the health benefits would be lost. There are no further records of any discussion on Mr Browning's suggestion but in May the Pilot Service was increased to 26 men. Mr Browning became renowned for some of his none too erudite suggestions.

The Rotary System, like all new systems, had its early problems, none were insurmountable, but ways to achieve a smoother working of the Rota system were constantly being proposed and investigated. One such proposal, in June 1930, found favour with all the Pilots and Mr Hindle (Pilots' representative) proposed at the Pilotage Committee a trial should be given to working half the Pilots up from Eastham to Manchester and the other half to work down from Manchester to Eastham each month. He stated that it was the general opinion that it would greatly improve the present working system. This working system was introduced on 1st September 1920 and Mr Bennion reported to the Pilotage Committee in October:

"The system of working the Pilots half up the Canal and half down the Canal has suffered in comparison with the single Rota system through the leave periods and a fourth Pilot being away through illness (three Pilots were on leave during the summer in the new leave system). The advantage of the double Rota appear to be that the Pilots know from which end they are working, a saving very often in travelling, and those on the outward Rota are fairly sure of the week-ends at home. The disadvantage appears to be that with a heavy volume of traffic moving from either end the time between each service is reduced due to the lesser number of Pilots to draw upon when in distinct groups. In either case it is quite evident that the service calls for more Pilots in order to maintain the required standard of efficiency and I would suggest

that at least four more Pilots be appointed as soon as possible, for which I advance the following reasons:

1. *The present complement is the absolute minimum: there is no margin or reserve for expanding trade and in my opinion the demands of the Port call for better provision to cope with the trade present and prospective (in August 1919 there were 30 Pilots against 26 today). The situation will deteriorate in the shorter days of the winter even with the full number of Pilots on the Rota.*
2. *It is well known that the trade arrives not in a steady stream but at times in abnormal numbers and it is better to be prepared than risk the possibility of being unable to handle it.*
3. *In the service there are 8 Pilots who are 60 years of age and over and they cannot be expected to maintain the same standard as the younger Pilots in travelling to and from the different points where the work lies. The risk of ill health or possible defection altogether in this number of senior men is liable to cripple the service at any time."*

In explanation of this case Mr Bennion quoted an example of Mr W Peacock, aged 61, who left Eastham with the S.S. *"Barfond"* at 0130 hours and was detained by fog on the passage to Manchester. When he reached home at Runcorn at 1700 hours he found he was on turn again at Eastham for the tide high water at midnight and he refused to go stating that he required a night's rest, and justly so.

Arising out of Mr Bennion's report, consideration was given to the need for the appointment without delay of further Pilots by the Pilotage Committee. The Pilots agreed it was essential that further Pilots be appointed and an increase in Pilotage Rates to provide for payment of same. The Pilotage Committee resolved that an additional four Pilots should be appointed as soon as possible. The Pilot Service was duly increased to 30 men in December 1920. There was one curious note of dissent. Mr Hindle desired it placed on record that in his view it was not necessary that there should be any increase in the number of licensed Pilots on the Canal. One wonders if his well-known dislike of Messrs Gorst and Bennet, the two senior helmsmen to be promoted, had any bearing on his statement.

It is interesting to note the swiftness with which the Pilotage Committee acted on the recommendations of the Chief Pilot Clerk. Had the Pilots' Association put forward the same proposals it would have resulted in the inevitable long and procrastinated negotiations lasting six months or more with the time honoured result of the Pilots achieving only half what they requested. This bears out the importance the Pilotage Committee and the Pilots' Association viewed the position when it was first instituted. (See Chapter on Pilotage Clerks).

Courtesy Captain P Dunbavand
August Monday Bank Holiday 1931 at "Jacks Castle", Hooton Wharf
Vessel passing tanker Anglo-American "Appalachee" GRT8826, Length 477', Beam 63' 8". Sunk by U-boat in 1940 in position 54° 30'N 28°00'W.

A quiet day at 'Jack's Castle', Hooton Wharf

In October 1923 the question of the appointment of further Pilots, once again became very important. It was thought essential that additional Pilots should be at once appointed in view of the approaching winter and having regard to the number of Pilots 60 years of age and over. Nearly 50% of the First Class Pilots were over 60 years of age, Mr Marker 72, Mr G Green 69, Mr Hankinson 66 were the eldest and all three were in indifferent health. The Pilotage Committee considered it was their duty to see the Pilot Service was fully maintained and in their opinion with the present limited number of Pilots, the service during the coming winter would be seriously prejudiced. This was a refreshingly different attitude from that of the past 25 years.

The Pilots' representatives, whilst agreeing that they were occasionally working under very high pressure and long hours, strongly objected to further Pilots being appointed, especially in view of the fact that it was their intention to apply to the Board of Trade for an enquiry into the Pilot Service in Manchester. The Pilotage Committee however insisted the appointment of further Pilots should not be left any longer and even suggested to the Pilots that their case to the Board of Trade might be strengthened by two further Pilots being appointed. The Pilots' representatives still protested and suggested the matter be left over until the Board of Trade enquiry. A high incident of sickness in November and December precipitated the appointment of two additional Pilots on 1st January 1924.

Concern was once again expressed at the Pilotage Committee in August 1929 regarding two of the most senior Pilots, Mr George Green (aged 74 years) and Mr William Onion (aged 66 years). Representations had been made to the Authority by the Steamship Owners to the Authority, and the Chairman was of the opinion that the licences of these two Pilots should not be renewed. Mr Hughes (Steamship Owners' representative) supported the views of the Chairman and said the Shipowners felt strongly that the Pilotage Byelaws which gave the Authority power to refuse or renew a licence should definitely be adopted and licences not granted to Pilots after they had attained the age of 65. The Chairman replied that the Authority would continue to reserve to themselves the right of retiring Pilots when they reached the age of 65 years but could not agree to the Shipowners' suggestion that all Pilots should be definitely retired at that age. Mr Young (Pilots' representative) asked if these licences in question could be granted for three months but it was ruled that it could not be done. After consideration it was resolved that the licences held by Messrs. Green and Onion would not be renewed with the exception of the Manchester Dock Pilots Licence - this licence was phased out in 1934. After this decision no further Ship Canal Licences were renewed to Pilots over 65 years of age.

In May 1925 certain anomalies in the working system were corrected. Firstly, the practice of requiring a Pilot on inward turn who piloted a vessel to Partington, 28 miles, to stand by and bring the vessel back to Eastham Locks, the whole service counting as only one turn on the Rota, was considered grossly unfair. The Pilots requested that the pilotage service should be considered completed on arrival of the vessel at Partington. If it was absolutely necessary for the same Pilot to stand by to bring the vessel back to Eastham this pilotage service should be counted as a second turn on the Rota. It was pointed out that unless a Pilot arrived at Partington with his vessel before 2200 hours he had to stand by for six to seven hours and the Pilots thought arrangements could be made for them to leave the vessel. It was agreed in Pilotage Committee that in future if a Pilot has to take the vessel outward he would be credited with an additional turn on the Rota otherwise an outward Pilot would perform the service.

There also existed the practice of Pilots boarding small vessels at Eastham Locks bound for Stanlow Oil Docks for the purpose of loading and or discharging within the limit of eight hours and afterwards returning with the vessel to Eastham Locks, and counting as only one Rota turn. The Pilots proposed that the inward Pilot should only be required to take the same vessel back to Eastham Locks if it was not possible for him to be relieved by an outward Pilot in which case the double service should count as two Rota turns. This proposal was accepted by pilotage Committee and put into practice.

Great inconvenience was also being caused owing to Second Class Pilots (9 in all) getting behind their "Turn" on the Rota especially when on *"Station Duty"* at Eastham awaiting a vessel of their restricted tonnage licence to arrive. In consequence First Class Pilots were frequently called out for duty although sixth or seventh on "turn" in the Rota. In an attempt to alleviate this problem two Second Class Pilots were promoted to First Class Pilots.

As ever the Choice Pilots continued to cause diverse problems to the new working Rota and in February 1929 they instigated a ruling, with the full backing of the shipwoners, that a Choice Pilot should not be given a "Turn" on the Rota for at least 24 hours before any of their vessels were expected to move in the Canal. Their reasoning was that it was unfair to the Choice Pilot and their vessel, to go from another vessel straight on board their own vessel. This situation was frequently faced by the ordinary Rota Pilot, due in no small measure to Choice Pilots being absent from the Rota through attending their "Choice" work or having an accumulated "turn" off the Rota. The people involved in this ruling chose to completely disregard the fact that a vessel's estimated time of arrival or departure was historically, notoriously unpredictable and unreliable. Fortunately commensense prevailed, the Pilotage Committee could not agree to this ruling but did indicate that everything possible would be done to facilitate the Choice Pilots in boarding their vessels without being unduly fatigued. How this infuriated the Rota Pilots throughout the years. The Choice Pilots were "Sacred Cows" indeed.

In 1932 it was again discussed at the Pilotage Committee in August. A proposal was made that:

"If a Choice Pilot was to transit the complete length of the Canal with his vessel he would not be given a "turn" on the Rota for at least 24 hours and if a Choice Pilot was to transit a portion of the Canal eg Eastham to Stanlow or Manchester to Partington, he would not be given a "Turn" on the Rota for at least 12 hours prior to his commencement of his Choice work."

This proposal was passed by the Pilotage Committee and came into the Pilot's Working Rules on 1st September 1932.

By February 1930 great concern was again being expressed at Pilotage Committee that the Authority might be considered to be running the Pilot service too fine and that the ability of the 32 Pilots (25 First Class, 7 Second Class) to maintain the Rota system was in question. The Pilot's Rota had on a number of occasions come perilously close to breaking down completely. A memo from the Chief Pilot Clerk was submitted:

"For the purpose of working the Rotary system the 32 Pilots are divided into two groups of 16, working inward and outward during alternate months. Group 'A' consists of 9 Choice Pilots, 3 Rota Pilots and 4 Second Class Pilots. 'B' Group consists of 8 Choice Pilots, 4 Rota Pilots and 4 Second Class Pilots. The total number of Choice Pilots being 17 is therefore more than half the full strength of the whole Pilot service and is a very difficult ratio to support. The remedy appears to be less Second Class Pilots, by promotion of some of the present numbers or more Pilots appointed. The reason for this is the disruption of the two Rotas by the Choice Pilots (as ever) *some of them being required to to work on their vessels on the opposite Rota or they are kept in reserve for Choice work arriving some time later or that they have "Turns" in hand and clear of the Rota Duty. It is very often difficult to get sufficient Pilots to man the Pilot Station at Eastham. The matter has been aggravated recently by prolonged bad weather and by sickness amongst the Pilots which, in combination, has created many difficult situations."*

Courtesy Mrs W Yates Collection
High Water at Eastham. SS "Cornwall" in lock. "Salford City" manoeuvring to enter small lock.
SS "Imber" inward bound passing "Syrian Prince" moored to quay awaiting tugs.

Courtesy Mrs W Yates Collection
"Belpamela" Grt.3215 L.330 B49'

Norwegian Heavy Lift Vessel with a deck cargo of railway carriages for South African Railways. The derricks were secured upright to the cross-trees of the mast to accommodate the deck cargo. Note the overhang of the carriages.

The Chairman thought the position could be temporarily met without appointing more Pilots by the promotion of two Second Class Pilots to First Class. Mr C F Young (Pilots' representative) replied that the Pilots had been discusssing this matter and agreed they should promote four Second Class Pilots to First Class. It was eventually agreed to promote two Second Class Pilots and give the Pilots' Association a month to consider what further should be done. The system whereby a Choice Pilot gained "Turns" which were placed to his credit was considered very unfair and it was suggested that all turns in hand at the end of the month should be cancelled. This suggestion was not followed up. In later years all accumulated "Turns" were automatically cancelled at the commencement of Summer and Winter leave periods.

At the March Pilotage Committee it was stated that although some difficulty had been experienced recently in working the Rota, this was mainly due to exceptional weather conditions. The sickness incidents within the Pilot Service had improved coupled with the additional First Class Pilots being promoted from Second Class. The Pilots were of the opinion that there was at that time no necessity for the appointment of additional pilots. it is unusual to record that although the pilots were being called upon for duty too frequently and in consequence did not get sufficient rest time between one pilotage service and the next, they showed great reluctance to appoint additional pilots.

The high incidence of sickness was unusual, as the service was now comparatively young with only three Pilots over 60 years of age. There has always been an unconfirmed theory that a cabal of Pilots had conspired to disrupt the Rota and pooling system to such an extent it would not function efficiently and the Pilotage Committee would be forced to return to what those Pilots fondly called the "good old days" of "catch as catch can". Although this has never been corroborated, the high incidence of sickness, tiredness and general abuse of the Rota system from a recurring group of Pilots does tend to place a certain amount of credence to this speculation.

A deputation of four Pilots and the secretary of the Pilots' Association informally met the Chairman of the Pilotage Committee early in April 1930 to discuss the subject of appointing additional Pilots. The Chairman pressed the Pilots to put forward proposals which in their view would ease the strain on the Rota. He also remarked that he was not very sanguine that they would be able to put forward anything which would give relief and concluded that something concrete must be proposed, not later than the third week of the month. The Pilots' Association duly presented a list of proposals to the April Pilotage Committee. The Chairman said that the proposals had been carefully considered by Captains Acraman and Perry (Canal Superintendents), Mr Bennion (Pilot Clerk) and himself and they were all of the opinion that they would not provide the number of Pilots to give an efficient service. Mr Browning continued that during the past month three Pilots had been ill, one in January, who had recently died (Mr J D Shaw who was 64 years of age) and quite recently a Pilot had refused duty because he said he was tired. All these circumstances forced him to the conclusion that more Pilots must be appointed against the wishes of the Pilots.

If the Pilots' proposals were adopted they would no doubt be of some assistance, but they did not remedy the situation sufficiently and therefore two additional Pilots would be appointed forthwith and the senior Second Class Pilots promoted to First Class. The Pilots were only naturally incensed at the heavy handed attitude of the Chairman and the Pilotage Committee in over-ruling their proposals without further discussion and stated at the May Pilotage Committee:

"In view of the difficulties which appear to exist in giving effect to the proposals submitted by the Pilots' Association and the fact that the Pilotage Committee decided to appoint two additional Pilots we wish to withdraw the proposals referred to."

The Pilotage Committee refused to withdraw the proposals until after the effect of the additional Pilots had been ascertained. This made the Pilots even more incensed. In December 1931 the powers and duties of the Pilotage Committee, previously vested in the Canal Company, were increased, when the Canal Company delegated those powers and duties to be the entire responsibility of the Pilotage Committee.

4

THE ABUSE OF THE ROTARY SYSTEM - PART 3

The secretary of the Pilots' Association tabled this letter in January 1933 at the Pilotage Committee:

"I am directed to call your attention to the practice of certain Choice Pilots , having two vessels belonging to their Company moving at the same time, leaving the vessel which is proceeding to Manchester on the rota and taking the vessel which is proceeding to a less distant point."

Captain Acraman explained that usually the Steamship Company decided which ship their Choice Pilot must attend and in any case the decision was invariably in favour of the Choice Pilot attending the most important vessel. Mr Hughes (Ship owners' representative) thought it should be left to the owners to say which vessel their Choice Pilot should attend. It was resolved that the Choice Pilots would have the necessary information regarding tankers, as to which was the most important or carrying the most dangerous cargo and his choice of vessel should be accepted. It is strange to relate that no tankers of importance or carrying dangerous cargos for these companies ever went to Manchester!

A Pilot refused to attend the tanker *"Comanchee"* from Manchester to Eastham in August 1938. His explanation was to the effect that his refusal was intended as a protest against the action of the Choice Pilot in electing to attend the tanker *"Pan Scandia"* also consigned to the same company, from Stanlow to Eastham. He alleged that it had been the Pilot's practice to abuse the rota in this manner for some time and to confine his activities as far as possible to pilotage between Eastham and Stanlow and steering his Choice vessels in the river (for which he received extra payment) leaving the longer and more exacting services to the Rota Pilots.

The explanation from the Choice Pilot was to the effect that it was his Company's desire he should preferably attend to the vessel carrying a highly inflammable cargo. It was pointed out that the *"Pan Scandia"* was Norwegian owned and was sub-chartered to the Company. The Pilotage Committee ruled that when two vessels in which this Pilot, or any other Choice Pilot, were interested and they required the service of the Choice Pilot, the vessel which was actually owned by them must take precedence as far as his attendance was concerned. This termporarily plugged a loophole in what the Choice Pilots could manipulate and abuse the Rota system to their advantage. It was never ever completely eradicated from the working system.

The Pilotage Committee arranged for particulars of the absences of two Pilots during the period January 1935 to March 1940, due to recurring sickness, to be placed before the Committee. It appeared that extra strain was being placed on the Rota because of continued absence similar to those under notice. Three points were put forward:

1 A Pilot was allowed to be absent from duty not more than three days without a doctor's certificate and was permitted to make up any turns he might miss during his absence.
2 It might not be in the best interests of the service to allow this practice of making turns up to continue.
3 Pilots should be subjected to a deduction from their earnings in respect of periods of absence within the three days.

These were severe measures for the rest of the Pilot service to suffer for the wanton abuse of two Pilots. However both Pilots were asked to attend the Pilotage Committee in August 1940. The Chairman explained he had before him the sickness records of the Pilots which showed that they had rather bad sickness records and this reduced the effective strength of the service by one Pilot. There was also the question as to whether the Pilots were suffering from any infirmity rendering them unfit to carry out their piloting duties. Both Pilots made lengthy statements complaining of the working conditions, viz unfair allocation of turns, inability to obtain reasonable notice of the duties assigned to them, irregular meals, lack of sleep and the general attitude of the Pilot Clerk.

Courtesy of the Warren family
1930s
The first visit of Royal Naval vessels to Manchester.
Arriving at Eastham Lock

Courtesy of the Warren family
1930 Under way in the Canal

The Chairman informed them that all the other Pilots had to work under the same conditions as they did, but did not have the sickness records attributed to them. After some discussion it was agreed that the sickness records of these Pilots be submitted to the Committee at its July meeting every year, and the Committee hoped that in the future they could look forward to a much better attendance record and the Committee would watch their progress with interest. These two Pilots became amongst some of the healthiest Pilots of their day in the Pilot service.

Another Pilot from 1941 to 1943 had been absent from duty for appreciable periods and the Chairman of the Pilotage Committee asked him for an explanation. The Pilot stated 45 days of his absence last year was due to an injury he had suffered while on duty moving a vessel at Eastham. He had received the discharge from a tug's funnel full in his face and owing to getting something in his eye he had to attend hospital in Liverpool to get it removed and his eye treated. The Chairman remarked that his absence seemed to be due to gastric trouble and colitis according to the doctor's certificates. The Pilot replied that he blamed that trouble on night work, but the Chairman pointed out his piloting records showed that he had not done any night work for a few years. The Pilot made no comment. The Chairman went on to say the Pilot's case was one that demanded attention. The Pilot assured the Committee that he had been feeling very much fitter for some time and he hoped to continue so. The Chairman remarked he hoped this would be so but a careful watch would be kept on his medical record in future.

A Pilot was ordered to attend a vessel drawing 25' 11" and a beam of 59' 6" from Eastham to Irlam Steel Wharf, a passage of at least 8 hours or more. He persuaded the Master to moor at Ellesmere Port as he did not think the vessel was handling very well and either discharge some of the cargo or obtain more powerful tugs. None of these options were available, therefore the Master cancelled the sailing till the morning and the Pilot left the vessel. The vessel proceeded from Ellesmere Port to Irlam Steel Wharf the next morning with the same tugs and in the same trim as the previous day the only change being the Pilot, and the vessel made a good and safe passage. Some Pilots were masters at getting out of their share of the work on the Rota.

THE OLD BRIGADE 1933

Left to right: Bob Green Snr., John Green, George Young Snr., Fred Onion, Bill Langley, Joe Lamey

5
THE PILOTAGE TARIFF 1926 - 1933

The partial success of the Pilots obtaining a 15% increase in their tariff did not deter shipping from using the Ship Canal. Indeed from 1925 to 1926 the actual tonnage using the Canal rose from 5,881,691 tons to 6,830,879 tons, an increase of nearly 1,000,000 tons. The Ship Canal revenue from this tonnage reflected this increase from £1,496,544 in 1925 to £1,592,219 in 1926, an increase of nearly £100,000. It must follow that the Pilots' earnings also reflected this most welcome increase in shipping. This did not go unnoticed by the *hawks* of the Manchester Steamship Owners' Association. At the Pilotage Committee on 9th August 1926 the Chairman reported that a letter had been received from the Manchester Steamship Owners' Association which read:

"At a meeting of this Association I was instructed to write to you with regard to the Pilotage dues, which you will remember were fixed by the Board of Trade for a trial period of twelve months expiring on 5th August next. The members of this Association accepted the trial period, but still remain of the opinion that the Pilots are overpaid for the services they render, and this Association therefore wishes to make application for a reduction in the Pilotage charges by 15%".

The Pilots' representatives said that they thought any application for a reduction should be made to the Board of Trade. The Chairman pointed out that in the first place the Board of Trade would require observations on any applications for a decrease in Pilotage Rates from the Pilotage Authority and asked the Pilots' representatives for any observations their Association may make and the matter reported to the next Pilotage meeting.
The September Pilotage Committee were informed that a meeting was to be

convened shortly with the Pilots when this matter of a 15% reduction in the rates would be dealt with and the representatives would be in a position to reply fully. The chairman impressed on the Pilots' representatives the uttermost urgency required for this matter to be dealt with. Speed was always of the essence in any negotiations with respect to a reduction in Pilotage Tarriff and in any negotiations for an increase in the tariff the order of the day had always been "both anchors down and holding with all engines going full speed astern". The October Pilotage Committee received the following letter from the secretary of the Pilots' Association:

"I beg to inform you that the letters regarding the proposed reduction in Pilotage Rates, were brought before a meeting of this Association and it was resolved to oppose any application that may be made to the Board of Trade for a reduction in the Pilotage Rates. It would appear that the Manchester Steamship Owners' Association put forward their application as a matter of course at the expiration of twelve months from the date when the existing rates came into force without giving any reason for their dissatisfaction with the operation of the rates. I am further to state that in the event of the Steamship Owners making a formal application to the Board of Trade for the proposed reduction the Pilots reserve the right to renew the demands put forward by them last year and any other demands they may deem proper."

A PILOT'S MONTHLY EARNINGS - DECEMBER 1925

Mr Thomas Lamey

Date	Vessel	Net Tons	From-To	Fee
3 12 25	JLuienan	1393	East-Manc	£6. 1s.0d (£6.05)
5 12 25	Maron	303	Manc-East	£4. 6s. 0d (£4.30)
7 12 25	Belgian	364	Manc-East	£6. 11s. 0d (£6.55)
9 12 25	Inverpool	660	East-Manc	£5. 3s. 6d (£5.17)
11 12 25	Vestfos	826	Manc-East	£5. 3s. 6d (£5.17)
13 12 25	Kristin	636	East-Manc	£5. 3s. 6d (£5.17)
15 12 25	Cato	700	Manc-East	£5. 3s. 6d (£5.17)
16 12 25	Holywell	2127	Manc-East	£5. 6s. 0d (£5.30)
18 12 25	Hindsholm	895	East-Manc	£5. 3s. 6d (£5.17)
19 12 25	Marg Lubersac	449	Manc-East	£3. 1s. 0d (£3.05)
22 12 25	Rugulus	649	East-Manc	£5 3s 6d (£5.17)
23 12 25	M/C Merchant	3635	Manc-East	£7 1s. 0d (£7.05)
25 12 25	M/C Corporation	3586	East-Manc	£7. 1s. 0d (£7.05)
28 12 25	Shakristan	1860	East-Manc	£6. 1s. 0d (£6.05)

Total earnings for month £78.18s 1d (£78.92).

The pooling system was in operation in 1925, therefore Mr T Lamey would only receive approximate £68. *The above by kind permission of Mr Peter Lamey*

Courtesy of Mrs W Yates Collection
SS King Edward Grt 5217 L 400' B 52'
A good example of the size of vessels that were regularly piloted in the 1930s.

Courtesy of Mrs W Yates Collection
SS Trewidden Grt 4381 L 400' B 52'

This situation now became the total reversal of the 1921-1925 saga, now it was the Pilots' turn to resist, by all means available to them, any alteration in the tariff suggested by the Steamship Owners. The Pilots were well versed in the tactics of procrastination having seen it at first hand being put into practice so efficiently by the self-same Shipowners' Association not so long ago, when the Pilots struggled to obtain an increase of $33^{1}/_{2}$% in their tariff. The Pilots did have some success holding back the negotiations and it was not until the Pilotage Committee in May 1929 that the following letter was read:

"At the monthly meeting of the Steamship Owners' Association I was instructed to call your attention to the recent reduction of Pilotage charges at Liverpool and to make application on behalf of this Association for a corresponding reduction in Pilotage charges of 15%."

With so many extra meetings being held between the Pilots' Association and the combined committees of the Steamship Owners Association and Pilotage Committee a sub-committee consisting of Messrs Young, Lloyd, Bennet and Warren (Pilots) and the secretary of the Pilots' Association was appointed to assist in dealing with matters arising out of the application of the Shipowners for a reduction of Pilotage Rates. This sub-committee was allowed the necessary time off the Rota without loss of "Turns" or pay providing their attendance at the sub-committee did not interfere with the efficient running of the Rota.

The Manchester Steamship Owners Association having been continually frustrated in their attempts to reduce the Pilotage Tariff - it was over six years since the original negotiations had been instigated - attempted another ploy by putting pressure on certain Pilots, their own Choice Pilots. The Chairman of the March 1933 Pilotage Committee reported the receipt of a letter from the British Tanker Company with reference to the Appropriation/Choice fee of £100 per annum for the services of their Choice Pilot. They felt that under existing circumstances a revision was necessary and expressed the wish that the charge be reconsidered with a view to a substantial reduction being made. It was proposed that the fee be reduced to £50. The Chairman remarked that the fee was not fixed by byelaw but had been adopted in 1899 by the various Steamship Owners who wished to appropriate a certain Pilot to their service. It was agreed that the British Tanker Company be informed that the question of Pilotage Rates was under review at the present time and until that question was settled it was not considered opportune to disturb the existing arrangements relative to Choice Pilot fees. The Pilots' Association's reply on 27th stated:

"The matter was considered and a ballot of the service was taken which resulted in the Pilots being unanimously opposed to any reduction made in the amount of the retaining fee for Choice Pilots at present in force."

Meeting after meeting passed away and it became increasingly obvious that through the intransigence of all the parties involved in the negotiations only a Board of Trade enquiry would bring about a conclusion to these meetings. Accordingly a Board of Trade inquiry was instituted to be held on 23rd May 1933. The following Byelaw was published as a result of that inquiry:

"The Pilotage rates, including those for extra services, set out in the schedule annexed to the Byelaws made by the Manchester Ship Canal Company as the Pilotage Authority for the Manchester Pilotage District, on 28th January 1929 and confirmed by the Board of Trade on 1st February 1929 shall be reduced by 10%. This Byelaw shall come into force seven days after the date of its confirmation by the Board of Trade."

What a blow to the Pilot Service, one from which it would take years to recover. With the success that the Manchester Steamship Owners' Association had achieved after the Pilots' success in 1926, both at reduced percentages originally desired, in tennis parlance it was "Love all" but there was to be precious little love between these two antagonistic Associations in the future years.

It must be pointed out that these negotiations did not preclude the Pilotage Committee or the Pilots' Association from their normal everyday business. Damage reports still had to be assessed, complaints to be attended to and diverse Pilotage matters to be dealt with. One such pilotage matter was resolved in July 1931. At the Pilotage Committee a letter from the Pilots' Association was read:

"I am requested to inform you that a number of the Pilots find the present method of monthly payment of their earnings inconvenient, more especially as once in each quarter a period of five weeks elapses between payments. I am therefore desired to ask whether arrangements could be made, in those cases where a request to that effect is made by any Pilot, for a cheque on account to be sent on the 14th day following the regular settlement day. The amount suggested on account is £15 for a First Class Pilot and £10 for a Second Class Pilot."

This format of payment was adopted and remained for the next 15 years. In 1947 the format changed to all Pilots receiving a cheque on account for £30, twenty-five years later it had increased to £150 and by 1977 the cheque on account stood at £300. The system of a payment on account was phased out in February 1983.

6

THE SEARCHLIGHT CONTROVERSY 1931 - 1939

From the very first day the Manchester Ship Canal was opened in 1894 the Pilotage Authority harboured a secret desire that the Canal should be open for navigation 24 hours a day - weather permitting - to all vessels irrespective of type or size. With this end in mind the Pilotage Authority and the Shipping Agents constantly badgered Pilots to proceed with vessels during the hours of darkness. Conversely the Manchester Pilots steadfastly refused every attempt to try and persuade them to do so, even to the point of not accepting ex gratia payments from Masters and/or Shipping Agents, a most heart-breaking and difficult decision to make for some Pilots. It was not hard to understand why the Pilots refused to participate in night navigation. There were few leading lights or marker buoys, and oil lanterns provided the only illumination for the very few leading lights. Even the swing bridge signals and lock signals were all illuminated by oil lanterns, the clarity of which depended entirely on the expertise of the resident Lamp Trimmer and the standard of lamp oil used in them.

In October 1932 some desk bound genius of a clerk - whose name has never been recorded - in the Pilotage Authority conceived the brilliant idea - or so he thought - of placing searchlights at the disposal of larger vessels wishing to navigate the Canal by night. The Pilotage Authority were delighted with this new innovation but the Manchester Pilots' Association were appalled. The experiment was to prove from the outset an utter disaster, both in attempting to navigate the Ship Canal by night with a searchlight, and in terms of the fragile relationship that existed between the Pilotage Committee and the Pilots' Association.

The first Pilot to attempt such a night transit on a large vessel to Manchester with a searchlight collided with all manner of objects and went aground on numerous occasions between Eastham and Runcorn. The Pilot was forced to go to a lay-by berth for the remainder of the night, utterly exhausted and completely chastened. Other Pilots had similar experiences, but the Manchester Pilotage Authority persisted with their attempts to introduce night navigation on the Ship Canal.

THE SEARCHLIGHT SHIPS
1931-1935

SS *Blairdevon*
Courtesy Mrs W Yates Collection
Grt 3282 L 338' B 49'

SS *American Importer*
Courtesy Mrs W Yates Collection
Grt 6897 L475' B 59' 6"

The first serious complaint against a Pilot, Mr J Lee, aged 36, an inexperienced First Class Pilot was that of not proceeding to Manchester during the hours of darkness when his vessel was fitted with a searchlight. This complaint was placed before the Pilotage Committee Meeting in December 1932. The complainant was Sivewright Bacon and Company, Shipping Agents and brokers, who had objected to the inordinate length of time taken by the SS *Blairdevon* when transiting the Ship Canal inward bound on 19th/20th December. The vessel had arrived at Eastham at 1650 hours on 19th December and after taking aboard searchlights, left at 1845 hours. On reaching Moore Lane - 17 miles from Eastham - at 2250 hours she was tied up until 0630 hours the next morning and eventually arrived at her berth in Manchester Docks about 1430 hours on 20th December. Captain Acraman said the Master of the vessel had seen him in regard to this matter and had stated that as the weather was not very good, he agreed with the Pilot's suggestion to moor the vessel up until 0600 hours the following morning. The Chairman (Mr Browning) said that when a ship took searchlights all concerned should try to get the vessel through with as little delay as possible. He suggested that there should be an enquiry into this case and it was agreed that a sub-committee consisting of himself, Mr Hughes, Captain Acraman and one of the Pilots' representatives (either Mr J Warren or Mr M Green) should interview the Pilot, Mr Lee, and thoroughly investigate the matter.

At the subsequent enquiry into this case held in Manchester, Mr Lee stated that the piloting in the dark of the *Blairdevon* to Moore Lane lay-by, a distance of 17 miles through the most hazardous parts of the Ship Canal had taken over five hours to complete. On arrival at Moore Lane he was extremely exhausted and the visibility on the Ship Canal had become impaired due to low lying mist, a climatic condition notoriously renowned in that area, thus making the use of the searchlight impracticable. He considered that it was a prudent and seamanlike decision to remain at Moore Lane rather than risk any damage to the vessel or Canal Company property in the narrow confines of the rock cuttings to Latchford Locks and beyond in the upper reaches of the Canal.

The Chairman of the sub-committee did not appear to sympathise with the Pilot's reasons for not proceeding to Manchester with the *Blairdevon* . He read the reports of the weather conditions from the Lock Master at Latchford and the bridge Masters on the four swing bridges over the Canal between Moore Lane and Latchford Locks. They were all unanimous that in their opinion the weather was clear and a vessel could have proceeded without due risk. The Chairman concluded by saying that Pilots must make every effort to reach their destinations during the night hours, provided weather conditions permitted and in this case he thought the Pilot did not. It was most important that no time should be lost in the transit of the Canal and this could only be done by the full co-operation of the Pilots. He further stressed that the Canal Company looked to all the Pilots to co-operate to the maximum and that on every occasion the fullest help should be offered and no hindrance placed in the way of night navigation. He hoped Mr Lee would bear this in mind on future occasions. The meeting was closed.

The Manchester Pilots' Association objected strongly to the conclusions drawn by the Chairman of that sub-committee, in particular to his references towards the Pilots in general. A letter was sent to the Pilotage Committee by Mr A Evans (Secretary, Pilots' Association) on 28th March 1933, protesting on behalf of the Manchester Pilot Service, firstly on holding such an informal enquiry and secondly the blatant attempt of that committee to coerce a Pilot against his own judgement to proceed during the hours of darkness. The letter was acknowledged by the Pilotage Committee and its contents noted.

Although over the next two years approximately 240 vessels navigated the Ship Canal during the hours of darkness, with the aid of searchlights, not all these larger vessels transited the full length of the Canal. A number of Pilots continued to oppose night navigation in any shape or form and other Pilots would not attempt a complete transit of the Canal in the dark, always arranging for a lay-by berth at some mid-way point even before they commenced their pilotage. Often the most favoured berths selected were those in close proximity to a local inn or hostelry.

Tales of happenings at lay-by berths on such occasions have become part of the folklore of the Manchester Pilot Service and Towage Department over the years.

At the February 1935 Pilotage Committee Meeting the Chairman reported the receipt of a complaint from the Blue Star Line with reference to the inward passage of the *Trojan Star* on the 16th/17th January 1935. The vessel left Eastham at 1245 hours on the 16th and the owners desired the vessel to reach Manchester Docks for 0800 hours the following morning and arranged for the searchlights to be provided at Latchford. On arrival at Moore Lane the vessel was made fast to the dolphins where she remained until the next morning and subsequently arrived in Manchester at 1645 hours on 17th January. On hearing that the vessel proposed to tie up at Moore Lane, Captain Acraman offered to send the searchlights to that point, but the Master and Pilot decided that they would remain at Moore Lane for the night. The matter was taken up with the Pilot concerned, Mr G Richardson, and the Chairman read the following letter received from the Pilot.

"The only explanation I have to offer for not proceeding beyond Moore Lane with this vessel is that having regard to her size and the fact that she had twin propellers, I considered it would have been imprudent to proceed further after nightfall with or without searchlights. I advised the Master accordingly and he agreed that if I thought there was any risk the vessel should be tied up until daylight."

Captain Acraman (Harbour Master) stated he understood Mr Richardson had informed the Captain that his ship was too large to proceed at night even with searchlights and also that it was dangerous to navigate the four miles from Moore Lane to Latchford Locks with a twin propeller vessel in the dark owing to the rock cutting. The Chairman said he was not satisfied with the action of the Pilot, who appeared to have gone out of his way to turn the Master against night navigation in the Canal. After further consideration the Committee were of the opinion that Mr Richardson should have made a greater effort to get the vessel through to Manchester and if he had even managed to reach Latchford Locks on the night of January 16th he would have in all probability have been able to reach Manchester Docks in time to commence discharging.

THE SEARCHLIGHT SHIPS
1931-1935

TS Trojan Star
Courtesy World Ship Photo Library
GRT 9025 L 474' B 60'

TS Pacific Grove
Courtesy World Ship Photo Library
GRT 7114 L 450' B 61'

The secretary was requested to communicate the Committee's findings to Mr Richardson.

This was the first of four major complaints investigated by the Pilotage Committee - by way of an informal enquiry and it was to lead to a very serious constitutional crisis between the Manchester Pilots' Association and the Pilotage Committee. In September 1935 another informal enquiry was convened to enquire why Mr F Onion (Senior First Class Pilot) had objected to leaving the berth in Manchester No 9 Dock with the SS *Matheran* GRT 7652 L 470' B 58' Draft 25' in the dark without a searchlight having already been informed that the searchlight would be awaiting the vessel's arrival at Mode Wheel Locks, a distance of three quarters of a mile away. Mr F Onion contended that the most hazardous part of the pilotage was navigating stern first down No 9 Dock. At that particular time every berth was occupied with barges laying alongside some of the vessels. He was further questioned as to why after a tug boat had been despatched to Mode Wheel Lock to bring the searchlight to the vessel he still refused to sail. Mr Onion replied that by the time the searchlight had arrived and was placed in position on the vessel there was not sufficient time for the vessel to arrive at Eastham and sail on the early morning tide. He had, therefore, arranged with the Master of the vessel to sail from Manchester in the morning in sufficient time to sail on the afternoon tide out of Eastham. This arrangement would prevent any possible damage to the vessel or Canal Company property that might occur during a night transit of the Canal and would also save additional cost to the ship owner of boating fees and pilotage shifting fees at Eastham.

The sub-committee did not feel that these answers could be accepted and that the Pilot showed no co-operation whatsoever with the Port Authority to assist in the sailing of the *"Matheran"*. His refusal to sail was prejudicial to the efficient governing of the Manchester Pilot Service. They warned Mr Onion that any such further refusal to obey and execute all lawful orders given by the Pilotage Authority, in like circumstances, would necessitate a more serious view being taken and a withdrawal of his licence under section 13 of the Manchester Pilotage Bye-laws.

THE SEARCHLIGHT SHIPS
1931-1935

SS Manchester Division
GRT 6048 Length 418' Beam 60' Draught 25' 6"

SS Manchester Citizen
GRT 5336 L 418' B 57' Draught 24' 9"

Photographs by Courtesy of Mrs W Yates Collection

Before an answer could be compiled and sent to the Pilotage Committee from the Pilots' Association a complaint from Captain Acraman that when interviewing the Master *of the MV Pacific Grove* (Furness Withy Line) on 18 October 1935 in respect of searchlights, he was informed that Mr W H Langley had stated to the Master that Captain Acraman was of the opinion that the searchlights were no good. Captain Acraman considered this to be a gross mis-statement. He had consistently advocated the use of searchlights. It was agreed that the matter be left to the Chairman of the Committee to investigate with the parties concerned.

On 2 November 1935 Mr Langley was interviewed in Manchester by the Chairman of the Pilotage Committee and Captain Acraman. Mr Langley denied that he had informed the Master of the *Pacific Grove* that Captain Acraman had told him that "he had tested the new searchlights aboard the *Manchester Division* and was of the opinion that they were no good". He admitted having informed the Master that the searchlights were of no use for his purpose. Mr Langley further stated that in his view ships's clusters over the forward and after ends of a vessel were of more use for night navigation than were the searchlights. He had navigated part of the Canal on a clear night with a Pacific vessel without using lights. Mr Langley said that when lights were put aboard the *Manchester Division* at Latchford Locks recently it was the first time he had heard he was to have them. He did not make much use of them that night as he thought he could proceed better without their aid having regard to the prevailing weather conditions.

The Chairman said it appeared to him that Mr Langley was opposed to the use of searchlights but he did not think Mr Langley's attitude was that of the Pilots generally. The Chairman then asked the Pilots' Representatives for their observations on the use of searchlights. Mr R Lloyd said in his opinion vessels of the type being discussed should not move in any other light than daylight, but admitted, however, that the searchlights were very useful at the locks and when passing through the narrow rock cuttings. Mr Bennet said he had quite a fair experience of searchlights and had come to the conclusion that by using them the risk of damage was reduced but with a ship like the *Manchester Citizen* or any other deep drafted vessel he thought it unwise to navigate during darkness even with searchlights. Both he and Mr Lloyd wished the Pilotage Committee to understand that the Pilots were not prejudiced against the use of searchlights or any other means which could be found to help them to get vessels through with as little delay as possible.

The reference to the *Manchester Citizen* at that meeting was prompted by the fourth complaint, this time from the vessel's owners, the Manchester Liners.

They expressed great concern over the exceptional length of time occupied by their vessel when navigating the Canal from Eastham to Manchester on 21st October 1935. The vessel had been moored at a lay-by berth during the night. The Chairman of the Pilotage Committee had written to the Pilot concerned expressing his disappointment at the unusual length of time during the transit of the Canal.

Here one must pause to reflect upon the many nuances of the searchlight controversy. On the one hand the Manchester Ship Canal Company, with the heavy responsibility to their shareholders forever in the forefront of their minds, were trying by every means to attract shipping to the Canal at a time of increasing economic torpitude in the United Kingdom. That they managed to maintain an average of 6,000,000 tons of shipping per year bringing in an average revenue from that tonnage of over £1,300,000 between 1931 and 1937 was a miracle in itself. It was then, as it is today, essential for a vessel to have the least possible delay in Port coupled with the least possible delay during the Pilotage. That was the main reason they were so keen to establish a 24 hour port.

On the other hand the Pilots were divided, this time into three factions, those who were totally opposed to night navigation on the grounds it was too dangerous, those who were against it for no other reason than there was no extra remuneration for this new work and those who were in favour, seeing it as a way to ingratiate themselves with the Pilotage Committee and/or Shipowners in the hope of being offered a "Choice/Appropriate Pilotage". There were a significant number of personnel changes in "Choice" pilotage during those years.

On 12th November 1935 the Pilots could contain themselves no longer and instructed the Secretary of the Manchester Pilots' Association to write the following letter to the Chairman of the Pilotage Committee to be placed before the Pilotage Committee:

"The Manchester Pilots have for some time been very concerned about their position in view of the attempts which are made from time to time by Representatives of the Port Authority to interfere with the exercise of their discretion with regard to the navigation of the Canal and in particular the night navigation. The Pilots wish to place on record their serious apprehension that a continuance of the sort of things which have been happening for some time and of which there has been a recent instance, will lead to trouble.

A Pilot when in the performance of his duties occupies a very responsible position and anything in the nature of dual control, which can be brought about in more ways than one, is to be avoided at all costs. The Pilots therefore insist that they are left free and unfettered in the exercise of their discretion at all times when in the performance of their duties. I regret to learn also that arising out of these efforts to interfere with a Pilot in the performance of his duties there has grown a practice of requesting the Pilots to attend informal enquiries before certain representatives of the Port Authority for the purpose of investigating some complaint which may have been made. This is neither desirable nor in the spirit of the Pilotage Act and it is not in the interest of the Canal that Pilots should be constantly harassed by representatives of the Port Authority to navigate vessels in bad weather conditions or at a speed which the Pilot considers excessive in the conditions existing at the time.

The Pilots further resent being called to informal enquiries before representatives of the Port Authority for the purpose of a discussion, which should take place, if at all, before a properly constituted Committee of the Pilotage Authority. In particular, they object to being required to discuss matters arising out of a complaint of which no proper notice or particulars have been given to the Pilot.
I am sure that the Pilotage Committee will receive and consider this letter in the spirit in which it is written and that they will believe that the Pilots are only anxious to serve what they believe to be the best interest of all concerned."

The Chairman reported that a letter had been addressed to the Pilots' Association on 15th December for particulars of any cases in which the Pilots alleged the Port Authority officials had exceeded their authority in interfering with the discretion of the Pilots and for instances to support the complaints contained in the third and fourth paragraphs of the Association's letter. He also reported that the only alternative to the method at present in operation would be to put the Pilots to the expense of appearing before this Committee. The almost contemptuous attitude adopted by the Chairman of the Pilotage Committee in asking for particulars and support of the Pilots' complaints was totally unbelievable. The Chairman, the Harbour Master, and some shipowners' representatives had all sat on the informal committees to judge the rights or wrongs of a Pilot not transiting the Canal during the hours of darkness. They already fully understood all the circumstances and particulars that the Pilots had complained and objected to. The Manchester Pilots' Association's reply could ill conceal their wrath, and a letter was read to the December Pilotage Committee Meeting.

"Referrring to your letter of the 15th ultimo, the question contained in the second paragraph hardly permits of a direct answer, but I am to state that the Pilots do not take exception to directions being given by officials of the Port

Authority in pursuance of any powers conferred on them by Statute. The question of suggestions from the officials is however a different matter as the propriety of such suggestions depends upon the circumstances in which they are made and the extent to which any such suggestions may be regarded as an interference with the discretion of the Pilots and that is one of the matters of which complaint is made.

The alleged interference referred to in my letter related more particularly to night navigation and in this connection, what the Pilots take exception to is the assumption underlying the practice of lights being put aboard vessels, in conjunction with the ordering of tug boats; it being apparently expected both by owners or agents and Canal officials that the provision of lights will ensure that the vessel will proceed, without regard to the opinion of the pilot as to the prudence of doing so in such weather and other conditions as may exist.

I am informed that in some instances verbal messages, amounting almost to orders, are received aboard a vessel intimating that the vessel must reach a certain destination by a given time and although the officials of the Port Authority are not responsible for such messages, any failure on the part of the Pilot to conform to the wishes of the Agents is frequently followed by a complaint which leads to the Pilot being called to account by officials of the Authority. I understand that minor officials of the Port Authority have expressed the view that a Pilot can be relieved of responsibility for any untoward incident if, in circumstances in which pressure is brought to bear on him to proceed against his own judgement, he obtains from the Master a written statement that he will not be held responsible. It will I am sure be appreciated a Pilot cannot be relieved in this way of his duty to exercise his own judgement and discretion.

With reference to the question of informal inquiries or investigations by officials of the Port Authority, I would refer you to the inquiry held in connection with the navigation of the SS "Blairdevon"*. The recent holding of an informal inquiry, which will be within your knowledge, led the Pilots to fear that their protest in the case of the* "Blairdevon" *had not been effective and thus prompted a renewal of their objections in this connection. I trust that what I have stated above will sufficiently indicate the reasons which prompted my letter on behalf of the Pilots Association, without further reference to particular cases and I again assure the Pilotage Committee that in referring to these matters the Pilots are only actuated by a desire to serve the best interests of all concerned in the safe navigation of vessels on the Canal."*

After **briefly** discussing the matter and the contents of the letter the committee were of the opinion that the complaint had not been substantiated, and the Secretary of the Pilotage Committee was requested to inform the Pilots Association to that effect.

Once more the total disdain shown by the Pilotage Committee towards the Pilots Association and their complaints angered all Pilots. The fact their complaints were only **"briefly discussed"** and then summarily dismissed as **"unsubstantiated"** was evern more infuriating to the Pilots. This astonishing attitude of the Pilotage Committee can only be attributed to their belief that the Pilots were so divided on the point of night work for large vessels that there would be little or no resistance to such a dismissive statement. For once the Pilotage Committee completely misread and misjudged the Pilots' reactions. The Pilots immediately saw a threat to their jealously guarded autonomy and realised, at last, if a united front was not presented against the Pilotage Committee's attitude towards night work with the assistance of searchlights, they would without a shadow of doubt lose their automomy for ever.

At the Pilotage Association's meeting held in January 1936 it was proposed that should the Pilotage Committee continue to attempt to force night work with searchlights by interfering with the Pilot's discretion with regard to the safe navigation of large vessels during the hours of darkness, the question of a withdrawal of the Pilot Service, by way of a prolonged General Meeting for all Pilots, should be considered. This is how serious that situation had become. [Author's Note: *It is forbidden by Parliamentary Law, from the days of King Henry VII, for a Pilot to withdraw his services or, in modern day idiom, to go on strike. Hence a General Meeting would be called for all Pilots to attend, such a meeting could then last as long as required.]*

There was only one more criticism recorded against a Pilot for not proceeding with a large vessel at night and one must deduce from this that the Pilots' united stand and proposed action had been successful. Nevertheless, the searchlight episode did much towards the estrangement between the Pilotage Committee and the Manchester Pilot Service which from that time onwards was never truly healed. The other sad fact was, although this united stand should have proved to all Pilots for all time the wisdom and the power of a united service, alas, it did not. This new found unity would disintegrate once again in the not too distant future.

The outbreak of the Second World War in 1939 saw the withdrawal of all searchlights from the Ship Canal and night navigation ceased completely for all large vessels. In June 1944 it was suggested at Pilotage Committee that the beams from the guiding lights on either side of the Canal should be so arranged that they converged one with the next thus providing a continuous line of light along the Canal banks. The chairman expressed his opinion that the restoration of these lights as suggested was doubtful as the expenditure would be difficult to justify. A form of flood lighting was also suggested along the banks of the Canal, but like many more ideas of illuminating the Canal they all came to nought.

For the next twenty years, with the exception of the United State Line - Mr N C Callister was the *Choice* Pilot for that Company - which had special Canal searchlights permanently fitted on the port and starboard wings of their vessels' navigating bridges, no large vessels made a night transit on the Canal. In 1959 Shell Oil Company at their own expense, installed guiding lights at regular intervals on each side of the Ship Canal between Eastham and Ince Oil Berth, a distance of 6 miles, to enable their large tankers to proceed in the dark to their oil complexes at Stanlow and Ince. The Shell Oil Company had four *Choice* Pilots. The Manchester Ship Canal Company completed the extension of this lighting system for the next 30 miles of the Ship Canal in 1964, when night navigation became a normality and the Port of Manchester was able to advertise a 24 hour port, nearly 70 years after the Port was opened.

SHIPS TO REMEMBER

Nearly a Submarine!
"San Casto"

"Springdale H" - ex Britmex 7
Propelled by Two Outboard Motors

7

PILOTAGE TARIFF 1934 - 1939

The Pilotage Act 1914, the Pilots Bible, stated unequivocally:

"A licensed Pilot, who has given a bond in conformity with the Byelaws made for the purpose under the Act, shall not be liable for neglect or want of skill beyond the penalty of the bond and the amount payable to him on account of pilotage in respect of the voyage in which he was engaged when he became so liable."

It is something of an enigma that no such bond appears to have been in existence for the Manchester Ship Canal Pilots since their inception in 1895. In June 1934 a draft Byelaw from the Board of Trade in London, had been transmitted to the Pilotage Committee in a form which had been adopted by other Pilotage Authorities. A copy of this Byelaw was sent to the Pilots' Association, who replied that as the Byelaw now put forward by the Board of Trade, made the execution of the bond obligatory, a ballot must be taken of all Pilots to ascertain the general desire. The ballot resulted in over 75% of the Pilots agreeing to the form of the Byelaw proposed by the Board of Trade - agreed by the United Kingdom Pilots Association and the Manchester Ship Canal Company solicitors - and that it should be put into force at the earliest possible time, in the terms agreed. The Byelaw read as follows:

"Every Pilot on being Licensed, and every Pilot already licensed shall execute a bond for £100 (One hundred pounds) in such form as the Pilotage Authority may direct, with a view to the limitation of his liability for neglect or want of skill to that amount as provided in Section 35 of the Pilotage Act 1913."

The Byelaw was duly confirmed in August 1934. During the year of 1934 the depression still lingered on in the United Kingdom, and the United Kingdom Pilots' Association promoted a revision in the present method of levying pilotage dues - a more inopportune moment could not have been chosen, the shipowners being in the depths of recession.

Know all Men by These Presents

THAT I DEREK AVERELL CLULOW

of 1 KINGSVILLE ROAD, BEBINGTON, WIRRAL am held and firmly bound to the Manchester Ship Canal Company as the Pilotage Authority for the Manchester Pilotage District (hereinafter called " the said Authority ") their successors and assigns in the sum of One Hundred Pounds to be paid to the said Authority their successors or assigns upon demand and for the due payment whereof I hereby bind myself and my heirs executors and administrators.

Dated this Sixteenth day of December 1960.

WHEREAS the above bounden DEREK AVERELL CLULOW is a pilot duly licensed by the said Authority AND WHEREAS this Bond is given under the provisions of section 35 of the Pilotage Act 1913 and in conformity with the bye-law made for the purpose by the said Authority under the said Act.

NOW the condition of the above written Bond or obligation is such that if the above bounden DEREK AVERELL CLULOW shall not be liable for neglect or want of skill when acting as a licensed pilot in the Manchester Pilotage District then the above written Bond or obligation shall be void but otherwise the same shall remain in full force and virtue and that without prejudice to all or any of the powers of the said Authority to suspend revoke or require to be given up any licence granted by them to the above bounden.

Signed, sealed and delivered by the above named

DEREK AVERELL CLULOW,
1 KINGSVILLE ROAD,
BEBINGTON, WIRRAL.

in the presence of

JOHN N.GIBSON, PILOT MANAGER,
PILOT OFFICE,EASTHAM LOCKS,
EASTHAM, WIRRAL, CHESHIRE.

A Pilot's Bond Certificate

Briefly the suggestion was that every Shipowner, irrespective of whether his ships availed themselves of the Pilotage Service or not, should pay something towards its maintenance. The proposals, if adopted, would mean that the administrative expenses of the Pilotage service would be met from a direct levy on every ship using the Port, with the possible exception of regular coasting vessels, instead of by a deduction from the Pilots' earnings as at present. This would enable the Authority to make a reduction in the scehedule of Pilotage charges without adversely affecting the Pilots. It was agreed to defer further consideration until after the Shipowners and the Port Authority had an opportunity of studying these proposals.

A large number of Pilotage Authorities replied to the Board of Trade stating they were not in favour of adopting the proposed scheme for levying Pilotage dues. The Manchester Pilotage Committee decided, in time honoured fashion, to let the proposals lie on the table. The Manchester Steamship Owners' Association replied on 5th July 1934 stating that in conjunction with the Chamber of Shipping they had considered the proposals, and felt that the scheme as a whole meant such far-reaching alterations, with the necessary sequel of increased costs, that it was not acceptable to them and they wished to oppose the proposals. They also stated that some of the proposals were not applicable as there were no pilot cutters in the Manchester Pilotage District and a Pilots Benefit Fund had already been established. It was also understood that proposals relating to Masters and Mates contributions to the Pilot Fund had been abandoned by the United Kingdom Pilots' Association. The Manchester Port Authority were not in favour of the proposals and notified the Board of Trade accordingly. The matter was not referred to again in the Manchester Pilotage District.

Between 1930 and 1935 the great depression years, the tonnage using the Ship Canal did not unduly fluctuate, averaging just over 5.5 million tons per year. The lowest tonnage recorded was in 1932 when a total of 5,318,935 tons used the Canal. This tonnage was in excess of 1.5 million tons less than in 1926, but that particular year was a record year for the Ship Canal; it was not exceeeded until 1937. From 1932 the tonnage increased yearly and by 1940 had reached 8.5 million tons. Pilots' earnings remained stable during this period of unprecedented misery and hardship for the nation. A First Class Pilot (Rota) maintained an average income of £45 per month, an additional £10 to £15 could be added to this figure for an Appropriated Pilot, Second Class Pilots averaged £33 10s 0d (£33.50) and Helmsmen £26 10s 0d (£26.50). Even in the bleakest year of 1932 the monthly income of all Pilots and Helmsmen was reduced by only £1 10s 0d (£1.50).

It is interesting to compare the income received by sea-going personnel during the depression years, on a vessel of 6,000 tons to 7,000 tons which frequented the Ship Canal.

Master	£30 per month
Chief Mate	£18 per month
Chief Engineer	£27 per month
Able Seaman	£8 per month
Galley Boy	£4 per month

It was no small wonder that the differential in earnings of these two maritime professions made a Pilot's life so desirable to many officers of the sea-going fraternity.

There had been an unprecedented wave of sickness amongst the Pilots during 1934 and 1935, culminating in as many as eight Pilots being off the Rota through illness, some Pilots for as long as one month. Coupling these absences from the Rota with four Pilots on leave, other Pilots on Committee work and certain Pilots attending to their appropriated vessels, the thirty-two Pilots on the working Rota were soon dramatically reduced by half, a situation which must have brought the Pilot Service perilously close to breaking point. It is a matter of conjecture as to whether the sickness phenomenon had been caused by the strain of work imposed on an already undermanned pilot service. Certainly the strain on the Pilots' working on such a reduced Rota was immense. The Pilots had gone some way to alleviate the strain by terminating forthwith, in June 1935, the agreement whereby the attendance by a Pilots' representative at Committee meetings counted as a turn on the Rota.

Correspondence on this subject and the pilotage tariff had been on-going for some months. In December 1935 at the Pilotage Committee meeting the secretary (Mr Eyre) referred to letters which had been exchanged between the Authority and the Pilots' Association regarding Pilotage Rates and he read a letter written on behalf of the Authority on 15th August 1935 informing the Pilots' Association that the Authority had given careful consideration to the question of the restoration of the 10% reduction in Pilotage Rates, but did not think the time had arrived for this to be done. Further correspondence followed and on the 11th September the Association wrote intimating that the Pilots were disappointed with the decision and stating that the level of earnings had only been maintained by imposing an undue strain on the personnel of the Pilot service as evidenced by the large amount of sickness experienced during the past two years. The Pilots' Association stated that after giving careful consideration to all aspects of the situation the Pilots had decided to ask that the service be increased forthwith by not less than two Pilots and at the same time renewed their request for a restoration of the 10% reduction made in the rates in 1933, or such other revision of the schedule of rates as might be adequate for the proper remuneration of the increased number of Pilots asked for. The matter was left in abeyance pending a reply from the Steamship Owners Association.

The Manchester Steamship Owners' reply was fairly predictable in that they were totally opposed to a restoration of the 10% reduction made in the Pilotage Tariff in 1933 and to an increase in the Pilotage Service. Once more the long and laborious pattern of negotiations and meetings were reopened, following the well worn path of all the previous occasions. A special meeting was held on the 16th March 1937 between the representatives of the Pilotage Authority and the representatives of the Manchester Steamship Owners' Association.

The Chairman (Mr L Roberts) opened the proceedings by stating that with regard to the question of discontent among the Pilots, the shipowners would no doubt have some idea of the atmosphere which the Canal Company certainly sensed.

1938

No 9 Dock with the famous Grain Elevator. On the port side of the Dock SS "Sofie Bakke" Grt 4729 L 436' B 59' Twin Screw. Horror to steer in the Canal. On the starboard side the German vessel "Merganser" - note the Nazi Swaztika flying on the stern.

1938
The coal burning "Albingia" Grt 3309 L 398' B 42' bunkering at Partington Coal tip No 4

Mr Hughes (Manchester Steamship Owners' Representative) said he thought the question would be answered by asking how the Pilots could be satisfied, as he had heard no comments from them. Mr K Stoker (Manchester Steamship Owners' Representative) said he thought the Pilots had a very legitimate grouse, in so far as that they were the only members of the shipping community who had not had some portion of their cuts in 1933 restored. Some discussion took place as to the number of services performed by the Pilot service, viz 3,701 services performed by 28 First Class Pilots and 8 Second Class Pilots in 1936 compared with 3,256 performed by 26 First Class Pilots and 8 Second Class Pilots in 1931. Mr Hughes contended that the increase in the number of services was mainly accounted for by the increased number of vessels using Stanlow Oil Docks. Mr Roberts pointed out that the Pilotage Committee had thought it wise to appoint additional Pilots in 1935 because of the extra amount of work and this rather contradicted Mr Hughes' argument. Mr Stoker thought the idea of amending the schedule of rates was preferable to a restoration of the 1933 cuts, to avoid creating a precedent for other Pilotage Districts.

The suggestion was only put forward in an attempt to provide a figure which would give the Pilots a general increase. Mr Kissane (Secretary to the Pilotage Committee) stated there appeared to him to be three points at issue.

(a) Was any alteration necessary?
(b) If so, what amount was involved?
(c) What was the best way of distributing it?

Mr Hughes still reiterated he did not think the Pilots were entitled to any increase. Mr Roberts expressed something of the view previously put forward as to travelling expenses (it being suggested that instead of increased rates, some contribution might be made towards the Pilots' travelling expenses). The question of a Late Booking Fee already in force in Liverpool (£3. 3s 0d - £3.15) was raised and that a fee of £1.1s 0d - £1.05) should be established at Manchester. Mr Kissane said he thought no case had been made for any increase in the Pilotage rates but if Mr Evans (Secretary of the Pilots' Association) could agree to the proposals now made being put forward as a tentative arrangement, it might meet the case. The meeting was closed.

This committee meeting did not really grasp the seriousness of the situation nor did they really get down to the basic understanding that what the Pilots wanted was a straight increase in their rates. The pitiful suggestions put forward to increase their renumeration was derisory to say the least. All the negotations inevitably reached a deadlock and once more a Board of Trade inquiry was called for, to settle the question of the Pilots' Tariff. The inquiry was duly held in December 1938 under the auspices of Sir Julian Foley. Resulting from that inquiry the Manchester Pilotage Authority amended the June 1933 Byelaw to read:

"A reduction of 2 ½% in lieu of the 10 ½ in the Pilotage Rates, including those for extra services, to be operative on and from 23rd February 1939. This was confirmed by the Board of Trade."

War clouds had once more begun to gather over Europe, Hitler was on the march and the United Kingdom was frantically scrambling to get their act together under the Chamberlain banner of appeasement. One wonders if the political situation in Europe had any influence on the making and passing of this Byelaw. While the Byelaws were open it proved a golden opportunity for all the Pilots to introduce a measure to curtail the annoying and disruptive practice of dilatory shipping agents/brokers placing orders for Pilots to attend a vessel - some hours hence - after office hours. This practice had become increasingly prevalant over the years and could seriously disrupt the order of the rota. The Byelaw read:

"When a vessel is ordered for a Pilot after office hours, ie 1700 hours Monday to Friday or after 1300 hours Saturday and Sunday an additional late booking fee of £1. 1s 0d (£1.05) shall be payable to the individual Pilot concerned."

This Byelaw did much to curb this unnecessary practice and in 1956 the late booking fee was incorporated into the Pilots' Tariff. The introduction of travelling expenses did not commence until January 1947 when a fee of 7s 0d (35p) was payable.

The Pilots' Association in 1938 had continued to press relentlessly for the restoration of the 10% cut in Pilotage Rates that occurred in 1933 or an increase in Pilotage rates, either of which would give a welcome increase in the Pilots' remuneration. On Sunday evening, 13th November 1938 a meeting of the Pilots' Association was convened at Rock Ferry under the Chairmanship of Mr J H Warren with Mr C Rhodes as Secretary. Both Pilots were representatives on the Pilotage Committee. At that meeting twenty-two Pilots attended and they unanimously passed a resolution that the Pilots would not move any large vessels on the Canal between dusk and one hour to sunrise. Since the great searchlight controversy that raged between 1931 and 1936 large vessels moved only spasmodically during the hours of darkness, those vessels that did so were usually with *Choice* Pilots in charge. This action was reportedly taken as an instrument to hasten the already protracted negotiations on earnings to a conclusion. The resolution was officially notified to the Harbour Master (Captian Howard) at 1400 hours on Monday, 14th November and duly relayed by him to the Chairman of the Pilotage Committee. At the Pilotage Committee meeting in November a somewhat aghast Chairman (Mr W Browning) expressed the view of all members of the Committee and he hoped he was correct in including the Pilots, that the Pilots' action was very much regretted from every point of view and it could well adversely affect the Shipowners, Canal Company and even the Pilots themselves. There appeared to have been a recurrence of statements to the national press and he emphasised the damage that a campaign of this nature might cause and he deprecated very strongly any extension of it.

The Pilots' proper course would be to make their representations through the Pilotage Committee. The Chairman in retaliation to the Pilots' actions pointed out that any Pilot who refused or wilfully delayed without reasonable cause to pilot a vessel when required to do so by the master, owner or agent or by an officer of the Canal Company (Pilotage Authority) rendered himself liable to a fine under section 48 of the Pilotage Act in addition to any liability for damages and also to the suspension or revocation of his licence under Section 26 of the Act. This veiled threat, when issued, was usually sufficient for the Pilots to moderate their demands and it appears in this case it was equally successful.

Runcorn "Riviera" 1938
Courtesy Captain P Dunbavand
Note the segregation - all the men on the grass knoll (top left), women and children on the beach.

The Chairman explained that the application for increased rates was taking its proper course and he thought more harm than good would be done by the Pilots adopting the attitude indicated in the newspaper articles (no night work). He went on to say that the Pilots should write to the National press and state that the statements had not been with the authority of the Pilots' Association and asked Mr Warren as Chairman of that Association if he would undertake to do it. Mr Warren declined saying that without the authority of the Pilots he could not do so. Mr Warren also remarked that the Pilots considered they had been taking an undue risk for many years moving vessels at night, and now decided to exercise more caution. One of the reasons, he said, why they had decided that they were risking their licences was when a Pilot had to pay £160 for doing damage whilst navigating in the dark.

Mr Warren's reply to the Chairman's statements was enlightening to say the least, because he refuted the allegations that the Pilots were responsible for the press release and counter-suggested that someone in the Canal Company could have passed the information to the National tabloids (in modern day parlance "a mole"). Mr Warren felt that the articles in the press contained quite a lot of truth and he thought the Pilots would not wish to disassociate themselves from them entirely. Both Pilots' representatives emphatically denied that the Pilots had agreed to the resolution referred to. This statement was in direct contradiction to the resolution that Mr Rhodes had hastily conveyed to the Harbour Master on the afternoon of 14th November. Why there were such contrasting statements has never been solved. The confrontation between the Association and the Pilotage Committee came to nought. Large vessels continued, occasionally, to transit the Canal at night but in September 1939 when war was declared the threat of no night navigation as a strong position to bargain from, ceased to be a threat at all.

8

THEY DON'T MAKE PILOTS LIKE THIS ANY MORE

They broke the mould after they made Noel Clifford Callister. No other Manchester Ship Canal Pilot came even remotely close to the unique manner in which he piloted vessels, especially the United States Line who were some of the largest vessels to navigate the canal and to whom he was the appropriated pilot.

Noel Clifford Callister (Cliff Cal to everyone on the Canal) was born on May 1st, 1896, in Douglas, Isle of Man. He was educated at Douglas High School and although there were no previous seafarers in his family, the long tradition of following the sea by Manxmen stirred within his breast. Little did he know or realise what traumas or experiences lay ahead of him when he made his decision to follow a seagoing career.

At the age of 14 years he was apprenticed to the Galgate Sailing Ship Co., of 13, Tower Chambers, Old Church Yard, Liverpool, and on June 3rd 1910, sailed out of Liverpool for the Far East on board the "LYDGATE", a steel hulled four masted barque under the command of Captain J. Jones. The "LYDGATE" was built in Jarrow-on-Tyne in 1893 and was fitted with double top gallants and main royals, she was 304 feet long with a beam of 43 feet and a gross tonnage of 2534 tons.

He spent his entire apprenticeship on board the "LYDGATE" sailing to such diverse places as India, China, Australia, South and North America and many countries in Europe and the Mediterranean. He had experienced rounding the

Mr. Noel Clifford Callister
Manchester Ship Canal Pilot Service
1921 - 1966

fearsome Cape Horn on more than one occasion during his days as an apprentice. In November 1914 he sat and passed his examination for a second officer in sail and was immediately appointed 3rd watch keeping officer on board another of the company's ships, the "INDIA". She was of similar dimensions and rig as the "LYDGATE" but was ironed hulled.

On the 12th June 1915, under the command of Captain Gilbert, on passage from Barry, South Wales to Pernambuco with a full cargo of coal she was intercepted by U.C.35 off St. Annes Head in 50 55' N 6 35' W. The crew and officers were allowed to take to the boats and she was then sunk by shell fire. The crew and officers were picked up by a passing fishing vessel and taken to Swansea.

On a historical note in 1915 the German fleet had two classes of submarines the U.B. and the U.C. they were about 90 feet in lenght with a beam of 10 feet and a draught of 9 feet 6 inches with a surface speed of 6 ½ knots. when submerged they could keep up a speed of 5 knots but for only an hour after which they had to surface and charge their batteries. They were armed with two torpedoes and eight mines and a 2 pounder gun was mounted close to the conning tower.

The enormous cost of torpedoes in those days, hundreds of pounds, meant that most of the U. Boat Captains when attacking sailing ships, which were in the main unarmed, allowed all on board to abandon ship and then either went along side and placed a mine on board and blew the vessel up or sank it by shell fire. The gunners on these submarines were experts lent from the German High Seas Fleet and their shooting could not have been bettered. The advent of British "Q" ships curtailed much of this German strategy but that is another story.

Mr. Callisters next sailing ship was the pride of the Galgate Sailing Co., the "GALGATE". She was built at Whitehaven in 1888, an iron hulled, four masted, square rigged ship. The "GALGATE" was one of the best known ships afloat at that particular time, having a good turn of speed but "rolled heavily when pressed". In 1895 she made the fastest passage from Calcutta to New York in 102 days at an average speed of 13.5 knots. Her best days run was 295 miles.

Her master was Captain W. Griffiths of Milford, a tall, lean and hard man, but just and fair, and a superb sailing Master. Mr. Callister learned a lot from this wonderful seaman. On May 6th 1916 whilst on passage from Portland Oregon, U.S.A. to Falmouth she was intercepted by U.B. 19, 170 miles West by North from Ushant and was sunk by shell fire.

"INDIA" G.T. 2057
Four masted barque - Iron hull - L. 277' - B. 41'

"GALGATE" G.T. 2361
Four masted square rig - Iron Hull - L. 294' B. 43'

In December 1916, Mr. Callister passed his examinations for a Chief Officer's Certificate. In late November 1918, he travelled overland with a full crew to Hamburg to join the company's last sailing ship, the "IRBY", under the command of Captain Gilbert. The reason for this, the "IRBY" had been captured and detained at Hamburg throughout the war. Fate dealt another cruel blow when on passage from Hamburg to the Tyne, she struck a mine and sank off the Dogger Bank. The "IRBY" was Mr. Callister's last sailing ship after a most eventful eight years sailing before the mast.

He then joined the Standard Oil Co., vessel "DONAX" as third officer. In 1920 he passed his Master's Certificate in sail and steam and sailed on the "MINNIE DE LARRINAGA" as second officer. At the age of 25 years he applied and was accepted as helmsman on the Manchester Ship Canal in October 1921. He steered his first vessel, S.S. "TYRO" (net 698 tons) from Manchester to Eastham under Pilot J.W. Heath for which he received payment of £1 13s 9d (£1.67p) for his services.

Mr. Callister for all his sufferings during World War 1 could not avoid the 'slings and arrows' of a totally vindictive pilot service (see Vol.2 Chapter 19) but nothing the Pilots could and did do ruffled this man's aimiable nature one iota. He attained his second class licence in 1928 and his First Class licence in 1931. He was appointed appropriated/Choice Pilot to the United States Line in 1935. It was during this appropriation that he became the first pilot to use the aid of a form of search light for night navigation when at that period of time all large vessels moored up at nightfall.

Mr (Cliff) Callister became one of the most loved and respected Pilots in the Manchester Pilotage District. A lifelong teetotaller and lifelong friend of all helmsmen who held him in such high regard. The stories of his unique approach to piloting are legendary and still recalled in ports all over the world wherever seamen meet. One such story deserves such a mention. At the A.G.M. dinner of the United States Line, held in New York, pilots and piloting were being discussed. A master of that company was heard to say "You guys have never really experienced being piloted until you have been piloted by our company's Pilot in the Manchester Ship Canal. He is the only pilot that can nearly rip the bilge keel off your ship on the canal banks whilst going full ahead and continue to discuss the nesting habits of the sand martins burrowing into that self same bank".

Mr Callister was indeed one of the most colourful characters ever to grace the ranks of the Manchester Ship Canal Pilot Service. It was indeed a sad day for many people when he retired back to the Isle of Man in September 1966. The

3rd Officer Mr. N. C. Callister
August 1920

S.S. Donax
Standard Oil Company

Manchester Pilot Service would never see the likes of such a man again and the service is all the more poorer for this. He will always be remembered with the greatest of affection. He died on November 14th 1968, aged 72 years. They certainly don't make Pilots like him anymore.

A PILOTS PRAYER

The Lord is my Pilot
I shall not strand nor shall I flounder
He steers me thro safe channels in deep
waters and by the stars of righteousness
For His names sake.

Yea through the peril of fog or tempest
I fear not for Thou art with me
Thy care and skill encompasseth me
Thou preparest a haven for me in the land
of the mariners gone before me.

My courses are true, the anchorage certain
Surely my life's voyaging will end in peace
So I may shelter in the harbour of the Lord forever.

Amen.

9

"THEY SHALL NOT GROW OLD"

One glorious sunny day in June I had been to pay my last respects to departed merit of a dear and close friend. On returning from his graveside I came across the grave of a Pilot colleague who had died all too young. For a minute I was overwhelmed with the sadness of remembrance and as I walked around that grave I saw on the curb stone, engraved almost as an afterthought, the inscription *"Fell Asleep"*. It suggested a peaceful image, entirely at odds with the agonizing death he fought so valiantly against in those last tortuous months.

The inscription on the headstone *"Loved with an everlasting Love"* betrayed the stark sorrow and pain that was felt with his passing. He had died never having seen grandchildren, never to reap the rewards of piloting with a long and contented retirement, never to have fulfilled all his ambitions that I knew he had. To have left life after having seen so little seemed a tragic waste.

The sun that beat down and warmed the white marble chippings on the grave failed to warm my body or soul, as I thought, what good does a warm sunny day do to you if you are dead? Everything has it seasons, and eventually we all have to die, tragically some much sooner than others, but what a waste if we neglect to live our lives to the full during our sojourn in life. As I left that sad place I prayed fervently that those Pilots who had pulled up their anchor in life so early had not neglected to live their short lives to the full.

I dedicate this Chapter to them with deep affection.

DEATH IN SERVICE

Name	Date	Age
Adam Cartwright	January 1902	52
C Stringer	January 1905	51
P Sinnot	April 1905	68
J Hynes	April 1905	60
J Thompson	August 19o5	62
J Ellis	November 1905	53
T F Smith	February 1908	55
J Hill	December 1906	66
J Batty	February 1908	47
H Stuart	March 1909	55
H Boxer-Jones	March 1911	49
J Abram	February 1912	52 (Drowned in the river)
B Whitehouse	June 1913	54
W J Huntington	February 1914	42
E Taylor	November 1914	61
E R Blake	June 1916	55
H Limb	July 1918	37 (On active service in France)
A Yates	January 1921	42
C Young	December 1922	70
T N Gorst	June 1924	33
J A Hindle	November 1925	66
J Barnes	June 1927	67
W P Dudley	June 1927	36 (Shooting accident)
J D Shaw	March 1930	63
R Southwood	February 1932	52
W D Southwood	March 1935	56
T J Lamey	May 1935	54
T E Woodall	August 1942	51
R Southwood	September 1963	51
J Clarke	May 1968	56
L Davies	December 1972	48
W Walker	February 1972	63
C E Bowell	April 1973	45
H Whitehead	November 1975	64
A Green	March 1975	53
D Armitage	November 1979	50
D Brown	December 1982	50
C Broom	August 1985	58
J Wainwright	April 1985	58
H Davies	June 1986	59
A Gleeson	December 1987	60
J J Pierpoint	February 1988	49

1912-1918
Captain Harry Limb RE

1917-1927
Mr W P Dudley

1919-1942
Mr T E Woodall

1904-1921
Mr A Yates

1950-1985
Mr J Wainwright

1949-1972
Mr L Davies

1928-1968
Mr J Clarke

1930-1975
Mr H Whitehead

1954-1979
Mr D Armitage

1954-1985
Mr C Broom

1959-1982
Mr D Brown

1951-1973
Mr C E Bowell

1944-1975
Mr A Green

Mr A Green

A CAPTAIN'S PRAYER

The storms may roar around me
My heart may low be laid
The pilots help surrounds me
How can I be afraid.

Wherever he may guide me
No danger turns me back
The pilot is beside me
And nothing can I lack.

His knowledge is for ever
His sight is never dim
His word deserts me never
And I will sail with him.

Shallow waters are before me
Which yet I've never seen
Deep channels will he steer me
Where threat'ning rocks have been.

My trust I cannot hide
My course to port is free
My pilot is my guide
And he must sail with me.

From Hymns Ancient and Modern
With apologies.

10

Accident Reports 1896 -1990

Pilots must not submit to pressure at any time, when this is in conflict with their judgement. Their discretion holds good whether their vessel is supplied with "lights" or any other aids to navigation. It would avail a pilot nothing to plead that "He was told to get the vessel on berth by a certain time" or "That the vessel was supplied with searchlights" or that the "Master persisted", if damage resulted from his handling of that vessel at a time when such influences were against his better judgement. The Pilot not the Master or any other individual has the "last word" and he has the law on his side.
Judgement by Sir John Inskip and confirmed by Messrs Batesons & Company, Solicitors.

In 1895 although the Manchester Ship Canal was the newest pilotage district in Europe, a number of aspects in the district had not been envisaged. one was that no consideration had been given to the formation of a Committee to assess the liability in an accident in the Ship Canal and to apportion the blame. At the Pilotage Committee held on 7th April 1896 it was reported that several complaints had been received from shipowners and agents whose ships had met with accidents whilst navigating the Canal in charge of a licensed Pilot. The Chairman (Mr Marshall Stevens) requested the Committee to consider the best method of dealing with such complaints with a view to ascertaining who was to blame in such cases. The Committee recommended that all the reports of accidents be laid upon the table at the meetings of this Committee and any case where the Committee thought an enquiry should be held in respect of the conduct of the Pilot of any vessel meeting with an accident in the Canal, they should hold such an enquiry and if it was thought desirable should summon the Pilot to attend and give evidence.

On Monday 18th May 1896 at the offices of the Manchester Ship Canal Company at 41 Spring Gardens the first Accident Report Committee was convened. Those present were:

Chairman of the Pilotage Committee	Mr Marshall Stevens
Deputy Chairman	Mr J C Wilson
Canal Superintendent	Captain Heasley
Canal Superintendent	Captain Waring
Canal Superintendent	Captain Dudley
Canal Superintendent	Captain Whitehouse
Canal Superintendent	Captain Williams
Mersey River Pilot	Mr Backhouse
Mersey River Pilot	Mr Lewis
Canal Pilot	Mr Adam Cartwright
Canal Pilot	Mr H Hill
Secretary, Canal Company	Mr Eyre

It was stated that this inaugural meeting had been called to enquire into the cause of the accident to the *SS Genova"* (Grt 743 tons, Length 198', Beam 28', Draft 15') when passing up the Canal on 13th March 1896 in charge of Mr George Clark, a Liverpool Pilot. The Chairman said that in the event of any member of the Committee being called upon to give evidence in the case he could not vote on the decision. The facts of the case was reported as follows:

"The vessel had just passed Runcorn Railway Bridge and was proceeding along the Canal in charge of the Canal Pilot, when the vessel appeared to be touching the ground on the port side of the Canal. Increased speed was ordered to give the vessel steering way. The vessel sheered over to the starboard side of the Canal which was met by hard starboard helm. The vessel then sheered to the port side striking the Old Runcorn Quay sustaining serious damage to upper work of forecastle, two plates being indented badly and deadlights broken. The quay was also injured. About a minute before the casuality, when a collision with the Quay seemed imminent, the engines were reversed full speed. Subsequently in passing through the first Lock (Latchford) the vessel collided slightly with the starboard side of the Lock damaging her rail on the starboard bow.

The damages stated had incurred a bill of £300 which the owners have had to pay and there is a further bill from the Ship Canal Company of £14. 3s 4d ((£14.17)."

To avoid any confusion to the reader arising from the helm orders given in the above statement viz. *"The vessel sheering to starboard being met with hard to starboard helm"*, it should be pointed out, in 1896 orders were completely opposite to those of today. In 1896 to change course to starboard you placed the wheel to port and vice versa. This manoeuvre was carried on from the days of the tiller when a tiller would have to be pushed over to starboard to give port helm to a vessel in order for that vessel to turn to port. This system remained in force until it was internationally changed in 1932 although a few rogue ships still existed until the mid-1950s. The phraseology of the report is symptomatic of its time in its quaintness viz *"The quay was also* ***injured*** and *A minute before the casuality"*.

The Captain of the *"Genova"* stated the casuality was caused by the action of the Pilot, that it might have been prevented by the Pilot properly handling the vessel and that he (the Captain) would have done better without the Pilot. The Pilot's report was read out to the meeting:

"Whilst proceeding up the Canal, just before arriving at Saltport I had occasion to complain about the man at the wheel. I told the Master to send another man to the wheel but he told me the man was the best helmsman in the ship. A minute or so afterwards the Chief Officer came to the wheel to steer until we arrived at Runcorn Railway Bridge when he gave up the wheel to the man I had previously found fault with: he did this after I had requested him to remain at the wheel until we had cleared Runcorn Bend. The cause of the accident in my opinion is that the vessel is a bad steering vessel and also the man at the wheel giving the vessel too much helm after me repeatedly telling him not to do so. The slight accident at Latchford Locks was caused by the vessel not answering the helm and the men on the forecastle head not holding on to the bow rope when I told them to."

The Pilot was subjected to an examination by several members of the Committee particularly on the speed of the vessel passing Runcorn and approaching Latchford Locks. The Committee told the Pilot, Mr G Clark, that when piloting the *"Genova"* he was going too fast with an untried vessel round Runcorn Bend and in entering Latchford Locks. The Pilot did not appear to have had the assistance from the officers to which he was entitled and it was considered, that as requested by the Pilot, the Chief Officer should have remained at the wheel until the vessel had rounded Runcorn Bend, but, at the same time it was felt that he should be severely reprimanded for the accident. This being the first enquiry the Committee had held they did not desire to take any more serious steps but they hoped that it would be a warning to him for the future as they considered they had dealt very leniently with him. The

Committee thought he should know that it was not judicious to go too fast and that when a vessel did not steer well he should have gone rather slower than faster.

PILOTING ODDITIES

A Chinese Junk
Courtesy The MSC Co

PILOTING ODDITIES

A Futuristic Sphere
Courtesy The MSC Co

A Floating Night Club
Courtesy The MSC Co

PILOTING ODDITIES

MV Aberthaw Fisher
Courtesy World Ship Society
Grt 2355 Length 276' Breadth 56' Max Draught 17'
"To see where you are going you have to look where you have been"

A Thames Barge "Will"
Courtesy The MSC Co
MV Aberthaw Fisher

A replica of Sir Francis Drake's famous warship "Golden Hind"
passing under Runcorn Bridge
1993
Courtesy of the Daily Post, Liverpool

PILOTAGE OF THE *SS "TRIGGA"* 25TH MAY 1896

This accident report brought to the attention of the Pilotage Committee and the Pilots' representatives, for the first time, the Auxiliary or *"Danube"* rudder to assist in the steering of a vessel in narrow waters such as the Ship Canal. Senior Pilot, Mr R Iddon, in his report stated "*Even in the river I could see the vessel was a bad steering one*". He then catalogued the incidents in the Canal.

1 Went aground in the Rock Cutting at Ince.

2 Went aground passing the Weaver Sluices

3 Struck Old Quay Wall at Runcorn, damaging two port bow plates and starting rivets. Total damage to the extent of £90 or thereabouts.

4 Went aground between Chester Road Bridge and Latchford Locks.

Mr Iddon went on to say *"The vessel's rudder was of no use to her. I am very sorry for the misfortunes but I had no control of the vessel as she was unmanageable"*. He added the classic Canal Pilots' rider *"Each place the vessel went aground the bottom was soft"*! A similar report from a Pilot, Mr N Morgan, who had piloted the *SS "Godwit"* was also read.

The question of the steering of these vessels when navigating in the Canal and the advisability of the Masters of same using an auxiliary or *"Danube"* rudder when passing along the Canal was discussed and the general opinion was expressed, that by using an auxiliary rudder these vessels would be less liable to accidents. It was decided to write to the owners on this subject pointing out that the Pilotage Committee had concluded that if an auxiliary rudder had been used the damage would have been avoided. The owners were asked to notify their Masters by letter to use an auxiliary rudder when navigating the Canal in future. The following notice was issued to all Canal Pilots.

"That all Pilots on boarding any vessel be required to ascertain whether such vessels have an auxiliary rudder available and if so to give their careful consideration as to the advisability of requiring its use during the piloting of the vessel in the Canal with a view to lessening the danger of her going against her helm and colliding with the banks or other objects in the Canal."

There was no disciplinary action taken against Mr Iddon or Mr Morgan.

PILOTAGE OF THE *SS "COANWOOD"* (GRT 1105 L 226' B 30') 8TH JULY 1897
THE FIRST SUSPENSION OF A CANAL PILOT'S LICENCE

On 8th July 1897 the *SS "Coanwood"* under the advice of Mr W Huntington (Pilot First Class), when entering Modewheel Lock inward bound caused considerable damage to the port and starboard wall of the Lock. At the same time damage was incurred to the port and starboard bows of the vessel. The Pilotage Committee, under the Chairmanship of Mr J C Wilson, deliberating on this accident report, heard Captain Williams (Canal Superintendent) a prime witness to this accident state that he was extremely critical of the positioning of the vessel when approaching the Lock. In Captain Williams' opinion the vessel should have been *"nearer the shore with a straight course for the Locks"*.

The Pilot stated his reason for the positioning of his vessel prior to entering the Lock was that he was afraid that if he came any nearer to the Canal bank he would lose command over the vessel and that if she had answered her helm as she ought to have done the course taken by him would have brought her safe into the Lock. He considered the vessel taking a sudden sheer as the cause of the accident and not to any mismanagement on his part. The Captain stated that on approaching the Lock the vessel took a sheer to port and a sheer to starboard and before the vessel could be straightened up she struck the Lock walls on both sides. The Captain thought the vessel had taken a sheer to port in consequence of some under current or disturbance of the water. Captain Williams said this could not be so as the sluices had been down for three and a half hours and no locking had taken place for a period of 25 minutes. Captain Williams' views were that the vessel was improperly navigated and if she had been brought up to the Locks nearer the shore and with a straight course for the Locks the accident would have been avoided.

After discussion it was moved by Captain Dudley that the licence of Mr Huntington be suspended for two months. It was then moved by Mr Stuart (Canal Pilot) and seconded by Mr Colquitt (Mersey River Pilot) that the licence of Mr. Huntington be suspended from this date to the 21 August next inclusive. This motion was carried. How a Canal Superintendent with no Pilotage experience whatsoever could so openly criticise a Pilot's navigational judgement in positioning his vessel prior to his entering the Lock - especially as Mr Huntington was one of the original Pilots examined and appointed a Pilot in February 1896 - and how the Pilotage Committee could come down so heavily in favour on the side of Captain Williams' evidence, is beyond comprehension. Nevertheless they did and I wonder if they were trying to make an example of someone to show the rest of the Pilot Service that the Accident Committee did have strong powers and were prepared to use them.

(230)

THE MANCHESTER SHIP CANAL COMPANY

PILOT'S CONFIDENTIAL REPORT TO The Harbour Master,
Manchester Ship Canal Company,
Dock Office, Manchester 17.

..................................19......

In accordance with the provisions of Pilotage Bye-Law 17, I have to report that the undermentioned Vessel, on which I was engaged as a pilot, met with an accident, the particulars of which are given below.

Signature..

Name of Vessel Piloted ....

Date of accident .... Time ....

Where accident occurred..

Name of Agent..

Draught of Vessel: Forward.................. Aft.................. Net Reg. Tonnage..................

Names of Tugs: Ahead.. Astern..

Where boarded.. Where bound..

Wind: Direction.................. Force .... State of weather....................................

Speed of Vessel through the water before accident ....

Speed and direction of engines before accident..

Speed of Vessel through the water at time of accident ....

Speed and direction of engines at time of accident..

Sound Signals given..

Sound Signals received..

Did Vessel sustain damage, and if so, where? ....

....

Damage to other Vessel or Property (if known)..

Did Vessel ground; if so, for how long? ....

How was Vessel re-floated?..

[P.T.O.

(*To be forwarded to Owners/Agents by the Authority*)

MANCHESTER PILOTAGE DISTRICT

Report by Mr. ....to Owners/Agents of

s.s./m.v. ....

I wish to report that the above mentioned vessel, on which I was engaged as a Pilot, met with an accident, the particulars of which are given below.

(1) Place where accident occurred..

....

(2) Nature of accident..

....

(3) Damage to Vessel (if known) ....

....

(4) Damage to other Vessel or Property (if known)..

....

(5) Date of accident ....

(6) Time of accident ....

Signature of Pilot ....

Address ....

....

....

PILOTAGE OF THE *SS"LIVORNO*" 22nd APRIL 1899 (Grt 1463 Beam 34' Draught 18')

This was the first fully comprehensive record of an adjudication of an accident report in the Manchester Ship Canal by the Pilotage Committee. The disciplinary action taken was the severest ever meted out and no such disciplinary action has ever exceeded this before or after in the history of the Manchester Pilot Service. At the meeting of the Pilotage Committee on 1st May 1899 the Chairman (Mr Collins) reported that the *SS "Livorno"*, piloted by Mr Albert Lever of 3 Whitfield Street, Higher Tranmere, Birkenhead, on her passage up the Canal to Manchester had met with a series of accidents, although only 860 tons net registered. The following are the particulars:

1 Runcorn Railway Bridge. Collided with river wall damaging fender on same also damage sustained to vessel.

2 Between Old Quay Locks and Old Quay Swing Bridge took a sheer to port and grounded on estuary side of Canal.

3 Near Moore Lane Wharf ran on shore north side of Canal - was re-floated after about two hours.

4 Warrington Dock: entrance to Twenty Steps Bridge. opposite to Warrington Dock entrance sheered to south side then across to the north side when she appeared to strike the Canal bank - rubbed along the south abutment of Twenty Steps Bridge and then sheered across the Canal to the north side striking the Canal bank.

5 Latchford old Station. Struck the north side of the Canal bank.

6 Barton Locks. When entering 65ft Lock collided with Island Bullnose damaging a plate on her starboard bow.

Mr Albert Lever had managed to go through the whole gamut of accidents that could happen to any Pilot in a lifetime on the Ship Canal in just one passage up the Canal. How I would have loved to have heard the conversation between the Master and Mr Lever when they finally arrived in Manchester Docks, utterly bewildered and exhausted.

The Pilot however only mentioned in his accident report the grounding off Moore Lane Wharf and colliding with Barton Locks. On arriving at Manchester Docks the vessel was found to be making water and the Agent had found it necessary to commence her discharge on the Sunday afternoon in order to prevent her sinking. The Chairman stated that he considered the matter so serious a nature that he had suspended the Pilot's licence forthwith, pending this investigation by the Committee.

The Chairman then submitted and read the detailed reports of the accidents from Mr Lever (Pilot) and Captains Heasley, Waring and Williams (Canal Superintendents). From these reports the following points arose:

1 The Anchor Line vessel *"Britannia"* delayed in Latchford Lock and missing the tide at Eastham due to the *"Livorno"* being aground for two hours at Moore Lane Wharf.

2 Captain Waring had never seen the Pilot, Mr Lever, before, neither had any of the lock staff at Latchford Locks.

3 The Lock Master at Barton Locks stated as the vessel approached the Locks he observed the Pilot and the Master having *'high words'*. (Rather quaintly put again!).

4 The vessel was piloted by a Liverpool Dock and Harbour Board Pilot holding a Canal licence and had been assisted by the Canal Company's tug the *"Agnes Seed"* from Latchford to the Docks.

The Chairman called the attention of the Pilot to his having omitted to mention in his report several cases of the vessel colliding with the banks of the Canal and he (the Chairman) was prepared to hear any further statement the Pilot had to make. Mr Lever stated that the vessel being only fitted with hand steering gear, and that of an antiquated style needing two crew members at the wheel, he found the vessel very bad to steer. There was no indicator on the steering gear to show the position of the rudder after an order had been executed by the men. He also stated that he considered the rudder chain was somewhat impeded by the cargo on deck (timber planks) which prevented the helm having proper play. The vessel was continually taking sheers across the Canal and he said he could only attribute the cause to the men at the wheel being unable to get the helm over as he ordered it to be put quickly enough. A case in point, he mentioned that on leaving Modewheel Lock he had instructed the men to port the helm and that although they appeared to carry out the order the Lockmaster, who had heard the order given, hailed him that the rudder was still amidships. The Pilot continued that several times when the vessel was taking a sheer the Master neglected to at once pass his instructions for the working of the engines, when he found the vessel sheering for the Canal bank an engine movement ahead as ordered by him would he thought have recovered her position, but the Master declined to give the order and instead ordered the engines to go astern thereby causing her to cant and strike the Canal bank.

The Master of the *"Livorno"* was invited to reply. He stated:

"I took the Pilot on board in the River and on entering Eastham Locks collided with the inner bullnose of the Lock. In my opinion this was due to the vessel having too much speed." He considered the damage to his vessel in the Canal was caused by the excessive speed at which the vessel was navigated and the Pilot's want of experience in navigating the Canal. He had informed the Pilot on several occasions that the vessel was going too fast but the Pilot did not seem to take any notice. He considered the vessel was very badly handled by the Pilot. The Master also laid great stress upon the point that he had been informed that the Pilot had not been up the Canal for a period of two years. With regards to the bad working of the helm he admitted there was no indicator on the steering gear but said both himself and the men at the wheel were so accustomed to its working that they could at any time tell from a mark on the chain working round the wheel the exact position of the rudder.

The Pilot's reply to these accusations was that the cause of the vessel striking the Locks at Eastham was the fact the crew could not get a bow rope out quick enough on account of the deck cargo and when the Lockmaster asked for a stern rope, no notice was taken of the request by those on board. The Pilot added that on arrival at Latchford Locks he had asked the Master if he preferred to have another Pilot to take him to Manchester but the Master had replied that he was satisfied he had done his best and that he must complete the journey. The Master's answer to these two points rather evasively admitted that in getting a bow rope out it had got jammed. With respect to the obtaining of another Pilot he considered that as he (Mr Lever) had engaged to Pilot the vessel to Manchester he ought to fulfil his contract. The Pilot was asked why, when the vessel was steeering so badly he did not moor the vessel and inspect the steering gear himself to ascertain its accuracy. He replied that he had not thought of doing so. Mr Sinnot (Senior First Class Pilot) stated that he had piloted the vessel from her berth into the Manchester Dry Docks and got the Master to try the wheel for him when it worked perfectly and seemed in good order.

The particulars of the pilotage performed by Mr Lever on the Canal since he received his licence in January 1896 was submitted, from which it appeared that he had only piloted ten vessels from March 1896 to September 1896 - two of these pilotages were of the full length of the Canal - and one vessel only in 1897, and had not piloted on the Canal since. The Pilotage Committee then considered the accidents which had taken place and the consequent damage to the vessel, to decide if they were the result of inexperience, carelessness or neglect of the Pilot or whether they were more attributable to the bad steering appliances of the vessel. After a lengthy discussion the Pilotage Committee concluded:

1 The Pilot, when he had observed the vessel steering so badly was very much to blame in not having moored his vessel and examined the working of the helm and so have satisfied himself as to the actual cause of the vessel sheering about in the manner she did.

2 The Pilot's want of experience in navigating the Canal had contributed greatly to the series of accidents which had taken place.

In the Pilot's defence Mr Colquitt (Mersey River Pilot) expressed the opinion that whilst proof of inexperience in navigating the Canal had been submitted against the Pilot it could not be said that he had been proved guilty of neglect or carelessness in giving orders.

The Pilotage Committee pronounced their verdict that it had been proved that the Pilot Mr Lever through his inexperience of the Ship Canal and the laxity he had shown in personally inspecting the working of the helm, was in a great measure responsible for the accidents. The Pilotage Committee therefore to mark their sense of disapproval suspended the licence of Mr Lever for three months. An amendment moved by Mr Colquitt and Mr Sinnot that the complaint against the Pilot be dismissed was defeated.

This suspension of a Canal licence for three months seemed to set the criteria for all future serious misdemeanours whether they be for neglect in piloting a vessel and causing damage or for not complying with Pilotage Byelaws and Regulations. Mr W Edmonds (Pilot First Class) was suspended in August 1899 for three months for neglecting to obey Canal Company sailing instructions and therefore incurred damage to his vessel and company property.

March 1954 Acton Grange Wharf
Collision between sand barge "Saxondale" and Everard Coaster SS Amenity.
Due to failure of steering gear aboard the ""Saxondale"

March 1954
Damage to SS "Amenity" GR 499 L 187 B 20'

Damage to "Saxondale". This vessel left Acton Grange Wharf to proceed to Pomona Docks to discharge. Her steering gear promptly broke down and she collided with the Canal bank as shown above. Tugs were sent to assist her to her discharge berth.
All photographs courtesy of Captain P Kennilworth

PILOTAGE OF *SS "ODD"* GRT 737 L187' B 28' 26TH MAY 1899

A more irate accident report from a Master of a vessel cannot be found in the records and considering the damage sustained to his vessel one can only totally sympathize with the Master's infuriation. It read as follows:

"I beg to give you notice that my vessel this morning received very serious damage whilst in charge of a Canal Pilot named Jones. This was caused by the signal on the Old Quay swing bridge being hoisted for 'to come ahead' or 'to proceed' but on approaching the Bridge same did not open, as usual, evidently being jammed or out of order again. My vessel being under-way came in collision with the Bridge carrying away her fore lower mast, level with the deck, damaging both bridges, breaking the pole compass, binnacle compass, steam whistle, engine telegraph and other various damages. I have had a survey held of the damages and if you desire you can also do same, as I am holding the Manchester Ship Canal Company liable for all cost of repairs, detention, loss of profit, etc. etc. etc."

It is hard to visualise the utter destruction and chaos that reigned at the time of collision on the bridge of the *"Odd"*. After the end of all the correspondence and deliberations surrounding this accident report the Pilot was informed that although the signal on the swing bridge had been hoisted, indicating his vessel may proceed ahead, he should have used extreme caution. In accordance with the byelaws he should have refrained from approaching too close, until the bridge had fully swung open and it was clear for him to pass through the bridge hole. The Pilot was severely reprimanded for his handling of the vessel and causing so much damage and warned if a similar accident of this nature occurred he would be automatically suspended.

PILOTAGE OF THE *SS "INVERLEITH"* GRT 1152 L 225' B 35' 8th APRIL 1902

Masters of vessels were not the only persons to vent their fury on Pilots' errors. The following letters of complaint were submitted to the Pilotage Committee from the Master of the vessel and the Owners:

"When approaching Runcorn Railway Bridge the Pilot in error put the helm to starboard instead of port to bring the vessel round the bend. My attention at the time being drawn to a large vessel coming down the Canal. The Second Officer noticing the Pilot putting the helm the wrong way at once went and put it to port but seeing the vessel would not recover the engines were put full speed astern, but before way could be got off, the vessel collided with the quay

doing considerable damage to the port bow and quay. It is my considered opinion the damage sustained was through the Pilot in error putting the helm the wrong way." Signed Geo Pickering, Master.

The vessel was inward bound and the Runcorn Bend is a notorious 45° turn to starboard. The mistake by the Pilot putting the wrong helm on probably stemmed from confusion with different steering mechanism as explained earlier in this chapter.

The letter from Mr E A Wiener of the Halmstad Shipping Company left no doubt about his feelings and what action should be taken and read as follows:

"We learn from the Master of our vessel that whilst proceeding up the Ship Canal in charge of a Pilot licensed by you, who was himself steering the vessel, he ran the vessel into the Quay Wall causing considerable damage to the vessel and whilst the vessel was being taken down the Canal after discharging her cargo again in charge of a Pilot licensed by you she was put ashore but fortunately on this occasion sustained no damage. This is the third occasion within twelve months on which our vessels the "Inverleith" *and* "Halmstadt" *have been run ashore by Pilots licensed by you and considerable loss and damage has been incurred by reason of their palpable incompetency.*

Under these circumstances we think you are fairly liable to compensate us for the losses sustained as it is quite palpable that the Pilots licensed by you and we are bound to employ, are grossly incompetent and we shall be glad to hear from you that you are willing to compensate us in this matter. We suggest that it is your duty to hold a formal inquiry into the conduct of these Pilots and whereas in the present case, it is absolutely proved that these damages result from absolute incompetence on the part of the Pilots, these Pilots ought to be mulched in the damages which ensue and ought to be suspended from further pilotage duties seeing that the circumstances prove that they are grossly incompetent and not fit to be trusted with the navigation of vessels in your Ship Canal."

The accident report from the Master was a clear and concise statement of facts, just as one would have expected from the Master of a British vessel. This cannot be said, unfortunately, about the owner's letter. It was full of histrionics, was heavily biased against Pilots in general - a practice still perpetuated to this day - and passing judgement on the Pilots before an inquiry had been held and all the facts revealed. The result of the accident reported at Runcorn Railway Bridge was that the Pilotage Committee found the Pilot guilty of a serious neglect in his piloting and he was suspended for three months.

In the case of the other two incidents reported by the owners both Pilots were severely reprimanded for their pilotage of the vessel.

1935
US Lines "American Importer"
Grt 7590 L 437' B 50'

Gulf Oil Co *"Belgian Gulf"*
Twin Propellers Grt 8401 L 450' B61'

COLLISIONS AND DAMAGE

13 7 1895	*S/S "Maranga"* ran into the Pontoon Dry Dock at Ellesmere Port, knocking the Barge "No 5" off the keel blocks, doing considerable damage
22 7 1895	*SS "Swan"* collided with dredger *"Mersey"* at Runcorn Bridge. Dredger was in tow of tugs *"Pioneer"* and *"Florida"*.
9 8 1895	Judgement given today by Justice Barnes and Trinity Masters re *"Beta"* and *Stanley Force"* (5 7 1895). The *"Beta"* was entirely to blame. Mr Forbes considered this a monstrous verdict.
14 8 1895	*SS "Gwillam Thomas"* inward, collided with the Barque *"Flora"* at Saltport. Damage considerable.
22 9 1895	*SS "Isabella"* entered the canal at Weston Mersey, stern first, and backing across the Canal damaged the bollards on the Barge *"No 5"*.
30 10 1895	*SS"Clan Macrae"* ran into dredger *"Medlock"* near Randle sluices, stove in 3 plates on port bow and parted the bucket chain. Damage considerable but will not prevent work when buckets are re-connected.
7 11 1895	*SS"Kirby Hill"* outward, collided with barque at Saltport.
13 11 1895	*"Alpha"* dropped down on the bows of dredger *"Bollin"* broadside. Extensive damage to *"Alpha"*. Cause was defective propeller and a heavy squall.
20 11 1895	Tug *"Minnie"* with steel barges *"No 2"* and *"No 14"*, collided with the Flat *"Laura"* and the barque *"Sherwood's"* boat, Saltport.
26 12 1895	*SS"Egret"* collided with *"Beta"*.
11 1 1896	Steam Barge *"Gertrude"* collided with Barge *No. 22"* at Runcorn Bridge.

3 2 1896	*SS "Swan"* collided with dredger *"Medlock"*. Considerable damage.
7 7 1896	Hopper *"Alpha"* collided with the tug *Queen of the Mersey"* at Bridgewater Pier Head (Fog). Damaged the latter's sponson and stove in a plate on the *"Alpha's"* bow.
30 7 1896	*SS "Courier"* collided with dredger *"Bollin"*, Section 55.
7 7 1896	Dredger *"Manchester"*. Rope in propeller, cut out by diver.
31 7 1896	*"Rubic"* collided with derrick barge *"Elin"* at Weston Mersey. *"Elin"* sunk. Lifted by *Ayres* using dredging men, etc. Lifted 1 8 1896. First Sinking in Canal due to a collision.
12 1 1900	Steam Flat *"Maggie"* (Liverpool Lighterage) sunk by the Tug *"Castlegarth"* in Eastham cutting.
10 12 1902	*SS "Winkfield"* went over the bottom gates at Barton sending them to the bottom and sinking the head Tug *"Flying Breeze"*.
27 6 1906	At 6.00 pm *SS"Cassia"* struck the lower 65 ft gates at Irlam and all the gates in the lock were carried away. Except for small traffic, the Canal was closed for 8 days.
Feb 1910	Barge *"Hawthorne"* (Rochdale Canal Co) sunk in river near E2 buoy. Mate's wife drowned in forward cabin.
23 5 1910	*SS "British Empire"* sunk at Ellesmere Port.
10 6 1910	Flat *"Annie"* with barbed wire sank at Acton Grange. Dredged up piece by piece by Dredger *"Medlock"*.
5 6 1913	While widening at Runcorn Bridge, the *"Camel"* and *"Scow"* picked up large tree, uncovered by *"Elk"*. Dimensions were 32' by 4' diameter.
17 3 1915	Tug *"Minnie"* was struck and sunk by *SS "Fleswick"* in Pool Hall rock cutting near No 2 Mile Post. Crew all taken on board *"Fleswick"* who was outward bound. Cause of collision - steering gear on *"Fleswick"* failed.

23 12 1919	*SS"Canadia"* (cargo of newsprint) ran ashore on West Bank, Eastham Channel, midway between the Ferry Stage and Eastham Locks. She broke her back on the ebb.
16 11 1925	Tug *"Carlgarth",* stern tug to *"Otorama"* was sunk on west side of Eastham channel. Salvaged on 21 11 1925.
23 2 1933	Steam Barge *"Bounty"* (Cooper's) sunk at Ellesmere Port in collision with *SS "Sentry".*

PILOTAGE OF THE *SS "SKRIM"* Grt 761 L 210' B 31' 2ND SEPTEMBER 1896

This accident report is included as a little light relief. It was reported that the *SS "Skrim"* arrived at Eastham at 0300 hours being brought in by the Mersey Pilot. After waiting until daylight 0600 hours, the vessel proceeded to Manchester in charge of the Mersey Pilot although his Canal licence had expired the previous day and was not renewable owing to him not having done any piloting on the Ship Canal for the previous twelve months. It was stated that the Canal Pilot, Mr Marker, had received instructions from the vessel's agents to pilot the vessel to Manchester but on his way to join the vessel he had met with an accident in Liverpool. He had been knocked down by a horse drawn cab which incapacitated him from attending the vessel. It only proves accidents do not happen to vessels alone, but also to Pilots and both can suffer damage.

There was no inquiry into the action of the Mersey River Pilot's actions in proceeding with the vessel to Manchester although he was not licensed to do so.

The accident report committee dealt with all forms of disciplinary measures. In May 1899 the Pilotage Committee was greatly concerned by the number of vessels navigating on the Canal with Pilots on board who were not displaying their pilot flag, therefore they were in contravention of the Pilotage Byelaws. The Committee considered this flouting of the Byelaw to be a particularly heinous offence and having in the past tried all lenient means to persuade Pilots to exhibit their pilot flag, and finding them by and large ineffectual, had recourse to more severe means. Every Pilot was sent the following letter:

"The Pilotage Committee wish to inform you that strong complaints have been made that Pilots very often navigate vessels along the Canal without flying their pilot flag and to draw your attention to No 7 of the Canal Company's byelaws:

> *'7. Every Pilot to whom a licence has been granted shall provide himself with a flag of the usual dimensions and of two colours the upper horizontal half red and the lower horizontal half white. On taking charge as Pilot of any vessel and so long as he remains in charge he shall cause his flag to be hoisted on board such vessel where it may be conspicuously seen and shall keep his flag continually flying until he is discharged or relieved by another Pilot'.*

The Pilotage Committee will deal with all future cases reported to them of a contravention of this byelaw, as provided for in Byelaw No 18:

> *'18. Every person offending against or contravening any of the byelaws shall, for every offence forfeit or pay a sum not exceeding five pounds.' "*

In June 1899 it was reported to the Pilotage Committee that a fine of ten shillings (fifty pence) had been imposed on a Pilot for not exhibiting his pilot flag requesting him to forward the amount of the fine but had not received a reply from two subsequent letters sent to him. They decided that strong measures must be taken against Pilots disregarding or disobeying the instructions of the Pilotage Committee. Therefore the Committee informed the Pilot that unless he at once remitted the fine of ten shillings they would recommend the recall of his licence for piloting on the Canal, **permanently**. The Pilot paid by return of post. This was the only case of a Pilot every being fined for not displaying his pilot flag in contravention of the byelaws.

The reluctance of Canal Pilots to exhibit their pilot flag whilst piloting a vessel has always remained a mystery, when everywhere else in the world it was flown as a matter of pride. In May 1925 the Pilotage Committee expressed concern to the Pilots for not flying their pilot flags whilst on duty. In November of that year the Chairman of the Pilotage Committee stated there was a serious complaint against Pilots not exhibiting their pilot flags. Records had been kept over a period of six days and these showed that out of 35 vessels in charge of Pilots, four only had flown the Pilot flag and ten the International Code Flag "H". Reference was made to Byelaw 7 once again. A further letter to all Pilots was sent out reminding them to pay better attention to this matter in future.

This long running saga continued and in October 1928 the Chairman of the Pilotage Committee said that he understood that very few Pilots were exhibiting their pilot flag and that generally they were not complying with the resolution of the Pilotage Committee in January 1908 which required a Pilot to wear a distinctive Badge on his cap when on duty. The Pilots Association replied that although formerly all the Pilots provided themselves with a pilot flag in accordance with Byelaw 14 it was found that the flags were frequently lost either through forgetfulness or through there being insufficient time to regain possession of the flag before leaving the vessel. The Pilots requested if consideration would be given to the use of the International Code Flag "H" - composed of red and white in vertical instead of horizontal sections - in lieu of the Trinity House Flag. The Pilotage Committee flatly refused to consider this proposition especially having regard to No 14 of the Manchester Byelaws requiring a Pilot to have his own flag with him when on duty. Captain Perry, Canal Superintendent, asked what would happen in the case of a vessel concerned in an accident/collision if she was flying the International Code Flag "H" instead of the pilot flag and the opinion was expressed that the code flag "H" would not be recognised by a court. It was finally agreed that the Committee could not sanction any variation from the regulations laid down by the Board of Trade and the Pilotage Authority. The matter was considered closed. The Canal Pilots continued to flout the relevant byelaws by refusing to exhibit their pilot flag for reasons only known unto themselves.

THE PILOTAGE OF *SS "STERK"* AND *SS "HALFDAN"* - 17th MAY 1907

A collision occurred between the above named vessels in the Ship Canal near Weston Mersey Lock. The trial of this collision took place before Mr Justice Bargrave Deane in the Admiralty Court. This was the first trial to be held in the Admiralty Court concerning a collision in the Manchester Ship Canal. The report and the judgement were recorded in the *Shipping Gazette* and *Lloyds List*. It read as follows:

COLLISION IN THE MANCHESTER SHIP CANAL - RULE 19

The Sterk(s) v The Halfadan (s) *Sterk* Grt 762 L 189' B 27'
Halfdan Grt 1307 L 240 B 37'

(Before Mr Justice Hargrave Deane and Captains Bell and Marshall; Elder Brethren of the Trinity House, February 20 and 21).

This action arose out of a collision in the Manchester Ship Canal between the Norwegian steamship Sterk and the Swedish steamship Halfdan. According to the statement of claim, the Sterk (Hanmer-Master) is a steamship of 759 tons gross register and at or shortly after 3 pm on May 17 last, was proceeding slowly down the Canal towards the sea, having loaded cargo at the Runcorn lay-by. She was under her own steam and in charge of a pilot. In those circumstances a steamer, which proved to be the Halfdan, was observed about a quarter of mile astern of, and following and overtaking, the Sterk. The Sterk

"CIS Brovig Grt 8996 L 506' B62'"
Entering the 90' rock cutting between Latchford Locks and Irlam Locks, inward bound for Barton Oil Berth
Courtesy Mrs W Yates Collection

blew a long and a short blast of her whistle several times, thereby indicating that she was proceeding down the canal, but the Halfdan gradually overhauled her and when abreast of Delamere Dock, attempted to pass her on her starboard side. The Sterk was then in the middle of the canal under a slightly starboard helm and her pilot shouted to the pilot in charge of the Halfden, "Why don't you keep astern? You'll have us both ashore". No reply was received and the Halfden drew abreast of the Sterk, leaving about 8 feet of water between the two steamers. As those in charge of the Halfden persisted in attempting to pass the Sterk, the helm of the latter vessel was kept to starboard and her engines put "dead slow ahead", but when nearing Weston Mersey Locks, as the 'midships of the Halfdan came abreast the starboard bow of the Sterk, the suction caused by the Halfdan drew the bows of the Sterk towards the Halfdan. The Sterk's helm was immediately put hard a-starboard, but the bluff of her starboard bow collided with the port side of the Halfden, and the Sterk sustained considerable damage by the collision and was driven ashore on the bank of the canal on her port side. The plaintiffs charged the Halfdan with attempting to pass the Sterk in an improper manner and at a place where a bend in the canal rendered it unsafe to do so and with neglecting to attend to the warning of the pilot of the Sterk.

According to the Defence and Counter-claim, the Halfdan (J A Forslund, Master) is a steamship of 690 tons net register, belong to the port of Gothenburg, and shortly before 3.5 p.m. on the day in question was about half-a-mile above the Runcorn lay-by, proceeding down the canal in the course of a voyage from Manchester to Gothenburg, manned by a crew of 17 hands all told. She was heading straight down the canal and was making about three knots. In these circumstances those on board observed, slightly on the port bow, a steamship which proved to be the Sterk and which with her head down the canal was brought up in the Runcorn lay-by. The Halfdan continued down the canal and shortly afterwards a small tug was observed coming out from ahead of the Sterk, whereupon the whistle of the Halfdan was sounded one long and one short blast, which signal was subsequently repeated several times and her engines were put to dead slow and subsequently stopped.

The Sterk made no signal in reply and as she appeared to be waiting for the Halfdan to pass, the engines of the latter vessel were put slow ahead and she, keeping well over on her starboard side of the canal, shaped to pass well clear of the Sterk and of the small tug which was apparently made fast to the Sterk and was angling athwart the canal. The Halfdan continued proceeding slowly down the canal and shortly afterwards when she was close to the Runcorn lay-by, those on board her observed the Sterk, which gave no whistle signal, canting her head out from the lay-by. She came away from the quay and directly afterwards the vessels were alongside of each other, proceeding down the canal. Immediately the Sterk was seen to be coming away from the quay the engines of the Halfdan were stopped and her helm ported and then steadied and directly afterwards her engines were again put slow ahead and worked as necessary to keep steerage way. The Sterk, which had dropped a little astern then, without any warning, increased her speed, whereupon the pilot of the Halfdan hailed the pilot of the Sterk, "Who is to go ahead, you or I?" and received the reply, "I am going ahead, you can do as you like".

As it was seen that the pilot of the Sterk was determined to go down the canal first, those on board the Halfdan decided to tie up, but before this could be done the Sterk, acting as if under port helm, began to sheer to starboard, causing serious danger of collision. The engines of the Halfdan were at once put full speed ahead as the best chance of avoiding collision, but before they had any effect, the Sterk, with her starboard bow, struck the port side of the Halfdan about amidships a heavy blow, forcing her starboard quarter against a fender on the Weston Mersey lock quay wall and causing her damage. The defendants alleged that the Sterk at an improper time and improperly and without giving any warning came away from the lay-by, instead of waiting until the Halfdan had passed clear; that she ignored the whistle signals of the Halfdan and failed to allow that vessel to pass down the canal; that she increased her speed and ported her helm at an improper time.

Mr Bailbache, KC and Mr H M Robertson (instructed by Messrs Cooper & Co, agents for Messrs Hill Dickinson and Co of Liverpool)appeared for the plaintiffs; Mr Laing, KC and Mr D Stephens (instructed by Messrs Stokes and Stokes, agents for Messrs Bramwell and Bell of Newcastle) for the defendants.

THE COURT pronounced the Halfdan alone to blame.

Mr Justic Bargrave Deane, in giving judgement, said "This is an action for damages arising out of a collision between the Norwegian steamer Sterk and the Swedish steamer, Halfdan. The collision took place in the Manchester Ship Canal at a point which is just opposite the Weston Mersey lock. The Sterk had been loading at a place called Runcorn lay-by and having completed her loading somewhere about 3 o'clock she came away from the quay, assisted by a tug for the purpose of going down the canal and out at Eastham. She seems to have been hampered by a barque which was taking in cargo and was laying ahead of her, and although she tried for some time to get out under her own engines, she failed to do so and eventually a small tug coming up the canal was hailed to take a rope from the starboard bow and tow her starboard bow off. Having done that, the tug helped her to straighten down the canal and then she proceeded down and got into collision off the Weston Mersey lock. I ought to mention that I find as a fact that before she came away from the quay she gave three blasts on her whistle and after she came away from the quay she obeyed the rule in giving on several occasions a long and a short blast which is a signal that she was a vessel proceeding down the canal. That is the story of the Sterk.

The other vessel, the Halfdan, had come down from Manchester. She had tied up for the night at Partington and as she came down, leaving Partington, according to the log, at 1.15 in the afternoon, she came past Runcorn and after she had rounded the bend she saw this vessel the Sterk, at the quay. She also saw a tug which at first she could not make out - she could not make out what the tug was doing - but eventually she could and was satisfied that the tug had got a rope to the starboard bow of the Sterk and was pulling her head off into the canal; and the evidence is that she saw that operation when a quarter of a mile away. Now, if so, she was aware at that distance that this vessel was coming away from the quay. We are told that she stopped and moved ahead again slow and then stopped and then undoubtedly she moved ahead again after she had seen this tug towing this vessel's head off from the quay. The tug having straightened the Sterk in the channel, we are told that at the moment she got straight the stern of the Halfdan was level with her taffrail. Now, that was half a mile or so from the place of collision. According to the log of the Sterk, she went full speed ahead from the time she was straight for five minutes and in the log of the Halfdan you will find the same thing stated - that the Sterk proceeded full speed ahead.

Notwithstanding that the Halfdan, at a half mile from the quay, had passed ahead of the Sterk to this extent, that from having her stern level with the taffrail of the Sterk, she had got her midships level with the bow of the Sterk; in other words, she had passed a length and a half forward of where the vessels were when off the quay. It shows that in that distance of half a mile the Halfdan had travelled at a speed which was a length and half faster than that of the Sterk. Now, I find as a fact that the Halfdan sounded all the necessary signals and therefore so far as the signals are concerned, neither vessel can be held to have broken the rules. Then comes the question of the crossing rule, Rule 19, of the Canal Rules which is as follows:-

"Whenever vessels under way require to depart from the course laid down for them in those regulations for the purpose - for instance, of proceeding to or from any quay, wharf, works or lock for any other reason - the responsibility of doing so in safety, having regard to passing traffic and to works in operation or otherwise, will rest upon the person in charge and the owners of such vessel".

This is a matter which I raised myself in the course of Mr Laing's address to the Court, not because I felt very clear about it, but because I thought it was a matter which, if this case happened to go further, might be raised elsewhere; therefore I thought we ought to consider it here. The Sterk undoubtedly was moving away from a quay and she was intending to pass down the canal. The Halfdan was also proceeding down the canal and although if the Sterk had passed so as to sanction the overtaking ship passing her she ought to have gone over on to the starboard side of the channel, as a fact she never did, and therefore it cannot be said, I think, that the Halfdan was a crossing vessel. By the time the Sterk had got out into the channel as I have said, the stern of the Halfdan was level with her taffrail on her starboard quarter and therefore, at no time can it be said that these vessels were crossing - that their courses were crossing courses.

Therefore it cannot be said that at any time the Sterk was crossing the Halfdan; and that being so in my opinion, the rule does not apply to the facts of this particular case. I rather think that the rule applies to vessels which are going in different directions - that is to say, that if the Sterk had been going down and the Halfdan coming up, then there would have been perhaps a reason why the rule should be made to apply; but in the facts of this case I do not think that the rule does apply.

Then whose fault is it that this collision took place? I confess that when the evidence of the Sterk was given it did not strike me as being very first-class, and the Elder Brethren say the same, but you have got to take it in its entirety. On the other hand I think that the evidence given by the Halfdan was very well given and very honestly and fairly given, especially by the Master. With those remarks, let me proceed to state what in the opinion of the Court is the true judgment to give upon what did happen. The Sterk intended to come out and she was blowing proper signals and she came out and her bow was out very near mid-stream - I am told the channel is only 120 feet wide here - when the other vessel coming down was a quarter of a mile off. Was she justified in going out and down as she did? In our opinion she was. If she was justified in going out and the other vessel coming down saw her a quarter of a mile, coming out, as they admit and well knew she was a vessel intending to go down, what ought the other vessel to have done? The evidence from the engineer of the Halfdan is this - he said "our movements of the engines were these - full speed, stop, full speed, stop", and so on. Now, the Elder Brethren advise me that that was improper - that it ought to have been slow, stop, slow, stop, the result of which would have been that the Halfdan would not have overtaken the Sterk. She would have allowed the Sterk to get way on her and having way on her, the Sterk could have got over to the starboard side of the channel so as to enable the Halfdan to pass her as she ought to have passed her - on her port side.

Going full speed, stop, full speed, stop, prevented that operation being performed and it struck us very much as though the two pilots were a bit hostile to each other. Each wanted to get down first and neither would give way. That is what it looks like. We have got on one side a Norwegian ship limited in speed by the rules and on the other hand we have a Swedish ship not limited, which might go down at full speed. Therefore the pilot of the Halfdan might think "I can go down at a speed of 8 or 9 knots and this other vessel cannot and why should I go down behind him" and he thought he would pass him. On the other hand the pilot of the Sterk said "No you shan't" and so far as I can see, so far from giving him room, he if anything, bored the Halfdan over because we find that immediately after the collision, the starboard quarter of the Halfdan was against the Western Mersey lock quay wall. I think that was very wrong conduct on the part of both of them but the Halfdan ought not to have been there at all, whereas the Sterk was entitled to do what she did. It was her proper side of the channel and the Halfdan had no business to be there. Therefore, I cannot find that the people on the Sterk were to blame. I think it was a very wrong spirit which animated both these pilots, but that does not affect the rights and wrongs of the collision. in my opinion, upon the evidence and in the opinion of the Elder Brethren with regard to what ought to have been the navigation of the Halfdan, the Halfdan is alone to blame."

The litigation over the claims for the responsibility of the accident and therefore the compensation claim, carried on over a few months and went through several law courts. After all these appeals the judgment of the Admiralty Court that the *"Halfdan"* was to blame in the end remained unaltered. The Pilotage Committee's action towards the two Pilots was to issue a severe warning with regard to the piloting of these vessels. Only if a similar complaint came before the committee in the future would a more serious view of the matter be taken, with the prospect of either one or both pilots having their licences suspended indefinitely.

The comments made by Mr Justice Bargrave Deane regarding the conduct of the two pilots *"it struck us very much as though the two pilots were a bit hostile to each other"* and *"I think it was a very wrong spirit which animated both these pilots"* proved only too clearly the animosity that existed between some pilots in the Manchester Ship Canal. This lack of co-operation and comradeship has been recorded a number of times within the pages of these volumes and this instance bears out the truth of those statements.

THE *SS "CALEDONIA"* - BARTON LOCKS - 5TH NOVEMBER 1952

The following is an account of the above incident given in the *Manchester Guardian* the following day.

STEAMER FALLS 15 FEET AFTER BURSTING LOCK GATES
Big Vessels Delayed on Ship Canal

Divers and engineers were working last night to repair the large lock at Barton on the Manchester Ship Canal, which was damaged yesterday afternoon when the Swedish steamer *"Caledonia"* collided with the outer gates. The *"Caledonia"* outward bound from Manchester had entered the lock which is 600 feet long and 65 feet wide when her bow struck the gates at the seaward end with such force that they were lifted off their sockets and sank to the bottom of the canal.

SS "Caledonia" Grt 1242 Length 228' Breadth 37'

The height of the water in the lock when the ship entered it was 15 feet more than the canal below. As the gates were forced off, the water rushed out and the *"Caledonia"* dropped suddenly to the lower level with such force that she sprang a leak. Cheshire County Fire Brigade was called out to pump water out of the ship and she was eventually towed to Irlam Dolphins and moored there.

An official of the Ship Canal Company said last night "The *Caledonia* had so much way on her that she struck the lower gates before the lockman had any chance of closing the top or intermediate gates". The upper and intermediate gates were eventually closed but the pressure of water behind them was so great that they buckled slightly under the strain and water continued to seep through.

Two vessesl which were due to leave Manchester Docks at 0700 hours today will now be delayed until the lock is working again. They are the *Dalesman* (6343 GRT) and the *Essex Trader* (7237 GRT). Inward bound vessels which are held up by the accident are the *Manchester Explorer* and the *Manchester Spinner*, both owned by Manchester Liners and used on the Manchester to Canada run and the *Clan MacQueen*. A smalller vessel the *Rylands* may be able to pass through the smaller lock.

Last night a 25-ton floating crane, brought from its berth at Mode Wheel two miles away, was being used to try to lift the gates. *"Divers are going down to attach hawsers to the gates so that the crane can bring them up to the surface"* a Ship Canal official said, *"but the operation is not quite as simple as it sounds. Until the gates are raised it is impossible to say how extensively they are damaged. It may be possible to replace them on their sockets but if extensive repairs are needed a spare pair of gates will be put into position as soon as possible. From our point of view the accident is a serious one"* the official said *"because until the gates are replaced no large ships can either enter or leave the terminal docks in Manchester and Salford. It is difficult to say what the delay will be but it may be about two days"*. Barton Lock where the accident happened is about five and a half miles from the terminal docks in Manchester. According to a Ship Canal official the stretch of water which it controls is used daily by between forty and fifty vessels of which about twelve are large ocean-going ships.

23RD FEBRUARY 1933   SUNK IN SHIP CANAL
BARGE COLLIDES WITH STEAMER

THE CREW'S ESCAPE
Barge was "Sinking under us"

The Manchester Ship Canal, at Ellesmere Port, was the scene of a collision between a steam driven barge and a steamer, early this morning, which resulted in the barge being sunk and the members of her crew having to make their escape in a small boat.

The vessels involved were the steam driven flat *"Bounty"* (owned by William Cooper and Sons Ltd, sand ballast merchants of Widnes) and the *SS "Sentry"*, 1,014 tons (owned by Messrs Fisher, Renwick Ltd of Manchester and London), Length 231' Beam 35'.

The *"Bounty"* was going up the canal, towards Manchester shortly after 5 o'clock this morning, with a cargo of 210 tons of sand, and the *"Sentry"* was going in the opposite direction. The impact was so severe that the *"Bounty"* sank in fifteen minutes, but fortunately, having been slewed round by the force of the collision, her final resting place does not block the canal.

EFFORTS TO REFLOAT

She now lies on the shelving slope of the Ellesmere Port bank of the canal, partly submerged, and efforts are being made today to refloat her. The *"Bounty"* carried a crew of four: Richard Lee, skipper of 9 Oakland Street, Widnes; Robert Files, St Mary's Road, Widnes; William Brown, Westmorland Avenue, Widnes and Peter Johnson, Highfield Terrace, Runcorn.

When it was seen that the barge was sinking, the small boat attached to the barge was hauled alongside, and the *"Bounty's"* crew hurriedly entered it and rowed ashore.

Interviewed by the Liverpool Echo, Mr Lee said they left Ellesmere Port at five o'clock this morning bound for Manchester with a cargo of sand. When opposite Stewart's Wharf a collision occurred with the *"Sentry"* and so severe was the impact that the *Bounty* began to sink rapidly. "*We just had time to collect a few belongings and get away in the small boat, as the barge was sinking under us*" he said.

The *"Bounty's"* bows are now lying on a sandbank where the sides of the canal slope down into deep water. The canal at this point, however, is about 250 feet wide, and, although the barge's stern is overhanging the middle of the canal, the passage of other traffic is not impeded. Canal divers are now at work attempting to raise the vessel, of which only the top of the mast is showing.

The *"Sentry"*, after standing by and finding there was no danger of loss of life, proceeded on her outward trip. She had suffered little damage.

THE SALVAGE OF THE *MARY P COOPER*

The account of the accident and the complex salvage operations that followed will clearly illustrate not only the inherent danger of piloting in confined waterways, but also the additional strain and responsibility placed upon the expertise of a pilot when passing a vessel with only metres of clearance between the vessels - especially a ship which does not have a licensed pilot on board, due to an exemption certificate as in this case.

The serious consequences, due to the delays occurring to shipping in the canal and the rerouting of Manchester bound vessels to other ports through such an accident as this, are only too obvious and are of vital concern to all pilots whilst on duty.

It is also a magnificent record of a salvage operation and co-operation between the Liverpool and Glasgow Salvage Association and the Engineering and Harbour Staff of the Manchester Ship Canal Company.

The Accident

It was 6.15 in the evening on Tuesday, 21 March 1961, when the steam vessel *Mary P Cooper*, 1250 DWT, L 194' B 33' made her way up the Canal with a full cargo of Mersey River sand bound for Pomona Docks. Outward bound for Ireland with a cargo of cattle food was the coaster *Foamville* 1140 DWT L 190' B30'. As they passed 200 yards upstream of the Northwich Road Swing bridge a collision occurred which resulted in the *Cooper* sinking immediately, the crew making a timely escape.

The Harbour Master was quickly informed of the accident by Shipping Movements who in turn had been alerted by Northwich Road Swing Bridge via Latchford Locks. At once arrangements were made for all vessels on passage in the Canal to be halted and within a very short time of the sinking there were eight outward and five inward bound ships held up. Meanwhile arrangements were made for the *Foamville* to be towed back to Latchford Lower Layby by the MSC tug *Arrow* for the damage to be assessed.

21st March 1961
Courtesy of Captain P Dunbavand
The Sinking of the Mary P Cooper by the SS Foamville
Note the Cooper Vessel's propeller still rotating

Preliminary Salvage Action

Shipping Movements notified the Company's officials who immediately decided the vessel was outside the capabilities of the Company's plant for removal and that the Liverpool and Glasgow Salvage Association should be called in. The Association's Manager was contacted and very shortly afterwards the Principal Salvage Officer left for the site.

Further action by the Company included the carrying out of a survey of the Canal at the site and arranging for the attendance of the Company's divers for a preliminary examination and attachment of emergency mooring ropes to the wreck.

By 11.30 pm discussions were in progress between the Company's Engineers and the Salvage Officer. Soon after midnight, arrangements were made to bring the salvage vessel *Dispenser* into the Canal and for Warrington Wharf to be kept free for any necessary preparations connected with operations. The *Dispenser* arrived at Warrington Wharf the following afternoon, 22nd March, and was in position on the south bank of the Canal immediately astern of the *Mary P Cooper* by 11.45 am the next day.

In the meantime, work started on the provision of anchorages for the mooring wires in the south bank opposite the wreck. Fresh moorings had to be installed because dredgers do not normally work at this point and therefore no such mooring existed. The moorings were placed and tightened by 4 am on 23rd March.

The *Grab Hopper No 1* arrived on the scene on 22nd March and began grabbing to remove the cargo of sand. The sand was very compact and grabbing under water proved an extremely difficult task.

Before daylight a preliminary examination of the *Foamville* by our divers took place at Latchford Locks and it was found that there was extensive damage on the port bow. fortunately, however, flooding was held by the bulkhead. A later examination revealed the damage to extend below the water line and it was therefore agreed that part of the cargo should be discharged to barge by dock workers from Manchester. This brought the damage clear of the water and it was possible to pump out the fore peak. After temporary patching, the vessel sailed for Manchester where she was discharged prior to dry docking.

At about mid-day it was decided that certain small vessels which would normally proceed without assistance of tugs could navigate without danger; movement to begin at 7 am on the following morning.

During the day a control point was established on the canal bank opposite the wreck. The site office was provided with a telephone and became the headquarters of the Company's operations. An experiment was also tried with "Walkie-Talkies" but they did not work well owing to the proximity of the bridges. (Note: For "Walkie-talkies" modern day parlance would read "Mobile phones")

By the afternoon of 22nd March, sufficient information was available to show that underwater repairs were impossible and thoughts were given to the possible employment of the 250-ton crane. This idea had to be abandoned however as it readily became apparent that the crane's lifting wire would be too close to the *Cooper's* bow and within the area of damage.

A call therefore was sent out to Liverpool for salvage pontoons and again frustration, for those at our neighbouring Port were too large to use in the confined area of the wreck. Quick contact, therefore, was made with Admiralty's Salvage Department and fortunately they could give immediate help and would send up four suitable pontoons from Pembroke Dock accompanied by Admiralty Tugs. These pontoons arrived during the afternoon of 26th March at the same time as other ancillary equipment reached us from Portsmouth.

Before describing the final and successful salvage plan, it should be mentioned here that consideration was given in the early stages to breaking up the vessel by means of explosives. Owing, however, to the proximity of houses and the difficulty of locating dispersed sections of the wreck, this plan was abandoned.

Salvage Plan

The final plan decided upon by the Salvage Officer entailed as a first step the sealing of the engine room together with the side buoyancy tanks which flooded when the vessel sank. Admiralty Salvage pontoons were then to be moored alongside, whilst the *Dispenser* would take the weight of her stern.

It was realised that the bows of the *Cooper* would have to come up first owing to practically the whole of the damage being centred there. It was then necessary for the *Dispenser* to control any listing by attaching two 6-inch wires to the propeller shafts from her own winches.

It should be borne in mind that the *Cooper* had a 10 degrees list to port when she sank.

Next, two greenheart logs were placed vertically down the starboard side of the *Dispenser* to prevent the side of the vessel from scraping the bank. A further stage in the plan involved the placing of lifting wires under the hull of the *Cooper* and this was one of the most difficult and lengthy operations of the whole plan. It must be appreciated that the vessel was lying on a hard rock bottom and the lifting pontoons had to be placed in exactly the right positions, two to port and two to starboard to ensure that the head of the sunken vessel would come up first. Once the wires had been placed in position under the hull, the pontoons would be filled with water and sunk; wires would then be attached to the pontoons by divers and finally, once the hull had been made watertight, compressed air would be blown into the pontoons which would then rise to the surface with the vessel cradled on the lifting wires between them.

Mary P Cooper Salvage Operations
Courtesy of The MSC Company

To seal off the holds and make them watertight, two prefabricated hatch covers, each in two sections weighting approximately 9 tons with dimensions of 22 feet x 20 feet x 2 feet, were designed by our Engineers at Head Office and constructed in our Mechanical Engineer's Workshops at Old Quay. These covers were made particularly robust as the *Cooper* sank in 30 feet of water which meant that they had to withstand considerable pressure. After fitting and sealing them, suction pumps would be used to clear the holds of water and so give additional buoyancy.

The camber of the hatch coamings on the *Cooper* had to be measured up under water by the Salvage Association's leading diver and these measurements had to be exact in order to ensure perfect water sealing operations which were carried out in their entirety by the Salvage Association.

Diving Operations

As far as our own divers were concerned they had the particularly unenviable task of clearing a way to both the forward and rear bulkheads so that the Salvage Association's divers could get at the buoyancy tanks to seal them. In the case of the forward bulkhead, and it must be remembered here that the main damage had been sustained by the bows where the crew's quarters were situated, they had to force their way in full diving kit down a companion way, normally a tight fit for anyone in ordinary clothing, and then piece by piece rip apart bunks, wardrobes and other cabin furniture, not to mention a thickness of wooden sheeting protecting the bulkhead itself and to pass it up to the top of the companion way, a formidable job when working by feel under 15 feet or so of inky black canal water.

The rear bulkhead which was protected by the coal bunkers, could not be reached until all the coal had been removed. This consisted of 25 tons which had to be smashed up into small pieces prior to being sucked up by suction pipes. Larger pieces, which could not readily be broken up, were placed to one side away from the bulkhead. During the actual sealing operations, which involved the use of standard type burning equipment, several of the Salvage Association's divers suffered burns to their hands. Our divers, on the other hand, were continually cutting their clothing while clearing away the debris and each time this happened the diver concerned had to make a rapid ascent to the surface for obvious reasons. As the diving tasks became more numerous the diving team had to be increased by the addition of two Admiralty divers from Rosyth. This made a total of 10 divers, the team consisting of four from the Salvage Association, four from the Manchester Ship Canal Company and two from the Admiralty.

The Intervening Days

During the days that followed there were many frustrations caused by the breaking of messenger wires attached to the lifting wires and the continual emergency of fresh leaks in the *Cooper*, each of which had to be plugged before the next stage of the operations could be commenced. Throughout this time vessels were allowed to pass the wreck at restricted periods, those requiring tugs being supplied with them. The most notable passage was that of the *Amfithia* inward bound on 3rd April with a beam of 57 feet and a draft of 18 feet 8 inches. This was the largest vessel to proceed past the wreck for the channel, which had been marked by beacons, was only 70 feet wide.

As time went on the surplus of Dock Workers in Manchester continued in the ascent and at one time the figure reached 1,500. To a small extent this situation was relieved by additional work at Ellesmere Port which became a hive of industry through certain vessels discharging their Manchester cargo there. There was also one instance, the first time in its history when the Queen Elizabeth 11 Dock was used as a general discharging berth by the *Manchester Merchant*, the cargo being discharged into barges overside.

There were, however, no less than 24 known cases of diversion of vessels to other ports which meant a very large tonnage lost to Manchester, the repercussions of which will be felt for a long time.

The Final Lifting

On Sunday, 16th April, at 5.20 am the blowing of compressed air into the forward pontoons commenced. This was to ensure that the bows would be the first portion of the vessel to clear the water. By 7.05 am a small section of the bows emerged, by 12.40 pm two-thirds of the vessel were above the water line and by 4.05 pm the *Cooper* was afloat.

It will be appreciated that there were many thousands throughout the country awaiting news of this moment and quick advice was given by the Public Relations Department to both the BBC and ITV which resulted in pictures of the final raising being transmitted on the same night with news that the Canal would be clear the following morning.

During the remainder of Sunday, the Salvage Officer stayed on the bridge of the *Dispenser* checking the list of the *Cooper* and making corrections by taking the strain on the appropriate lifting wire when required. It is important to realise that the whole lifting operation was staged in periods of about

Courtesy of the MSC Co

The Scottish Prince GRT 3364 L 364' B51' outward bound, passes the sunken vessel. The bows of the salvage vessel Dispenser can been seen at the bottom left. Note Helmsman on Upper Open Bridge

Courtesy of the MSC Co

The final lift, Sunday 16th April. Note the lifting pontoon and the specially constructed watertight hatch covers

twenty minutes, commencing with the bow and working gradually aft. At 5.05 pm the Salvage Officer decided to move the wreck to Warrington Wharf at first light of day the following morning, meanwhile draining operations with the aid of pumps continued throughout the night.

During the whole of the time the *Cooper* lay in her somewhat inglorious state she acted as a magnet to hundreds of thousands of people who were drawn from all over the country to view her. A local ice-cream vendor is reported to have said that he'd never had it so good and a lady from Winwick, who brought her four children there each day with thermos flask and sandwiches, said that although it cost her half-a-crown ($12^1/_2$p) in bus fares it was better than taking them to the park.

The Removal

Thick fog heralded the dawn of Monday, 17th April and in consequence the removal of the wreck was delayed. However, soon after 10 am it began to clear rapidly and at 10.30 am two Ship Canal tugs the *Onset* and the *Quest* arrived to take up positions at her bows and her stern. Meanwhile, the *Dispenser* cast off and sailed for Latchford where she was to turn prior to proceeding to Acton Grange Wharf. Finally, at 11.45 am amidst the thunderous handclapping and cheers of the onlookers together with the whirring of press cameras, the *Cooper* began her journey to Naylors Wharf, Warrington.

The Canal was clear again after 27 days and nights of frustrating heartbreaking work. It was fitting that the crowd should cheer for what they had witnessed was a victory achieved over formidable odds. A victory of most vital concern to thousands throughout the country and not least to our own Company.

As the ships sail freely again and the accident becomes but a distant memory the grave and costly effects both to shipowners and ourselves, the Port Authority, will be felt for some time ahead.

A NIGHT TO REMEMBER
Sunday 16 March 1969, 2305 hours

The *Manchester Courage* outward bound for Montreal entered Irlam Locks, collided with and went through the lower lock gates, and wedged herself in the lower lock entrance. Through its 75 year life the Ship Canal has suffered very few serious accidents but this constituted the worst calamity to befall the Ship Canal. An early estimate forecast that the passage of large vessels would be held up for at least eight weeks, as it turned out due to the Herculean efforts from all departments of the Ship Canal Company the port was back in business within five weeks.

The accompanying photographs show the scenes that faced the port officials on that cold and wet Monday morning. The Pilot was completely exonerated of all blame for this accident, an engine malfunction was designated the cause.

Manchester Courage GRT 11,899 L 529' B 63' 9"
The Lower Lock Gate, Irlam Locks Port Side
Dimensions of Irlam Lock 600' x 65'

1969
The Complete Destruction of Irlam Locks Lower Gates

Port Side Lower Lock Gate at Irlam Locks

1969
Irlam Locks Top Gates forced inwards by the sudden release of water

BOB'S LANE FERRY, CADISHEAD, DISASTER - 14TH APRIL 1970

A REPORT ON THE CORONER'S INQUEST AT THE ECCLES TOWN HALL ON THE 25TH AND 26TH JUNE, 1970

In his summary of the evidence heard at the inquest the Coroner, Mr Leonard Gorodkin, commented as follows:

1 It was known that the six men died as a direct consequence of the fire on the Manchester Ship Canal in the vicinity of the Bobs Lane Ferry.

2 That the material which caused the fire was almost certainly that same material which had overflowed from the petroleum barge *Tacoma* berthed at No 4 berth Partington, some two and a half to three hours earlier.

3 That it was not known what had ignited the material, but that he hoped that this would not prevent a verdict being reached.

4 That "papers" in this case have been sent to the Director of Public Prosecutions and he considers there is insufficient evidence to bring manslaughter charges against any person.

5 That no person involved in the loading of the *Tacoma* could be said to have been recklessly negligent and that this being so a manslaughter verdict was out of the question.

Verdicts of death by misadventure were then returned on all six deceased.

The Coroner then added "Throughout this inquest we have heard a most horrifying story and although a deep tragedy has occurred it could have been far worse - a local disaster, with shore installations and habitations involved. It is to be hoped that a serious lesson will have been learned: that safety regulations are not just pieces of paper but are meant to be complied with to save life and property. Where human beings are concerned mistakes can happen but it is to be hoped that in the future if such a spillage occurs, however large or small and whatever the consequence to the people involved, they will not, as in this case remain silent but will bring it to the notice of the Authorities.

I feel that having reported as above I could well let the matter rest were it not for the fact that the operations of *Tacoma* in particular and Low Flash petroleum carrying vessels in general having been and indeed still are a matter of real concern to the Pilot service, special emphasis being put on the safety in navigation aspect. It is a common belief among Pilots that the most likely way that inflammable material can find its way into the Canal in any significant quantity is as the direct consequence of a navigational accident. The Authority have been made well aware of the Pilots' views on the subject and are agreed that a better system of traffic guidance is desirable for the future.

Regretfully however no mutually satisfactory system has been agreed for the present or near future, although negotiations have been promised. The matter of safety in navigation being for the time being still left to the individual discretion of Duty Harbour Master, Ship Master and or Pilot where employed.

The Pilots have been consistently advised that their fears with regard to the dangers involved in the handling and carriage of inflammable materials are groundless and in particular that the normal safety precautions are adequate to meet all the demands ever likely to be made on them.

In other words the Bob's Lane Ferry tragedy could never happen! IT DID THOUGH! *and consequently I must offer the following comments:*

(i) That the death of six men is proof enough that the danger is real and that the Pilots' fears are not groundless.

(ii) *That the evidence produced at the inquest proves that the normal safety precautions are not always adequate to the needs and certainly not when allied to admitted human failings.*

(iii) *That the shortcomings of the Mate and 2nd Engineer of* Tacoma *so patently revealed by the enquiry must permit of the gravest doubt being entertained as to the ability of that vessel to be safely navigated* ***at all times*** *as required by Byelaws and etc. Further even than this, one can now feel entitled to enquire "is any such vessel being safely navigated when those in charge lack the extensive specialised local knowledge that is required to cope properly with the traffic problems frequently arising and a full appreciation of all the Regulations?"*

(iv) *That we as Pilots and indeed as responsible members of society should both heed the Coroner's warning and also have the courage of our own expressed convictions and insist that the Authority agree with us the conditions necessary for maximum safety in the navigation of such vessels in the Canal.*

(v) *That not even our own self-interest must be allowed to interfere with the establishment of a such safe system.*

In conclusion may I say that having sat through the whole of the Inquest and having heard all the evidence, I personally shall need a terrible amount of convincing that there is no need for me to worry about the ability of the "system" to operate safely and it will certainly be my intention to do my bit in the future.

(Signed)
ROBERT S BOYLES

Pilot First Class

This was one of the most tragic accidents ever to occur on the Manchester Ship Canal, although it had nothing to do with Pilots or piloting it does show the inherent danger these unpiloted vessels with their lethal cargoes could pose to other vessels being piloted up or down the canal. The "TACOMA", a small petroleum barge was loading a very highly toxic and inflammable cargo at No. 4 berth at Partington during the evening of April 13th and because of the safety regulations imposed by the Manchester SHip Canal Authority, the transport of highly inflammable cargoes was regulated to day light sailing only. The "TACOMA" was was scheduled to sail at 0730hrs. During the loading, towards the completion of the cargo, for some reason that has never been explained, none of the crew of the vessel were in attendance on board the vessel which resulted in a significant overflow from the full tanks and the inflammable liquid drained into the Canal and floated down stream for about one mile towards Bobs Lane Ferry. No one from the vessel or ashore reported this highly toxic spilage to the Manchester SHip Canal authorities or to the Oil installation it was being pumped from.

It was 0700hrs, on the morning of April 14th,., the ferry service across the Canal had just commenced. A total of six persons including the ferry man, the macimum number the ferry was licensed to carry at any one time had just left the ferry stage. A few people standing at the top of the stage landing steps smelt strong fumes emanating from the canal waters and one or two felt rather faint. They suddenly noticed that some of the people on the ferry, which was about a quarter of the way across, had collapsed and they immediately hailed the ferry man to turn round and return to the stage.

Before the ferry man could complete the manoeuvre the whole of the canal exploded into a raging inferno, so intense was the heat the steel and the glass on the navigational guiding lights on the canal fused together., The vegetation on both sides of the canal for about two miles was completely destroyed. No one on that ill-fated ferry survived.

There have since been many rumours and much conjecture on how and why it happened, but none of it could be satisfactorily substantiated a lot of intimidating questions have remained unanswered and it all ended very sadly and very unsatisfactorily.

11
THE SOUTHWOOD GENERATION

1902-1932
Mr Robert Southwood
Courtesy of the Southwood Family

Daniel Southwood came to Eastham from Devon in 1888 to work on the construction of the Ship Canal. He was born in Exeter and had been a seaman on deep sea sailing ships. He bought a picturesque house at Eastham facing over the River Mersey. He had three sons who all went deep sea in sailing and steamships and they all eventually became Ship Canal Pilots.

The first son to enter the Pilot service was Robert Southwood, born in 1880, he became a steersman in 1902 and successfully obtained a Second Class licence in 1905. In 1909 he passed the examination for a First Class Pilot at the age of 29 years. He was appointed Choice Pilot for Marwood and Robertsons - the Federal Line - in 1919 and frequently piloted some of the largest vessels to then transit the Ship Canal to Manchester viz, *Argyllshire, Somerset* and *Armagh* all in excess of 7,500 tons net eg. He died very young aged only 52 years in February 1932. In the minutes of the Pilotage Committee held in February 1932 the following is recorded:

"The secretary of the Pilotage Committee regretted to have to record the death of Mr Robert Southwood, which took place on February 10th, the service thereby losing one of its most efficient Pilots. The Chairman (Mr W Browning)said he was sure the Committee would agree with him in saying the Pilot Service had indeed lost one of its best Pilots by the passing of Mr Robert Southwood and he asked the Committee to stand for a minutes silence in tribute to departed merit. This the Committee did."

It was the first time and the only time such a tribute was accorded to a Ship Canal Pilot by the Pilotage Committee.

Mr Wilfred Daniel Southwood, the eldest of the sons, started his career on the Ship Canal as a steersman in 1905 at the age of 26 years. He was successful in his examination for a Second Class Licence in 1910 and a First Class licence in 1913. In 1905 Mr W D Southwood had a telephone installed in his home to enable him to be in constant touch with Eastham Locks, Liverpool Pilot Station and Point Lynas. Such a communication network gave him valuable information of vessels arriving and sailing in those early chaotic days of the "catch-as-catch-can" system of pilotage. His telephone was one of the first to be installed in Eastham Village and consequently was used by many of the villagers, and children would rush to the house if they heard the telephone bell ringing just to see the instrument being used. Legend has it that Mr Southwood's mother would run out of the house - if alone in the house - every time the telephone rang afraid to answer it. The telephone appeared to be a mystery to some of the Pilots as you will have read in this book!

1905-1935
Courtesy of the Southwood Family
Mr Wilfred D Southwood

Mr W D Southwood was appointed Choice Pilot to the Prince Line in 1919. Always the perfect gentleman, when a vessel he was piloting moored at Estham for the night - it was the custom to do so in those days - he would invite the Master to his home for dinner. Through this courteous gesture he became a close friend of Captain Jameson, Master of the *Lancastrian Prince* whose daughter became the famous authoress, Sorm Jameson. Mr W D Southwood died in March 1935 aged 56 years.

The last of the three sons to become a Ship Canal Pilot was Mr Ernest Southwood. He was born in 1891 and commenced steering in the Canal in 1911. He obtained a Second Class licence in 1920. Unfortunately his sight was deteriorating and continued to do so over the next four years. In August 1924 he failed the Board of Trade eyesight test prior to sitting for his First Class licence and was not allowed to proceed with the examination for his licence. Under these circmstances the Pilotage Committee had no alternative and they refused the renewal of his Second Class licence.

It had been reported that Mr Southwood smoked an excessive number of cigarettes daily and the opinion of the Committee was that his sight might improve if he smoked considerably less. The Chairman of the Pilotage Committee said although Mr Southwood could not continue to act as a Second Class Pilot he did not wish to see him thrown out of the service altogether. He thought the matter might be met by allowing him to act as a Helmsman. The Committee unanimously agreed with this proposal. The name of Southwood still meant something in Pilotage Committee for if he could not see properly as a Pilot how would it be different as a Helmsman?

Mr Southwood never regained his sight sufficiently enough to pass the stringent Board of Trade eyesight test and he retired from the Pilot Service in 1924 aged 33 years. He did however establish a mooring service at Eastham that became very successful and is still in operation to this day under the supervision of his sons and cousins.

Mr Robert Southwood (1902-1932) had one son born in 1912 who was named after his father, but was always known throughout his piloting life as Robin. He was a quiet, thoughtful person, of a kindly disposition to all he met during his piloting duties, especially to Helmsmen. He was never known to have ever raised his voice, even in anger. Robin commenced his career at sea in October 1928 as a cadet with the New Zealand Shipping Company serving his apprenticeship aboard the *Northumberland* and the *Devon.* On 24 August 1931 his father sent an application form for him to become a Helmsman, duly signed by his son and also signed by Mr George Cartwright (Senior No 1 Pilot), Mr J Robertson (Director and Owner of Marwood and Robertsons) and Captain Acraman (Senior Harbour Master) as character witnesses. His father died in 1932 but his mother, concerned that the Southwood name should still grace the Port of Manchester, kept her son's name in the minds of the Pilotage Committee by constantly writing to the Chairman reminding him of her son's application and her son's progress at sea.

1911-1924
Courtesy of the Southwood Family
Mr Ernest Southwood at the wheel.

1935-1963
Courtesy of the Southwood Family
Mr "Robin" Southwood

In January 1933 Mr Robin Southwood obtained his Second Officers Certificate and notified the Pilotage Committee accordingly. The Chairman's reply was not encouraging, stating that there was little prospect of a vacancy in the Helmsmens Service for some considerable time. The 1930s recession was deeply entrenched in shipping and Mr Southwood, because of his desire to join the Pilot Service, was not re-engaged by the New Zealand Shipping Company. In other companies during that dreadful period only men with Masters Certificates could hope to find an officers position of any rank. He therefore served for five months as an AB (Able Seaman) in the Elder Dempster Line and three months as a quartermaster with the T & J Harrison Line. He found employment ashore in November 1933 as a gateman at Stanlow Oil Refinery until March 1935 when he at last joined the Helmsmens service. On 1st April 1949 he successfully passed his Second Class licence and four years later was successfully examined for a First Class licence. In December 1959 he suffered a Coronary Thrombosis. He was strongly advised by his doctors to retire immediately to ensure a longer life, but for some inexplicable reason Mr Southwood had never contributed to the Pilots Private Pension Fund. This

5 9 1931

MANCHESTER SHIP CANAL COMPANY.

APPLICATION FOR EMPLOYMENT.

Applicants for situations with the Manchester Ship Canal Company are requested to reply, in their own handwriting, to the following questions.

QUESTIONS.	REPLIES.
Name (in full)	Robert Southwood
Address (in full)	Selby, Spital Rd, Bromborough Cheshire
Date of Birth and Height	Date 15th Oct 1912 Height Ft. 5 Ins. 4
Nationality	British
State if married and what family?	
Are your Health, Hearing and Sight good?	Health good Hearing good Sight good
State description of Employment and salary required	Helmsman
State in what capacity and by whom you have hitherto been employed, and how long you were in each place.	Apprentice. New Zealand Shipping Co. Two years ten months. S.S. Northumberland and S.S. Devon.
Present employment, and when and why leaving; or if out of employment, state last occupation, and why you left.	
Names and Addresses of three persons to whom reference may be made as to character, including last employer.	I L Acraman Dockmaster M/C J. Robertson 11 Albert Square Manchester George Cartwright. Pilot. 12 Falkland Rd. Egremont.

Signature of Applicant Robert Southwood

Date 24th Aug 1931

obviously precluded him from drawing a pension and his commitments to his family were such that he could not retire. This situation undoubtedly hastened the end of his life immeasurably.

He returned to work in mid 1960 but only for brief spells and was constantly in and out of hospital with his debilitating problem. On the night of 2nd July 1963, after completing a pilotage service from Partington to Eastham, he had another serious heart attack and was ordered to remain in bed. Mr Southwood's condition deteriorated during the weeks that followed and he was eventually transferred to the Hoylake Cottage Hospital where on 17th September 1963 he died aged 51 years. It was not until eighteen years later that Mrs R Southwood was granted a small widow's pension from the Pilots National Pension Fund.

On the death of Mr Robin Southwood in 1963 the widow's gratuity from the Pilot Service still remained at £50. This had remained so since 1933 when it was first granted to the widow of Mr T N Gorst. The Manchester Pilot service has never been renowned for its generosity in supporting charity or relief funds. As far back as 1914 an application was submitted from the Port Talbot Pilots asking for a subscription to a fund in aid of the dependants of the men who recently lost their lives through the disaster to the Cardiff Pilot Cutter the *W W Jones*. It was allowed to lie on the table, a much used euphemism rather than an outright refusal.

The sum of £50 constituted a contribution from 75 Pilots of 66p per man whose earnings were in excess of £1,500 per year. The first gift to Mrs Gorst constituted a contribution from 32 Pilots of £1.60 per man whose earnings were £600 per year. One can draw their own conclusions from that comparison. A minority of Pilots of a more compassionate and charitable nature were disgusted with such a trivial amount and expressed their feelings in writing. "£50 is contemptuous treatment from 75 Pilots" Mr W Yates. "The figure should be a minimum of £500" Mr T H Clugston. "Paltrey, an utter disgrace to the Manchester Pilot Service" Mr A Marshall Dick. "It is a great pity the Association Committee of the Pilots did not really do something worthwhile and deduct £50 per man towards a contribution" Mr D A Clulow. The Pilots Association did not attempt to alter the contribution one iota. The comments made by the minority of Pilots must have troubled the Association's moral sense of obligations. In 1972 on the death of Mr L Davies in service, a contribution of £10 per man from the 75 Pilots was proposed and accepted by a two-thirds majority.

Mr Robin Southwood had one son, John Robert, born in Stornaway in 1940, an unexpected arrival whilst his parents were holidaying there.

1965-1985
Mr John Robert Southwood

At the age of fourteen he passed the scholarship to enter the training ship HMS *Conway* in 1955. He joined the Liverpool Pilot Service in 1957 and left that service in 1960 to join T & J Harrisons. He gained his second officers certificate in 1961 and joined Townsend and Thorensons Ferries plying across the English Channel. In 1965 he joined the Helmsmans service. He was a most competent Helmsman for twenty years, but his prospects of ever attaining a Pilot licence on the Ship Canal were virtually non-existent due to the rapid decline of the Port of Manchester. A vacancy arose for the position of a Pilot on the River Dee serving the Ports of Mostyn and Shotton. In November 1985 he successfully passed all his examinations and was appointed a First Class Pilot for the River Dee.

Thus ended the generations of the Southwoods after 83 years of exemplary service to the Manchester Ship Canal Pilot Service.

12

A NICE LITTLE EARNER

One of the more pleasant "spin offs" from main stream piloting on the Ship Canal were the private Docking Fees to be earned within the Runcorn and Weston Point Dock systems. Both systems, being owned by the Bridgewater Canal Company (now the North West Water Authority) and managed by the Manchester Ship Canal Company were outside the jurisdiction of the Manchester Pilot District with regard to having an official Pilotage Tariff. The normal procedure, from 1895-1928 was for the Dock Master and his men to move all vessels within the systems, charging such fees that could be arranged between the Master of the vessel and the Dock Master.

When the Pilots realised the potential for additional personal revenue in 1928, they set an unofficial tariff of £1 for every dock a vessel passed through whilst going to or coming from her berth in the Runcorn or Weston Point Dock systems and immediately took over the pilotage. This tariff was flexible, being entirely dependent on the persuasive powers of the Pilot on the Captain, that his (the Pilot's) expertise was essential for a safe and damage free passage through the dock systems. It goes without saying the Dock Masters were far from pleased with this infringement on what they had always clearly regarded as their own private domain.

The Pilotage Committee were none too pleased with this new situation either. The very thought of uncontrolled pilotage fees escalating in Runcorn and Weston Point Docks, where none had been before, becoming detrimental to attracting traffic to the Ship Canal, filled them with great consternation. In September 1928 the Pilotage Committee formulated, submitted and passed

unanimously the first official tariff in the Runcorn and Weston Point Docks systems. It read as follows:
A special tariff applying to movements between points lying entirely within Runcorn Docks, Weston Point Docks, and Weston Canal between Weston Point Docks and Weston Marsh Lock (including Marsh Lock Lay-by Berth) and the channel between Weston Marsh Lock and the Manchester Ship Canal:

RUNCORN DOCK TARIFF FOR VESSELS NOT EXCEEDING 500 TONS GROSS

Between the Ship Canal and Francis Dock	£1.10s. 0d (£1.50)
Between the Ship Canal and Alfred/Fenton Dock	£2. 2s. 0d (£2.10)
Between Alfred Dock and Fenton Dock	£1. 1s. 0d (£1.05)
Between Alfred Dock and Francis Dock	£1. 1s. 0d (£1.05)
Between Fenton Dock and Francis Dock	£1. 10s. 0d (£1.50)
Between berths in any Dock	£1. 1s 0d (£1.50)

WESTON POINT DOCKS ETC TARIFF FOR VESSELS NOT EXCEEDING 500 TONS GROSS

Channel between Ship Canal/Weston Marsh Lock	£1. 1s. 0d (£1.05)
Weston Marsh Lock to the Old Basin	£1.15s 0d (£1.75)
Weston Marsh Lock to Tollemache Dock	£1. 15s 0d (£1.75)
Weston Marsh Lock to Delamere Dock	£2. 2s 0d (£2.10)
Ship Canal to Tollemache Dock	£1. 15s 0d (£1.75)
Ship Canal to the Old Basin	£1.15s 0d (£1.75)

In all cases charges for th Helmsmans service shall be at a rate of 75% of that of a Pilots fee.

This tariff catered for all vessels of that era who would normally be expected to use these docks, that is to say seldom exceeding 500 tons gross. As time progressed so the tonnage of vessels increased and in 1937 the following addition was made to the above tariff:

1 In the case of vessels over 500 tons gross the scale of fees shall be increased by 50%.
2 In the case of vessels over 1,000 tons gross the rate shall be increased by 100%.
3 In the case of vessels over 1,000 tons gross being manouvered stern first the rate shall be increased a further 25%.

This gave birth to the proliferation of vessels of 499.99 tons gross and 999.99 tons gross that used these docks. Shipowners were frequently planning and thinking how to reduce their costs, particularly in the direction of harbour dues and pilotage dues. Over the years they devised many methods of reducing a vessel's tonnage until it bore no relationship to the actual size of the vessel and as pilotage dues were traditionally based on the tonnage of vessels this new type of vessel seriously reduced a pilot's income from Docking Fees.

1890
Courtesy British Waterways, Gloucester
Weston Point Tollemache Dock

1938
Courtesy Captain P Dunbavand
Runcorn Alfred Dock and Fenton Dock

1938
Courtesy Captain P Dunbavand
Runcorn Tidal Dock or Francis Dock

1980
Courtesy of The MSC Co
The New Tidal Dock Entrance at Runcorn
Polish Vessel Wolin GRT 1272 L 284' B 40' entering Dock

1978
Courtesy of The MSC Co
The Hey-day of Runcorn Docks looking down from the top of Fenton Dock

1955

Courtesy British Waterways, Gloucester

Weston Point Tollemache Dock. Dock Office on the left foreground. Note Canal Long Boats ready to sail to Northwich.

1924

Courtesy British Waterways, Gloucester

The Entrance to the Old Basin in Weston Point Docks (now ICI) Works in the background.The Canal ahead leads to Marsh Lock and the River Weaver to Northwich.

1977
Courtesy MSC Co
Another Busy Day in Runcorn Docks

1934
Courtesy British Waterways Gloucester
Full House in Delamere Dock

1900
Courtesy British Waterways, Gloucester
The Norwegian SS Norana GRT 1322 L 232' B 33' undocking at Weston Point Delamere Dock

No greater example of this was in the tariff for the Runcorn and Weston Point Dock systems, so much so, it became incumbent to alter the whole structure of the Dock tariff to take into consideration the size of vessels now being built. In the 1970s the tariff was completely altered to a vessel's length and breadth criteria instead of the tonnage. In 1980 this "Nice Little Earner" for a pilot's personal pocket was withdrawn, when the Pilotage Committee proposed and accepted unanimously to absorb all the Runcorn and Weston Point Dock fees into the general tariff of the Manchester Pilot District by placing a surcharge of 5% on all Pilotage Rates. There was a reason why this proposal was given a unanimous vote of acceptance at the Pilotage Committee. The two Manchester Pilots' representatives on that committee were Appropriated Pilots and they seldom, if ever, had the opportunity to earn "Docking Fees". With the absorbing of the fees into the Manchester Pilots' schedule for services, the Appropriate Pilots would receive, albeit indirectly, such fees without having ever to perform any service in the Docks. They found this a highly satisfactory state of affairs. The very last Runcorn and Weston Point Dock Schedule and the manner it was calculated is reproduced overleaf.

THE LAST RUNCORN AND WESTON POINT DOCKS TARIFF 1970

PILOTAGE SERVICES PERFORMED BETWEEN	A	B	C	D	E	F	G
	TARIFF GROUPS (SEE FOLLOWING TABLE)						
Alfred Dock and Francis Dock	13.55	20.32	26.56	33.34	39.57	46.36	54.72
Alfred Dock and Fenton Dock	13.55	20.32	26.56	33.34	39.57	46.36	54.72
Fenton Dock and Francis Dock	17.83	26.74	35.65	44.57	53.11	61.87	70.61
Shift within any dock	13.55	20.32	26.56	33.34	39.57	46.36	54.72
Movements in the Channel between the Ship Canal and Weston Marsh Lock	13.55	20.32					
Weston Marsh Lock & (Castners) (Nitrate Shed) (Stone Quay)	8.92	13.37					
Castners (Nitrate Shed) & Delamache Dock Stone Quay	13.55	20.32					
Weston Marsh Lock & Delamache Dock	22.11	32.26					
Weston Inner Dock & Weston Marsh Lock	14.80	22.28					
Delamache Dock & Weston Inner Dock	13.55	20.32	26.56	33.34	39.57	46.36	54.72

OWING TO PHYSICAL LIMITATIONS VESSELS WILL NOT NORMALLY FALL WITHIN THIS PART OF THE TARIFF.
ANY EXCEPTIONAL CASES TO BE CHARGED PRO RATA.

Subject in **all** cases to a minimum total fee of £13.55
In the case of Runcorn Docks — one fee is charged
In the case of Weston Point Docks — fees are point-to-point and may be added.

TARIFF GROUPS : TABLE 2

TO READ TABLE, TAKE VESSEL'S OVERALL BEAM, FIND COLUMN INCLUDING VESSEL'S OVERALL LENGTH, AND USE COLUMN FIGURE IN TABLE 1

N.B. ALL FIGURES IN FEET — LENGTH AND BEAM TO NEAREST FOOT (6ins. TO HIGHER FOOT)

TARIFF GROUP	LENGTH OVERALL IN FEET						
	A	B	C	D	E	F	G
EXTREME BREADTH IN FEET	UP TO AND INCLUDING	BETWEEN	BETWEEN	BETWEEN	BETWEEN	BETWEEN	ANY VESSEL NOT COVERED BY GROUPS A TO F
25	237	238 - 309	310 - 383	384 - 457	458 - 531	532 - 615	
26	226	227 - 297	298 - 368	369 - 439	440 - 510	511 - 581	
27	217	218 - 286	287 - 354	355 - 423	424 - 492	493 - 561	
28	209	210 - 275	276 - 342	343 - 408	409 - 472	473 - 536	
29	202	203 - 266	267 - 330	331 - 394	395 - 458	459 - 522	
30	196	197 - 257	258 - 319	320 - 381	382 - 443	444 - 505	
31	189	190 - 249	250 - 309	310 - 369	370 - 429	430 - 489	
32	183	184 - 241	242 - 299	300 - 357	358 - 415	416 - 473	
33	178	179 - 234	235 - 290	291 - 346	347 - 402	403 - 458	
34	173	174 - 227	228 - 281	282 - 335	336 - 389	390 - 443	
35	168	169 - 221	222 - 274	275 - 327	328 - 380	381 - 433	
36	163	164 - 214	215 - 266	267 - 317	318 - 368	369 - 419	
37	158	159 - 208	209 - 258	259 - 308	309 - 358	359 - 408	
38	154	155 - 203	204 - 252	253 - 301	302 - 350	351 - 399	
39	150	151 - 198	199 - 246	247 - 294	295 - 342	343 - 390	
40	147	148 - 193	194 - 239	240 - 285	286 - 331	332 - 377	
41	-	Up to 188	189 - 233	234 - 278	279 - 323	324 - 368	
42	-	Up to 184	185 - 228	229 - 272	273 - 316	317 - 360	
43	-	Up to 179	180 - 222	223 - 265	266 - 308	309 - 351	
44	-	Up to 175	176 - 217	218 - 259	260 - 301	302 - 343	
45		Up to 171	172 - 212	213 - 253	254 - 294	295 - 335	
46	-	Up to 168	169 - 208	209 - 248	249 - 288	289 - 328	
47	-	Up to 164	165 - 203	204 - 242	243 - 281	282 - 320	
48	-	Up to 161	162 - 199	200 - 237	238 - 275	276 - 313	
49	-	Up to 157	158 - 195	196 - 233	234 - 270	271 - 308	
50	-	Up to 154	155 - 191	192 - 228	229 - 265	266 - 302	
51	-	-	Up to 187	188 - 224	225 - 260	261 - 297	
52	-	-	Up to 183	184 - 219	220 - 256	257 - 291	
53	-	-	Up to 178	179 - 214	215 - 252	253 - 286	
54	-	-	-	Up to 210	211 - 247	248 - 280	
55	-	-	-	Up to 205	206 - 243	244 - 275	
TARIFF GROUP	A	B	C	D	E	F	G

The only other “Nice little earner” was the Manchester Dock Shifting Fee. The secretary of the Pilots Association wrote to the Pilotage Committee in March 1925 stating:

“I understand that occasionally when no Dock Pilot is available at Manchester, rotary pilots are called upon to move vessels in the Manchester Docks. This matter has been before a meeting of the Pilots Association and it is their wish that any dues earned by rotary pilots so employed should be paid to the individual Pilot who performs the shift. I trust this will be agreeable to your committee.”

It was decided that the Pilots request, that the fees be retained by the individual Pilots and not paid into the pool as previously had happened, be agreed to. This system did not last very long, on the retirement of the last Dock Pilot all the Dock Shift Fees reverted to be being paid into the pool once more.

DOCK PILOTAGE RECEIPT

DOCK PILOTAGE

Messrs. F. ARMIT & SON Agent

dr. to D. A. CLULOW *M. S. C. Pilot*

for services rendered to mv

"BLEIK VASSLI"

CANAL TO DELAMERE DOCK

£2-0-0.

Pilot Master

DATE: 18.6.61

A GENTLEMAN PILOT

Mr W (Bill) Yates Pilot 1st Class
1940-1973

Mr W (Bill) Yates was an exceptional Pilot who had exceptional talents. Apart from his natural ability piloting vessels he was a gifted artist in oils and water colours. Many of his paintings depicting scenes of vessels on the Ship Canal adorn the Eastham Pilots Station and many homes of past and present Pilots. Mr Yates was born in Runcorn on 19th December 1916, the second son of Captain William Yates, who was Captain of the MSC tug *"Cornbrook"* his grandfather also named William was Captain of the MSC tug *"Old Trafford"*. He commenced his sea life working on the Mersey Dock and Harbour Board dredging craft in the River Mersey and in May 1934 he joined the mv "Shellbrit" and served on several coastal vessels until November 1940 when he joined the Helmsmens Service. He passed his 2nd Class Pilots Licence in 1952 and became 1st Class in 1955.

Bill Yates was admired by all; he had that rare quality of being thoughtful, kind and considerate. He had that wonderful knack of getting the best out of all who worked with him by his quiet and unassuming demeanour. He had to retire in March 1973 - due to a heart condition - and went to live in Ilfracombe, Devon. Sadly his retirement was all too short and he died on 16th August 1981 aged 65 years. He left a wife, Doris, two daughters Susan and Linda and 5 grandchildren.

1920s
Courtesy Mrs W Yates Collection
Stanlow No 1 Oil Dock
Note the oil boom across the entrance. Removed about 1936.

13

THE PILOT WORKING SYSTEM 1936 - 1939

During 1935 the Pilot Service struggled on, often hopelessly undermanned to maintain an efficient rota system with their present limited number of 32 Pilots. It taxed the Pilot Service to the limit and December 1935 was the month "the straw broke the camel's back". Out of the complement of 32 Pilots, on some days, the effective working number was reduced to 20. Sickness was responsible for one Pilot being off the rota the whole of the month, another Pilot 21 days, yet another 17 days and one Pilot was sick with acute Bronchitis between 24 December and 2 January (**Note the dates**). Other Pilots had absented themselves from the Rota for divers reasons. At the Pilotage Committee Meeting held in January 1936 the Chairman (Mr Browning) submitted a letter from the Manchester Steamship Owners Association stating that the shipowners looked to the Authority to provide an efficient and adequate supply of pilots but were opposed to any increase of Pilotage Rates. The Chairman thought the Committee should consider whether two additional Pilots should be appointed as suggested by the Pilots Association. He was of the opinion that it was only when Pilots were absent owing to sickness that any undue strain was imposed on the remaining Pilots. He referred to the number of services performed during the last 10 years.

Mr Evans (Secretary of the Pilots Association) accepted the view expressed by the Shipowners that it was for the Pilotage Authority to determine the number of Pilots required to provide an efficient and adequate service and stated that the Pilots trusted that the Authority would not be deterred from proposing such increase of Pilotage Rates as they considered proper, by the unwillingness of the Shipowners to acquiesce in an increase. The Pilots renewed their application for an increase of two Pilots. The Chairman gave further particulars of the average number of turns performed by Pilots during the years 1920-1935 and said that while the number of services had increased, he thought the increase was in the main attributable to services of short duration chiefly in the lower reaches of the Canal.

Note - In 1920, 26 Pilots performed 3234 services. In 1926, 32 Pilots performed 4292 services. By 1935 34 pilots performed 4198 services.

18 September 1938
Courtesy MSC Co
"Manchester Progress" Grt 5620 L431' B57' on her maiden voyage entering Barton Lock. Stern tug "Old Trafford". Far right the original sewage vessel "Salford City". In 1942 she struck a mine in the River Mersey and sank.

NOTICE TO MASTER MARINERS AND PILOTS
AMENDMENT OF GENERAL BYE-LAWS

(1800) **MANCHESTER SHIP CANAL.**

NOTICE TO MASTER MARINERS AND PILOTS.

Whenever a Steamer is navigating any portion of the Ship Canal or Docks, **every order telegraphed to the engine room must be at the same moment conveyed verbally to the engine room.**

For this purpose a man must always be stationed below the steamer's bridge, and every order must be given to him simultaneously with the telegraphic order loud enough for the man to hear, and he must instantly repeat the order in a voice loud enough to be distinctly heard in the engine room.

No infringement of this regulation can be permitted for any reason whatsoever.

BY ORDER.

Dock Office, Manchester,
13th December, 1902.

With reference to Minute dated 24th November 1938, the Committee discussed the proposed amendments of the General Bye-Laws of the Port of Manchester. Mr Stoker said he had an objection to raise to the amendment to Bye-Law 14 requiring orders telegraphed to the Engine Room to be confirmed by voice tube or telephone. He did not think this should be deleted from the Bye-Laws.

A very strange suggestion came from the Pilots' Representatives that the service of Piloting a vessel from Eastham to Ellesmere Port or Bowaters and vice versa should not count as a complete turn, and the Chairman promised that this would be considered and the matter brought up at a later meeting. The Pilotage committee were very sympathetic toward all the Pilots' requests and after further lengthy discussions it was unanimously agreed that two additional Pilots be appointed as from 1st February 1936.

The following year was one of continuing disenchantment for the Pilots Association. The Pilots were frequently called upon for duty without having the opportunity of reasonable rest and the general opinion of the Pilot service was that they were considerably overworked. The Chairman of Pilotage Committee had instructed the Secretary of the Pilots Association that his committee would be prepared to consider any concrete proposals which they might submit, with the approval of the Pilots generally, in an attempt to alleviate the pressing problem of overworking. At the December 1937 Pilotage Committee Meeting the Secretary of the Pilots Association stated that after consideration the Pilots suggested that the only method of relieving the present conditions of working was to increase the number of Pilots by promoting four of the Second Class Pilots and appointing a like number of Second Class Pilots. After some discussion it was agreed that for the time being one First Class Pilot be added to the service by promoting the senior Second Class Pilot and appointing one Second Class Pilot. It was also suggested that the promotion of two further Second Class Pilots to First Class without appointing two new Second Class Pilots might afford considerable relief without any serious effect on the earnings, but the Pilots' representatives said they had no authority to agree to such an arrangement. It was decided this proposal should be deferred for consideration of the Pilots. The two appointments to First Class were made on 6 January 1938.

The Pilots replied to the Pilotage Committee that they regretted to learn of the decision of the Committee to add only one Pilot to the service as they were still of the opinion that at least four additional Pilots were necessary, a fact they considered was borne out by the increase in the number of vessels piloted and rota turns performed during 1937 - a total of 4432 turns performed giving an increase of nearly 200 over the 1936 figure of 4239 turns. The Pilots did not approve the suggestion that two further Second Class pilots should be promoted without appointing two new Pilots neither did they approve of the suggestion that a service from Eastham to Ellesemere Port or vice versa should not count as a full turn on the rota. After further discussion it was agreed that the question of appointing additional pilots should be deferred until the result of the recent appointments was known. Further negotiations and meetings resulted in a stalemate and no further appointments of new pilots were made until 1940.

When the appointment of Mr Bennion as Chief Pilotage Clerk was made in 1920, at the commencement of the Rotary and Pooling system, his office was situated at Runcorn from where all orders from shipping agents' brokers requiring pilots to attend their vessels were transmitted. These orders were then sent to Eastham Locks and relayed to the Pilots at their home via the telephone by the personnel on Eastham Locks. In September 1938 the Pilots Association thought it was desirable that the office of the Pilotage Clerk should be removed from Runcorn to Eastham. They thought the present method of issuing orders to pilots was most unsatisfactory, as it was contended that they had considerable difficulty in obtaining their orders and eliciting information in relation thereto from the staff at Eastham Locks through whom such orders were obtained. The Pilotage Committee noted the request for a change of venue for the Chief Pilot Clerk but requested it remain in abeyance for the time being.

The continent of Europe was in turmoil once again, Hitler having marched into Austria and Czechoslovakia. The Pilotage Committee rightly deduced it would only be a matter of time before a full scale war with Germany would become a reality. On 2 May 1939 they reported that the question of a possible depletion of the Manchester Pilot Service in the event of a national emergency arising had been extensively discussed and stated that, with one possible exception they could not learn of any Pilot who belonged to the Royal Naval Reserve. They agreed that a letter should be addressed to each Pilot and Helmsman in relation to national service, stating that the Committee considered it of the paramount importance that the pilotage service at the Port of Manchester should be maintained at full strength and that they should be advised before any licensed Pilot or Helmsman volunteered for active service, as occurred in the 1914-18 war.

1938
"When Day is Done"
A tranquil picture of No 7 Dock looking towards Trafford Park wharf

14

THE HUBERT G PRINGLE STORY 1922-1967

Mr Hubert Pringle represented the archteypical Pilot - he was punctilious; he was abstemious and he was meticulous, but above all he was a superb natural ship handler. The expertise he showed in piloting all manner and sizes of vessels and the speed at which he safely transited the Manchester Ship Canal was admired and often envied by all in the Manchester Ship Canal Pilot Service. Not for nothing did he earn the sobriquet "The Flying Scot".

He expected the same high standards that he had set himself, from all who assisted him whilst he was in attendance on a vessel. Such was his dedication to his piloting duties. The most fortunate attribute of this remarkable man was his passion to catalogue, in the minutest detail, every vessel he attended during the 40 years he was connected with the Manchester Ship Canal Pilot Service. These diaries chronicling the history of a Manchester Ship Canal Pilot were so detailed in the information contained within them that to say Mr Hubert Pringle was the Samuel Pepys of his time in the Pilot Service would not be an understatement.

Mr Pringle commenced his sea-going life at the tender age of 14 years. On 24 May 1922, Empire Day as it was called in those times, he accepted a berth as a deck boy on the three masted schooner *"Black Cat"* sailing out of the port of Runcorn. He was subsequently berthed on two other three masted schooners the *"Mary Watkinson"* and the *"Bidsie E Bell"*. His wages during that period were £2 per month. On 24 January 1924, he joined the steam tug *"Clarendon"* working in the Ship Canal for £2 per week until 24 April 1924 when he became apprenticed to the Stag Line of West Hartlepool, joining his first vessel the ss *"Gloxinia"* of 1961 net reg tons that same month. His wages for the first year were 16s.7d (82 1/2p) per month plus one shilling (5p) per month in lieu of soap. This magnificent remuneration rose in small increments to £1.13s.2d (£1.65) per month plus his one shilling per month in lieu of soap in the fourth year.

He served three years and three months with the Stag Line sailing to such diverse places as Russia, Texas, Canada, Denmark and Africa. On completion of his apprenticeship in July 1927, he applied to join the Manchester Ship Canal Helmsmen's Service - was accepted and placed on the list of awaiting applicants to join the Helmsmen's Service. He then joined the British and Continental Steamship Company - colloquially known as *"The Cork Boats"* - whose steamers traded between the continent of Europe and the Port of Manchester. This was to prove a most judicious move on his part towards his future as a Helmsman. He was appointed a probationary helmsman on 18 August 1928 and became an authorised helmsman on 19 September 1928 when the famous diaries began.

Mr Pringle's first entry in his diary read *"19 September 1928 0600 hrs. Steered first vessel ss Sirius 466 net reg tons. Eastham to Manchester. No wheelhouse. Weather overcast but dry. Pilot Mr John G Baxter aged 62 yrs of Liscard. Received the sum of £1.13.9d* (£1.68) *for my services, calculated as follows:*

Initial Fee	*7s.6d*	(37 1/2p)
Mileage charge at 9d (3 1/2p) *per mile*	*£1.6s3d*	(£1.31)
Total:	*£1.13s9d"*	(£1.68)

Note: Mr Pringle had earned on his first day as a Helmsman a sum equal (all but 2p) to what he had earned in one month a year previously. October 1928 was his first full month as helmsman.

He completed the year earning £69.0.2d (£69.01) for his Helmsman's services. In 1929, his first full year as a Helmsman, he earned £310.18.2d (£310.91) for steering 167 vessels a distance of 4,511 miles in a total time of 1,788 hours. He paid no Income Tax. A Chief Officer of a vessel with the average tonnage Mr Pringle was steering, would have earned £216 per annum, whilst a Master would have earned £306 per annum. A pint of beer cost 4d (2p) and a bottle of whisky 4s.9d (23p).

OCTOBER 1928

NB: MANC = Manchester, EAST = Eastham, PART = Partington, RUNC = Runcorn

All vessels had no Wheelhouse

DATE	VESSEL	NETREGTONS	FROM-TO	FEE	DECIMALFEE	PILOT	COMMENTS
2 10 28	KATHOLM	876	EAST-MANC	£1.13.9d	£1.68	Thos.Lamey	
3 10 28	COBURG	471	MANC-EAST	£2.3.9d	£2.18	W Musker	Detention 10s0d (50p)
6 10 28	LANGFOND	865	MANC-EAST	£1.13.9d	£1.68	C S Rhodes	
9 10 28	ICELAND	722	EAST-MANC	£2.13.9d	£2.18	G V Davidson	Detention 10s0d
11 10 28	ASTRID	660	EAST-MANC	£1.13.9d	£1.68	D H Hughes	
13 10 28	ASTRID	660	MANC-EAST	£1.13.9d	£1.68	D H Hughes	
15 10 28	FLORINTINE	1032	EAST-RUNC	£1.1.6d	£1.7½p	J Inglesfield	
18 10 28	HOLSTEIN	471	PART-EAST	£1.8.9d	£1.48	J D Shaw	
19 10 28	SIRIUS	466	MANC-EAST	£1.0.9d	£1.07	J Lee#In ballast	
22 10 18	POLLUX	724	MANC-EAST	£1.13.9d	£1.68	A P Bennet	
24 10 28	TEXELSTROOM	967	EAST-MANC	£1.13.9	£1.68	W Onion	
26 10 28	SAGATIND	907	EAST-MANC	£2.0.9	£2.07	P J Morton#Detention 7s.0d(35p)	

Total	£21.15.6d	£21.77
Less Collection Fees	£1. 2.lld	1.15
Balance	£20.12. 7d	£20.62

Mr. Pringle's first full month earnings

Courtesy Mrs W Yates Collection
"Arabian Prince" Grt 5764 L 405' B 52'

VESSELS MR PRINGLE STEERED

1930
"Iceland" Grt 1236 L241' B36'
Note the Open Bridge and Wheelhouse

1928
"Katholm" Grt 1510 L253' B39'
Chain and Rod Steering Gear

On 19 March 1929, he was promoted to a First Class Helmsman to steer vessels of all tonnages. His services with the British and Continental, sailing in the Ship Canal, had stood him in good stead; his excellence as a Helmsman was quickly recognised by all pilots. All the Appropriated Pilots - the most fastidious group of pilots to say the least - accepted his services and in all the years he was a Helmsman, his services were never once refused. The diaries record that he steered his first large vessel on 22 March:

"ss DARIAN 4058 NRT 6639 GRT. Eastham to Partington. In Ballast.
Pilot: Mr G Cartwright aged 59 years
No Wheelhouse. Steering Fee: £3."

The other highlight in 1929 was his marriage to Miss Celia Wileman on 16 October. Helmsmen were not pooling their earnings in those days and his diary tells us his week-long honeymoon cost him £7.4.9d (£7.23) in lost steering fees. Mr Pringle was averaging £27 per month for fourteen steering services - proof enough his services were always in demand - and his weekly domestic expenses were as follows:

Rent	£1. 0. 0d	(£1.00)
Coal	0. 5. 1½d	(26p)
Electricity	0. 3. 0d	(15p)
Gas	0. 1. 0d	(5p)
Insurance	0. 2 0d	(10p)
Cleaning Lady	0. 2. 6d	(12½p)
Food	0. 14. 6d	(88p)
	£2. 8. 1½	(£2.41)

It is a delight to record Mr and Mrs Pringle celebrated their Diamond Wedding Anniversary in 1989.

During the next ten years he performed 1,774 steering services in a total mileage of 47,905 miles, for which he earned £3,201.5.10d (£3,201.29). During that decade he steered the following number of Appropriated vessels:

90 Tankers (Shell/Eagle Oil/BP, etc)
57 Furness Withy (Pacific Boats)
54 USA Lines
25 Prince Line
24 Leyland Line
23 Thor Thorenson Line (Foss Boats)
16 Manchester Liners
16 Knudsen Line (Holm Boats and others)
13 City Line
11 Clan Line.

Courtesy Mrs W Yates Collection
Another type of vessel piloted by Mr H G Pringle, "Fjordass" Grt 13,325 L 465' B 63'

Courtesy Mrs W Yates Collection
"Pacific Fortune" Grt 9400 L 499' B 63' 6" manouvering to enter Irlam Locks inward bound for Manchester.

Norwegian Vessel "Skotfoss" owned by Thor Thoresen Line

His complete steering record for 12 years 8 months, states that he steered 2,190 vessels and a total mileage of 56,390 miles. He was absent from duty through sickness a total of 83 days. Considering the conditions he had to steer under, no wheelhouses on 75% of the vessels, an average of seven days a year off duty because of illness, was indeed remarkable.

Mr Pringle steered his last vessel on 12 May 1942, the ss *San Dario* 594 NRT from Stanlow Oil Dock to Partington with Mr W W Milsom. The steering fee was £1. 3. 9d (£1.18). He proceeded on leave, and on 27 May 1942 successfully passed the examination for a Second Class Licence. He piloted his first vessel on 29 May, the mv *"Shell Spirit 2"* 234 NRT from Eastham to Stanlow. His pilotage fee of £2.12.3d (£2.61) went into the pooled earnings scheme. He was promoted to a First Class Pilot on 19 September 1946 and piloted his premier first class vessel on 27 September and was as ever recorded thus:

SS *Empire Jet* 4728 NRT
Stanlow to Eastham
Tugs *"Cornbrook"* and *"Rixton"*
Helmsman: Mr Harvey Clugston
Vessel fitted with wheelhouse
Pilotage Fee: £8. 9.11d (£8.50)
No damage
Weather: Fine and Clear

Courtesy MSC Co
1958
SS Clan Maclean Grt 6017 L 466' B 61' on Moore Lane straight outward bound. Head tug MSC "Stanlow"

Twenty years after joining the Manchester Pilot Service his earnings were as follows for the year 1948:

Total Pilotage Fees Earned:	£969.8. 6d	(£969.42½)
1 Total Pooled Balance received	£885.7.6d	(£885.37½)
2 Travelling expenses	£35.6.8d	(£35.34)
	£920.14.2d	(£920.71)

This was nearly a 300% increase on his first full year's earnings.
On a nostalgic theme, on 9 June 1949, Mr Pringle purchased a car, an Austin 10, registration number CKD 146, from a certain Mr Joshua Davies, for the then princely sum of £175. His running costs are calculated in his diary as follows:

Car Insurance	£6.15.0d	(£6.75)
AA Fees	£2.12.0d	(£2.60)
Motor Tax	£1.16.8d	(£1.83)
Petrol June (6½ galls)	13. 5d	(77½p)
Petrol July (9½ galls)	19. 5d	(97½p)
New Petrol Pump on car	£1.10.0d	(£1.50)
Car Cover	£1. 5. 0d	(£1.25)

Motorists of today must wonder at petrol 2s.1d (10½p) a gallon and can only sigh for a car insurance fully comprehensive for £6.75.

Mr Pringle was appointed as Appropriated Pilot for Clan Line on 24 July 1952 and on 31 July performed his first pilotage service for the Clan Line:

SS *Clan Macquarrie* 4259 NRT 7131 GRT
Eastham to Manchester
Draught 25'6"
Helmsman Mr P Rule
Tugs *"Arrow"* (Capt. Rowlands); *"Quarry"* (Capt. Halewood)
Pilotage Fee £13.17.6 (£13.85)
Travelling Expenses 7s.0d (35p)
No damage
Weather fine, warm and clear.

His retaining fee as Choice Pilot for Clan Line was £100 per annum and was increased to £200 in 1958. As one would expect of this remarkable pilot, he served Clan Line with the same dedication he approached all things in life. From his appointment as Appropriate (Choice) Pilot until he retired in August 1967, he had piloted 1,020 Clan Liners and their associated companies, having covered 32,490 miles on board those vessels transiting the Ship Canal.

Between 1942 and 1957, Mr Pringle only absented himself from duty through illness 15 days - an average of one day a year - but in October he became seriously ill with pneumonia which necessitated his absence from the rota for 30 days. His only other prolonged absence from duty was between 21 December 1963 until 6 September 1964 due to a heart condition. On his return to the rota until he retired, he never again absented himself from duty due to illness.

From May 1942 until August 1967, Mr Pringle piloted 4,455 vessels for a distance of 80,730 miles during which time he never once refused the services of a Helmsman. His last full year as a pilot, 1966 - nearly 40 years after commencing on the Manchester Ship Canal - his diary tells us:

Total Pilotage Fees earned	£3,153.8.2d	(£3,153.41)
1 Total Pooled Balance received	£2,496.18.3d	(£2,496.91)
2 Travelling expenses	£54.15.0d	(£54.75)
3 Appropriated fee	£200.0.0d	(£200.00)
	£2,751.13.3d	(£2,751.67)

Mr Pringle had come a long way since he was a deck-hand on a three-masted schooner for £2 per month. He had accomplished this feat through his own expertise and single minded dedication to become a Pilot and above all, a master of his chosen profession.

Courtesy of Mr H Pringle
1967
Mr H G Pringle about to board one of his last appropriated vessels "Clan Alpine" Grt 7163 L 442' B 57'

A Chief Officer during this year, with a Master's Certificate on a foreign-going (Deep Sea) vessel between 7,000 and 9,000 GRT would have a salary of £1,985. A Master's salary would have been in the region of £2,293 per annum. Beer was 1/11d (10p) a pint and a bottle of Scotch Whiskey standard brand was £2. 9 .0d (£2.45). Income Tax was 4s 0d (20p) on the first £100; 6s 0d (30p) on the next £200 and 8s 3d (42p) thereafter. Mr Pringle did pay tax.

On 28 August 1967, Mr Hubert G Pringle boarded his last vessel before retiring. This sad moment, for he truly loved his pilotage life and work, was recorded - like the many thousands before it in his diary - thus:

MV *Clan Magillivray* NRT 4908 9039 GRT
Eastham to Ellesmere Port
Tugs *"Talisman"* (Capt P Dunbavand) *"Tarn"* (Capt G Perris)

Helmsman Mr N Pickwell
Pilotage Fees £37.11. 0d (£37.55)
Weather - A lovely Summers day
No damage
The diary closed for the final time but on the last line written in hold capital letters, was the legend: "**THE END OF AN ERA.**" How true that was!

Mr H G Pringle died on 23 May 1994 aged 87 years, Mrs Pringle having died two years previously.

I shall always be eternally grateful to Mr Pringle for allowing me to see and use his copious diaries for the purpose of writing this book. His dedication to such minutae within them throughout his life on the Manchester Ship Canal, has been invaluable in recording the history of the Manchester Ship Canal Pilot Service. I sincerely hope that his diaries will be preserved in a suitable Maritime Museum. They are too valuable a record to be lost to future generations, of an era such as the likes we will never see again nor will ever be recorded again in such detail.

Courtesy of Mr H Pringle
"Clan Macindoe" GRT 6,957 L 494' B 62', one of the last vessels of that Company to enter the Ship Canal.

15

THE MANCHESTER SHIP CANAL TUG FLEET 1894 - 1990

PADDLE TUGS

Tug	Years in Service	First Captains
Bridgewater	1894-1895	T Leach
Earl of Ellesmere	1894-1926	S Edwards
Brackley	1894-1926	W Yates
Helen	1894-1903	G Jones
Dagmar	1894-1927	Not known
Gower (wooden hull)	1894-1905	W Banner
St Winifred	1894-1927	T Smith
Queen of the Mersey	1894-1905	W Smith
Barton	1903-1948	W Peck
Irlam	1903-1953	Not known
Rixton	1905-1953	Not known
Eccles	1905-1952	Not known
Acton Grange	1907-1948	Not known
Old Trafford	1907-1950	W Yates (Snr)

SINGLE SCREW STEAM TUGS

Mercia	1895-1935	
Charles Galloway (Twin screw)	1895-1930	
Pomona	1896-1960	
Agnes Seed	1899-1930	T A Seed

Eastham	1899-1947	
Partington	1899-1946	
Bridgewater	1905-1959	
Cornbrook	1905-1963	W Yates (Jnr)
Modewheel	1907-1939	
Old Quay	1907-1938	
Stanlow	1924-1965	
Cadishead	1926-1960	
Mount Manisty	1926-1960	
Firefly	1935-1965	D Clifton
Archer	1938-1967	
Arrow (1963 altered from steam to diesel)	1938-1970	
Badger	1939-1967	A Steele
Bison	1939-1967	

TWIN SCREW DIESEL TUGS

Mallard	1940-1968	J Rowles
Merlin	1940-1968	P Kortens
Neptune	1941-1970	J Guard
Nymph	1942-1970	W Clifton

The four tugs above were given the sobriquet *"The Donald Ducks"*

Onsett	1948-1973	
Onward	1948-1975	
Panther	1950-1975	J Garvie
Puma	1950-1975	J Banner
Quarry	1952-1975	
Quest	1952-1975	
Ranger	1953-1976	
Rover	1953-1978	
Sabre	1956-1986	R W Blyth
Sceptre	1956-1984	P Kortens
Scimitar	1956-1986	J Garvie
Sovereign	1957-1984	J Banner
Talisman (First and only tug fitted with Radar)	1961-1980	R W Blyth
Tarn	1962-1980	E Hancock
Ulex	1965-1983	
Undine	1965#1983	The 'V' class
Victory	1974-1989	were the last
Viceroy	1975-1989	traffic tugs
Viking	1976-1989	the M.S.C.
Volant	1976-1989	had built

1903

MSC "Irlam" A steel paddle tug built by Rennoldson of South Shields. Dimensions L 100' B 11'. Entered service 1903 withdrawn 1953. The picture above is taken from a painting by Peter Kortens. Later he became a well-known Captain in the Tug service for very many years.

"Lord Stalbridge" A steel, twin screw steam tug built by the Dublin Dockyard Company, North Wall, Dublin in 1909. Off No 124625. Registered at Chester No 2/ 1909 then at Manchester No 54/1922.
105' 6" x 22' 6" x 10' 2". 164-49 Gross. 60-95 Reg. Sold 1946.

1894
MSC "Earl of Ellesmere" An iron paddle tug built by Ogle at Preston in 1857. Dimensions L 109' 9" B 20' 110 GRT 60 BHP. Entered service in 1894 broken up in 1926.

1901
MSC "Dagmar" An iron paddle tug built in 1863 at Lairds, Birkenhead. Dimensions L 138' B 21' 183 GRT. 95 BHP. Entered service 1896, broken up at Garston 1927.

msc "Charles Galloway" A steel twin screw tug built by Eltringham of South Shields in 1895. Dimensions L 90' B 19' 8" 128 GRT 9 knots. Engine size 450 IHP. The first twin screw in the MSC service. Entered service 1895 withdrawn from service 1929. Named after an early Director of the Canal Company. Pictured on her maiden voyage in the Canal.

1939
MSC "Partington" A steel single screw tug built in 1899 at Southampton. Dimensions L 80' B 19' GRT 103 430 BHP 11 knots. Sold to Lamey Tugs, Liverpool 1946. Broken up 1959.

1939
The galley on the "Partington" A coal stove open to all weathers, Chef Mr Harold Horton - Deck Hand.

1894
MSC "Brackley" An iron paddle tug built by Vernons of Liverpool in 1859. Dimensions L 116' B 17' 6" 122 GRT. 50 BHP. Entered service 1896 broken up in 1926.

1912
MSC "Barton" A steel paddle tug built by Rennoldson in South Shields in 1903. Dimensions L 100' B20' 166 GRT 400 BHP 10 knots. Entered service 1903 withdrawn 1948. Captain W Peck is third from the right, Mate P Kortens 2nd right, S Rushton, deck hand, last in line on the right.

1963
Re-fitted M.S.C. ARROW

1957
Foreground "Sabre" Background "Onsett" and "Mallard"
MSC "Arrow", a steel single screw steam tug built in August 1938 by Henry Robb at the Victoria Dockyard, Leith. Registered at Manchester No 2/1938. First date was 26 August. Off. No. 147433. 85' 5" x 23' 1" x 11' 2". 144-22 gross. A reciprocating steam compound engine by Aitchison 2 cyl 19 1/2" - 42", 27" stroke. 90-5 NHP 850 IHP 11 knots 750 BHP.

The *"Arrow"* arrived at Runcorn via the Caledonian Canal on 1 September 1938 and the crew were alleged to have seen the Loch Ness Monster on passage through there. She entered service on 5 September, the Captain being George Maddocks who was in charge for abour 15 years. When *"Archer"* and *"Arrow"* arrived they had two large tall vents on the stokehold casing, these with the double casing funnel gave a poor stern view. Later the vents were cut down, the view was still restricted and so they were removed and a screw-in type fitted. The wheelhouse had no rear to it and consequently in a stern wind it was very draughty. A back was fitted after the War. Until 1946-47 The Captain and Chief lived forward with a room each and sharing a large mess room. The Mate and Second had a room each after, with the Deckhand, Lad and Fireman in cramped quarters over the prop shaft. It was decided to alter the accommodation and to move the officers aft and the Crew forward. This didn't go down very well with the Captains but nevertheless it went ahead, *"Arrow"* first, *"Archer"* later. The Galley was on the starboard side forward with the WC and Lamproom on the port side.

In 1946 the *"Arrow"*, as with many steam tugs, was infested with an insect known as a Jasper. These were about the size of a cockroach and they lived and bred near the Boiler but not on humans. My sister obtained 7 lbs of DDT from Randle Works and in two days we shovelled thousands of these insects out of the Galley. None were ever seen again.

In 1963 the *"Arrow"* was extensively re-fitted and altered from steam to diesel at Old Quay Yard. She was never as manouverable after that. The time lapse from ahead to astern was too long. Fitted with a Ruston & Hornsby oil engine, 8 cyl 10¼", 14½" stroke 800 BHP 10¾ knots 162 gross. She was sold to Malta in 1970, her registration being transferred to Malta on 18 January 1972 (she left Runcorn in November 1970). Re-named *"San Pietru"*. Sold again to Midmed Towage Company of Greece in 1983 and re-named *"Irene K"*.

1947
MSC "Mallard" A twin screw diesel tug built by Robbs of Leith. dimensions L 85' B 23' 131 GRT Engine 770 BHP 10.25 knots. First diesel tug in the fleet. Entered service 1940 withdrawn 1968. One of the "Donald Ducks".

1938
MSC "Archer" A steel single screw steam tug built in 1938 by Robbs of Leith. Dimensions L 85' B 23' 144 GRT 850 BHP. Entered service July 1938 withdrawn 1967. Sister ship to the "ARROW"

1980
The Fleets in Port
Foreground "Sabre". Background "Viking", "Tarn, "Talisman"

1965
M.S.C. "Ulex"
L 86' B 24' Twin screw 11 Knots 1300 BHP.

The last of the paddle tugs was the *"Old Trafford"*. In their early days they had a painted or carved emblem on their paddle boxes, of the coat of arms of the town they were named after. The paddle tugs carried a crew of eight consisting of the Captain and Chief Engineer who had spacious quarters aft with a large cabin each and sharing a dining room. The rest of the crew lived in a large cabin forward, the Mate, Deck hand and lad on the starboard side and the second engineer and two firemen were berthed on the port side. The wheelhouse was open to all the elements for many years so was the galley which was set on the starboard side abaft the paddle wheel and in bad weather it was a case of covering your head and as much of the meal you were cooking, with a coat.

The toilet arrangements were extremely primitive at first, a tundish shaped bowl open at the bottom and washed down with a bucket of Canal water. One did not linger in there very long in winter. Some of the faults were rectified but not until their working lives were nearly over. The tugs contributed immensely to the safe passage of large vessels transiting the Canal and in manouvring vessels into locks and docks. Their assistance was invaluable to all Pilots in the execution of their duties. I hope some day someone will record their history for posterity.

All the photographs of the tugs and the information on them are by courtesy of Mr P (Percy) Dunbavand, ex Captain in the tug fleet and I wish to acknowledge with grateful thanks his contribution to this history.

The Power Unit

1974
M.S.C. "Victory"
L 86' B 24' Twin Screw 11 Knots BHP 1280

(223)

THE MANCHESTER SHIP CANAL COMPANY

TUG REQUISITION AND AGREEMENT

EASTHAM. Station,

1300 hours 20/7/64. 19.....

To THE MANCHESTER SHIP CANAL COMPANY

Please supply 2. *Tug(s) for my vessel the* HALIA.

to be at EASTHAM. *at* 0530 *hours on the* 21ST. *day*

of JULY. 19 64. *cargo* CRUDE OIL *net registered*

tonnage 6931 *draft of water aft* 28'

from EASTHAM. *to* STANLOW.

on the conditions named herein, and upon the terms specified in the Company's Schedule of Towage Charges for the time being in operation.

MASTS AND/OR FUNNELS
NOT MORE THAN 7/8' FEET
ABOVE WATER LEVEL

CONDITIONS UNDER WHICH THE MANCHESTER SHIP CANAL COMPANY PROVIDE TUGS.

The Company, its servants and agents are not to be responsible or liable for delay, damage or injury to any ship, vessel or craft, or the persons or goods on board thereof of which the Company may undertake the towage, assisting or docking in the River Mersey and/or the Manchester Ship Canal, or which may be piloted to or from any place in the River Mersey and/or the said Ship Canal, or for any loss sustained or liability incurred by any one by reason of such delay, damage or injury or for any loss or liability incurred in consequence of any such ship, vessel or craft colliding with or otherwise damaging any other vessel or thing or for any damage, loss or liability of any kind whatsoever arising from the towing, docking, assisting or piloting, whatever may be the cause or causes of such delay, damage, injury, loss or liability, or under whatever circumstances such delay, damage, injury, loss or liability may have happened or accrued, even though arising from or occasioned by the act, omission, incompetence, negligence or default, whether wilful or not, of the Company, its servants or agents or any other persons, or any defect, imperfection, insufficiency of power or unseaworthiness in, or any delay, stoppage or slowness of speed of any tug or vessel, her machinery, equipment, appliances or gear engaged in towing, docking, assisting or piloting any ship, vessel or craft, even though such defect, imperfection, insufficiency of power or unseaworthiness be in existence before or during the said services.

It is further agreed that on the hiring of a Tug for towage, docking, piloting or assistance services the master and crew of such Tug become in all respects the servants of and are identified with the Ship and are under the control of the person in charge of the Ship whilst the towage, docking, piloting or assistance services are being performed.

Further the hirer agrees to indemnify the Company against all losses, damage and claims whatsoever including damage sustained by the Tug and her machinery, equipment, appliances and gear, even though caused by any defect in such Tug, her machinery, equipment, appliances and gear or by the neglect or default of the master or crew of the Tug or of the servants or agents of the Company.

If a Tug is engaged to tow a ship, vessel or craft to any place and through stress of weather or any other unavoidable circumstances, she runs short of fuel or is separated from such ship, vessel or craft and the service is not completed the Company shall nevertheless be paid *pro rata* according to the time occupied as compared with the ordinary period of the intended services.

The Company reserve the right to substitute one Tug for another and to supply a Tug or Tugs not belonging to the Company and the terms hereof shall apply to such substituted or other Tug or Tugs.

Signature,

Master.

The Company's form of printed Towage Requisition must be signed by the Master of the vessel and deposited at any of the following Offices of the Company:—

Dock Office, Manchester 17; Eastham Locks;
319 India Buildings, Water Street, Liverpool 2; Stanlow Oil Docks;

at least 12 hours before the service is required, and not later than 4 p.m.

Upon receipt of a signed Towage Requisition the Company will endeavour to supply Towage Power at the time required, **but cannot guarantee to have Tugs always at liberty** and will not be responsible for delay that may arise from any cause.

When Tugs are in attendance at the time ordered and the ship is not ready to proceed, or Tugs are ordered and not required, a charge will be made at scheduled rates.

Dock Office, Manchester, February 1955.

The tugs' home base at Runcorn. Quays and workshops can be seen left of the bridges, near the top of the picture

16
THE PILOT SERVICE AT WAR 1939-1945

On 3 September 1939 Europe was again plunged into war and the Manchester Pilot Service prepared themselves for whatever eventualities they would have to contend with. On 15 September the Secretary of the Pilots Association, Mr Evans, placed before the Pilotage Committee a six point charter to meet the demands of wartime conditions.

1 The supplying of service respirators and steel helmets to all Pilots by the Port Authority.
2 The supplying of priority passes to enable the Pilots to travel in conjunction with their work, without avoidable delay, to be obtained by the Manchester Port Authority and issued to all Pilots.
3 The Chief Pilotage Clerk be stationed at Eastham forthwith.
4 A special telephone line devoted entirely to Pilotage enquiries to enable Pilots to obtain direct and immediate information.
5 Co-ordination with the Authorities at Liverpool to enable information to be made available to the Manchester Authorities regarding vessels bound for the Ship Canal, passing through the Port of Liverpool.
6 If sufficient increases in traffic due to the war occurred, further Pilots would be appointed at once.

The Chairman of the Pilotage Committee replied to these six points by saying he was not aware of the existence of any form of priority pass either for rail or bus travels and that it was not possible, at the present time, to obtain information in regard to vessels passing through Liverpool bound for the Canal due to security reasons. All the other points would be fully investigated and he assured the Pilots' representatives that if such a position arose as mentioned in point 6 it would receive immediate attention.

At the October Pilotage Committee meeting the Pilots' representatives stated that the provision of an additional telephone at Eastham did not cover the desire of the Pilots that there should be some person at Eastham who had authority and whose duty it would be to issue orders to Pilots and to furnish them with authentic information as to their duties. It does not sound unlike a situation from the TV series *"Dads Army"* with the blustering Captain Mainwaring. Nevertheless the Chairman of Pilotage Committee replied that the question of establishing a person at Eastham to perform the duties referred to had been previously raised, but was being held in abeyance pending the retirement of the present Pilotage Clerk. The committee agreed that if the Pilots considered there were new conditions necessitating the matter receiving immediate attention, they should submit their suggestions for consideration. With regard to the question of supplying the Pilots with Service Duty Respirators it appeared from the advice received that the ordinary civilian respirator was just as effective as the Service Duty Respirator, the latter being intended for persons engaged in connection with ARP (Air Raid Precaution) duties, necessitating their being actively engaged during or immediately after an Air raid. It did not appear to the committee that a Pilot would be "actively" engaged and further as the Pilots were not connected with the ARP there would be considerable difficulty in obtaining the duty masks free of charge. If the Pilots, however, were prepared to pay the cost themselves or purchase through the Pilot Fund Account, the matter would be followed up. Steel helmets could also be supplied on similar conditions at a charge of 8s. 6d (42½p) each. Not one Pilot applied for either item.

In June 1940 the Port Authority announced that they were now prepared to provide each Pilot and Helmsman with a steel helmet and civilian duty gas mask free of any charge. By this time the Ministry of Shipping issued Merchant Navy Badges to officers and men in the Merchant Service and all sea-going Pilots, who were not in uniform - no crews and precious few officers of coastal shipping had uniforms in those days - from being classed as armed civilians. If they were captured by the Nazi regime after their vessel had been sunk and were out of uniform or not bearing any insignia of their profession, they were not protected by the rules and regulations of war under the Geneva Convention and were liable to be summarily shot by their captors.

The Manchester Pilot Service could not in any way be described as sea-going and were not included in this scheme. A number of the Pilots took this as a personal slight against their war effort and felt they were entitled to wear such a badge. Those Pilots who thought they should be entitled to all the war-time paraphernalia only wished to wear them - service mask, steel helmet, badges et al - to promote the sense of their own importance, no other reason than that. A circular letter was sent to all Pilots and Helmsmen from the Chairman of the Pilotage Committee. It read as follows:

Courtesy of the MSC Company
1943
"Give us the tools and we will finish the job" Winston Churchill
American Liberty Ship (Sam Boats) entering No 9 Dock May 1943

"I am directed by the Board of Trade to inform you that it has been brought to their notice that foreign seamen calling at British Ports who are not allowed ashore frequently hand letters to Pilots with a request that the letters may be posted. It is undesirable that such letters should be sent without being first censored and I am accordingly to request that you will be good enough to deliver any such letters to the Customs and Excise Authorities who have been requested to forward them to the Chief Postal Censor." The Fifth Column movement was taken very seriously in those early days of the war.

Despite the country being at war and everyone in every walk of life pooling their resources and skills, united together for the good of the war effort, the Manchester Pilot Service was out of step with the rest of the nation. They must have been the only professional body to be at loggerheads with themselves. Certain Senior First Class Pilots were disgruntled with the manner in which the Pilots Association were running the affairs of the Pilot Service. Since 1936 the unity of the Pilots Association had always been a most fragile and volatile liaison and in February 1940 that uneasy union collapsed when eight Pilots were signatories to the following letter.

"The undersigned wish to bring before the notice of the Pilotage Authority, that they are no longer members of the Manchester Ship Canal Pilots Association. We wish it to be understood that our resignation or what would be more appropriate, our expulsion from that Association, does not imply that the deliberations of the Pilotage Authority have ceased to be our interest. On the contrary, we are whole-heartedly interested in all matters concerning the mutual welfare of the Authority and the Pilotage service, but feel that to remain members of the Pilots Association is tantamount to conveying to the Authority an existent spirit of agreement, sanction and co-operation between all Associates, which we are not.

You will note that our members consist chiefly of the Senior members of the service, to whom Piloting on the Ship Canal is somewhat a heritage, whose opinions concerning Pilotage on the Canal because of long service, experience, and inborn enthusiasm, should be permited to be on record,but who are allowed no voice or place in the government of our affairs, being out-voted at all Association meetings and ostracised on all occasions. We respectfully ask that the Authority, when conferring with the remaining members through their representatives have a mind for we Pilots who are not represented.
We are Sir,
Yours respectfully

Matthew Green	*C G Killender*
William Lamey	*G V Davidson*
William H Langley	*R Green*
A P Bennet	*J E Lamey"*

In the discussion which took place on this letter it was pointed out that apart from the obvious administrative difficulties which would be occasioned by the secession of these Pilots from the Association the influence of the Pilots in the governing of the Pilotage service could not fail to be weakened by the existence of what would be in effect two Associations instead of one and the hope was expressed that a way would be found to remove the causes of dissension and restore that united spirit which had been so beneficial to the Pilot service, especially now, having regard to the existing wartime conditions.

No such *esprit de corps* was forthcoming from these eight dissidents. On the contrary, they completely ignored all pleas and negotiations from different sources for a reunification of the Pilot Association. Strange though it might seem their request to have a representative on the Pilotage Committee was sympathetically received and Mr W Langley was appointed as representative, thus reducing the Association's representation to one, Mr J H Warren. Their influence on other Pilots, especially junior First Class Pilots and most certainy

1936-1980
Mr H H Harrington, Pilot
One of only two Helmsmen called up for active service in the 1939-1945 War.

1966-1987
Mr G Harrington, Helmsman
A Pilot on the River Dee. The last person to pass a Trinity House Pilots Licence Examination. Returned to the Manchester Pilot Service in 1994

all the Second Class Pilots was shown in December 1940 when five more Pilots resigned from the Association and again in June 1941 twelve more resigned making a total of twenty-five Pilots non-members of the Pilots Association, well over half the Pilot Service. This very unsatisfactory state of affairs lasted for six years and caused on more than one occasion lengthy delays in the Pilots Association's negotiations with the Pilotage Committee, for this division in the Association was exploited at every possible opportunity and from every possible source.

The Pilotage Committee soon realized the ludicrousness of a divided Pilots Association and the considerable waste of vital time when conferring with both sets of Pilots to reach any agreement. They could also see that the breakaway Pilots were deeply entrenched in their beliefs and nothing, in the near future, would make them see otherwise. The Secretary of the Pilotage Committee (Mr Eyre) suggested in regard to membership of the Pilots Association, the Association should frame its constitution and rules for the approval of the Pilotage Committee and such approval having been given the Committee would thereafter be in order in submitting any matter direct to the Association for its opinion, thus bypassing the non-members of the Association. The Pilotage Committee agreed unanimously that a properly constituted Association would be the appropriate channel of communication with the pilots on questions affecting the efficiency of the service and the welfare of the Pilots.

In October 1940 the Pilots Association duly presented its new constitution and rules to the Pilotage Committee who tabled certain amendments that were not acceptable to the Pilots Association. The Pilotage Committee prompt rejoinder was that the Committee could not recognise the Pilots Association as the proper channel of communication with the Pilots on all matters affecting the general interests of Pilots and the efficiency of the Pilots service, but would have to revert to taking such steps as they considered proper in each case. What caused this sudden and complete U-turn is not recorded but the situation remained unchanged until 1946.

For some time the Pilots had been complaining that the service was undermanned and with the increase of shipping movements since the commencement of the war, there appeared to be justification for the appointment of additional Pilots as promised by the Pilotage Committee in September 1939. The Pilotage Committee had gone some way, in March 1940, to relieve the pressure of work on the rota, by increasing the Second Class licence tonnage restriction from 1,000 tons net reg to 1,200 and promoting two Second Class Pilots to First Class. It was pointed out by the Pilotage

Committee that there was great uncertainty as to the course of the trade in the near future. While European trade had practically been cut off, a good deal of overseas shipping had been diverted to Manchester and further diversions might be expected. It was agreed that steps should be taken to enable additional Pilots to be provided on a temporary footing, and that this should be done by granting temporary First Class Licences to a number of the Second Class Pilots and temporary Second Class licences to a similar number of Helmsmen. Captain Richardson (Harbour Master) was requested to proceed with the engagement of six helmsmen on probation, subject to termination at short notice and to discuss the details of their training and employment with representatives of the Pilots and Helmsmen.

The restricted tonnage for second class Pilots was reverted to 1,000 net reg tons in october 1942 on the grounds that the present Second Class Pilots and the temporary Second Class Pilots had insufficient experience, two years and one year respectively. The previous seven Second Class Pilots had upwards of five years experience and since then had become First Class Pilots or temporary First Class Pilots thus reducing the strain on the rota.

In June 1940 draft byelaws were drawn up somewhat similar to the provisions that had been made at Liverpool and on the Clyde and modelled on a code received from the Ministry of Shipping on the appointment of additional Pilots. The only persons who would be brought in on a temporary footing from outside the service would be Helmsmen. Such Helmsmen would not participate in the pooling system but would retain all their individual earnings. It was questioned why powers were being sought by byelaws under the Pilotage Act instead of a navigation order under the Defence Regulations. It was explained that Liverpool and the Clyde had obtained powers under the Pilotage Act and that was considered to be the proper procedure as far as the Authority was concerned. Even after all these years as a Pilot Service, Manchester still looked for guidance on pilotage matters from the Liverpool Service. The byelaws were approved on 5 August 1940 (see Appendix No I).

By August the number of "Turns" per Pilot had risen to 144 per annum, whereas 120 "Turns" had been regarded as a normal average. However the earnings of the Pilots had shown a proportional increase. Nevertheless the Pilots Association pressed for an increase in the number of Pilots and that the increase should not be less than four. It was suggested by the Pilotage Committee that it would be prudent to appoint the additional Pilots on a temporary basis but the Pilots' representatives were opposed to this. A compromise suggestion, again from the Pilotage Committee, that two of the additional appointments should be temporary was similarly resisted. The Pilots were really digging

NOVEMBER 1943
Courtesy MSC Company
The Docks at War

their heels in on this matter and would not be fobbed off with any watered down compromise. The Pilots had felt for a long time that an increase in their number was necessary and they thought four permanent appointments should be made immediately. The Pilots' representatives also stated if it was later found that four were not sufficient, then more could be appointed on a temporary basis.

From the Shipowners point of view, forever cost conscious, they replied the more men there were the lower the Pilots' earnings would be and they wished it to be put on record that in any future negotiations respecting pilotage rates the Shipowners would not be prejudiced by the present increase in personnel. It was then unanimously agreed that four additional Pilots be appointed on a permanent basis as from the 1 September 1940. Four of the temporary Helmsmen at present on probation to be absorbed into the Helmsmens Service on a termporary basis and participate in their pooled earnings, subject to the usual conditions as to probation.

The year 1940 was to prove a particularly busy one for the Pilots' representatives, already overworked as a Pilot on the rota and assailed on all sides by all manner of divers problems and schemes dealing with pilotage. In May a subject dear to the heart of all Ship Canal Pilots, **compulsory pilotage**, was raised at the Pilotage Committee Meeting. The Chairman said that the question of the desirability of instituting compulsory pilotage for all foreign and Irish vessels had been considered by the Board of the Ship Canal Company and remitted to the Committee for such action as it would deem necessary. It was agreed that as a first step the Flag Officer at Liverpool should be consulted. The Naval Authorities consulted in Liverpool stated that the institution of compulsory pilotage for all ships not British owned would be very desirable but, however desirable compulsory pilotage was, it would seem there were no sufficient Pilots available to cope with the increased demands which this would impose on the service. Captain Richardson (Harbour Master) was asked to enquire as to the number of vessels of foreign ownership using the Canal, in order to get an approximate idea of the number of Pilots required.

[AUTHOR'S NOTE: The reason the Ship Canal Company could not institute compulsory pilotage when the Canal was opened in 1894 was that a Parliamentary Law made in the 1700s stated "No Pilotage within the confines of Lock Gates can be made compulsory." This applies worldwide with the exception of the Panama Canal and the Welland Canal in Ontario, Eastern Canada].

In July the total number of British, foreign and Irish vessels entering the Canal, in the first six months of 1940, was submitted to the Pilotage Committee Meeting. It appeared from these figures that if compulsory pilotage was introduced an increase of 50% would be required in the service, which was not considered practicable. Moreover, it was doubtful whether compulsory pilotage would be effective for the purpose in view. Having regard to all the circumstances it was agreed that no further action need be taken and the once in a lifetime opportunity to establish compulsory pilotage in the Ship Canal, thereby consolidating the security of the Pilot Service livelihood, was allowed to quietly slip away to be lost for ever. It was the greatest single mistake ever to be made in the history of the Manchester Ship Canal Pilots Service. The subject of compulsory pilotage was never seriously debated again at Committee level.

Amongst all these negotiations in mid-1940 a proposal for a better regulation of the Pilot service by a revision of the Pilotage Rota System was submitted to the Pilotage Committee by Mr C S Rhodes (First Class Pilot). The Chairman mentioned that the Pilotage Clerk was at the moment completing a trial scheme on paper. The basis of the scheme was that the first pilot off duty became the first pilot on turn for duty again and it was hoped that it would be possible to incorporate some week-end leave. Mr Rhodes' scheme was adopted in May on the basis that it would provide a more equitable distribution of the work as opposed to the two watch system then in operation. Rules were drafted by Mr Rhodes, whose scheme it was, ably assisted by Mr J H Warren (Pilots' representative) and considered by Captain Richardson and Mr R Bennion (Chief Pilot Clerk).

At the June Pilotage Committee the new scheme was submitted. It was pointed out that the proposed working rules would be incompatible with the 'choice' Pilots - forever and a day a constant thorn in the side of the Manchester Pilot Service as a stumbling block to all negotiations and progress - and if the proposals were acceptable to the Pilots generally it was the intention to abolish the appropriation of Pilots, at any rate for the duration of the war. What a bombshell that was to the posturing choice Pilots. It would also follow that a Pilot absent from duty on account of accident or illness or for any other reason would not be allowed to make up his turn and byelaw 33 would apply which provides that a Pilot shall not be entitled to any share of the Pilotage earnings in respect of any day upon which he shall be absent from duty or in order to give evidence as a witness. It was agreed that the proposed scheme should be submitted to all Pilots with a letter informing them that the Pilotage Committee proposed to adopt it unless the Pilots generally were opposed to it.

In the course of the discussion it was stated that the abolition of 'choice' pilotage would mean a saving of £100 a year to ten shipowners, or an aggregate of £1,000, which was equivalent of approximately 5% of the total earnings of the Pilots and the view was expressed that there should be in equity a corresponding increase in the pilotage rates. What a shock these proposals must have been to the Pilotage Committee, their beloved **"choice"** Pilots who they could manipulate so easily for their own ends would no longer be at their beck and call. The *"Sacred Cows"* were about to be put out to grass and some Pilots with their three day sickess bouts - so conveniently occurring between Friday and Monday - and known as the *"Weekend Welchers"* - cancelled out.

In July it was reported to the Pilotage Committee that twenty-six of the Pilots had intimated that they were in favour of the adoption of the proposed alteration of the Rota System. Four Pilots were not in favour of the proposed scheme; one objected, because as a Choice Pilot it would deprive him of his appropriation fee; another suggested that instead of Pilots trying to proceed first after having been tied up for the night or any other reason would now endeavour to be last underway, thus vessels would be delayed unnecessarily; the other two objectors did not consider any drastic change from the present system necessary and expressed the opinion that certain Pilots who did not live in the vicinity of Eastham would be involved in heavier travelling expenses. Mr Hughes (Shipowners' representative) said that he had mentioned the possibility of an increase in rates to compensate choice Pilots for the loss of fees but no comment had been made by any members of that Association. His own opinion was that such an increase was not feasible. The Pilots' representatives - both Choice Pilots - thought it might be possible to work the new scheme or a modification of it without abolishing choice pilotage. After further lengthy discussion it was agreed that the matter be investigated further by Captain Richardson, Mr Bennion and the Pilots' representatives.

In their deliberations it was agreed to abolish "Choice" pilotage and the requisite three months notice be given to the Shipowners concerned. They also agreed to pursue a 5% increase in Pilotage rates to compensate for the abolition of the appropriation fees. The new Rota system of first to finish, first on duty again was introduced on 1 September and the two watch system phased out. Mr Bennion gave his first report on the new system at the October Pilotage Committee Meeting stating that the new system was apparently working satisfactorily and seemed well suited to the abnormal conditions brought about by the war. After the experience gained during the first month it had become apparent that certain clauses in the Pilotage Working Rules would have to be changed, the main alteration being Pilots on Eastham Station Duty remaining on duty for four tides instead of two.

1943

Courtesy of Mr H Clugston

Pilot, Mr W Milsom. Helmsman Mr H Clugston. The vessel was the American Liberty (Sam Boat) *"Helen Hunt Jackson"*. Passage time from Eastham to Manchester four days, due to air raids and no night navigation. Both Pilot and Helmsman received a gift of a food hamper from the Master, Captian R J Bronswki III on the completion of the passage.

At the October Pilotage Committee, in order to meet the objections of the Shipowners' representatives to the abolition of "Choice Pilotage" the Committee agreed for an experimental period, to the adoption of the new rules with modifications permitting the continuance of "Choice Pilotage". It was decided that although choice pilots might continue to be appropriated where desired by the shipowners, such appropriation would have to be subject to the general condition that it must not interfere with the smooth working of the pilotage service. Accordingly the provisions in Rule 13 of the working rules whereby choice pilots vacate the list for 24 hours (or in some cases 12 hours) ahead of the known time of his vessel moving should be rescinded.

The war was not without its compensations to the Pilots, at least they were made exempt under "Certificate D" from fire watching duties! The control of traffic navigating the Canal was greatly improved in 1941 when a semaphore signal on the north bank of the Canal opposite the upstream end of Ince Oil Berth, to indicate to outward bound vessels whether or not they may pass Stanlow Oil Docks was installed, also the provision of mooring bollards in Ince High Cutting in order that vessels stopped by the signal could make fast if necessary. It was also considered necessary to provide a voice amplifier at Eastham to facilitate the passing of orders to vessels approaching the locks outward bound. Steps were also taken to secure the passing of messages to vessels passing the Weaver Sluices. All shipping movements between Eastham and Runcorn would in future be controlled by the Lockmaster at Eastham under the supervision of the Assistant Harbour Master.

An amusing sequel to these innovations was that the messages relayed to vessels regarding shipping movements when passing the Weaver Sluices, Weston Point Locks etc were all given by a hand-held megaphone not unlike the ones used by a coxswain of a rowing eight in size and range. Any wind above Force 2 complemented by a rich Runcorn/Cheshire accent made such vital information unintelligible to the Pilots or Masters.

At the December 1941 Pilotage Committee, Mr F Davenport (Pilots' representative) assured the Chairman all the Pilots were concerned that the appropriate action to take, to alleviate the under-manning, was to make the temporary Pilots permanent. He said that the three vacancies which had been filled by the appointment of temporary Pilots were caused by the retirement of three permanent Pilots and the Pilots considered they should be filled by permanent men. The Chairman said that in his opinion the Pilots were aggrieved because their application for an increase in rates had been unsuccessful and he thought the effect upon their work and their relations with the Canal Company and the Shipowners was most apparent. If their application for an increase was still refused and later they were committed to additional permanent Pilots during a period of declining trade their grievance would be aggravated. He thought the Authority, acting as guardian, should not allow the Pilots to mortgage their future.

The Pilots' representatives stated they fully realised what they were asking and still insisted that the positions be made permanent.

The Chairman continued and said that despite his note of caution, he wondered if the Pilots had considered these two points:

a) That as far as the Authority knew the traffic now carried on by the petrol barges was an emergency traffic and would probably cease immediately after the war.
b) The large volume of coal traffic appeared to be purely wartime traffic, and as soon as the railways were free, would cease to come up the Canal.

With these features before them the Pilots' representatives might wish to have further consultations with their colleagues. Mr Davenport stuck to his guns, reiterating that the Pilots were most definite in their views and according to his calculations the appointment of the additional pilots would at worst involve a diminution of only 6 ½% in the average earnings. Mr Roberts, just as insistent, stated that while this might not appear serious on their present earnings it might be very much more so in a period of stringency. He was not anxious to delay this matter unnecessarily but he thought the Pilots should take away the aspects he had now mentioned and place them before their Association. The Pilots' representatives reluctantly agreed, but they would raise the matter again at the January meeting.

It was a masterly piece of oration by Mr Roberts. He had studied his subject well, touching on all the fears he knew - loss of trade in the future, less earnings, etc - deterring the Pilots from pressing home their demands for additional Pilots. It was possibly one of the finest deterring arguments ever put forward by a Pilotage Committee member and it won the day. At the next meeting of Pilotage Committee it was unanimously agreed that this matter should rest until the cessation of hostilities. What a debt the Manchester Ship Canal Company owed to Mr Roberts.

In a minute recorded on 20 December 1943 it was agreed by all parties that upon completion of four years' service as a Second Class Pilot he should be automatically called for examination and if found to possess the necessary qualifications he should be granted a First Class Licence. It was also decided that in future in order to enable the Committee to consider the qualifications of Second Class Pilots for promotion under the four year service rule, the records of the Pilot concerned together with the result of the examination should be submitted at every August meeting. On 4 September 1944 the four temporary licences made in 1940 - Messrs C M Oliver, N R Colvin, H Stott and W Sharp - were successfully examined,and under the new four year ruling were made permanent First Class Pilots.

In June 1944, when the war was seen to be drawing to a victorious conclusion, the secretary of the Pilotage Committee mentioned that the Committee might at some future date have to consider breaking up the present pooling system and reverting to the system of each pilot working for himself. In his opinion it was possible to work on a rota without pooling earnings. What possessed him to suggest such a retrograde step is not recorded. It can only be assumed that the Canal Company, thinking ahead to peace time conditions, decided this type of system would break any new found unity that may have developed during the war. The Pilots' representatives replied that they presumed powers would have to be sought under the Pilotage Act and a majority of Pilots would have to reach agreement on the subject before any change could take place and finally, that if such a change were made, Choice Pilotage would most certainly have to be abolished. That last sentence killed off any more suggestions of non-pooling piloting. It was never mentioned at the Pilotage Committee again.

At that same meeting the Committee decided to restore the leading and guiding lights - as far as they were permitted under war time restrictions - for the purpose of aiding night navigation. Mr Davenport expressed the opinion that no useful purpose would be served in doing this considering the size of vessels now navigating the Canal, their deep draught, boxed in bridges and views restricted by gun platforms and life-rafts. The Chairman said it should be borne in mind by all Pilots that the question of night passages on the Ship Canal, by large vessels, after the war would most certainly have to be considered. He went on to say that the Pilots must not overlook the fact of the desirability of bringing the Port of Manchester as near as possible to the sea by minimising delays to shipping during their Ship Canal transit. The Pilots did adopt a particular ostrich-like attitude towards night navigation, reasoning that if the Port of Manchester had survived the depression years and had continually grown for 50 years without night navigation, why should it be introduced now. This sort of attitutde was taken by many of their generation who were unable to cope or appreciate a fast changing world. To be fair it must be recorded that at this particular time the Pilots were performing twenty services a month with little or no rest between each service. Night work was not a priority to them.

On a lighter note in May 1944 the wily ways of a Manchester Pilot was exposed again, when it was reported that on the 12th May First Class Pilot Mr G V Davidson had piloted a US Coastguard vessel from Manchester to Eastham with three other US Coastguard vessels in line astern and had claimed that he was entitled to the appropriate pilotage rates in respect of all vessels. Mr Davidson also claimed four late booking fees and four detention fees. Section

51 of the Pilotage Act 1913 states that a Pilot is entitled to charge for the four vessels but was only entitled to one Late Booking Fee and one Detention Fee. Mr Davidson was claiming £24 in Pilotage Fees, his revised fee was £19. 7s 0d (£19.35).

On 12 July 1945 a historic event occurred that had never happened before or would ever be repeated again. A German Submarine U-1023 sailed from Eastham to Manchester, the Pilot being Mr C Callister and the Helmsman Mr W Yates. The end of the war saw the return of Mr H H Harrington to the service and Mr R C Cheshire, but the latter stayed briefly as a Helmsman, before departing to South Africa to train air-crew in the South African Air Force.

One of the many frustrations of the war to a Pilot was the restricted travel facilities. Few if any Pilots had private cars and if they had would never have thought to use them in the pursuit of their Pilotage duties. Taxis were either prohibitive through cost or non-existent due to lack of petrol. The possibility of providing a motor car or cars or a motor launch to convey Pilots to and

Courtesy Mrs W Yates Collection

12 July 1945. The only German submarine U1023 to transit the Manchester Ship Canal. Pilot Mr C Callister, Helmsman Mr W Yates.

from vessels was suggested by the Pilots, but when it was pointed out that the cost of any such facility would have to be borne by the Pilot Service, the suggestion was quickly withdrawn. There was also a suggestion that Mr Stoker (Shipowners' representative) as the Ministry of War Transport representative might notify the Police of the necessity of Pilots being provided with travelling facilities especially at weekends and national holidays. Nothing more was heard of that suggestion either.

The Regional Transport Commissioner was brought into the negotiations and he wrote to the main public transport companies used by the Pilots, ie Crosville Motor Company and the Salford Corporation and Warrington Service. Their reply to the Commissioner was to the effect that if a Pilot would make himself known to the bus inspectors, they would do their best for the Pilot according to the circumstances prevailing at that time. The Commissioner was not clear whether the Pilots had been refused transport because the vehicles were already fully loaded or because priority had been given to other important passengers. In the latter event he would ask the operators to give the Pilots similar treatment as to other essential passengers, on production of a means of identification. It was agreed that as a means of identification and establishing his identity to the conductors of the buses a Pilot should produce his wartime Canal Pass and the secretary of the Pilotage Committee would furnish specimens of the pass to the bus companies. This system was also arranged for travelling by the railways.

In September 1943 the Steamship Owners Association agreed that in cases of emergency only, intimation would be given, when the Pilot was being ordered to a vessel that the owner or agent was prepared to pay for the hire of a taxi to enable the Pilot to reach the vessel for an urgent sailing. The Chairman of the Pilotage Committee said in regard to expenses incurred by a ship which worked overtime in order to finish and which might be delayed because the Pilot was unable to get to her in time, due to travel difficulties, the Pilot, having taken reasonable steps to get to his ship by bus or train, and through no fault of his own might be unable to reach the ship by any other means than a taxi, then he thought the Pilot should have the authority to take a taxi, when absolutely necessary. If the Shipowners did not wish to take the responsibility upon themselves then the Port Emergency Committee would have to give instructions to the Pilots to do this. All that was necessary was that when on occasion a Pilot might be delayed and in consequence the sailing of the ship might also be delayed and the tide lost, then the Pilot should have the authority to take a taxi to a point which would enable him to get there in sufficient time. Mr Stoker said the Ministry of War transport agreed a Pilot should make use of a taxi when the need arose and the owner or agent should pay the fare. The Pilots' representative pointed out that the Pilots were primarily concerned with the Stanlow, Ellesmere Port and Ince sections.

The following month it was proposed and accepted at Pilotage Committee that:

"When a Pilot was unable to reach his vessel he would be empowered to make use of a taxi, after first receiving authority from Captain Bennet or the Pilotage Clerk who would be in the best position to judge the urgency of the case and the genuineness of the Pilot's requirements. This arrangement should apply only to Pilots who are joining ships at Ellesmere Port, Stanlow or Ince Oil Berth and should only be picked up at agreed points."

Two taxi proprietors had been contacted, Leedhams of Ellesmere Port and Station Taxis at Hooton and they were willing to provide the necessary conveyance. The scheme was given a trial for a period of three months. The scheme was never withdrawn.

There was one small question posed by the Shipowners. It appeared they were a little concerned in regard to the possibility of accidents in which Pilots travelling by taxi might be involved. Their fears were unfounded, as no liability could accrue to them by common law and as regards Workmen's compensation Act liability it was pointed out to them that all Pilots were at present earning considerably more than £420 per annum, under which amount they must earn to be able to claim under the Workmen's Compensation Act.

This was the first time in the history of the Pilot Service that official sanction had been given for the use of taxis during normal public transport times, albeit very stringently and in a very limited way. What the Pilots did not realise at the time was that this was the beginning of an era when taxis to and from vessels at all times of the day and night would become more the rule than the exception. With changing times and changing aspects of Pilotage on the Canal, eventually no public transport was used at all and in 1990, Pilots were conveyed to and from their vessels anywhere on the 36 miles of the Canal by car, 24 hours a day.

Pilots and Helmsmens Travel Arrangements 1958

The arrangements for the use of Taxis by Pilots and Helmsmen have been extended to include Old Quay, Runcorn Docks and Weston Mersey Docks under the following conditions:

1. If a Pilot or Helmsman are unable to reach a vessel owing to lack of normal travelling facilities.
2. If a Pilot or Helmsman is unable to return to the Eastham Pilot Station owing to lack of normal travelling facilities.
3. Sections 1 and 2 only apply when there is no suitable sleeping accommodation on board.

Under section 3, the two taxi accounts were returned to be paid by the respective Pilots, as shown overleaf.

THE MANCHESTER SHIP CANAL COMPANY

PILOTAGE DEPARTMENT, QUEEN ELIZABETH II DOCK,
EASTHAM, WIRRAL, CHESHIRE

Telephone: "EAStham 1242"

JNG/T.

9th March, 1963.

Leedham's Taxis,
4a, Meadow Lane,
Ellesmere Port,
Wirral.

Dear Sirs,

I enclose copies of letters addressed to the following Pilots:-

Mr. Clulow : Engaged taxi between Runcorn Docks & Rock Ferry at 0130, 25th February - Fare £2.12. 6d.

Mr.L.Davies : Engaged taxi between Old Quay and Rock Ferry at 0145, 26th February - Fare £2.12.6d.

In each case the Pilot should arrange payment direct with you. Your invoice therefore, dated 2nd March, 1963, has had to be amended accordingly.

Yours faithfully,

(John N.Gibson)
Pilot Manager.

THE MANCHESTER SHIP CANAL COMPANY
Harbour Master's Office,
Dock Office, MANCHESTER, 17.

Ref: H.M./H. 24th August, 1953.

Dear Sir,

PILOT AND HELMSMEN'S TRAVEL FACILITIES.

The arrangements for the use of taxis by PILOTS AND helmsmen when they are unable to reach vessels at Ellesmere Port, Stanlow or Ince Oil Berth owing to lack of normal travelling facilities are as follows:-

A PILOT OR helmsman who is under the necessity of making use of a taxi because of the lack of normal facilities must ring either Captain Colebrook, or the Pilotage Clerk, at Eastham Locks to obtain authority, and upon receiving this, he should then ~~'phone~~ CONTACT either:

Leedham's Taxis, 4a, Meadow Lane

Messrs Gregory's, Taxi Proprietors
47, Station Road

Eastham Taxi Service,
60, Crosthwaite Avenue

W. McNally, 111a, Princes Road

Lester's Taxi Service,
Railway Station Yard

S. Crump (Station Road Garage)

and after identifying himself, specify his requirements, and intimate at which of the following points he has to be picked up:-

Bedford Road, Rock Ferry;
New Ferry Toll Bar;
Allport Road, Bromborough;
Stanley Lane, Eastham;
Ellesmere Port;
Stanlow Lay-Bye;
Ince Oil Berth.

The service will extend from Bedford Road, Rock Ferry, to Ince only, and PILOTS AND helmsmen must not ask to be picked up at any other than the points indicated above.

It is also permitted to use a taxi between Ellesmere Port and Bowaters' Wharf, and vice versa, when the necessity arises.

On arrival at his destination, the PILOT OR helmsman will be required to sign a chit which will be presented by the driver. The account for the service will be forwarded by the Taxi people to the Dock Office for verification, and will subsequently be forwarded to the Owner or Agent responsible for payment.

PILOTS AND Helmsmen are expected to make every endeavour to reach their ships by normal means, and the arrangement outlined above is only to apply in case of extreme urgency. If at all possible PILOTS AND helmsmen are expected to co-operate in the economical use of taxis.

Yours faithfully,

F. HOWARD.

1953
Courtesy of the MSC Co
The opening of the Queen Elizabeth Oil Dock, the largest oil dock in Europe at that time.

1955
Courtesy of the MSC Co
The Queen Elizabeth Oil Dock fully operational

17

THE ALLAN GREEN AND PETER ONION AFFAIR 1941-1943

The history of this affair goes back as far as the inception of the Manchester Pilot Service in 1895 when families such as the Greens, Onions, Lameys, Youngs and Cartwrights dominated the Pilot Service in the Ship Canal. These very close knit families piloted only for their own avarice, often to the detriment of other families and over the years, it naturally followed, considerable animosity was engendered between these warring families. Bitter controversy between pilots lasted long after an incident had occurred and any injustice, real or imagined, suffered by a Pilot's family, was never ever left to be forgotten. The Helmsmens Service was still suffering from the contemptuous treatment of certain pilots who resented any new helmsmen entering the service who were remotely related to any of the Pilot families in any way.

Into this crucible of malcontentment stepped Allan Green and Peter Onion. Both these men were sons of serving Pilots, both had grandfathers who had been original pilots in 1895 and both had fathers who were the original instigators of refusing helmsmen's services. To them it must have been akin to Daniel stepping into the lion's den but with no help from Him above.

It all started in August 1941 when they applied to become probation helmsmen. The Helmsmens Service was considered by the Government as a reserved occupation and their fathers had obviously recruited them to be Helmsmen to avoid them being recruited for active War Service. The fact that neither of these applicants had ever been sea-going was conveniently overlooked. Considerable lobbying by their fathers had been carried out at various levels and at various times, to accept them into the Helmsmens Service. Certain

Pilots made certain promises to the Helmsmen that if these two men were accepted into their service, their attitude towards the Helmsmens Service would considerably change. True to form those promises were never kept.

From the commencement of their probationary service they never were really given a chance to prove their ability as helmsmen, family differences are hard to reconcile, after all blood is thicker than (canal) water. They went through a particular torrid time during the first twelve months of their probationary service, resented by pilots and helmsmen alike. They never knew from one vessel to another if their services would be accepted. It was not an unknown occurrence for a Pilot knowing either Green or Onion was the helmsman for his vessel, to allow him to travel from Eastham to Manchester Docks, in wartime conditions - black out, air raids, uncertainty of public transport etc etc - then refuse his services when that helmsman came on board his vessel. This would have incurred seven hours of travel and possibly a night away from home plus the expenses which were not allowable for helmsmen in those days.

The Helmsmens Service came under unjustifiable accusations. A letter dated 14th July 1942 addressed to the Pilotage Committee from Mr W Roberts complained that when he went aboard the MV *"Drupa"* to steer her from Eastham to Stanlow the Pilot, Mr F Onion, accused him in a most vehement manner of unfavourable actions towards his son, who was a probationary helmsman. He also intimated that if he (Mr Roberts) did not change his attitude he would in future refuse his service on all types of vessels. Mr Roberts was a Senior Helmsman.

At the Pilotage Committee Meeting held on 26th August 1942 the secretary reported that owing to the reluctance of certain pilots to accept the services of temporary helmsmen Green and Onion, who were at present serving a period of probation, they had been given notice that their services would be terminated on 31st August. A letter had been received subsequently, however, signed by nine of the Pilots intimating they were prepared to utilise the services of these two men: three other pilots had also intimated that they were prepared to accept the services of Mr A Green only (the family feud syndrome). It was agreed on this information the notice should be withdrawn.

Mr Hughes (Pilots' Representative) suggested that the two men should be allowed to continue to steer vessels on the Canal, but until such time as their earnings reached the average of the Helmsmen's pooled earnings they should retain their earnings and not participate in the pooling system. The committee agreed on this motion. It was also suggested that if a pilot of a vessel under 1,000 tons net reg refused to accept the services of either helmsmen Green or

Onion, he should not be allowed to engage the services of another for that particular vessel. This suggestion, that might have ended the "Turning Down" practice, was not agreed upon but the shipowners would consider it and report back at a later meeting. The Committee decided that two further temporary helmsmen be appointed and the Harbour Master was requested to make the necessary arrangements.

1950
Courtesy of the MSC Co.
Barton Locks
"Pacific Reliance" (Grt 9942 L482' B63'4") outward bound.
Pilot Mr W Langley
"Senator" inward bound. Pilot Mr W Sharp.

The suggestion by the Pilots' representatives, and its acceptance by the Pilotage Committee that Messrs Green and Onion should not participate in the helmsmen's pooling system is indeed puzzling. Surely this was a decision purely under the jurisdiction of the helmsmen themselves and of no concern of the Pilots. What is more puzzling no record of any objection from the helmsmen is minuted. What is not so puzzling is the real reason for preventing them from participating in the pooling system. The average earnings of a helmsman at that time was £32 gross per month. If so many pilots refused the services of them and they retained their personal earnings only, their monthly earnings would be drastically reduced, thereby placing more pressure on them to leave the service. The arrangement to appoint two further temporary helmsmen suggests that the Pilotage Committee had already concluded that this latest move against Green and Onion would precipitate their leaving the service.

The Pilots' representative's proposal that if a Pilot refused the services of Messrs Green or Onion on vessels under 1,000 tons net reg they should not be allowed the services of another helmsman for that vessel was particularly galling to the helmsmen. It had to be the most grandiosely, hypocritical proposal ever made by a pilot and they made quite a few regarding the helmsmen. This particular pilot was always recognized as the first and foremost instigator in refusing the services of helmsmen on vessels below 1,000 tons net reg. Throughout his piloting years, before and after this affair, he steadfastly refused to accept helmsmen on small vessels. He caused no end of trials and tribulations with his proposals that pilots should not be forced to take helmsmen on vessels under 1,000 tons net reg. This was beyond belief. One must raise the question "Did this Pilot make such a proposal because he was such an intimate confidant and long serving colleague of the fathers of these two men who were desperately trying to keep their sons out of the war?". The answer was **"Yes"**.

At the Pilotage Committee Meeting held on 21st December, Captian L G Richardson (Assistant Harbour Master) made the following statement:

"Helmsmen Green and Onion had been given authority on 26th August to act as temporary helmsmen under the condition that until their earnings averaged those of the other helmsmen they were not allowed to share in the pooled earnings of the helmsmen. They have not succeeded in attaining the average of the other helmsmen's earnings and a large number of the pilots still refused to accept their services."

The Committee agreed that two new helmsmen should be engaged and when this had been done suitable notice would be given to Messrs Green and Onion terminating their engagement. That Messrs Green and Onion never succeeded in earning as much as other helmsmen was not surprising. Indeed one of them earned only £44 between October and November. It hardly bears thinking about the quality of life these men endured. The hostile atmosphere surrounding them in the Pilotage Service coupled with the mental stress of knowing the Pilotage Committee was shortly to terminate their engagement and therefore they would be faced with the prospect of all the horrors of war in one of the armed services must have put them in the very depths of despair.

It was reported at the Pilotage Committee Meeting of 18th January 1943 that the services of one new temporary helmsman had been obtained and it was not anticipated that any difficulty would be experienced in engaging a second. After a short discussion it was agreed that as the services of the temporary helmsmen Green and Onion could not be fully utilised they should be given notice that their engagement would terminate on the 28th February 1943. The reaction from the Pilots' Association to this decision was to say the least truly amazing, confounding everyone and contradictory to all that had been discussed previously regarding Messrs Green and Onion.

The Pilotage Committee Meeting in February must have found it hard to believe what they were hearing when the Chairman reported the receipt of a letter dated 12th February from the secretary of the Pilots Association, forwarding a protest regarding the proposed dismissal of Helmsmen A G Green and C F Onion. The document bore the name of 37 Pilots and it was stated that in those cases where the names were not the signatures of particular pilots they had been added with the Pilots' consent. The petition in addition to protesting against the Committee's action in terminating the services of these two helmsmen referred to, stated that the signatories wished it to be known that they would not undertake to train and would not utilise the services of any helmsmen the Authority might introduce into the service other than those who were appointed before Messrs Green and Onion.
[Author's Note: *Just what amount of training a pilot gave to a helmsman is highly debateable and often ludicrous. The training consisted of constant abusive criticism of a helmsman's inability to steer a vessel.*]

The Pilotage Committee were somewhat taken aback by this letter but nevertheless were not prepared to accept the statements contained in the Pilots Association's petition neither did they believe that all the pilots concerned would be so irresponsible as to subscribe to the statement regarding the training and utilising of future helmsmen. The Chairman stated the decision to dispense with the services of the two helmsmen was forced upon the Committee because of the large number of pilots who refused to utilise their services. In fact one

1965
Courtesy of the MSC Company
An impressive view of Stanlow Oil Docks - Ellesmere Port

helmsman had already been engaged to replace one of the helmsmen in question and another would be engaged shortly.

The contents of that letter from the Pilots Association were extremely dubious. It was hardly likely that the entire complement of pilots (37) would have agreed to the statements made in it. The threat not to utilise the services of any new helmsmen was pure bluff. A report was presented from Captain Richardson analysing replies to a circular letter sent to all pilots. This questioned the pilots' willingness to utilise the services of either or both of the helmsmen in question and over half the pilots said they would not use the services of one or the other helmsman.

This statement only went to prove the duplicity of the persons who sent the letter to the Pilotage Committee. Captain Richardson further stated that though these two helmsmen had been steering vessels on the Canal for more than one and a half years, over half the Pilots did not consider them competent to steer vessels over 3,000 tons net reg, a qualification usually attained in 12 months. After some discussion it was agreed that Captain Richardson should ascertain the helmsmen's views on this contentious affair.

Captain Richardson asked the Helmsmens Association for their opinion as to whether their present strength of seventeen men was sufficient to meeting the requirements of the service and if they desired the number to be raised again to eighteen and whether they would consider either Green or Onion should be reinstated. The April Pilotage Committee meeting heard that the helmsmen had desired their numbers to be brought up to eighteen men. With regard to Messrs Green and Onion, the helmsmen considered these men had never been allowed by the Pilots to successfully contribute towards the helmsmen's work load. They also stated that the practice of engaging men with seagoing qualifications should be maintained and as neither Green or Onion possessed such qualifications they should not be considered. At that April meeting the services of Mr A G (Alan) Green and Mr C F (Peter) Onion were dispensed with.

This was the end of a very sad and tawdry affair which did nothing to enhance the reputation of the Manchester Ship Canal Pilot Service, and it only fueled the deep bitterness that had always existed between Pilot families. It also proved once again the great gulf that existed between the pilots' and helmsmen's working relationship, a gulf that would never be bridged in their history. One legacy that did remain from this affair was the continuation of harrassment of helmsmen. Certain pilots infuriated by the inability to retain the services of Messrs Green and Onion, concentrated their wrath on the first helmsman to be engaged as a replacement for Green or Onion. They made his life as unbearable and as uncomfortable as possible, but they bit off more than they could chew for Mr T H Clugston was made of sterner stuff than they were.

Mr Clugston (sobriquet Frisby Dyke) commenced his probationary service in December 1942, completing it in November 1943. He made three applications from December for promotion to steer vessels of any tonnage, on each occasion permission was refused by the Pilots Association on the grounds he needed more experience. At last in July 1944 the Pilots' Association intimated their willingness to accept the service of Mr Clugston with any vessel of any tonnage (there was one Pilot who dissented and did so until he retired) with a rider that it was subject to his suitability for any particular vessel for which he might not be considered sufficiently experienced. During the rest of his steering service he was continually harassed and heavily criticized by pilots but he rose above all this to eventually attain a First Class Pilot's Licence and became one of the "Messiahs", an appropriated Pilot. He was a joy to steer for and when he retired in 1982 he was greatly missed by the Helmsmens Service.

The final word on this affair relates to a letter written to the Pilotage Committee and read out at their September meeting in 1944. In the letter Mr A G Green stated that on leaving the Helmsmens Service in February 1943 he had joined the RAF but that he had now been strongly recommended for discharge from that service. He inquired whether there was any possibility of his regaining his former position as a helmsman. The Pilots' representative intimated that so far as the Pilots were concerned there would be no serious objection to the return of Mr Green. It was pointed out that at the moment there were 17 helmsmen operating on the Canal. With the possible return to the service of Mr G D Young (temporarily acting as Second Class Pilot), Mr R C Cheshire (with the RAF and Mr H H Harrington (with the Merchant Navy), all of whom would have to be reinstated, there were no vacancies at the moment in the service. The normal strength of the service was 20 men. Mr A G Green was told of the situation and his application to rejoin the Helmsmens Service was refused.

Mr A G Green was discharged from the RAF in November 1944, and subsequently went into the coal mining industry as a wartime "Bevan Boy". He did not rejoin the Helmsmen's Service until January 1947 and became a First Class Pilot in October 1956. He was appointed an Appropriated Pilot for Shell Tanker Ltd in 1957. Mr Green's premature death at the age of 53 in March 1975 was a great loss to the Manchester Pilot Service and deeply lamented by all who were connected to the Pilot Service. Mr C F (Peter) Onion on leaving the Helmsmen's Service became employed as a deck hand aboard small barges carrying fuel oil and trading mainly between Stanlow Oil Docks and Barton Oil Dock in Manchester. He also rejoined the Helmsmen's Service in 1947. The legacy of bitterness between the piloting families still haunted Mr Onion. He was examined for his First Class Licence on two occasions and on each occasion he failed to pass a satisfactory examination. Mr Onion's father, who had been a Manchester Ship Canal Pilot, contacted the Pilot who was the Senior Examining Pilot on those two occasions, and heatedly accused him of still holding a grudge towards his family, by failing to pass his son in his examination for a First Class Licence. The Pilot, obviously categorically denied this accusation. However, when a new Senior Examining Pilot was appointed for Mr Onion's third examination, Mr Onion passed his examination successfully. Mr Peter Onion retired in 1984 and at the time of writing was alive and well.

August 1965
Courtesy of MSC Company
A superb air view of Manchester Docks showing 30 vessels in port. Compare this with the last air view picture in 1988 at the end of this volume.

18
THE PILOTAGE TARIFF 1940-1956

On 3rd September 1939 the British Empire once again became involved in a war with Germany. Once again all shipping transiting the Canal was immediately placed in control of the Naval Officer in charge of war transport, as decreed by the Lords Commissioners of the Admiralty under Regulation 43 for the Defence of the Realm Act. Suffice to say the lessons learnt from the scandalous manner in which the Admiralty system was conducted in the 1914-1919 war (see earlier Chapter) were not forgotten. It was conducted in a far more equitable way to the satisfaction of all pilots, but it must be said that the pilotage system was vastly different from that of the 1914-1919 war.

The Pilot Service had increased to 36 licences in 1939 and by September 1940 had further increased to 40 licences. It remained so until 1947. The Pilots were restless for an increase in earnings, true to form, war or no war. In January 1941 at the Pilotage Committee they applied for a 10% increase in the Pilotage Tariff, and true to form their request was totally opposed by the united front of the Pilotage Committee, Chamber of Shipping (UK) and both the Manchester and Liverpool Steamship Owners Associations. Not daunted by this massive rebuff the Pilots Association continued to press their claim for a 10% increase. On 28th May at the Pilotage Committee, Mr Kissane, the secretary, said that the meeting had been called for the purpose of obtaining the Committee's views in regard to questions contained in a letter from the Ministry of War Transport, on pilotage conditions.

It was pointed out that at the time of the 1938 Inquiry into pilotage rates at Manchester, three hours travelling time had been allowed, but under existing conditions it was felt this allowance should be increased to four and a half hours. Having due regard to the wartime conditions it was considered fair and unanimously agreed. The travelling time has never been changed and stood at four and half hours until 1990.The Ministry also queried the retention of the four pilots appointed in September 1940, having regard to the amount of shipping using the district but the Committee quickly dispelled any attempt to reduce the numbers stating the present strength of the pilotage service left no substantial margin for possible emergency.

Throughout the Summer of 1941 meetings were convened between the Association and the Pilotage Committee until eventually in September all the parties agreed to promote the Byelaw for an increase of 10% in the Pilotage Tariff and submit the same to the Ministry of War Transport (the old Board of Trade). On 1st November the Ministry refused to confirm the Byelaw. At the Pilotage Committee held in November a letter was read from the secretary of the Pilots Association expressing disappointment that the Ministry would not support a 10% increase and suggested that the Authority should consider whether an increase in earnings of the pilots could be brought about by some other means, recollecting Sir Julian Foley's views in 1938 in regard to extra services, viz minimum charge raised, abolition of half the initial fee. The Committee promised to look into this point.

Those pilots who were not members of their Association had affiliated themselves to the Transport and General Workers Union and for the first time ever a union voice was heard at a Pilotage Committee when this letter was read out:

"The Trade Group Secretary of the T & GWU wishes to express the dissatisfaction of the pilots with the position resulting from the decision of the Ministry in not confirming the Byelaw for an increase of 10%. I would like to point out that the majority of the pilots were not party to the application for the 10% increase as they were of the opinion that it would not meet the case. The pilots took exception to the Ministry basing the pilot's income on the number of hours worked and on a basis of a labourer paid by the hour. The pilots considered it a most unfair comparison to be used in calculating the remuneration of the pilots whose services were highly skilled. Finally the pilots intend to submit an application for a revision of the present tariff."

The secretary of the Pilotage Committee said the position was that the Pilots Association, representing a minority, had made suggestions and the Transport Union, representing a majority had stated they were dealing with the matter themselves and until some sort of order could be established between these two parties no further progress could be made at the Pilotage Committee.

How sad to recall that even in the darkest days of the war, 1940-1941, when Britain and her Empire stood alone against the might of Germany, losses to allied shipping having reached its highest tonnage and the U-boat blockade of Britain being almost complete, the Manchester Pilot Service still could not agree amongst themselves to present a united front in any negotiations regarding their earnings, when the whole of Britain was working in unison with each other. The deep rooted non-co-operation of certain pilots and the continuation of family feuds of years gone by, still remained firmly entrenched in their minds. That age old maxim *"United we stand, divided we fall"* could not be more amply illustrated. There are no further records of any attempt to gain an increase in the Pilotage Tariff during the war years and the tariff remained unchanged until 1946.

It appears hard to understand why the Pilots Association did not continue to apply for an increase in earnings, from one faction or the other, as they did continuously during the 1914-1918 war. The Pilots lack of forcefulness to pursue their claim could be explained thus.

Between 1940 and 1945 a First Class Pilot averaged £600 per year, a Second Class Pilot £474 per year and a Helmsman £360 per year. These figures do not take into consideration any personal earnings for extra services, eg Late Booking Fees, Choice Fees and Docking Bills (Runcorn and Weston Point Docks). A First Class Choice Pilot could expect an additional £150 per year from these extra services and a Rota Pilot about £60. By comparison a Master of a deep sea vessel facing all the dangers and rigours of the Atlantic, Arctic and Malta convoys averaged £480 per year whilst a Chief Officer averaged £324. I often wonder if the Ministry of War Transport, on refusing the 10% increase, told the Manchester Pilot Service a few 'home truths' about their standard and safety of living during the War.

When the victory of the British Empire and her allies over Germany and Japan had once more been attained and all hostilities had ceased the Canal Pilots did have two moments of financial joy. The Pilotage Committee decreed that on VE Day+1 and VJ Day+1 all pilots' and helmsmen's rates were to be doubled after which it was back to sanity. The war clouds had hardly time to disperse over Europe when the Pilots' Representatives proposed a new Pilotage Tariff which was submitted to the Pilotage Committee on 20th September 1945. The proposals would entail an all-over increase of approximately 40.18%. The Authority would not consider adopting this poposal and it was not considered that any useful purpose would be served by a discussion with the pilots' representatives and it was summarily despatched.

The last increase in the pilotage tariff (15%) was made on 5th August 1925, a decrease of 10% followed in 1933, on 1st March 1939 a decrease of 2½% was introduced in lieu of the 10% and on 27th May 1940 the 2½% decrease on all pilotage tariff was removed. After fifteen years the Pilot Service was back to the same Pilotage Tariff as in 1925, hardly what one would call a great advancement. The Pilots' earnings had been sustained by the extra war time tonnage transiting the Canal at a record average of nearly 8,000,000 tons per year. Now, twenty years after the last increase, an application for an increase was abruptly denied. This almost contemptuous dismissal came as a great shock to all the pilots, for after two decades and a war, they had hoped and anticipated a more sympathetic response from the Pilotage Committee and the Steamship Owners. How wrong they were.

Whether or not the Pilotage Committee or the Steamship Owners considered no useful purpose could be served by further discussions with the pilots, further discussions did take place with a very incensed Pilots Association, who were in no mood to be put off. Night lamps burned into the early hours of many a morning as tactics were devised, accepted or refused and the slow rounds of hard bargaining at Pilotage Committee dragged on. All the time progress was being made to a settlement agreeable to all concerned and at last on 1st June, the following Byelaw was duly published.

"The rates contained in the schedule Pilotage Dues for the Manchester Pilotage District, other than travelling expenses, shall be subject to a 35% increase".

The byelaw was confirmed by the Ministry of Transport on 6th July 1946 and came into force on 13th July.

The speed at which the byelaw was promulgated from the first promptings in nine months, contrasts sharply with the belaboured negotiations in 1925 and 1933, which took years as opposed to months. Perhaps the dramatic fall in tonnage transiting the Canal in 1946 - from the heady war years of 8,000,000 tons to just over 5,500,000 tons the lowest tonnage recorded since 1932-1933 - might have hastened the negotiations along.

The Pilots Association had been, for many years, very dissatisfied with the Schedule of Pilotage Dues implemented in 1921. It had become archaic, contained important omissions and did not truly reflect the fees charged to vessels now using the Ship Canal. The recommendations by Sir Julian Foley at the Board of Trade Inquiry in 1938 that the Association should consider different methods to increase their earnings other than an overall percentage, had gained considerable credence over the past seven years. A sub-committee was constituted as early as 1939 to consider Sir Julian's recommendations. It consisted of the following Pilots:

Mr J H Warren, Senior Pilots' Representative (Chairman)
Mr F Davenport, Senior Pilots' Representative (Vice Chairman)
Mr S Ratcliffe, Pilot First Class
Mr N Colvin, Pilot First Class
Mr J Green, Pilot First Class

The intervening war years curtailed any great development towards a new schedule of Pilotage Dues, but the sub-committee did meet regularly to exchange ideas and plan the post war reconstruction of the schedule.

1960s
Courtesy of the MSC Company
No 9 Dock at the height of its trading day. Ten vessels in dock.

1960s
Courtesy of the MSC Company
Full house in No 6, No 7 and No 8 Docks. Compare this photograph with the one taken in 1989.

After the cessation of hositlities in 1945 the sub-committee worked tirelessly for many months to produce a satisfactory Schedule of Pilotage Dues, acceptable to both their Association and the Pilotage Committee and hopefully also to the Manchester Steamship Owners Association. At the Pilotage Committee held in September 1946 Messrs Warren and Davenport placed before the meeting a twenty point charter of the recommendations for a change in the Schedule of Pilotage Rates. The following are the main reforms in that charter:

1 The initial fees for all vessels shall be payable according to the gross registered tonnage and not the nett registered tonnage.
2 The initial fees to be adjusted.
3 The tonnage limits for initial fees to be reassessed.
4 A rate of 1¼d (1p) per foot draft per mile or portion of a mile to replace the existing 1s 6d (7½p) per mile or portion of a mile.
5 The abolition of one half the mileage fee for vessels in ballast.
6 The minimum charge for a Pilot service of £1.10s 0d (£1.50p) to be introduced.
7 Moving a vessel from point to point in the Canal without leaving or entering the Canal, if in excess of 8 miles two-thirds initial fee shall be charged, not half as prescribed now.

Many other alterations of minor, but collectively significant, increases were proposed, eg Detention Fees, Swinging of Vessels Fees, Cancellation Fees, the final charge in the list, number 20, was an increase in travelling expenses to 7s0d (35p).

It was an excellently documented charter that fully modernised the Schedule of Pilotage Charges. Great credit must be accorded to that worthy committee not just for their commitment but for their foresight in a lot of the changes they recommended.

The Pilots Association had anticipated another long, hard, toilsome struggle to achieve any modicum of success, reminiscent of the negotiations in the 1920s and 1930s, due to the radical nature and thorough reforms the new Schedule contained and their demands coming so closely, as it did, on the heels of a 35% increase granted in July of that year. Any fear of a return to the style of the 1920 and 1930 negotiations was quickly dispelled with the total rejection of all the major reforms and increases in the twenty point charter by both the Pilotage Committee and the Steamship Owners Association. This total rejection brought a swift response from the pilots' representatives who immediately called for a Ministry of Transport Inquiry concerning all aspects of the Manchester Pilot Service.

The response to this call for an inquiry was equally swift from the Pilotage Committee and the Steamship owners who declared their willingness, there and then, to be participants in such an inquiry. The inquiry was arranged with the utmost expedition, so foreign from all the previous negotiations, and was held in November 1946. As in all negotiations some points are given away in order to gain others, this inquiry being no exception. At the conclusion of this inquiry it was the general opinion that the pilots had been dealt with most favourably by the Ministry of Transport, but time will show that this did not prove to be the case. The new Schedule of Pilotage Dues - which can be found briefly in Appendix II - was published on 21st November 1946 and came into force on 1st January 1947. The first major change since 1925.

It was to be six years before another percentage increase was imposed on the basic Pilotage Dues. This occurred on 1st August 1953 when an additional 14% was added to the existing 35% granted in July 1946. The opening of the Queen Elizabeth II Oil Dock at Eastham necessitated an additional Pilotage Tariff which came into force on 5th November 1953.

"For a vessel shifted from the entrance of the Oil Dock at Eastham to a berth in the dock or vice versa or from one berth to another with the dock the following dues according to gross registered tonnage shall be payable in respect of services rendered.

Not exceeding 500 tons	*15s 0d (75p)*
Exceeding 500 tons but not exceeding 1,000 tons	*£1.10s.0d (£1.50)*
Exceeding 1,000 tons but not exceeding 3,000 tons	*£3. 0s 0d (£3.00)*
Exceeding 3,000 tons	*£4.10s 0d (£4.50)*

All the fees are subject to a surcharge of 49%."

Two further percentage increases occurred one on 8th June 1954 of 20% and the other on 16th April 1956 of 36% thus bringing the total percentage increase on all Pilotage Dues and Charges other than travelling expenses to 105%.

In 1947 when the method of assessing rates was changed from net to gross tonnage, the assumption was that 1,000 net tons equalled 2,500 gross tons, when in actual fact the ratio is 1,000 net tons to 1,666 gross tons. Thus the present method of charging was grossly unfair to the pilots and did not now bring in the increase intended by the Minister of Transport in 1946. The calculations were worked out by Mr A L Shepherd, First Class Pilot. The existing schedule of rates was also full of anomalies which were detrimental to the pilots and rendered the schedule of rates incapable of bringing in the requisite remuneration to enable the pilots to provide an adequate or efficient service, because they could not afford to provide the required complement of pilots to deal with the work.

1930 - 1988
A Pilot's "Bill" presented to the Master on completion of his services

P
397)
Pilot's Name
A/C Ref.
Name of Vessel
Nationality
Agent
Date of Service
G.R.T.
N.R.T.
Max. Draft at commencement of Service.
Length O.A.
Beam
From
Initial Fee
To
Mileage
Via Swing
Disappointment Fee
Cancellation Fee
Extra Services and Detentions
Master's Signature
Scheduled Travelling Expenses
ONE
TWO
Taxi from
To and Time
J/N 10444

Maximum Height of Vessel's Mast and/or Funnels
Ft. Ins.
MASTS...........
FUNNELS........
Signature of Master.........................

This was the reverse side

PORT OF MANCHESTER MARINE OPERATIONS
VESSEL NAME & FLAG
AGENT
DATE OF SERVICE
DIMENSIONS GRT DRAFT
LOA BEAM
MAXIMUM HEIGHT OF VESSEL'S MAST/FUNNELS
SERVICE FROM
TO VIA
PILOT ORDERED FOR
SERVICE COMMENCED
SERVICE COMPLETED
PILOT DETAINED
ASSISTANT PILOT USED NAME:
DETENTION:
TUGS USED TUG 1:
TUG 2:
REMARKS
MASTER NAME & SIGNATURE
PILOT NAME & SIGNATURE

The 1990 Version

This had an adverse effect on the health of the pilots and had brought about a complete collapse of the service in February 1955. During the 1946 Inquiry Mr Kissane, secretary of the Pilotage Committee, stated that 120 Pilotage Services per annum was the maximum amount of work to be expected from a Ship Canal Pilot due to the long and arduous nature of the Pilotage. In 1948 the figure was 194 Pilotage Services and in 1956 it had risen to approximately 220. A Canal Pilot having navigated his vessel from Eastham into Mode Wheel Locks for 10 or 12 hours was tired and exhausted but he was still faced with the hazardous manoeuvre of docking the vessel on her berth, adding another hour or more on to the passage, for which he received no extra fee. There were still many other extra services which a pilot had to perform for no extra fee. The anomalies which existed in the tariff were ridiculous as the following examples will prove.

1 Mv *"Anterioty"* of 2,003 gross tons swung at Stonedelph and after at Stanlow Oil Docks. The fee for swinging at Stonedelph was only half the fee charged, according to the tariff, for the same vessel swinging at Stanlow Oil Dock and if the same vessel had been swung in the Manchester Docks, no fee would have been chargeable under the present tariff.

2 Manchester is an open port and only Eastham Locks are governed by tides, therefore vessels can leave the various points in the Canal at any time (weather permitting). During adverse weather conditions pilots, unlike other pilots in the United Kingdom, have to standby on board their respective vessels. The stress of weather clause in the present tariff is so designed that pilots receive one fee for their service. A pilot should not have to attend vessels and standby and earn no money, he should be paid detention fees when he is detained on passage for any reason. There are also many other anomalies too numerous to mention. The service provided by the Manchester Pilots is first class and the Manchester Ship Canal Company and the Shipowners benefit enormously from this service.

This dissatisfaction brought about the most dramatic change ever to occur in the history of the Pilot Service. A proposed new schedule of Pilotage Rates drawn up by the two Pilot representatives, Messrs R T Green and J Lee, was circulated to all pilots. It was inflammatory to say the least, being sent to an angry Pilot Service who were already clamouring for a review of the Pilotage Tariff and working conditions. Nevertheless the required result was obtained and the whole of the pilot service was united as one man and unanimously voted for a Ministry of Transport Inquiry. All the parties concerned knew full well that such great changes in the tariff and working conditions could only be satisfactorily and swiftly settled by an Inquiry. The Inquiry dates were fixed for 12th to 15th June and 18th to 20th June. This was the fifth occasion an Inquiry had been called and as the future revealed it was also to be the last.

1959
City of Newcastle Grt 7032 L 456' B 54'
Swinging at Stanlow Oil Dock

1960
Passing vessels in Eastham Basin

The Inquiry was far too long and complex to document in detail, but a brief summary of that Inquiry can be found in Appendix III.

The major changes in the Pilotage Rates gained at the Inquiry were as follows:

1 An overall increase in the percentage on Pilot Charges of 75%.
2 The Late Booking Fee to be discontinued but an increase of 5% included in the overall increase as compensation for its abandonment.

The new percentage was calculated to give a First Class Pilot £1,350 net per year, a Second Class Pilot £1,012.10s 0d (£1,012.50) net per year and a Helmsman £1,100 per year. The situation of a Helmsman earning more than a Second Class Pilot was quickly,and quite rightly, objected to by the Pilots Association. A letter was swiftly despatched to the Ministry of Transport calling his attention to this. The Helmsmen's increase in their rates was suitably adjusted. During this period a letter was sent to the Liverpool Steamship Owners Association pointing out that the appropriation fee for Choice Pilots of £100 had remained unaltered since 1919 and querying whether there was any reason they should not be brought into line with the present day conditions. The fee was in due course raised to £200 and eventually to £300. It was still at £300 when the Choice Pilot system was at last abandoned in 1989. The new Byelaws came into force on 21st September 1956. The cost of the Inquiryto the Pilots was in total £3,693.

The comparison of earnings at sea in 1956 had, and always would have, some bearing on any increases granted to any Pilotage District. A Master of a deep sea vessel regularly using the Ship Canal was earning £1,000 per year whilst a Chief Officer would have earned £768 per year. These figures are for the flat rate before bonuses etc.

To conclude this Chapter it is with great pleasure to record that the Chairman of the Pilotage Committee, who was also a member of the Steamship Owners Association, Mr R Stoker, sent a message of good wishes to all pilots and helmsmen. As far as the shipowners were concerned he wanted the pilots to know that there were no ill feelings and that the award from the Ministry of Transport was accepted and acknowledged.

19

APPROPRIATED/CHOICE PILOTS JUNE 1967

In June 1967 the highest number of Appropriated/Choice Pilots was recorded by the Manchester Pilotage Committee and is listed below.

NAME OF PILOT	COMPANY
G F Ashworth (Maersk Line)	A P Moller, Copenhagen
P A Barraclough	A/S Rederiet Odfjell
C M Broom	United Steamship Co. Copenhagen
C E Bowell	B I S C (Ore) Limited
G W Scully	" "
H Frith	" "
G Cartwright	Furness Ship Management Ltd
J H Warren	" " "
R Cashin	Esso Petroleum Co. Ltd
H Davies	" "
A G Green	Shell International Marine Ltd
R T Green	" " "
P K Rali	" " "
W J Maddocks	" " "
J H Law	A C Olsen, Sandefjord
C M Oliver	Transatlantic Carriers Limited
J A Patterson	F C Strick & Co. Limited
H G Pringle	British & Commonwealth
J E Morris	" "

W H Roberts	T & J Brocklebank Limited
L Davies	" "
A D Shenton	James Fisher & Sons Limited
N T Sigley	" "
A L Shepherd	Lykes Bros. S S Co. Ltd.
H Stott	Manchester Liners Limited
T W Lamey	" "
H Whitehead	" "
G D Young	" "
J T Wainwright	United States Line
W Walker	T & J Harrisons Limited
D Scholes	" "

HEAD HUNTING FOR CHOICE/APPROPRIATED PILOTS

The following letter shows the manner in which Choice/Appropriated Pilots were usually selected.

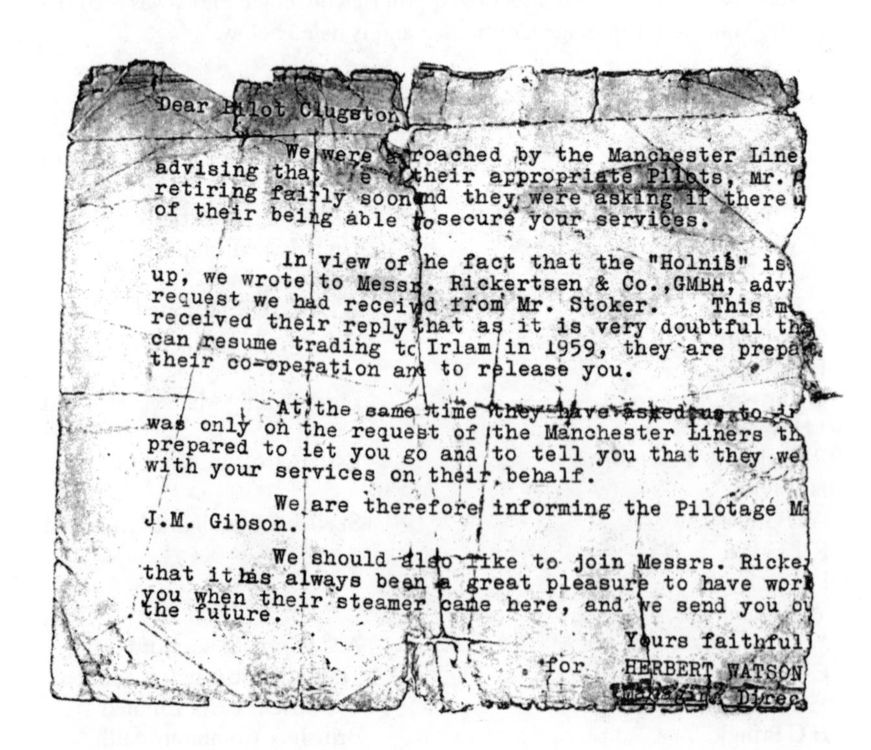

Dear Pilot Clugston

We were [illegible]roached by the Manchester Line
advising tha[illegible] their appropriate Pilots, Mr.
retiring fairly soon and they were asking if there
of their being able to secure your services.

In view of the fact that the "Holnis" is
up, we wrote to Messrs. Rickertsen & Co.,GMBH, adv
request we had received from Mr. Stoker. This m
received their reply that as it is very doubtful th
can resume trading to Irlam in 1959, they are prepa
their co-operation and to release you.

At the same time they have asked us to i
was only on the request of the Manchester Liners th
prepared to let you go and to tell you that they we
with your services on their behalf.

We are therefore informing the Pilotage M
J.M. Gibson.

We should also like to join Messrs. Ricke
that it has always been a great pleasure to have wor
you when their steamer came here, and we send you ou
the future.

Yours faithful

for HERBERT WATSON

Managing Direc

This is the type of vessel Mr Clugston would have been expected to pilot for his £100 per annum (Less Tax)
"Manchester Mariner" GRT 7850; L. 466'; B. 60' Draught 26'

For clear reading the letter is reproduced below.

Dear Pilot Clugston,

We were approached by the Manchester Liners advising that one of their appropriate Pilots, Mr P Bennet, would be retiring soon and they were asking if there was a possibility of their being able to secure your services. In view of the fact that the "HOLNIS" is laid up, we wrote to Messrs Rickersten & Co., advising them of the request we had received from Mr Stoker. This morning we received their reply that as it is very doubtful that they can resume trading to Irlam Ore Wharf in 1959, they are prepared to co-operate and to release you.

At the same time, they have asked us to indicate it was only on the request of the Manchester Liners that they were prepared to let you go, and to tell you they were very pleased with your services on their behalf. We are therefore informing the Pilot Manager Captain J Gibson. We should also like to agree with Messrs Rickersten, that it has always been a great pleasure to have worked with you when their steamer came here, and we send you our best wishes for the future.

Yours faithfully

HERBERT WATSON AND CO

Mr H Clugston declined the invitation from Manchester Liners on the grounds that he thought the retaining fee of £100 was too paltry a figure for what was virtually a 7-day working week, irrespective of the so-called prestige that went with the appointment as Choice Pilot for THE MANCHESTER LINERS. Mr Clugston was not easily impressed by such flattery. With his refusal, Manchester Liners appointed three extra Pilots, Messrs Young, Whitehead, and W Yates - providing they relieved each other at Latchford Locks inward and outward bound.

Courtesy the MSC Co

No 1 and No 2 Stanlow Oil Docks today

These docks, acknowledged to be a model of their kind, are connected by means of pipelines running through subways under the Canal to the tank storage farms on the opposite bank.

20
THE PILOT SERVICE 1946 - 1960

The future of the Manchester Pilot Service was going to be just as difficult and frustrating as it had been in the past. Continual and prolonged negotiations took place with the Pilotage Committee to obtain a more compatible working system, more leave entitlement and, of course, an increase in the Schedule of Earnings. Now that the exceptional wartime circumstances no longer existed the Ministry of Transport withdrew the power to issue Temporary Licences to pilots on the Canal. The Pilot Service was still fragmented by the resignation of the eight senior pilots from the Association in 1940. They were to become a continual source of delay and disruption to all future negotiations with the Piulotage Committee and the Pilotage Committee took full advantage of that situation. The Pilotage Committee would use this minority of pilots shamelessly to procrastinate on any of the advances - especially earnings - that the Pilots Association were attempting to procure for the betterment of the whole service.

Time and again the Pilotage Committee would reject any new proposals put forward by the Pilots Association on the grounds that it did not represent the wishes of **all** pilots. Time and time again negotiations with the Pilotage Committee on any proposal were delayed until the Pilotage Committee, on their insistence, heard the views of the individual pilots who were not members of the Association. Time and time again proposals and negotiations broke down due to the attitude these renegade pilots took. It would be over 20 years before the Pilots Association eventually became a united body, but because so much dissension had been caused over the years this united front was always to be exceptionally fragile.

With the war ending the pilots thought it desirable to revert to the former practice of issuing weekend orders, viz. that orders issued at 1300 hours on

Saturday should include all vessels booked up to 1300 hours on the following Monday. The present practice of weekend ordering was introduced in order to meet war conditions and therefore there was no justification for its retention. The Committee agreed that this was mainly a domestic matter and that the previous practice of weekend ordering could again be put into operation. On 19th November 1945 the Pilotage Clerk explained to the Pilotage Committee the difficulties which had arisen during the several weekends since the amendment in the issuing of orders. The Pilotage Committee considered it wise to revert to the arrangement whereby orders received up to 1300 hours on Saturday to cover work up to 1300 hours Sunday were given out to the pilots on turn and similarly at 1300 hours Sunday to 1300 hours Monday and any known work - inwards or outwards - being listed at Eastham. This arrangement was put into practice on 22nd December 1945 and remained so until 1988.

In 1946 a problem arose that was a legacy from the war years and was to bedevil the Pilot Service throughout the years ahead. This was the question of establishing the deepest draught that a vessel should have to safely navigate the Ship Canal. This question was never a real problem before the war because few vessels were capable of a fully loaded draught in excess of 24 feet, whilst transiting the Ship Canal. T & J Harrison of Liverpool had a company policy stating that none of their vessels, transiting the Ship Canal, must exceed a draught of 24 feet. They maintained this throughout their long association with the Ship Canal. Vessels that transited the Ship Canal at 26 feet or more - to Manchester - were usually piloted by their own Choice Pilots, who would have sailed to hell and back on dried sand for their measly £100 appropriation fee. During the war vessels - especially the American built *Liberty* ships - arrived in Manchester fully laden with a draught of 26 feet plus and the Pilot Authority could see no viable reason why in peacetime this practice should not continue.

The pilots in general objected to vessels having a draught exceeding 25 feet 6 inches inward at Eastham, if proceeding to Manchester and a draught not exceeding 26 feet outward from Manchester. The difference in the draughts, inward and outward, relates to the Fresh Water Allowance (FWA) of 6 inches. It has always been considered salt water (density 1025) between Eastham and Latchford Locks - because of the levelling tides - and fresh water (Density 1000) between Latchford Locks and the Manchester Docks. At a Pilotage Committee Meeting in February 1946 the pilots' representatives, Mr N Colvin and Mr C Acraman, stated that in their professional opinion and that of all the pilots, they were not prepared to pilot vessels whose draught exceeded the limits already stated. The Chairman said the Pilotage Committee was extremely

1970
Courtesy The MSC Company
The dry docks at Manchester with the small floating dry dock in the upper sluiceway of Modewheel Lock

1932
Courtesy Captain P Dunbavand
"Argyleshire" NRT 7526 Length 545' 3" Beam 61' 5". The largest and longest vessel to transit the whole length of the canal, a record she held until 1966. Head tug "Old Quay". Note tug boats Lifeboat Position.

disturbed that the pilots were unable to withdraw or modify their position. He further stated the restriction was not a view the Ship Canal Company took and doubted it was the view of the majority of the pilots. This was a direct reference to the pilots who were not members of the Pilots Association and the Choice Pilots who would willingly pilot a vessel at a draught exceeding the limits placed on by the Pilots Association. The pilots' representatives had attempted to show a united front on this matter but the Pilotage Committee had already driven a wedge into that very fragile front by perceiving the different factions within the service.

The Chairman continued by remarking that the draughts quoted by the pilots could be exceeded by fully 6 inches and as the Pilotage in the Ship Canal was not compulsory, the ultimate responsibility in these matters must rest with the Master of the vessel. The pilots are not jusified in stating they are not prepared, in any circumstances, to pilot vessels exceeding their stated draught. The representatives pointed out to the Chairman most forcefully that it was neither prudent nor seamanlike for the safety of a vessel navigating in enclosed waters, not to have a margin of at least 2 feet of water under the keel. This brought a sharp rebuke from the Chairman, who informed the pilots' representatives, it was not prudent, necessary or seamanlike to apply a hard and fast rule for all vessels, but that every vessel should be treated individually. He held the pilots' attitude to be injurious to the interests of the Port of Manchester and to themselves.

The pilots' representatives affirmed that their attitude was taken in the interests of shipowners, in preventing unnecesssary damage to their vessels. Nevertheless the Chairman said he was most concerned that the strict line of demarcation, laid down by the pilots as an ultimatum, was not helpful to the advancement of the Port of Manchester as a major port in the United Kingdom. He suggested that the pilots should withdraw their restrictions and he concluded that certain pilots are prepared to take vessels of 26 feet draught with the exception of twin propeller vessels which are very difficult to navigate in enclosed waters and he hoped the Pilot Service would take this attitude. The pilots' representatives retorted that the pilots the Chairman referred to would be the Choice Pilots, but agreed to put the Pilotage Committee's views before their colleagues and report at some future meeting.

The maximum draught problem was never resolved - as the Pilotage Committee always knew it would not be - the Choice Pilots continued to ignore the Association's limitations: pilots yearning for a company to appoint them as their Choice Pilot ignored the limitations and pilots who were not members of the Association ignored the limitations just for spite. This problem is no longer a matter of contention, with the decline of the Port of Manchester and the resulting silting up of the upper reaches of the Ship Canal the Manchester Authority reduced the official maximum draught for all vessels to 21 feet.

When all the temporary licences became permanent in 1944 the complement of the Pilot Service was 40 men and remained at this figure until 1947. This number was reduced to 38 men in 1947 but the Pilot Service achieved an increase of one pilot the following year. This new figure, of 39 men, was far from acceptable to the Pilot Service. The increase in tonnage over the last decade is shown in the following table:

Year	Pilots	Vessels	Tonnage	Tonnage per vessel	Miles piloted	Fees
1938	36	3,874	6,765,243	Av. 1,747	93,528	£16,828
1949	44	5,993	8,272,481	Av. 1,380	122,558	£31,252

Between 1939 and 1949 the complement of the Pilot Service had averaged 40 men but the increase in the number of vessels transiting the Ship Canal over that decade had placed an intolerable burden upon the physical condition of the individual pilots. The high rate of absenteeism due to sickness, especially from November to March of 1949-1950 was causing great concern, with the average pilot being absent from duty through sickness for fifteen and a half days during that period. The pilots were regularly performing 20 pilotage services per month - the official number of services per pilot was 12 - and one First Class Pilot, Mr H G Pringle, recorded he had performed 24 separate pilotage services for each of the months of July and October in 1948. In September 1949 the same pilot performed 27 separate services, a record never surpassed. A comparison was made between a pilot and that of a normal professional man on a five day week as to the number of working days per year.

Total days in a year	365
Less Saturdays/Sundays	104
Bank Holidays	6
Annual Holidays	10
Working Days	245

A pilot had only 28 days leave a year in which to relax without the fear of being called out for duty, his working days were 337 a year. A very illuminating comparison.

1966
Courtesy World Ship Society
mv "Serbistan" F Stricks. Dimensions Beam 63' 10" Length 503' 4" GRT 8985. This was the largest vessel to transit the whole length of the Manchester Ship Canal.

Courtesy World Ship Society
SS "Markhor" 11 April 1929 T & J Brocklebank. Draught forward 27' 1" Aft 27' 2". The above vessel holds the record for the deepest draughted vessel to transit the whole length of the Manchester Ship Canal.

From as early as 1946 the Pilots Association through their representatives had constantly pressed the Pilotage Committee for an increase in the complement of pilots, but their pleas had generally fallen on unsympathetic ears. At last in March 1949 after intense negotiations between the Pilotage Committee and the Manchester Steamship Owners Association they achieved an increase of five new licences. Messrs McIntosh, Cartwright, Green,RT, Patterson and Walker were all promoted from Helmsmen to Second Class Pilots. The corresponding number of Second Class Pilots were also examined and promoted to First Class Pilots. In May 1950 a further two licences - Messrs Harrington and Sheppherd - were granted to bring the complement to 46 men. Of these 46 men 39 were First Class Pilots and 7 were Second Class Pilots.

In that same year the present rota system and its operation showed a marked variation in duty time performed between one pilot and another per day. There was an average variation as much as 3 hours 34 minutes per day. In twelve months it would therefore be theoretically possible for one pilot to be on duty 1,3203 hours or nearly two months, more than another for the same remuneration. The following example was presented to the Pilotage Committee in September 1950.

Mr G V Davidson had become a Choice Pilot for Shell Tankers Ltd between Eastham and Ince. He lived in Manchester and his recorded average hours per day during May were as follows:

Duty	**Travelling**	**Total**
1 hour 39 min	2 hours 48min	4 hours 27min

Comparing this with the record of Mr R Southwood who lived at Eastham and was a First Class Rota Pilot:

Duty	**Travelling**	**Total**
10 hours 27 min	2hours 51 min	13 hours 18 min

Taking these figures to a theoretical conclusion over twelve months Mr Southwood would have been on duty 2,951 hours or 4 months, more than Mr Davidson for the same earnings. It very definitely indicated that the present rota system was most unsatisfactory. It was also revealed that of the present 46 pilots licensed 41 resided at the Eastham end of the Canal, 2 resided in Runcorn, 2 at Warrington and 1 in Manchester. The number of pilotage services in the first six months of 1950, in the six miles between Eastham and Ince, was 5,986 whereas vessels being piloted beyond six miles numbered only 3,741. Furthermore, shifting vessels in Eastham Basin totalled 1,099 against 459 services at Manchester Docks. Other shifts elsewhere in the Canal - Partington, Runcorn Salt Works, etc - numbered 714 vessels.

SS "Ravensworth" at Latchford Locks. The Fo'c's'le Head in the Winter of 1963-1964.

SS "Ravensworth" Grt 6805 L 426 B 58'. Freezing fog caused most of these conditions.

With all these facts and figures before them and diverse suggestions and advice from every member of the Pilot Service, the pilots' representatives formed a committee to investigate a more equitable Rota System. It was to take a full three years for this to be achieved. The Choice Pilots had always to be placated, more often about the security of their position as Choice Pilots with their corresponding fees, which to them came before anything else in the Pilot Service. The infighting and internecine strife from the group of senior pilots still not members of the Association caused a considerable amount of delay and the Pilotage Committee, who as always, viewed any new system promulgated by the pilots with great caution and suspicion, feared that it would necessitate an increase in Pilotage Rates.

Eventually a Rotary System was devised that was acceptable to all parties. It was named the *Ince Rota*, brief details of which can be found in the Appendix No IV. The *Ince Rota* commenced on 1 September 1953 and was quite happily and successfully worked until time and circumstances overtook its usefulness. The new *Ince Rota* did not, however, resolve the one major problem that had beset the Pilot Service since 1946, ie that of the number of services being performed each month by individual pilots and the continued high incidents of absenteeism through sickness. Certain pilots were still returning, on average, 20 separate services per month. The complement had very slowly risen to 54 men in 1954 whilst the tonnage of vessels piloted in the Ship Canal rose over 6,000,000 tons, a percentage increase of 70%.

Amongst all the other problems that concurrently ran with the manning complement, the Pilots Association, through their representatives, continued the unenviable negotiations of trying to persuade the Pilotage Committee for a further increase in the number of licences issued by them. The Association's recommendation was for an increase in complement of ten men, coupled with the necessary increase in the pilotage tariff to allow for such an increase. The Association considered this recommendation would reduce the present unacceptable work load on the Pilot Service, which was having such a detrimental effect on their well being. After many prolonged and frustrating meetings with the pilotage Committee, the pilots' representatives, finding their negotiations were ineffectual, had to resort to more vigorous action. In September 1954 they took the unprecedented step of withdrawing all Pilotage Services from the Ship Canal.

Because of Parliamentary Law dated as far back as the 1700s, a withdrawal of pilot services - a strike if one wishes to be blunt - was prohibited and was subjected to a term of imprisonment if such action was taken. Therefore the Pilots Association's withdrawal of services took the form of an *All Hands* meeting at the Eastham Ferry Hotel, which lasted four days. It is most gratifying to place on record that ALL pilots did concur with this meeting. Out of this adversity came unity, for the very first time in the history of the Manchester Ship Canal Pilot Service. Unfortunately it was only short lived. The withdrawal of all the pilotage services took the Pilotage Committee by surprise. Such action had never been envisaged by them and it was a situation they had never contemplated would ever arise. A *Hot Line* was installed between the Pilotage Committee in Manchester and the Pilots Association at the Eastham Ferry Hotel. This *Hot Line* had the dual purpose of keeping the Pilotage Committee fully updated on the progress of the meetings being held by the Pilots Association and secondly, it enabled the various Shipowners to contact their Choice Pilots in an attempt to cajole them to return to work. The Shipowners promised that as soon as a normal pilot service was resumed, they would reopen the negotiations on the pilots' pressing problems. It was as if three years had not already been endlessly spent in trying to solve the manning situation, with a completely negative response from the Shipowners. Several attempts were made by the Shipowners to entice their Choice Pilots to return to work, thus seriously undermining the Pilot Service's new found united front, but to their undying credit it must be said that they steadfastly and unanimously refused to return to normal pilotage services. How this must have tested a number of the less scrupulous pilots. Here was a golden opportunity to obtain the elusive Choice Pilot appointment, but the feeling of unity was running so high in the Pilot Service that even these vultures recoiled from contemplating a return to normal pilot services. In the forthcoming years, distressing as it may seem, some shipowners, viewing their Choice Pilot's action as disloyal never let it be forgotten.

I sincerely believe that if the Choice Pilots had weakened and returned to work, it would have signalled a defeat more catastrophic than Napoleon's at Waterloo. The Pilot Service would no longer have been recognised as a dominant power in influencing and conducting their affairs. This was to quote a Churchillian phrase "*their finest hour*". Had they faltered then they would have been subservient to the Pilotage Committee and the Shipowners from that moment onwards.

It also proved once and for all that the shipowners could not implicitly rely on the support or subservience of their Choice Pilots.

There was complete stagnation of traffic on the Ship Canal, with vessels anchored at the Liverpool Bar awaiting berths in the Canal, or being diverted to other ports. There was no such thing as *black legging* in those days and every berth in the Ship Canal was occupied. The Manchester Ship Canal

1986
Courtesy of the MSC Company
The last visit to Manchester of the Royal Navy. HMS "Orpheus" docking in No 9 Dock. Demolition of the dock had commenced as shown - top right Transit Shed.

Shareholders Association quickly made their feelings known about the apparent intransigence of the Pilotage Committee in settling this dispute one way or another. They informed the Pilotage Committee, in no uncertain terms, the effect a prolonged stoppage would have on their annual dividends. On 1st October 1954 the Pilotage Committee capitulated and the demands of the Pilot Service were met. The complement of Pilots now stood at 64 men.

The Pilot Service immediately instigated proposals for a new and revolutionary system of piloting on the Ship Canal, in addition to a substantial increase in the Pilotage Tariff. A working system whereby the service of a pilot - on certain vessels - was terminated at Latchford Locks and a relieving pilot took charge to complete the vessel's passage. This had always been viewed as an impossible dream. It was now about to be brought into reality. A letter dated 2nd September 1955 explained the Pilots Association's proposals and the manner in which they wished these proposals to be negotiated. The Ministry of Transport and Civil Aviation inquiry into the Pilot Service's problems was held in Manchester on 12th - 20th June 1956. A summary of that inquiry can be found in the Appendix III. Many of the observations and recommendations by the learned Mr Thomas Haworth bears out what the Author has already documented over the past 60 years.

The appointment of Captain John N Gibson as Pilot Manager on 1st September 1956 was a major step towards closer working relations between the Pilotage Committee and the Pilots' Association. This appointment was not without its trials and tribulations. It was almost a re-run of the saga of appointing the first Chief Pilot Clerk's successor in 1944. The Pilots' Association had insisted that they should be considered in all the deliberations in choosing a Pilot Manager and had once again put forward the name of Mr S (Sam) Hargrave for this new post. Mr Hargrave had, at considerable risk of incurring the wrath of his employers, the Ship Canal Company, and an even greater risk of being dismissed from his position in the Canal Company, supplied important information to the Pilots' Association to assist them in their case at the inquiry by the Board of Trade and Civil Aviation. The Pilots' Association had promised Mr Hargrave, because of his assistance, he would be appointed the new Pilot Manager after the successful outcome of the inquiry. Unfortunately, the Pilots' Association had not learnt the bitter lesson of 1944 and once again the Pilotage Committee overruled the pilots' candidate and placed their own man in the post of Pilot Manager. Mr Hargrave's position in the Ship Canal Company became untenable and he was demoted and slowly but ever so surely eased out of the Ship Canal Company under the guise of early retirement. A few years later, Mr Sam Hargrave died a sad, broken and disillusioned man, whose demise must be partly attributed to the Pilots' Association's failure to keep their promises.

Pilot Manager Captain John N Gibson

Pilot Manager Mr Robert S Boyles

What an onerous task it was to prove to be. Captain Gibson needed the patience of Job and the wisdom of Solomon when dealing with the many factions and individual grievances within the Pilot Service. I am sure many of the pilots looked upon the Pilot Manager as a form of "Agony Aunt" and brought all their petty complaints - both domestic and professional - to his door. Captain Gibson was always polite and sympathetic towards individual pilots and conducted himself in such a manner as to become a great credit to the position of Pilot Manager. On his retirement on 1st September 1978, Mr R S Boyles (First Class Pilot) was appointed his successor. Mr R (Bob) S Boyles maintained the high standards set by his predecessor in the most commendable manner, throughout his office as Pilot Manager. Mr Boyles had the most unenviable task of overseeing the disintegration of the Pilot Service and the complete abandonment of the Helmsmans' Service. He carried out all his duties without fear or favour, constantly championing the Pilots' and Helmsmans' services. Without Mr Boyles' dedication to these two Services, much would have been lost financially in the final negotiations between the new owners of the Ship Canal and the fast diminishing Pilot Service. Mr R S Boyles retired on 1st September 1989 when the office of Pilot Manager was phased out.

It took three years of negotiations before the first draft of a Relief at Latchford Scheme was placed before the Pilots' Association. It proved totally unacceptable to the pilots and a second draft was prepared on 25 September 1959. This also failed to meet the conditions set by the Pilots' Association (See appendix V). An ad hoc committee under the Chairmanship of Mr R T Green (first class Pilot) had been formed to deal exclusively with the Relief at Latchford Scheme and their recommendations were put to a general meeting of the Association on 18 January 1960. The recommendations were as follows:

1 Delete Clause 1 entirely and replace it with the following clause.
"A permanent Relief at Latchford will commence at 001 hours on a date to be nominated shortly".
2 All other clauses to be rewritten within the context of a permanent Relief at Latchford.
3 Clause 3. The Draft to read "24 feet or more, the beam of a vessel to exceed 55 feet to qualify for a Relief".

The recommendations were unanimously adopted by the Association.

Further meetings were held between the Pilotage Committee and the Association on the resolution and recommendations passed by the Association. Eventually, the Pilotage Committee agreed to all the recommendations. On

1st May 1960 the long-awaited dream became a reality and the Relief at Latchford commenced. It was to last for thirty years until the complete reorganisation of the Pilot Service in October 1990 forced the scheme to be abandoned.

The first vessel to qualify for a relief Pilot and Helmsman at Latchford was the S S CLAN MACLEOD Draught 25 feet 6 inches on 2 May 1960. The first Helmsman to provide a relief service was Mr D A Clulow. The Choice Pilot for the vessel was Mr H G Pringle.

SHIPS IN THE CANAL ON THE 31ST OCTOBER 1951 (WED)

9 DOCK

"CARLSLOGIE". (CARLSLOGIE S S Co) 2317 REG TONS. IS DISCHARGING 4325 TONS OF TIMBER FROM ARCHANGEL.
"OCEANSIDE". (ANDRES SHIPPING Co) 4310 TONS. IS DISCHARGING 5750 TONS OF TIMBER & 2500 TONS OF GRAIN FROM VANCOUVER & NEW WESTMINSTER.
"SEA FIGHTER". (TRANS PACIFIC NAV CORP) 4389 TONS. IS DISCHARGING 6375 TONS OF TIMBER FROM THE PACIFIC COAST.
"MANCHESTER MERCHANT". (MANCHESTER LINERS) 4621 TONS. IS LOADING GLASS, CHEMICALS, TEXTILES, MACHINERY ETC FOR MONTREAL AFTER DISCHARGING 8467 TONS OF WHEAT, BARLEY, ORE, FLOUR, FERRO SILICON, ASBESTOS ETC.
"CASLON" (RUNCIMAN) 3018 TONS. IS DISCHARGING 6031 TONS OF NEWSPRINT FROM PORT ALFRED.
"MANCHESTER REGIMENT". (MANCHESTER LINERS) 4652 TONS. IS LOADING GLASS, CHEMICALS, TEXTILES, EARTHENWARE, MACHINERY ETC FOR MONTREAL, AFTER DISCHARGING 5971 TONS OF WHEAT, BARLEY, FERRO SILICON, WOODPULP, TIMBER, FLOUR, COPPER ETC.

8 DOCK

"VANELLUS". (BRITISH & CONTINENTAL) 905 TONS. IS DISCHARGING 2500 TONS OF CORNFLOUR, STEEL & GENERAL FROM ANTWERP.
"SPEAKER". (T & J HARRISON) 4452 TONS. IS DISCHARGING 5718 TONS OF COTTON & STARCH FROM CORPUS CHRISTI.
"FINLANDIA". (FINSKA ANGFARTYGS A/B) 1149 TONS. IS DISCHARGING 2364 TONS OF WOODPULP, PAPER, PLYWOOD ETC FROM FINLAND.
"SARPFOSS". (THOR THORESEN). 877 TONS. IS DISCHARGING 1802 TONS OF WET PULP, CHEMICALS, PAPER, FELSPAR, TIMBER ETC FROM EAST NORWAY.

7 DOCK

"HOHEWEG". (W SCHUMANN) 609 TONS. IS DISCHARGING CORNFLOUR, CHARCOAL, TIMBER & MISCELLANEOUS CARGO FROM HAMBURG & BREMEN.
"SYRIAN PRINCE". (PRINCE LINE) 999 TONS. IS LOADING MACHINERY, EARTHENWARE, GLASS, CHEMICALS, STEEL ETC FOR MEDITERRANEAN PORTS.
"TEXELSTROOM". (HOLLAND S S Co) 651 TONS. IS DISCHARGING 850 TONS OF DEXTRINE, STRAWBOARDS, FARINA, CANNED GOODS ETC FROM AMSTERDAM.

6 DOCK

"ARDETTA".(BRITISH & CONTINENTAL) 586 TONS. IS DISCHARGING 1757 TONS OF FARINA, STRAWBOARDS, FRUIT PULP, CHEMICALS, PAPER FROM ROTTERDAM.

TRAFFORD WHARF

"COEN", (C V D MOLEN) 147 TONS. IS DISCHARGING 325 TONS OF TIMBER FROM OSCARSHAMN.

"GIOACCHINO LAURO". (ACHILLE LAURO) 4303 TONS. IS WAITING ORDERS AFTER DISCHARGING 9000 TONS OF SULPHUR FROM US GULF PORTS.

8 PIER

"ALAMAZAN". (CIA FRUTERO VALENCIA). 1413 TONS. IS DISCHARGING 2185 TONS OF TIMBER FROM GEFLE.
DRY DOCK

"BRITISH CONFIDENCE". (B T C) 4893 TONS. REPAIRING.

WEASTE OIL WHARF

"AUDACITY". (F T EVERARD) 291 TONS. IS DISCHARGING 620 TONS OF PALM OIL FROM LIVERPOOL.

Courtesy World Ship Society
1980
Thos & Jos Brocklbank vessel the "Maturata" trading from Manchester to India

Courtesy Mrs W Yates Collection
1966
Ship Canal cross ferry at Irlam. The ferry carried cars also. Passengers seen waiting until tanker clears.

1980's
No 2 berth. No 9 dock. Manchester Liners container quay. The "Manchester Clipper" (GRT: 1599; L. 307' ;B. 50') could be discharged and loaded again in 8 hours, by simultaneously loading and discharging. The gantries were dismantled in 1991.

ECCLES OIL WHARF

"ALCHYMIST". (EVERARD). 334 TONS. IS DISCHARGING OIL FROM HEYSHAM.

IRWELL PARK WHARF

"DIMITRIOS A KYDONIEFS". (N A KYDONIEFS) 2971 TONS. IS DISCHARGING 8050 TONS OF IRON ORE FROM WABANA.

BARTON OIL BERTH

"FRISIA". (N V VERENIGDE TANKKUSTVAARI) 587 TONS. IS DISCHARGING OIL FROM HEYSHAM.
IRLAM ORE WHARF

"KINGSBRIDGE". (KINGPORT SHIPPING) 4211 TONS. IS DISCHARGING 9900 TONS OF IRON ORE FROM LA GOULETTE.

Courtesy of Mrs W Yates Collection
Ellesmere Port docks around the turn of the century

Courtesy of the M S C Co.
Cawoods container terminal at Ellesmere Port. Dismantled and transferred to Liverpool in 1991.

PARTINGTON COALING BASIN

"MALEVIK". (W HARKISS & SONS). IS LOADING 2000 TONS OF SLURRY FOR DENMARK.
"GRANFOSS". (THOR THORESEN) 890 TONS. IS LOADING 1000 TONS OF COKE FOR NORWAY.
"JANET PLYM". (PLYM SHIPPING) 183 TONS. IS LOADING 380 TONS OF PITCH FOR FRANCE.
"MULTISTONE". (RICHARD GARDNER (LUNESIDE) LTD) 105 TONS. IS LOADING 270 TONS OF COAL FOR FALMOUTH.

WARRINGTON LAY BYE

"ATONALITY". (F T EVERARD) 548 TONS. IS DISCHARGING 1250 TONS OF WHALE OIL FROM BARRY.

WIGGS WORKS

"TUNISIA". (SOC TUNISIENNE FRANCO) 304 TONS. IS DISCHARGING 5400 TONS OF SULPHURIC ACID FROM BILBAO.

INCE OIL BERTH

"BRITISH HARMONY". (B T C) 4908 TONS. IS LOADING 11000 TONS OF FUEL OIL FOR KARACHI.

STANLOW

"SEA THRILL". FROM ARUBA. IS DISCHARGING 9500 TONS OF FUEL OIL.
"SHELBRIT 10". (SHELL MEX & B P) 383 TONS. IS LOADING 800 TONS OF SPIRIT FOR HEYSHAM.
"ESSO SUWANEE". (ESSO TRANSPORTATION) 105 TONS. IS LOADING 280 TONS OF SPIRIT & 80 TONS OF KEROSENE FOR CAERNARVON.
"LUCELLUM". (H E MOSS). 5726 TONS. IS DISCHARGING 13500 TONS OF CRUDE OIL FROM MENA-AL-AHMADI.
"WAVE PRINCE". (THE ADMIRALTY) 4569 TONS. IS DISCHARGING 10000 TONS OF CRUDE OIL FROM MENA-AL-AHMADI.

VESSELS IN TRANSIT

OUTWARD BOUND

"BELGIAN GULF". (BELGIAN GULF OIL Co) 5237 TONS. LIGHT. HAS DISCHARGED LUBRICATING OIL FROM PORT ARTHUR AT BARTON.
"LAGANFIELD". (FIELD TANK SHIPPING) 4375 TONS. LIGHT. HAS DISCHARGED NAPHTHALENE AT PARTINGTON.

INWARD BOUND

"ASTRONOMER". (T & J HARRISON) 4500 TONS. FROM BROWNSVILLE WITH 4400 TONS OF COTTON, COTTON LINTERS, CARBON BLACK FOR MANCHESTER.
"AMERICAN TRAVELLER". (U S LINES) 4833 TONS. HAS 1945 TONS OF LARD, ORE, TOBACCO, LAST BLOCKS, TIMBER, CHEMICALS ETC FROM BOSTON FOR MANCHESTER.
"OPEPE". (J FISHER) 131 TONS. FOR PARTINGTON TO LOAD 320 TONS OF COAL FOR EIRE.
"ASTERIA". (Wm ROBERTSON) 319 TONS. FOR PARTINGTON TO LOAD 740 TONS OF COAL FOR EIRE.
"MARSHALSEA". (HINDLEA SHIPPING) 150 TONS. FOR PARTINGTON TO LOAD 320 TONS OF COAL FOR FREMINGTON.
"DIANA.V". (H VAN DIR EB) 209 TONS. FOR MANCHESTER WITH 300 TONS OF TIMBER FROM KALMAR.
"IBERIA". (SWEDISH LLOYD) 790 TONS. FROM GOTHENBURG WITH 750 TONS OF FELSPAR, PAPER, HARDBOARDS, BOXBOARDS, PLYWOOD, TIMBER ETC FOR MANCHESTER.
"WELLIN". (Wm NEUMANN) 695 TONS. FROM DINGLE TO MODE WHEEL OIL WHARF WITH OIL

21
PILOTAGE TARIFF 1956 - 1990

During these years the Manchester Pilots' Association concentrated on steadily improving all aspects of the pilots' working system, although the Pilotage tariff was always inextricably linked with any alterations in the aforementioned systems. The Port of Manchester Authority was not alone in being beset with the diverse problems posed within their Pilot Service. Many pilot services throughout the United Kingdom were dissatisfied with their conditions and continually sought negotiations locally, for an improvement. It was a most unsatisfactory situation; there was no real co-operation between the various pilot services - no exchange of ideas - and certainly no united front to present to Pilotage Authorities and/or Shipowners. What was really needed was a representation of pilots on a national level, but in 1956 that was impossible to achieve.

Appeals were constantly being made from all parties concerned with pilotage, for the Government to set up a committee to investigate and establish a basis for the earnings of pilots in the United Kingdom. Such a committee was duly formed, and in May 1957 a report and recommendations of that committee, under the Chairmanship of Sir Robert Letch, on the earnings of all United Kingdom Pilots was published (see Appendix VI). The Letch Report, as it became known, was the criterion for all future negotiations on pilots' earnings and a constant thorn in the side of all shipowners. It superseded the Ministry of Trade Enquiries. The Letch Committee met every three years but only when pilotage matters were on a National Level. Their findings appertaining to Pilotage Rates were final - there was no provision for an appeal.

Courtesy Captain P Dunbavand
1976
MV "Monass Queen" GRT: 2998; L. 347'; B. 56'
The fastest vessel capable of making a record-breaking transit from Eastham to Manchester

Courtesy Mrs W Yates Collection
1897
Probably the slowest vessel to make a transit from Eastham to Manchester

A PILOT'S MONTHLY EARNINGS JANUARY 1961
Mr D A Clulow. Pilot 2nd Class.

A PILOT'S MOMTHLY EARNINGS JANUARY 1961

Mr. D.A. CLULOW. PILOT 2nd CLASS.

DATE OF SERVICE		VESSEL	AMOUNT £	s.	d.	TRAVELLING EXPENSES £	s.	d.	
Jan	1	Vacuum Pioneer	19	7	10		12	6	BARTON-DK-BERTH – EA
	4	Jade	12	14	5		12	6	EASTHAM – PARTINGTO
	5	Rondo	7	6	5				ELLS. PORT – EASTHA
	6	Britannia 7	8	14	7		12	6	IRLAM C.W.S. – EASTHA
	10	Guinness	15	6	2		12	6	MANCHESTER – EASTH
	11/12	Willem Cornelis	8	2	5		12	6	EASTHAM – MANCHES
	13/16	Wiedau	37	3	5		12	6	MANCHESTER – EASTHA
	17	Pointsman	8	5	4		12	6	PARTINGTON – EASTH
	20	Grazinella	5	7	8				BOWATERS – EASTHA
	24	Irish Heather	13	8	0		12	6	EASTHAM – PARTINGTO
	18	Ulefoss	7	19	9	1	5	0	MANCHESTER – EASTHA
	25	Valeria	10	0	7		12	6	MANCHESTER – EASTH
	27	Marwestad	3	19	11				CANCELLED
	27	– " –	5	6	6				EASTHAM – STANLOW
	31	Maritrapa	9	7	7		12	6	EASTHAM – MANCHES
	30	Somme	6	8	8				RUNCORN – EASTHA
	8	Britannia 7	9	4	4		12	6	MODEWHEEL – EASTHA
									17 SERVICES
			188	3	7	8	2	6	
Dec	29	Elmol	1	6	7	-	-	-	Overcredited in Dec per Am.
			186	17	0	8	2	6	TIME ON BOARD 70HRS

PARTICULARS OF PAYMENT

POOLED	£	s.	d.
FEES*	117	18	5
Travelling Expenses	8	2	6
Deductions	126	.	11.
Contributions to M.S.C. Pilots Association			
Assurance Scheme 3. 0. 0			
Less :			
Paid on Account ... 45. 0. 0			
....	48	.	.
	78	-	11
*After deductions for :			
Leave......................(days)			
Sick Leave ....(days)			

In line with the Letch Report recommendations that Pilotage Rates should reflect any increases granted by the National Maritime Board to its sea-going officers, the Manchester Pilotage Rates were adjusted as follows:

Date Commenced	% Increase on Basic Tariff	NMB % Increase	Total Increase
Nov 1957	17½%	7½%	25%
Jan 1959	12%	5%	17%
Dec 1960	23%	11%	34%
May 1961	5%	4%	9%
Oct 1962	8%	5%	13%
June 1963	10%	8%	18%

On a lighter note, in 1957 a new charge was introduced into the Pilotage Dues: "If a pilot has been ordered to attend a vessel entering the Pilotage District at Eastham on a specified tide, and does in fact attend at Eastham for the purpose of boarding such a vessel, and the vessel does not arrive on that tide, a fee of £1 2s 6d (£1.12½p) shall be payable".

The charge was quaintly named a Disappointment Fee, but one can only guess at just how disappointed a pilot would be at not having to leave the confines of a warm bed at 0300 hrs to board a vessel bound for Manchester on a wet, windy and freezing winter's morning!

In 1958, after fifty years, the retaining fee for Appropriated Pilots was increased to £200 and again in 1964 it was increased to £300. It stayed at this amount until the Appropriation System was phased out in 1988.

The Manchester Pilot Service had been far from satisfied with their grading in the Letch Reports of 1957 and 1962 (see Appendix VI). Their earnings had exceeded the Letch Report recommended level every year. The Secretary of the Manchester Pilots' Association, Mr H Frith (First Class Pilot) and Mr H Whitehead (First Class Pilot) the pilots' representatives, had initiated negotiations in an attempt to improve the Manchester Pilots' grading, and with Mr Peter Henderson (Solicitor's representative) they met the Chamber of Shipping in London in April 1963. The Chamber of Shipping refused to consider the Manchester Pilots' position in isolation, and further informed them that the Letch Report could only be reviewed if both pilots' unions, the Transport and General Workers Maritime Division and the United Kingdom Pilots' Association applied for a review.

The one very great danger in applying for a review was that the Shipowners Association would welcome this as an opportunity to get rid of the Letch Report, which they had come to regard as something of a millstone around their necks.

During the meeting with the Chamber of Shipping it became apparent to the Manchester Pilots' delegation that the UKPA and certain other Pilotage Districts in the T & GWU would oppose the Manchester Pilots' case, and that there was little hope of the Ministry agreeing to anything that would disturb the Letch Report. The Ministry had already set a precedent by refusing an application for an enquiry from the Hull Pilotage Association on the level of earnings. They had no alternative but to withdraw their application for a review of their earnings in the Letch Report.

The representatives were only too well aware of the significant benefits and important stability the Letch Report had brought to Pilotage earnings along with the high regard which many Pilotage Districts had for the Letch Report, including those districts which did not do as well in their gradings as they might have expected. There was a realisation that if one Pilotage District succeeded in altering the basis of the Letch Report, the agreement would be terminated. There could be no prospect of an agreement amongst Pilotage districts for its substitute. The greatest fear was the probability of the Shipowners refusing to negotiate another such progressive report. To have taken unilateral action in pursuing the Manchester Pilots' claim would have certainly failed and have alienated other Pilotage districts with which they would have to negotiate in the future to achieve any modicum of success when dealing with the Shipowners.

The Manchester Pilot Association directed their efforts into establishing their Pilot Service in as influential a position as possible in the new Maritime Division of the T & GWU (of which they were founder members), so that if the Letch Report was finally reviewed, they would not be dismissed as they were at its inception in 1957. This was, of course, a long-term plan: the immediate priority was for an increase in net earnings which might go some way to redress the pilots' grading grievance. At the Pilotage Committee Meeting held in April 1963, the pilots' representative stated that due to changes in certain areas of piloting on the Ship Canal, especially an increase in night navigation, it constituted a substantial change in the nature of piloting on the Ship Canal within the concept of the Letch Report, and requested a 10% increase on all Pilot Dues to be implemented at once.

The Pilotage Committee reply was predictable. Whilst conceding that there just might be an injustice in the Letch Report grading which they would try to remedy, there were also many other aspects of piloting to settle, and the whole conditions of service must be reviewed. The following is a summary of the procedure recommended by the Pilotage Committee for dealing with these problems:

1 On the assumption that the pilots have been unsuccessful in their approach to the Letch Report signatories for an improvement in their agreed level of earnings, the Authority, the Manchester Steamship Owners' Association and the pilots to accept that a positive and constructive effort must be made to resolve the question of earnings locally (bearing in mind, however, the limitations imposed by the Letch Committee Agreement).

2 As an immediate first step, renewed efforts to be made to remove the exisitng deficit between the actual level and the notional level of earnings which has developed since the last agreement was reached in May 1961. This to be achieved by an uplift in the rates designed to increase the earnings, based on the last 12 months' figures, by 5% (a figure which represents an over-correction, intended as a gesture of goodwill). This was implemented on 25 July 1963.

3 As a second step (to be commenced concurrently with the first) the whole question of the actual level of earnings to be included in the negotiations now taking place on relief at Latchford, night navigation, working arrangements and conditions generally, with a view to deciding whether or not there should be a furhter improvement in earnings within the toleration margin established by the Letch Report. Such improvemnt, if any, might be achieved in various ways and would be dependent on satisfactory and genuine understanding being reached on the issues under discussion, including the steps to be taken to ensure continued and further co-operation by all concerned in improving transit times and eliminating delays to navigation.

4 Because of their close interest in many of the issues to be considered, the Helmsmen whenever possible to be brought into the negotiations from the earliest stage. This was a completely new innovation and received with some displeasure by certain Manchester Pilots.

An increase of 15% on all Pilotage Dues was confirmed in October 1963.

Pilotage Tariff increases continued to proliferate, for one reason or another, over the forthcoming years. Every increase, as ever, was hotly contested by the Pilotage Committee and/or Manchester Steamship Owners Association. It is a pleasure to record that the days of long protracted negotiations had long since passed. In 1968, the surcharge levied on the basic charges of the Pilot Tariff had reached 61.8% and on 4 September of that year it was thought desirable that the Schedule of Charges for Pilotage and Helmsmens' services, incorporating this surcharge on the basic rate, should be published: (see Appendix VI Volume I)

The steady decline of world-wide merchant shipping brought about a similar decline in Pilotage Revenue throughout the United Kingdom. The Manchester Pilot Service was at a greater disadvantage than other pilotage Districts, not just because of the decline in shipping using the Port of Manchester - which had resulted in the port ceasing to be recognised as a major port in the United Kingdom, but because pilotage was by law not compulsory in the Manchester Ship Canal.

Ship owners and agents had begun to actively encourage the Masters of their vessels to dispense with the services of a pilot in the Manchester Ship Canal, irrespective of the inherent dangers this situation posed.

This twin curtailment of revenue, plus the new phenomenon called "inflation", seriously eroded the value of their earnings and the small percentage increase on the Pilotage Tariff every year to compensate for inflation could not possibly hope to keep pace with their rapidly declining earnings. The reduction in licences could only be achieved by natural wastage, ie retirements and deaths whilst in service, for in those days such phrases as early retirement, enhanced pensions or golden handshakes were not in the vocabulary of the self-employed. Between 1970 and 1980 the Manchester Pilot Service was reduced by natural wastage from 89 pilots to 72 pilots. It was not enough. On 1 July 1980 the Letch Committee published a new National Agreement on the Earnings of Pilots (see Appendix VII). It had no effect on the earnings of the Manchester Pilots.

Substantial discrepancies still arose in their earnings; in 1983 their net earnings decreased by £1,500 and again in 1984 they decreased a further £1,300 per pilot.

An article appeared in the *Times* newspaper on 7 November 1984:

WILL THATCHER TRIM THE PILOTS' SAILS?

Trinity House, the ancient body which has for more than 450 years supervised approaches to Britain's shores, will soon have to face the biggest shake-up in its long and distinguished history.
Along with 39 other pilotage authorities around the country, Trinity House provides the back-up service which enables Britain's 1,373 working pilots to guide ships of all shapes, sizes and nationalities safely into harbour. It is a job of which the pilots themselves are intensely proud and fiercely protective. But shipowners who have to foot the £43m annual bill say that this service is too expensive, over-manned and often unnecessary.

The Government has its own interest. Not only is it keen to keep British ports attractive to international shipping, but it seems in the archaic customs and practices of the pilots a ripe target for deregulation.

In the next two weeks the Transport Secretary, Nicholas Ridley, is to produce his department's proposals in a Green Paper. There is intensive interest in Whitehall as to what form these will take. Earlier this year it was expected that Ridley, one of the Government's most ardent advocates of deregulation, would advance swingeing changes. But faced with both the daunting complexities of the pilotage business and the Prime Minister's reluctance to fight another major battle during the miners' strike, it is thought that he may now be more cautious.

Two Cabinet committees, chaired by Minister without Portfolio Lord Young, are examining the whole area of deregulation and competition policy in the run-up to the spring budget. But as Mr Ridley is already discovering through the reception to his Bill on buses, deregulation has few immediate political attractions. In tackling the pilots he risks antagonising a highly vocal group of mainly Conservative supporters.

The pilot's job is essential and responsible. He is the man with expert local knowledge who guides all ships, apart from local vessels under 3,500 tons, into harbour, and if anything goes wrong, it is usually the pilot who carries the can. Experienced pilots with 20 years' service can count on the fingers of one hand the times a master has questioned their decision.

Most pilots are old merchant seamen up from the ranks, and as a body are tough, disciplined and dedicated to their craft. They are also often very awkward and argumentative, as shipowners and the Government have

A PILOT'S MONTHLY EARNINGS DECEMBER 1987
Mr D A CLULOW - PILOT FIRST CLASS

PILOT FIRST CLASS.

VESSEL	REFERENCE	DATE	EARNINGS	TRAVEL EXPENSES
LA PRADERA	A04622	2 DEC	213.99	EASTHAM - STANLOW
BAKCHISARAY	A04722	3 DEC	214.08	1 LATCHFORD - EASTHAM
STELLA ORICN	A04723	6 DEC	219.01	EASTHAM - RUNCORN
KAY L	A04747	12 DEC	214.08	1 PARTINGTON - EASTHAM
GONGORA	A04761	13 DEC	569.26	1 LATCHFORD - EASTHAM
PICO RUIVO	A04792	15 DEC	118.94	STANLOW - EASTHAM
LITZEN	A04868	19 NOV	179.13CR	2 MANCHESTER - LATCHFORD
LITZEN	A04871	19 NOV	179.13	2 " "
SAN BARTOLOM	A04919	23 DEC	339.96	1 PARTINGTON - EASTHAM
A THERESA	A05002	25 DEC	214.08	EASTHAM - RUNCORN
NORDLAND	A05003	26 DEC	238.19	1 PARTINGTON - EASTHAM
		TOTALS	2341.59	11 SERVICES
				5 TOTAL TIME ON BOARD
				32HRS

PILOTAGE FEES

POOLED

PARTICULARS OF PAYMENT

FEES • for the month of DECEMBER	1563	27
Travelling Expenses	30	70
Payment on account		
Choice Pilotage Fee		
Deductions		
Payment on account		
Insurance Premium		
M.S.C. Pilots' Association	19	00
General Purpose Fund		
Sickness and Accident Insurance	9	15
	1565	82

• After deductions for:

Leave .... (days)

Sick Leave .... (days)

discovered. A few lines of doggerel in the current issue of the Trinity House magazine paint an accurate portrait:

"Afloat, he's on firm ground: it is his decision
How best to ride the tides with deft precision:
Honest in his craft and proud of his ability
The pilot does not know - or show - humility".

For centuries pilots have been almost literally a law unto themselves, and it was only in 1913 that they were subject to any regulation at all. Even now they remain proudly self-employed with average earnings of some £20,000 a year. But over the years they have become enmeshed in a web of legislation and bye-laws administered by a small army of bureaucrats that the best brains in Whitehall are finding hard to untangle.

"The administration of pilotage defies belief", says Stuart Conacher of the General Council of British shipping, the shipowners' trade association. "There are 88 pilotage districts and 40 pilotage authorities, each with their own set of bye-laws, regulations and scale of charges".

What makes the situation even more complex is that responsibility for pilotage does not rest with the pilotage authority. Trinity House, for example, merely provides the boats and the shore stations from which the pilots work. The ports, the shipowners and in some cases the local authority, also have a finger in the pie. On top of the whole edifice sits a quango in the shape of the Pilotage Commission, created in 1980 and which so far, through no fault of its own, has made little progress in sorting out the mess.
The shipowners acknowledge the need for the service, but at the same time complain loudly about bearing the cost of a service, which, they argue, is lavishly overstaffed and which has failed to change with the times. "Over the last 20 years", says John Callen, chairman of the Pilotage Commission, "there have been dramatic changes in the business: a drastic decline in English merchant shipping, the growth of North Sea oil, containerisation and a closer alignment of the UK with the Common Market. But while the ports have adjusted to these changes, the pilots have not".

An examination of the official statistics tend to support the shipowners' contention that in many ports, pilots are underworked and overpaid. Last year, for example, each of the 53 Southampton pilots, whose net earnings were £19,994 apiece, did an average of 2.9 jobs a week, while the three pilots at the Scottish port of Peterhead handled 50 ships apiece a week for an annual salary of £23,279.

The pilots do not dispute these figures and agree that they are comparatively well paid. "But", says Neil Walker, chairman of the UK Pilots' Association, "if you want a Rolls-Royce service you have got to pay for it. Each of my jobs takes me 16 hours, with waiting and travelling time, and I'm on call 24 hours a day".

Both pilots and shipowners agree that there is scope for rationalization and that in the process several hundred pilots may have to hang up their oilskins. The real question is: how many and at what cost? Two years ago the merchant bankers Samuel Montagu were commissioned to study the problem. they came up with a scheme that involved paying off up to 600 pilots - 45% of the total - with handouts of up to £105,000 per man.

The overall cost was £43 million - just about what it costs to run the service for a single year. The shipowners thought this far too generous, so the Montagu scheme remained on the shelf and the problem was handed back to the Government.

Just how the Department of Transport will tackle the redundancy question remains unknown, but it is suggested that Whitehall is trying to simplify the whole field. The obvious solution would be to strip Trinity House and the other pilotage authorities of their responsibilites and hand the job to the ports. It is a move that would be welcomed by the shipowners but fiercely resisted by the pilots.

The following three years did see a mini revival in their fortunes due to two reasons. There was a slight increase in traffic using the Ship Canal and secondly and more significantly, there was a continuance of the reduction in pilots holding a Licence. In 1987 the strength of the Manchester Pilot Service had decreased to 58 men. In that same year of 1987, the old Manchester Ship Canal Company relinquished its control over the Ship Canal and all its ancillary departments to a development company. The wind of change that had been blowing so fitfully was about to become a hurricane.

Since 1980 the United Kingdom Pilots' Association, in conjunction with the United Kingdom Pilots' National Pension Fund, had been pursuing all avenues to implement a National Early Retirement Scheme incorporating all the enhancements that such schemes contain. The Manchester Pilot Service had, from the very onset of these negotiations, been the prime movers behind such a scheme. The negotiations had been painfully protracted, frustrating and demoralising. Seemingly interminable meetings and proposals had ended in disappointment and disillusionment and it appeared that no scheme could be found that would be equitable to all pilotage districts, the main prerequisite for an Early Retirement Scheme.

These negotiations had not gone unheeded by the development company who now owned the Manchester Ship Canal Company. In the cut and thrust of today's business conglomerates, accountants brook no arguments. The leisurely atmosphere of negotiations, coupled with an exchange of the ideas so prevalent in yesteryears, no longer existed. A fait accompli is presented to one party which is not negotiable. The Manchester Pilot Service found themselves in just such a "Might is Right" situation on 1 December 1988, when the Manchester Ship Canal Company placed before the pilots' representatives the following solution to all the contentious issues and problems appertaining to the Pilot Service in the Manchester Ship Canal.

"The Manchester Ship Canal Company were prepared to advance the money to fund and implement an Early Retirement Scheme on the following basis:

a) The Pilot Service to be reduced from 58 to 33 pilots.
b) A contract for services to be signed by all pilots agreeing to a fixed income of £2,000 gross per month.
c) All additional revenue generated from Pilotage Services to be used in repaying the money made available by the Canal Company to initiate the Early Retirement Scheme.
d) A review of the contract for services would take place on 1 October 1988 and 1 April 1989.
e) All pilots to remain self-employed.
f) The Early Retirement Scheme to be implemented on 1 March 1988. the offer would not be repeated, nor was it negotiable".

Courtesy of Mrs J J Pierpoint
1986
The once proud and prestigious No 9 Dock

Courtesy of Mrs J J Pierpoint
1986
No 8 Dock laid waste. The MSC Dock Office is the white building at the top of the dock. Manchester Liners Head Office is the tallest building on the left.

Courtesy Mrs J J Pierpoint
1985
A view of the derelict docks in Manchester. Even Hermann Goering's Luftwaffen did not achieve this in five years of war.

Courtesy Mrs J J Pierpoint
1985
A demolished No 7 Dock.

Courtesy of John Mills Photo, Liverpool
1989
The Dock System
A depressing view of a once great port.
At the top right of the picture the three Pomona docks also being re-developed.

The speed at which the Early Retirement Scheme had been introduced by the Manchester Ship Canal Company, considering the long years of deliberations between the UKPA and the UKPNPF, came as a considerable surprise to the Manchester Pilot Service, albeit a most pleasant one to the retirees. At the same time, the UKPNPF had at long last produced a most satisfactory pension scheme for all pilots who wished to accept early retirement, whereby they lost none of their entitlements and received a suitably enhanced pension equal to that which they would have received had they continued to work until they were 65 years old. The opportunity and the offer to accept early retirement was too good to refuse, and consequently on 1 March 1988 the Early Retirement Scheme was implemented.

From that date the Manchester Ship Canal Pilot Service became a limited company and was renamed the Manchester Pilots Ltd. The Manchester Pilotage Committee was renamed the Manchester Pilots Liaison Committee.

Courtesy of the MSC Co.
1980's
Approaching Latchford Locks.
Note third tug standing by to assist vessel into lock.

1980
The age of the container service. "Manchester Concord" outward bound for Canada entering Modewheel Locks.

22

THE LARGEST WORKING ROTA IN THE HISTORY OF THE MANCHESTER SHIP CANAL PILOTS' SERVICE

The list was compiled on 1st January 1971 and the names are placed in order of seniority.

NAME	PLACE OF RESIDENCE
G D YOUNG	WIRRAL
W WALKER	RUNCORN
J A PATTERSON	WIRRAL
R D RICHARDSON	NORTH WALES
A L SHEPHERD	WIRRAL
W H ROBERTS	WIRRAL
H WHITEHEAD	MANCHESTER
E CLARE	WARRINGTON
W YATES	FRODSHAM
G CARTWRIGHT	WIRRAL
R T GREEN	WIRRAL
W C MCINTOSH	WIRRAL
H H HARRINGTON	WIRRAL
J H WARREN	WIRRAL
H CLUGSTON	LIVERPOOL
S P JONES	LIVERPOOL
A GREEN	WIRRAL
P ONION	WIRRAL

J H LAW	WARRINGTON
G F ASHWORTH	ROSSENDALE
M E WARREN	WIRRAL
A D SHENTON	WARRINGTON
P K RALI	WIRRAL
H FRITH	MANCHESTER
P RULE	WIRRAL
H DAVIES	MANCHESTER
W MADDOCKS	WIRRAL
P BRIDGES	WIRRAL
L DAVIES	LIVERPOOL
J WAINWRIGHT	CHESTER
V FRY	CHESTER
D SCHOLES	WARRINGTON
E JONES	CULCHETH
R YEWDALE	MANCHESTER
P D COLES	MANCHESTER
A JONES	LIVERPOOL
F PENRICE	WARRINGTON
R CASHIN	WIRRAL
J E MORRIS	WIRRAL
I COLQUHOUN	WARRINGTON
L G VOLUME	MANCHESTER
G W SCULLY	WIRRAL
C E BOWELL	WIRRAL
A E GLEESON	LIVERPOOL
P A BARRACLOUGH	WIRRAL
J T PRITCHARD	LIVERPOOL
C M BROOM	CHESTER
N T SIGLEY	WIRRAL
D J ARMITAGE	WIRRAL
H H HIGNETT	WIRRAL
J M CLARKE	WARRINGTON
D A CLULOW	WIRRAL
V B POWNALL	WARRINGTON
D J FOSTER	MANCHESTER
J E RUSSELL	LIVERPOOL
J S EMBERTON	WIRRAL
R A GOLSBY	WIRRAL
R J BALL	FRODSHAM
M J DAVIES	WIRRAL
J GANNICLIFFE	LIVERPOOL

F K APPLETON	LIVERPOOL
J T KEYS	WIRRAL
D NECK	WIRRAL
G SMITH	WIRRAL
B WOOD	WIRRAL
M LIGHTFOOT	WARRINGTON
G GRAY	WIRRAL
R FOULKES	BLACKBURN
I C MCINNON	WIRRAL
B BELL	CHESTER
R S BOYLES	WIRRAL
P F WOODHEAD	WIRRAL
B WICHESTER	LIVERPOOL
W HOPKINS	WARRINGTON
J LAW	WARRINGTON
D HOPKINSON	WIRRAL
P BAINES	WARRINGTON
D ANDREWS	LYMM
D WILLIAMS	NORTH WALES

The Manchester Pilotage Committee granted 90 Licences on 1st September 1970, but only 84 were taken up in that licensing year. Shipping was beginning to decline even then in the Ship Canal.

Courtesy Captain P Dunbavand
1972 "Manchester Concorde" Latchford Locks
GRT 11,899; L. 529'; B. 63' 09"

When the canal was built they never envisaged vessels of this size entering the canal. On the left the M S C heavy lift crane is changing the small lock gates: hence the two tugs have to be lifted up first as the extreme length and breadth of the vessel prevents them all entering into one lock.

23
THE PILOT SERVICE 1960 - 1990

T & GWU
APRIL, 1974
TOL/HF/MH/436/Z3

MARINE PILOTAGE BRANCH

RELATIONSHIP OF THE PILOT TO THE MASTER, THE SHIPOWNER AND THE PORT

To the Master

Following the discussion of the draft section of the SCOP Report on March 22nd, and accepting that it was generally agreed that SCOP should not attempt to spell out the relationship between the Master and the pilot in a new Act, the Branch nevertheless feel that every effort should be made to describe the present situation as accurately as possible and the following extract from the Report of the Royal Canadian Commission on Pilotage, based on the definition of the term "pilot" found in S. 742 of the Merchant Shipping Act, 1894, ie "means any person not belonging to a ship who has the conduct thereof", might be of some assistance.

"...Therefore, to be a pilot as defined in the Act is not a question of qualification, profession, certificate or licence; it is the fact of actually navigating a vessel (and not of being capable or authorised to navigate a vessel). A pilot, whether licensed or not, ceases to be a "pilot" when, for any reason, he is superseded by the Master or by the person in command. Similarly, if anyone is merely used as an adviser and is not entrusted with the navigation of the ship, he is not the pilot of that ship. Therefore, the general provisions concerning pilots do not apply to him under such circumstances".

SHIPS OF TODAY

1990
"*Atria*" GRT: 500 L. 252'; B. 26'
Cargo of coal in containers for Northern Ireland. A regular trader.

1990
"*Robert*" GRT: 1599 L. 321'; B. 43'
Both Vessels in Eastham Channel

The Report also compares the <u>factual</u> situation with the above statutory definition of "pilot" in the following terms.

"...This factual situation which corresponds to the legal defintion of "pilot" is, in fact, the only realistic solution because, if pilots were used merely as advisers, navigation would be very hazardous and, at times, it would be impossible to proceed safely. For instance, there is no time for advice, consultation and deliberation when a supertanker is brought into the Courtenay Bay approach channel (St John NB) or when a larger ship is brought down from Fraser Mills through the New Westminster Railway Bridge.

A further statement by Sir John Inskip, confirmed by Messrs Batesons & Co., Solicitors, might also help to illustrate the position:

"<u>Interference with Pilot's Discretion</u>

Pilots must not submit to pressure at any time, when this is in conflict with their judgement and their discretion holds good, whether their vessel is supplied with searchlights or any other aids to navigation.

It would avail a Pilot nothing to plead that "He was told to get his ship there by a certain time", or "that his vessel was supplied with searchlights", or "that the Master persisted", if damage resulted from his navigation at a time when such influence was against his judgement.

THE "PILOT", NOT THE "MASTER" OR ANY OTHER PERSON, has the LAST word, and the LAW is on his side".

To achieve the maximum accuracy in describing the present relationship of the pilot to the Master, the Branch submit that the terminology used should, in the Section and throughout the Report, be carefully considered in the light of the above and other quoted opinions, and the following various suggestions are made to this end.

1 The pilot is considered to be in charge of the navigation of the vessel and the Master remains in command.

2 The pilot is responsible for the navigation of the vessel, the Master is answerable for the navigation of the vessel.

3 The description of the pilot as an adviser to the Master should be avoided.

4 The statement that quotes: "Most people think that there are not many Masters in this country who would doubt that, in a situation of emergency, they can take over from a pilot" should be reconsidered. Whilst this may be a sincere conviction on the part of some people, it is too general to be accurate in that it ignores the variety of skills and exactitude required between Districts and that approximately two-thirds of ships piloted in the UK are of foreign registry.

Since May 1957 when the first national report and recommendations for the United Kingdom Pilotage - the Letch Report as it was to become known - was published (see Appendix VI) the grading of the Manchester Pilot Service, in that table of thirty-two major Pilotage Districts, had always been regarded by the Manchester Pilot Service as a grave injustice. The years between 1960 and 1970 became a decade of intensive activity, with meetings between the Manchester Pilots' Association and the Manchester Pilotage Committee regarding their working system and Pilotage Tariff at an unprecedented level. On a National level meetings continued to be held with the United Kingdom Pilotage Authority and "ad hoc" committees proliferated at random. In all these diverse meetings the attempts by the representatives of the Pilot Association to rectify their position in the Letch report had proved singularly unsuccessful, both nationally and locally. The Shipowners and Pilotage Authority were ever mindful that any change in the grading for any Pilotage District would inevitably lead to enhanced earnings - and this they were determined to prevent. The Manchester grading was never changed.

In 1963 the Manchester Pilotage Committee produced a report on what in their considered opinion were the current problems besetting the Manchester Pilot Service, and put forward certain proposals to remedy them. Both the views and recommendations of the Pilotage Committee were found to be unsatisfactory to the Pilots' Association. Nevertheless, the report itself had significantly shown that the Pilotage Committee was prepared to consider the pilots' views and it represented a well-intentioned attempt to grapple with the problems which were bedevilling the Pilot Service. The report did not conceal the Committee's desire for a further increase in night navigation through to the Manchester Docks, or their wish for a realistic partnership with the Pilot Service in the best interests of mutual concern, the Port of Manchester. This latter process inevitably suffered setbacks and disappointments due to the attitude of some Pilotage Committee members and certain Manchester Pilots, which left much to be desired.

On the night navigation aspect, the Pilotage Committee made it quite clear that it was not, and never could be, their intention to encroach on the discretion

Manchester Ship Canal. Tuesday 3rd May 1955. A photograph from railway bridge No. 35 Latchford - former L & NWR Liverpool Lime Street to Manchester London Road - of a ship canal helmsman Mr. V. Fry - on open bridge, and pilot Mr. H. Scott about to enter Latchford Locks, inward bound

of the Pilots to navigate at night with any vessel. What they hoped for was that the Pilots would objectively and sensibly consider each vessel and the prevailing weather conditions and act accordingly in a prudent and seamanlike manner. On the other hand, what the Pilots wanted was the utmost financial benefit and a re-grading in the Letch Report under Paragraph 6 (ii). The inherent danger was that, as in the Eastham to Ince section of the Ship Canal, where night navigation had been established - due to the installation of a lighting system by the Shell Oil Company - the Pilots would receive no recognition financially or otherwise for this new service.

One of the most distressing aspects of this period (although hardly surprising looking back through the history of the Manchester Pilot Service) was the tendency of some individual Pilots to show their disagreement with the policies pursued by their Association, by resigning from the Association. It was significant that a large number of ex-representatives who were senior Pilots, no longer took any part or gave any support to their Association's negotiations. They were the very Pilots whose experience and constructive advice could have been invaluable to the Association. These individuals had no sense of allegiance to their Service, nor were they concerned one iota for the future of their fellow Pilots. As selfish individuals they craved nothing more than to perform as few pilotage duties as possible for the most financial return, in an unchanged working system in order to see them through the few remaining years before their retirement.

The Manchester Pilot Service was the only Pilotage District in the United Kingdom without 100% membership of their Association. After nearly 70 years the Pilot Service could still not display a united front, but this had always been their inherent weakness. By 1968 the complement of the Pilot Service had risen from 72 Pilots in 1960 to 84 Pilots, and a twenty-four hour pilotage had been established.

In that same year a further comprehensive study, in conjunction with the Pilots' Association, had been conducted by the Pilotage Committee into the future of the Pilot Service. The findings of this report were prepared, published and placed before the Pilots' Association. An agreement was eventually concluded on the many facets of this report, which resulted in an increase in the Pilotage Tariff of 14%, coupled with an increase in the complement of Pilots to 90. Little did the negotiating parties realise they were witnessing for the very last time an increase in the complement of Pilots in the Port of Manchester.

The decade of the 1970s saw the commencement of the remorseless, but inevitable, decline of the Port of Manchester as a major port. Its antiquated locks, docks, cargo handling equipment and the length of the Pilotage - in

Courtesy John Mills Photography, Liverpool
1989
No's 6 - 7 - 8 Docks
Far lower right in picture the white circle in the water was the pivotal base for the Trafford Road railway bridge now installed across No 9 Dock. The white circles in the yacht marina (No 6 dock) are made by the aeration pumps re-oxygenizing the water. This system to clarify the water is installed throughout the dock system. Compare this picture with the scene in 1960, earlier in this volume.

time as well as in distance from sea to Manchester Docks - all combined to make it less and less attractive and more and more expensive for a shipowner to bring his vessels and their cargoes to Manchester. In the fast modernisation of shipping, where quick and efficient turnrounds of vessels were of paramount importance, the Port of Manchester was losing its competitiveness. It was becoming faster and cheaper to discharge or load a vessel in Liverpool or any other port in the United Kingdom by using the network of motorways to convey their containerised cargoes, rather than transit the Ship Canal.

As early as 1976 there was concern expressed whether the Manchester Pilot Service would still be in existence in ten years' time. Mr D A Clulow (the author) produced a radical treatise for the future of the Pilot Service during that year, which contained many salient points that have now been incorporated into the present working system of the service in 1990. More importantly, it introduced the idea of an Early Retirement Scheme for the very first time (see Appendix No XIV). This dissertation was acknowledged by the Pilotage Committee and the Helmsmen's Association, but no such acknowledgement was forthcoming from the committee of the Pilots' Association, not even the courtesy of a letter acknowledging the receipt of same. It was never discussed at a General meeting of the Pilots' Association or any "ad hoc" committee so beloved of the Association at that time.

Because of this monumental lack of interest shown by the Association's committee - for reasons the Author has never been able to discover - it was, to coin a well worn phrase at Pilotage Committee, allowed to "lie on the table" and be forgotten. In June 1977 the last Helmsman, Mr G Kitchen - under the auspices of the the old Manchester Ship Canal company - was examined and promoted to Second Class Pilot, becoming a First Class Pilot in 1980. The decline of the Port of Manchester was now rapidly escalating, and by 1985 all the regular major shipping lines - T and J Brocklebank, F C Stricks, T and J Harrisons, Furness Withy, Clan Line and even the Manchester Liners to name a few - had deserted the Port of Manchester. The decline in tonnage was mirrored by the number of pilots required to provide an efficient service and a financially lucrative one. By 1987 the complement of the Pilot Service had been reduced by natural wastage to 58 men and yet it was still grossly overmanned.

The Manchester Pilotage Bye-laws stated that a pilot must serve until he is 65 years old before he qualifies for a full pension. The pilots with the exception of the 8 senior men were all under the age of 60 years and the only way to overcome this serious overmanning situation was by an enhanced Early Retirement Scheme. Compulsory redundancies could never be considered or implemented due to the pilots' self-employed status. Over the past 10 years many schemes had been promoted for an early retirement of pilots but all had financial obstacles to scale and none came to a successful conclusion. Nationally a financial framework was being put together on which to implement an Early Retirement Scheme for all the United Kingdom Pilots. Then in 1987 came a new threat to the Manchester Pilots' livelihood.

SHIPS OF TODAY

1996
"Leicester Brook" GRT: 1599 L. 305′; B. 43′
Entering Eastham Lock

1996
"Thuntank" GRT: 1670 L. 252′; B.26′
In Eastham Channel

In that year the first intimation came that the new owners of the Ship Canal were firmly committing themselves to the concept of a "Through Pilotage". This was from within the limits Bar Light Vessel/Mersy Bay to/from any berth within the Manchester Pilotage District. This situation had previously existed in 1895, the major difference being, in the 1987 system, there would be only one Pilotage Authority and only one Pilotage service for both Liverpool and Manchester Pilotage Districts.

The Ship Canal Company were totally unconcerned if they were to be the Competent Harbour Authority for Pilotage Administration or the Mersey Docks and Harbour Board. They looked upon it as merely an exercise for an immense saving of administration costs and in their world of acquiring declining businesses, a natural progressive step towards productivity. It was an ill-prepared and an ill-conceived project. Their advisers to a large extent were in the form of Harbour Masters in the Ship Canal, with dubious limited knowledge relating to ship handling in restricted waters, let alone in fast-flowing rivers. The Harbour Masters were equally ignorant of the immense impracticabilities that a dual pilotage would present. They were but lackeys to their masters calling.

The Pilots' Association immediately realised that the Ship Canal Company would brook little or no argument in the negotiations for pilotage reorganisation. They wisely adopted a step-by-step approach to all negotiations in an attempt to prevent the loss of all autonomy as a Pilot Service - or even the loss of the Pilot Service itself. In the November of 1987, with a suddenness that was both refreshing as it was remarkable, the United Kingdom Pilots' National Pension Fund and the Ship Canal Company made funds available to implement an enhanced Early Retirement Scheme, to commence on 29 February 1988. On that day 18 Pilots retired and three months later on 1 June a further 6 Pilots accepted early retirement, leaving a complement of 33 men.

On 1 June 1988, the Manchester Ship Canal Pilots' Association ceased to exist and all the functions and duties of same, together with all the funds and benefits, were transferred to the newly established Manchester Pilots Limited.

On 1 October 1988, a contract for pilots to provide services as self-employed contractors was drawn up between the Manchester Ship Canal Company (The Competent Harbour Authority) and the Manchester Pilots Limited (Appendix IX).

1990
No 6 Dock

1990
Top of No 6 Dock

24

THE FINAL PILOTAGE TARIFF: 1990

At the General Meeting of the Manchester Pilots Ltd, held on 20th September 1989 at the Eastham Conference Room, it was reported by the Pilots' representatives that during the past 18 months the money advanced by the Manchester Ship Canal Company to fund the Early Retirement Scheme had been fully repaid by the excess Pilotage Services revenue. Unfortunately, there had been a great reluctance by the Manchester Ship Canal Company to agree to a review of the contract of services, both in October 1988 and in April 1989, and it had become very apparent that the Manchester Ship Canal Company were not prepared to countenance any increase in pilots' earnings.

With the dawning of a new era of pilotage in the Manchester Ship Canal in March 1988, it was fervently hoped that an atmosphere of mutual trust, co-operation and harmony would be engendered between the pilot service and the Manchester Ship Canal Company. It was the predominant wish of all the pilots that they should never return to the acrimonious feelings that had bedevilled the two committees over the past 90 years. That this harmonious co-existence was not achieved is to their everlasting shame. What little trust, co-operation and harmony may have existed was completely eroded by the Manchester Ship Canal Company's intransigent attitude for a review of the contract of services. On the other hand, it must be acknowledged that the standard of the present day representatives of the Manchester Pilots Ltd left a lot to be desired.

The pilots were appalled and disgusted by the behaviour of the Manchester Ship Canal Company in their breaches of the contract of services which had almost contemptuously forfeited all goodwill from the pilot service. The meeting called for an "all hands" meeting but it was rejected by the committee on the grounds that an "all hands" meeting would really only be appropriate after the 1st October when the pilots' contracts of service would expire, after which time they would not also be in breach of contract. The meeting then requested the Committee to instruct their solicitors to issue and serve a Writ for breach of contract and make a direct approach to the Department of Transport in London.

The Secretary of the Manchester Pilots Ltd (Mr D R Wetherell) who was in attendance, advised the meeting that if the pilots and the Manchester Ship Canal Company could not reach agreement on renewal of the contract for services on the 1st October, the pilots would not be entitled to compensation under Section 28 of the new Pilotage Act. Since the pilots had been offered arrangements by the Canal Company for the provision of their services as authorised pilots, even though those arrangements were not acceptable to the pilots, the offer would still have been made. The frustration of the pilots at being unable to make any significant progress at this meeting came to the surface when various precipitous actions were proposed, from withdrawing their services altogether on the 1st October to issuing more writs.

In an attempt to defuse what was fast becoming a very verbose and volatile meeting, the pilots' representatives proposed to adjourn the meeting to give them every chance to explore every avenue to reach a satisfactory contract for services with the Manchester Ship Canal Company. They were also given an open mandate to approach any person or institution they felt might be of assistance in their deliberations. It was further proposed that they would instruct their solicitors (Lace & Mawer) to investigate the question of issuing a writ against the Manchester Ship Canal Company for breach of contract, and to ascertain the chances of the success of such a writ. The representatives promised the meeting that the actions taken by them would be referred to the Manchester Pilots Liaison Committee in accordance with the rules in the contract for services. These proposals proving satisfactory, the meeting was accordingly closed.

The meeting between the Manchester Ship Canal Company and the Manchester Pilots Ltd to review the contracts for service duly took place on the 1st October 1989 with predictable results. The Manchester Ship Canal Company resolutely refused any change in the contract of services and the representatives of the Manchester Pilots Ltd were left in a quandary as to how to proceed. After a lengthy discussion, it was resolved that the Manchester Pilots Ltd and the M S C Co should place their case before the national body ACAS for arbitration. The Manchester Ship Canal Company agreed that they would abide by any decision reached by ACAS. The date for the arbitration meeting was set for 4 January 1990.

1989

WALKWAY AND CHANNEL CONNECTING NO 7 TO NO 8 DOCK.

Note on the extreme right two Stoddart and Pitt cargo cranes erected as a reminder/ memorial to the great days of shipping and cargo handling that have gone for ever in Manchester.

1989

THE MIDDLE OF NO 7 DOCK

1989
LOOKING DOWN NO 7 DOCK

1989
LOOKING ACROSS NO 7 DOCK TOWARDS NO 8 DOCK

The Manchester Pilots Ltd took a calculated risk in going to arbitration. Firstly, ACAS was renowned for not giving 100% to one side or the other, and secondly, the Chairman of ACAS could be swayed on the day by the arguments of either party; also, the pilots might, by their honesty in presenting their case, do themselves an injustice. The representatives had no choice other than to proceed with the arbitration. The helmsmen had already received a 6% increase in respect of a period of 10 months, being part of the period during which the pilots had not received any increase, and for which the Canal Company were opposing any increase to the pilots. More importantly, it was the pilots' last avenue to achieve any success for any increase in the contract for services.

On 11 January 1990, an "all hands" meeting of the Manchester Pilots Ltd was convened at the Eastham Lodge Golf Club to hear the results of the arbitration meeting with ACAS. Mr J Connolly of the Transport & General Workers' Union requested that the matter of the ACAS arbitration should not be discussed at this meeting lest it be interpreted as any form of endeavour to put pressure on ACAS whilst they were still deliberating the case. It was agreed no discussion would take place.

On 23 January another "all hands" meeting of the Manchester Pilots Ltd was convened. The representatives reported to the meeting that they had that very morning been advised by telephone from London of the result of their claim for a 10.2% increase in their contract for services. The ACAS arbitrator, having due regard to all the arguments of both parties, had awarded the Manchester Pilots Ltd an increase of 6% of their present retainer (£24,000 gross p.a.) back-dated only to the 1st October 1989. The award was of course final. The representatives further stated that four factors led to the award being so low:

a) The award had been back-dated.
b) The representatives had had difficulty convincing the Chairman of the Arbitration Committee that the pilots had not had the 4.5% index-linked increase in 1988.
c) The representatives had considerable difficulty in replying to the Manchester Ship Canal Company's attack on their (the represntatives') case on the basis of hours worked.
d) These difficulties had obviously influenced the Chairman of the arbitration on the day.

All the fears entertained by the T & G W U representative (Mr J Connolly) and largely ignored by the pilots' representatives, had been amply realised; and although the Manchester Pilots Ltd were extremely disappointed with the percentage awarded, they had no alternative but to accept it under the conditions laid down in law to go to arbitration.

Courtesy N Trowler Photo Ltd
SHIPS OF TODAY
1990
MANCHESTER TRADER
Both vessels entering Eastham Channel

1993
GAS TANKER "BECQUER" GRT: 792 L. 286' ;B. 40'

In parallel with all the discussions, the review of the contract for services was a complex and far-reaching negotiation on the future of the Manchester Pilots Ltd. These negotiations continued in the months ahead, but, like so many other futuristic plans over the years for the Manchester Ship Canal Pilot Service, they were again floundering on the rocks of dissent, disagreement and disillusionment. When all avenues for a compatible scheme to amalgamate with the Liverpool Pilot Service had seemingly been exhausted and all negotiations had virtually broken down, the Manchester Ship Canal Company produced their second fait accompli and final tariff to the Manchester Pilots Ltd:

1) The Manchester Pilots Ltd to be reduced from 30 to 19 First Class Pilots.
2) The Helmsmen Service to be discontinued. The present 8 helmsmen to be examined and, if successful, be promoted to Second Class Pilots.
3) A sum between £860,000 and £900,000 to be allocated each year for the contract of service to the Manchester Pilotage Ltd and such other expenses, (transport to and from vessels and the maintenance of the Eastham Pilot Station) incurred in the pursuit of their pilotage duties.
4) A Second Class Pilot should not receive less than three-quarters of the contract for services received by a First Calss Pilot.

The Scheme was to be implemented on the 1st October 1990; it was not negotiable, nor was it to be repeated if it was found unacceptable to the Manchester Pilots Ltd.

There was absolutely no alternative but for the Manchester Pilots Ltd to submit to the conditions laid down by the Manchester Ship Canal Co for their future existence and new contract for services. The failure to accept the terms would have most certainly meant the end of the Manchester Pilots Ltd functioning as an individual entity. They would have been powerless to prevent any move by the Mersey Docks and Harbour Board from taking control of the Manchester Pilots Ltd and consequently the control of their own destiny.

The final tariff was as follows:

a) First Class Pilot: £2,220 gross per month plus £350 per quarter;
b) Second Class Pilot: £1,668 gross per month plus £260 per quarter.

It is interesting to compare these figures with the earnings in 1896 - the first year of a properly constituted Manchester Ship Canal Pilot Service - when Mr Adam Cartwright (No 1 Manchester Ship Canal Pilot Licence) earned the then princely sum of £280 for his pilotage services. Are the present-day pilots any more contented or any happier with their lot than that of their predecessors of long, long ago? I wonder....!!!

1989
LOOKING ACROSS NO 8 DOCK FROM NO 7 DOCK

1989
LOOKING DOWN NO 8 DOCK

1990
LOOKING DOWN THE NO 9 DOCK
The Trafford Road Railway was floated into position in 1989. The last working quay and the container gantries can be seen on the starboard side behind the railway bridge. The container gantries were demolished in 1991.

TOP OF THE NO 8 DOCK
House prices started at £100,000 rising to £250,000 plus

25
THE NEW ERA OF PILOTING

During 1989 the first joint meeting was held with the Liverpool Pilots' Association which laid the foundations for the mutual understanding which they hoped would inevitably develop between the Manchester Pilots Ltd and the Liverpool Pilots' Association in studying the complexity of a joint pilotage system. In November of that year, the representatives of the Manchester Pilots Ltd felt it was appropriate to bring to the notice of all their Pilots the hard and unbending business techniques of the new owners of the Manchester Ship Canal. The respective Pilotage Authorities in the estuary had not included Pilots in their deliberations about radical changes, and whatever emerges for the future in this direction would be, yet again, an ongoing trial of strength and tribulation.

All the bitterness and acrimony, all the resentment and mistrust that had soured so many relationships and negotiations with the old Manchester Port Authority, were about to be activated once more. It appeared as if no lessons had been learnt or heeded from the past. The proposed "through Pilotage" and amalgamation of the Liverpool and Manchester services was the most ill-conceived and hopelessly prepared document ever to be presented to these two services. The lack of any intelligent preparation invested into this scheme only resulted in a dismal failure. Why the Manchester Pilots' representatives ever considered such a hare-brained scheme only they can answer.

Consider the position of both those Pilotage Services at that time. The Liverpool Pilot Service was beset by its own traumatic problems, identical in every way to that which assailed the Manchester Pilots Ltd - ie a considerable reduction in vessels using the Port of Liverpool coinciding with the inevitable overmanning of their Pilot Service. In the glorious hey-day of shipping on the Mersey in the late 1950s and early 1960s the Liverpool Pilot Service was ranked as one of the largest Pilotage Districts in the United Kingdom, having a complement of 188 pilots. Their number had steadily decreased by natural wastage to 130 pilots in 1987. By 1990 their complement was 50 pilots and the Liverpool Pilot Service was deeply embroiled in embittered negotiations with a Pilotage Authority (the Mersey Docks and Harbour Board) who were a far more unreasonable and unrelenting Pilotage Authority than any the Manchester Pilot Service had ever had to contend with. The Liverpool Pilots were fighting to preserve a much cherished heritage of autonomy, held for over 200 years. Their negotiations for an enhanced Early Retirement Scheme to be offered to all pilots over the age of 56 years - to run in conjunction with a new working system based on a complement of 67 pilots - was being strenuously contested at Committee level. To be presented with another problem of amalgamating their Pilotage Service with another ailing Pilotage Service was not high on their list of priorities. A table of reduction in UK pilot numbers can be found in appendix X.

One of the many factors never considered by the Pilotage Authority in Manchester when preparing for a joint estuarial pilotage was the Manchester Pilots' age factor. A number of Liverpool Pilots over 55 years had reluctantly left the service to avoid the necessity for younger pilots to seek transfers to other Pilotage Districts - thus preserving the continuity of their Pilotage Service. If Manchester Pilots were allowed into a combined service over the age of 55 years - about 90% would have been - they would indeed feel justifiably aggrieved. It had been established that an amalgamated service would be achieved by 1st April 1991, but by then only 4 Manchester Pilots would have been below 55 years of age.

Other salient points of paramount importance had failed to be given any consideration:

1) What was to happen to the Manchester Pilots who did not wish to pilot vessels in the Port of Liverpool? Already in December 1989, 19 pilots had indicated their unwillingness to pilot outside the Manchester Ship Canal.
2) What of the Manchester Ship Canal Company's obligations to the Helmsmen's service? Were they to be indiscriminately abandoned? The final ludicrousness of this whole episode was the commencement date for this monumental folly, 1st April 1991, April Fool's Day - ironic indeed: whoever chose such a date must really have had a warped sense of humour.

One can only surmise that the Manchester Pilots' Representatives of that day were not of the quality or acumen they thought themselves to be, to even consider such an unworkable amalgamation.

Courtesy John Mills Photography Liverpool
1988
"WHERE HAVE ALL THE SHIPS GONE? GONE, GONE , FOR EVER"
Manchester and Pomona Docks

Before the time the Manchester Ship Canal had ever been built, it had taken an apprentice in the Liverpool Pilot Service seven years and upwards to train, learn and dedicate himself to gain sufficient knowledge of the intricacies of his Pilotage District - one of the most difficult in the United Kingdom - to enable him to successfully pass an examination for a third-class licence, restricting him to vessels not in excess of 600 net reg tons. Some four years later and two more examinations, he would eventually become a First Class Pilot, a total of eleven years. Many years would pass before that pilot was satisfied he had become proficient enough to pilot vessels of all tonnages - many such tonnages were far in excess of vessels that enter into the Manchester Ship Canal - in all states of tide and prevailing weather conditions. It takes many, many years to reach this pinnacle of ship handling - that is renowned throughout the world - achieved by a Liverpool pilot.

The Manchester Ship Canal Company now expected a man of 56 years of age to achieve this eminence of ship handling in the River Mersey in just 12 short months. It was as irresponsible as it was dangerous. No Manchester pilot is capable of performing the normal duties of a pilot outside the safe confines of the banks of his Ship Canal. He has no tidal ebb or flow to stem; he needs no compass to guide him; he has no concern for lack of water beneath his vessel; neither has he ever had to board a vessel on a dark night by way of a 30-foot pilot ladder from a small pilot launch being tossed about like a cork in a heavy swell and sea. Only years of practice teach a pilot the expertise of boarding or disembarking in such conditions. This art can never be taught from a text-book. One mistake can prove fatal, as it so tragically occurs from time to time in the Liverpool Pilot Service. One can appreciate the Author's - and many pilots' - utter despair as to why the Manchester Pilots' Representatives wasted so much valuable time and energy on such a nonsensical scheme.

Discussions with the Liverpool Pilots' Association continued fitfully throughout the early months of 1990 without any real conviction that a suitable solution would be found for a joint pilotage system. The two negotiating bodies soon realised there were too many unresolvable problems preventing a successful conclusion to their meetings. The Manchester Ship Canal Company's new masters were impatient for an early resolution to their pilotage problems. The Manchester Pilots Ltd, at last sensing this urgency and fearing that the Ship Canal Co. would suddenly foist a totally unsuitable and unacceptable scheme on to them by taking away the right to govern their own affairs or be masters of their own destiny, hurriedly convened meetings with the Manchester Pilotage Liaison Committee to present their scheme for the future of their Pilot Service. The whole scheme for a joint pilotage system with the Liverpool Pilot Service was aborted.

THEY WERE EXPENDABLE
The final muster 1st March 1988

From right to left:
Back Row: Peter Coles, Gordon Smith, Harry Hignett, Peter Rali, Ron Cashin, Ian Colcoquon
Middle Row: Geoff Ashworth, Tony Jones, John Keys, Dave Williams, Rex Yewdall, Derek Clulow, Peter Bridges, Ted Morris
Front Row: Vic Fry, Norman Sigley, Peter Barraclough, Derek Shenton, Don Scholes, Bill Maddocks, Mick Warren

In September 1990 the final document for the future of the Manchester Pilots Ltd was concluded and read as follows:

1) The present complement of pilots to be reduced to 19 pilots.
2) A new scale of earnings.
3) Retain the self-employed status.
4) A new working system.
5) Eight helmsmen to be promoted to Second Class Pilots to bring the complement to 27 pilots.
6) The Helmsmen's Service to be phased out.

All these points were implemented on 1st October 1990.

Fifty-eight licences were originally issued by the Manchester Ship Canal Authority in August 1896, for the pilotage year 1896-1897 - this number excluding any licences granted to the Liverpool River Pilots. In the pilotage year for 1988-1989, prior to the reformation of the Manchester Pilot Service, exactly the same number of licences were issued.

The Final Pilots' Rota on 1st October 1990 reads as follows:

NAME	PLACE OF RESIDENCE
G Andrews	Alvanley
J Astles	Ruthin
J P E Baines	Northwich
F M W Bartleet	Mold
D H Bernard	Bromborough
A E Cooke (Second Class)	Thornton Hough
G Collins (Second Class)	Hoylake
J Cahill	Denbigh
M J Davies (Senior First Class)	Mold
J F Davis	Whitchurch
D J Edwards (Second Class)	Liverpool-Formby
A A Elliot (Second Class) Died August 1991	Northop
W Hopkins	Warrington
D E Higgins (Second Class)	Chester
D H Jackson (Second Class)	Wrexham
J W Jarvis	Bromborough
G H Kitchen	Gayton
J H Law	Warrington
J M Lloyd	Warrington
F Penrice (Senior First Class)	Manchester
J D Reynolds (Second Class)	Warrington
G W Scully (Senior First Class)	Bromborough
D A Snowden (Retired ill health 1991)	Heswall
J G Taylor (Second Class)	Bromborough
L G Voloume (Senior First Class)	Warrington
M D Watts	Wallasey
B D Wood	Denbigh

The last of the old brigade
1990
Left to right- M.D. Watts D.A. Snowden D.H. Bernard G. H. Kitchen

PILOT

The Manchester Pilotage District invites applications from holders of a Class I Certificate and aged between 35 and 45 years. Closing date 8th February.

The Harbour Master,
The Manchester Ship Canal Company,
Queen Elizabeth II Dock,
Wirral L62 0BB.
Tel: 051-327 1461

1993
"and it came to pass, as foretold by the author in 1976"

CAPTAIN PHILIP HENDERSON
The first of the future pilots

Captain Henderson commenced his sea-going career in 1969, aged 16, as an apprentice to the Furness Withy S S Company, and by 1980 had attained his Master Mariner's Certificate of Competency. At the age of 41 he had gained command of vessels owned by the Belfast Freight Ferries. In answer to the advertisement in the Liverpool Daily Post, he applied for the position as a Pilot on the Manchester Ship Canal; he was accepted and served the statutory probationary period of one month as required by the Manchester Port Authority. This probationary period entailed 20 transits of the Canal of which 6 transits had to be in excess of 27 miles. After a successful examination he was duly appointed as a 4th Class Pilot on 20th September 1993. This licence allowed Captain Henderson to pilot vessels not exceeding 800 gross tons or 75m. in length for a monthly remuneration of £1,583 gross. A Master of a coasting vessel of similar size would also be receiving a remuneration similar to that of Captain Henderson's.

On the completion of six months Captain Henderson will be examined for a Third Class licence, and if successful will be allowed to pilot vessels not exceeding 1,600 gross tons or 120m. in length for which his remuneration will increase to £2,058 gross per month. There is one restriction to this licence: Captain Henderson will not be allowed to pilot vessels carrying dangerous cargoes, but he will be allowed to act as assistant pilot on all vessels by acting as a helmsman. Having served two years as Third Class Pilot, Captain

Henderson will be examined for a Second Class Licence which will enable him to pilot all vessels not exceeding 3,500 gross tons or 120m. in length with an increase in remuneration to £2,375 gross per month. A Chief Officer's pay on similar tonnage vessels would be receiving £2,500 per month. Captain Henderson's promotion to First Class will entirely depend on the whims of the now ruling First Class Pilots: likewise, so will his remuneration of £3,166 gross per month.

This method of gaining new pilots was proposed, almost in its entirety, by the Author as long ago as 1976 (see Appendix X), but was never acknowledged or acted upon at that time. The termination of the Helmsmen's Service, coupled with the induction of Master Mariners directly into the Manchester Pilot Service, was long overdue and can only bode well for the future of this service. Let us fervently hope and pray that 100 years of grievances - real or imagined - and of troubles and vexations between pilots that have haunted this service from its inception in 1894 will at last be laid to rest. Let the appointment of Captain Henderson signal the beginning of a new and enlightened Pilot Service that will uphold the great traditions of Pilotage throughout the United Kingdom. May the Manchester Ship Canal Pilots Ltd continue to prosper for another 100 years. I wish them well.

A MANCHESTER SHIP CANAL PILOT'S EPITAPH

Twix field and farms, through sluice and locks,
They quelled all qualms from sea to docks;
No tides have they to stem, on tranquil waters sail
No compass guides them in weathers that prevail
Gone days of work where dangers spurn,
Gone ships they'd piloted, they will never return.
So lie in your sleep: those days were best....
Home no ships will keep. you've earned your rest

Derek Clulow

"NO TIDES HAVE THEY TO STEM ON TRANQUIL WATERS SAIL"
T & J Harrison Vessel "Govenor" GRT:8202
L. 464'; B. 59' Head Tug "Arrow"
Courtesy the M S C Co.

THE REWARD OF A THING WELL DONE IS TO HAVE DONE IT

R W Emerson

APPENDIX I

CONDITIONS OF SERVICE OF TEMPORARY PILOTS

8 Except as by these Bye-Laws otherwise provided a Temporary Pilot shall be subject to all the provisions of the Principal Bye-Laws as though he were a Pilot who has received a Licence from the Pilotage Authority under those Bye-Laws.

9 Notwithstanding anything contained in Bye-Law 37 of the Principal Bye-Laws Temporary Pilots shall be granted such annual leave of absence (if any) as the Pilotage Committee may from time to time determine.

10 The provisions of Bye-Law 38 of the Principal Bye-Laws relating to sick allowances to Pilots shall apply to a Temporary Pilot only during the currency of his Temporary Licence.

11 Notwithstanding the payment into the Pilots' Benefit Fund provided for by Bye-Law 41 of the Principal Bye-Laws or anything contained in the Bye-Laws relating to that Fund, Temporary Pilots and the widows and children of Temporary Pilots shall not be entitled to any benefit or repayment out of that Fund.

12 A Second Class Pilot, not being a Temporary Pilot, who has been classed as a Temporary First Class Pilot shall be entitled only to the benefits out of the Pilots' Benefit Fund to which he could have been entitled in his capacity as a Second Class Pilot, and service as a Temporary First Class Pilot shall not be reckoned as service as a Pilot of the First Class.

13 Persons granted a Temporary Licence under these Bye-Laws shall obey all lawful orders given by the Pilotage Authority and undertake such employment as the Pilotage Authority in their sole discretion shall direct.

14 These Bye-Laws shall come into force as from the 5th August 1940.

APPENDIX II

SCHEDULE JANUARY 1st 1947

1946/47 JAN 1st FIRST CHANGE SINCE 1920

SCHEDULE.

(1) The Pilotage Dues for the Pilotage District shall be as follows :—

(*a*) For each vessel entering or leaving and navigating the Ship Canal under pilotage an initial fee shall be payable according to the gross registered tonnage of the vessel, as follows :—

Initial Fees.

For a vessel—

	£	s.	d.
Not exceeding 500 tons	1	0	0
Exceeding 500 tons but not exceeding 1,000 tons	1	5	0
,, 1,000 ,, ,, ,, 1,500 ,,	1	10	0
,, 1,500 ,, ,, ,, 2,000 ,,	1	15	0
,, 2,000 ,, ,, ,, 2,500 ,,	2	0	0
,, 2,500 ,, ,, ,, 3,000 ,,	2	5	0
,, 3,000 ,, ,, ,, 4,000 ,,	2	15	0
,, 4,000 ,, ,, ,, 5,000 ,,	3	5	0
,, 5,000 ,, ,, ,, 6,000 ,,	3	15	0
,, 6,000 ,, ,, ,, 7,000 ,,	4	5	0
,, 7,000 ,, ,, ,, 8,000 ,,	4	15	0
,, 8,000 ,, ,, ,, 9,000 ,,	5	5	0
,, 9,000 ,, ,, ,, 10,000 ,,	5	15	0

Exceeding 10,000 tons, 10s. for every additional 1,000 tons.

In addition there shall be payable a sum based on a rate of 1¼d. per foot draft per mile or portion of a mile for the distance the vessel has been piloted. Draft to be based on the maximum draft at the commencement of the pilotage service, and to be taken to the nearest foot (six inches and over to be charged to the higher foot).

Minimum Charge.

Minimum pilotage charge for services under Clause 1 (*a*) to be £1 10s. 0d.

Moving from point to point in the Canal.

(*b*) For each vessel moving from point to point in the Ship Canal under pilotage (except as otherwise provided) but without entering or leaving the Canal there shall be payable :—

(i) An initial fee calculated as follows :—

If the pilotage service is less than 8 miles at half the appropriate rate set out in clause 1(*a*) above;

If the pilotage service is 8 miles or over at two-thirds of the appropriate rate set out in clause 1(*a*) above;

and (ii) A rate of 1¼d. per foot draft per mile or portion of a mile for the distance the vessel has been piloted.

APPENDIX III

THE SUMMARY OF THE MANCHESTER SHIP CANAL PILOTAGE INQUIRY ON JUNE 12th-15th AND JUNE 18th-20th 1956 BY MR. THOMAS HAWORTH.

The Minister of Transport and Civil Aviation

I attended an Inquiry held in Manchester on the above dates. The Inquiry provided an opportunity for the pilots to state their claims and ventilate their grievances in full measure. It has also enabled me to appreciate the depth of human feeling and emotion which prompted the request for this Inquiry.

I cannot help getting the impression after listening to the evidence of individual pilots (Messrs R.T. Green, G. Young, C. Killender) that there is a feeling of frustration that pilotage as a service is such a small feature of the large interests and operations of the Manchester Ship Canal Company that it tends to become neglected and insensible to the interests of the pilots.

I cannot but feel that there is somewhere an absence of liaison in the day-by-day administration. I am satisfied that something must be done to establish a better feeling and atmosphere in working relations that, I am sure, is the goal which all interests are seeking. The key solution undoubtedly lies in the appointment of a Pilot Manager; it is the day-by-day contact that is missing.

For the foregoing reasons and for other reasons which go without mention, the appointment of a Pilot Manager is extremely urgent. The appointment of a Pilot Manager is agreed by all participating parties but the Pilots insist that he should be appointed and paid by them and be their servant whilst the Pilotage Authority and the Shipowners equally maintain that he must be the servant of theirs. Moreover, the pilots do not seem very clear about the type of man they want and his status and duties.

On this issue I have very definite views. He must be appointed by the Pilotage Authority and be their servant. He must be an Administrator of suitable talent to be able to present the grievances of the pilots and their difficulties in the proper quarter. He must be available to discuss and to settle day-by-day troubles, if any, between the pilots themselves; sanction leave periods and see that the Rota is working fairly and equitable. He must have frequent contact with the pilots and their work.

I am of the opinion that he should be a technical man and preferably a Master Mariner. He must be of personable disposition and he will have to work hard to gain the confidence and goodwill of the Pilots. With the right man, I believe it can be done and indeed it must be done.

Number of pilots

There is no direct evidence to establish the number of "attendances" or their duration under current conditions. The pilots themselves have no factual information to offer themselves as they admit they have kept no records but insist they are working harder than before the war. I was particularly interested to find out if possible, something of the range in the number of "attendances" of individual pilots and of their hours of duty. At my request a limited sampling of individual records was undertaken, producing three tables. The information disclosed by the tables was as follows.

	December 1955	February 1956
Mean time per hour	7 hours	8 hours
Mean turns per month	15	14
Mean hours per month	110	113

Against this picture of current conditions the pilots claim for the establishment to be regulated by reference to a standard of 120 Rota Turns per annum. The Pilotage Authority argued that before a previous Inquiry held in 1946 that changed conditions warranted 140 Rota Services. After much perusal of figures presented to me the real figure would appear to lie somewhere between 140 "Attendances" and 180 "Attendances" per annum.

In this dilemma, I cannot believe that pre-war "attendances" could have been less than 150 per annum per pilot. I have pursued this exhausting statistical examination with the desire to clear the air and to secure a more equitable working of the Rota. In this examination and finally in assessment of the pilotage strength it appears to me that a figure of about 70 pilots is reasonably established.

The Pilots' case asks for a remuneration of £1,500 per annum based somewhat on the prestige of Manchester in order of importance as a leading port. Contrariwise the Shipowners submit a formula based on the remuneration of Ships Officers of the average size vessel using the Ship Canal. The Chamber of Shipping put their figure at £1,350 per annum while Liverpool Steamship Owners Association set it at £1,265 per annum.

It is admitted that a pilot's occupation denies a regularity in home life and requires and insists upon attendance at call whatever the inconvenience; week-ends, Bank Holidays, Christmas are all the same. These are conditions for which adequate compensation can be expected and of which neither the Pilotage Authority nor the Shipowners are unmindful or insensitive.

The Ship Canal is almost unique in character and great care is required during its passage. All that one can say is that his work is different from that, for example, of a Master Mariner, but that is not to say it requires greater skill or is more exacting in other respects.

An assessor has made a trip along the full length of the Canal to see something of the actual conditions of a pilot's work. Fortified with this help and advice I give due weight to the evidence of the pilots who have appeared before me. One cannot deny that they feel their present duties impose a strain which, though it may be possible to qualify, is real and genuine.

I have endeavoured to approach the issue of remuneration between pre-war and post-war scales of pay. Examples can be given of ex-Master Mariners and other senior officers, in similar spheres of employment ashore, whose current scales are little more than twice their pre-war earnings. It seems to me on these figures, a relative remuneration at the present time, like for like, could be put at £1,250 per annum. I nevertheless felt that there must be some acknowledgement for the perhaps more exacting conditions pilots work under. I am inclined to put an additional £100 on that figure. I therefore conclude that a remuneration of the order of £1,350 per annum is fair and equitable and takes account of all representatives that have been put before me.

Relief at Latchford

I have found this the most difficult of all the representations put forward by the pilots. The through transit from Eastham to Manchester, under favourable conditions a large vessel occupies a pilot for about 12 hours and in bad weather or heavy shipping movements the transit can take days. Some relief is at least desirable on these long transits.

The pilots want the relief to be compulsory while the Shipowners and the Pilotage Authority feel that a voluntary arrangement would meet the difficulty. This issue could well be left for the prospective Pilot Manager to look into as one of his first duties. I am inclined to think that the relief should not be made compulsory. The Pilot Manager, under more favourable relations with the pilots which I hope will follow his appointment this very contentious and difficult matter could be amicably resolved. To my way of thinking, here is an outstanding example of the sort of difficulty that a Pilot Manager would be able to handle.

Late Booking Fees

This is a personal fee payable to the individual pilot and has been the bone of contention with the Shipowners for a long time. The Pilotage Authority have submitted that in substitution or in compensation for the withdrawal of the Late Booking Fee the pilots should receive into their pool of fees an amount approximately 5% of their earnings. The pilots do not think Late Booking Fees should be discontinued. I am on the other hand much in agreement and sympathy with the Pilotage Authority and feel it is fair and equitable and since it would remove long-standing grievances of the Shipowners, it would contribute to the establishment of a better relationship in the future.

Summary

The calculation of the ratio of surcharge to give effect to the remuneration of £1,350 is as follows.

60 First Class Pilots	@£1,350	£81,000
10 Second Class Pilots	@£1,012.50p	£10,125
Net remuneration reqd.	=80%	£91,125
Gross earnings	=100%	£113,900

The net figure of £1,350 per annum is the equivalent of a remuneration of £1,421 subject to a deduction of 5% for pension benefits.

I cannot conclude this report without referring to the urgent need for the cultivation and realisation of better relations between individual Pilots and also between the Pilots Association and the Pilotage Authority and the Shipowners. I much hope that on all sides there will be an endeavour and a goodwill to this very desirable end and that it will rebound to the enterprise and progress of the Manchester Ship Canal.

APPENDIX IV

THE MANCHESTER SHIP CANAL.

PILOTAGE WORKING RULES.

THE INCE ROTA

(1) The Pilotage Service shall be divided into two Rotas, one to be known as the "Ince Rota" and the other as the "Manchester Rota".

(2) The "Ince Rota" shall be manned by at least twelve pilots. The pilotage of all vessels bound from Eastham to Ince Oil Berth or any place Westward of Ince Oil Berth, or vice versa, or between any other places Westward of Ince Oil Berth shall be performed exclusively by pilots on the "Ince" Rota". This, however, shall not apply to a vessel piloted by a Choice Pilot performing an appropriated service.

(3) The "Manchester Rota" shall be manned by the remaining pilots. The pilotage of all vessels bound from Eastham to a place Eastward of Ince Oil Berth or from a place Eastward of Ince Oil Berth to Eastham or any other place Westward of Ince Oil Berth, shall be performed exclusively by pilots on the "Manchester Rota". This, however, shall not apply to a vessel attended by a Choice Pilot performing an appropriated service and shall not prevent a pilot on the "Manchester Rota" from attending a vessel which unexpectedly has to lighten or trim at Ellesmere Port or Stanlow before proceeding to her destination Eastward of Ince Oil Berth.

(4) The composition of the "Ince Rota" and the "Manchester Rota" shall be changed every four weeks in the following manner, viz: as soon as practicable after noon on every fourth Sunday the pilots on the"Ince Rota" shall (subject as mentioned below) be replaced by at least twelve pilots on the "Manchester Rota" who are due for transfer to the "Ince Rota" in accordance with the approved list current for the time being; and the pilots transferred from the "Ince Rota" shall take their place on the "Manchester Rota" list in their correct order for subsequent work in accordance with the approved list. If, however, any pilot due to be so transferred from the "Manchester Rota" is, at the time of the monthly change of Rotas, either on passage or attending tide, he shall not enter the "Ince Rota" until he has completed the service on which he is engaged; and the pilot whom he is due to replace on the "Ince Rota" shall remain on that Rota until he is relieved.

(5) To maintain the strength of the "Ince Rota" during periods of leave any pilot leaving that Rota during such a period shall be replaced as soon as possible by the first available pilot on turn and of the same Class on the "Manchester Rota" and the latter shall remain on the "Ince Rota" until such Rota changes or until the pilot whom he replaces has received his next orders. A similar arrangement shall apply if at any time the strength of the "Ince Rota" is, in the opinion of the Pilotage Clerk, unduly depleted by sickness.

- 1 -

(6) Both Rotas shall be worked on a turn for turn system with the object of securing that so far as practicable every pilot on the "Ince Rota" or the "Manchester Rota", as the case may be, shall perform an equal number of turns. But turns may not be accumulated after a pilot has been transferred from the "Ince Rota" to the "Manchester Rota" or vice versa, and any turns in hand at the date of such transfer shall be cancelled.

In the case of a Choice Pilot who is temporarily transferred from one Rota to the other, the turns which he performs shall be credited to the Rota to which he is attached.

(7) When a pilot on the "Ince Rota" has been temporarily transferred to the "Manchester Rota", he shall on his return to the "Ince Rota" be credited with the number of turns on that Rota which he missed by reason of the duty which he performed on the "Manchester Rota".

(8) In order to perform an appropriated service a Choice Pilot on either Rota may be withdrawn from that Rota twelve hours or a reasonable time before the expected arrival (as signified to him by the Pilotage Clerk) of his ship. After completing that service, wherever it terminates, he shall return to the Rota to which he is attached, so that if he performs an "Ince service" while he is attached to the "Manchester Rota" he shall complete that service and then return to the "Manchester Rota", and if he performs a "Manchester service" while he is attached to the "Ince Rota" he shall complete that service and then return to the"Ince Rota.

(9) (a) Orders for tide duty shall be issued at the termination of the preceding tide, i.e. four hours after high water. Each tide shall commence with two pilots (one from each Rota) on the station, or as many more as may be required for known or expected arrivals for the "Ince" and "Manchester" Rotas. Further pilots as may be required for tide duty shall be drawn from the pilots next in order on the Rotas.

(b) If at a time when tide duties are made up a number of second class pilots are grouped on the Rota ahead of a first class pilot who is required for tide duty, the number of second class pilots required to attend tides shall be kept down to two or as many more as may be required.

(c) When an inward bound vessel not subject to choice pilotage is lying in Eastham basin she shall be manned by the first pilot on the appropriate Rota.

(d) A pilot shall remain on tide duty until he is engaged. If, however, after completion of one tide he is not engaged he shall be credited with a turn and shall re-enter his Rota accordingly unless, at the close of the tide, a ship is in sight and preparations are made to lock her into the Canal, when he shall remain and perform that service.

- 2 -

APPENDIX V

THE MANCHESTER SHIP CANAL COMPANY

Ship Canal House : King Street : Manchester 2.

S E C R E T A R Y

Reference No ....S..........

September 25, 1959

Dear Sir,

Relief at Latchford.

The conversations which I mentioned in my letter of August 11 have now taken place and it has been decided, with the approval of the Pilotage Committee, that the experimental system of Relief at Latchford shall be resumed on a revised basis with effect from October 1. The initial experiment was suspended after the Pilots' Representatives had raised certain objections to the provisions concerning the size and draught of vessels taking part and the granting of extra turns. You will see that condition (3) has now been amended. Condition (1) has, of course, been affected and condition (4) has been slightly amended by the addition of a sentence relating to travelling expenses. Apart from these amendments the conditions are precisely the same as in the original scheme.

The conditions on which the experiment is to be resumed are therefore as follows :-

(1) The new experiment will commence at 0001 hours on October 1 and will end at Midnight on December 31, 1959. At the end of the experiment the results will be considered by all parties.

(2) The fact that the parties concerned have agreed to the experiment in no way prejudices their position in regard to a permanent arrangement, and if, during the experimental period, the Manchester Ship Canal Pilots' Association or the Manchester Steamship Owners' Association or the Company wish to do so they will be free to terminate the arrangement at any time.

2.

(3) The experiment will be carried out on all vessels having a draught of 23 ft. or more, at time of departure, and proceeding either inward bound from points below Knutsford Road Swingbridge to points above Barton Bridge or outward bound from points above Barton Bridge to points below Knutsford Road Swingbridge. The Pilots of such vessels will be entitled to ask for a relief at Latchford provided they indicate their intention before the time of departure. A Pilot who does not ask for a relief when entitled to do so or who, for one reason or another, is not relieved, shall not thereby be entitled to an extra turn.

(4) During the experimental period no Shipowner shall be put to extra expense as a result of the arrangements made under the experiment, except for travelling expenses in accordance with the Schedule of Charges. It therefore follows that each passage is to be regarded as one through service for charging purposes, and the second Pilot is to present the service card for signature by the Master. The first Pilot should have his card signed for travelling expenses only. It should be appreciated that during the experimental period there can be no charges for detention prior to sailing or cancellations on behalf of Pilots detained or cancelled at Latchford as a result of the experiment.

(5) It is to be a fundamental condition of the experiment that no ship will be delayed because of the experiment. It is anticipated that unexpected difficulties will arise from time to time, and that Pilots are bound to be inconvenienced as a result, but if a relief is not present at Latchford when the ship is ready to leave again the Pilot already in attendance must complete the passage beyond Latchford.

It is most important, if the experiment is to succeed and if it is to be allowed to run its full course, that it should be conducted as realistically as possible. The whole object is to endeavour to find out all the difficulties that arise and to assess the requirements which are essential to an efficient relief system.

- 3.

The Committee are confident that the Pilots will give their whole-hearted support and co-operation to this end, and any unexpected difficulties which might arise can be discussed between the Representatives of the parties as necessary.

(6) The Committee have agreed that the Pilot Manager shall have full control of the experiment and in the light of the exigencies of the service at any particular time he will be entitled to exercise his discretion in all matters connected with the experiment. He will decide in each case whether or not a Pilot's application for a relief can be granted.

It has also been agreed that Helmsmen shall take part in the experiment on the same conditions.

Yours faithfully,

D. K. REDFORD

SECRETARY.

<u>Sent to all Pilots.</u>
A.

APPENDIX VI

EARNINGS OF PILOTS.

REPORT AND RECOMMENDATIONS OF COMMITTEE UNDER CHAIRMANSHIP OF SIR ROBERT LETCH.

	Per Annum. £
Aberdeen	1,050
Barrow	1,250
Barry	1,200
Belfast	1,300
Blyth	1,100
Bristol	1,500
Cardiff	1,200
Clyde	1,650
Dundee	1,050
Falmouth (Sea)	1,500
Goole	1,300
Grangemouth (Including Bo'ness)	1,225
Hartlepool	1,050
Hull	1,400
Ipswich	1,100
Isle of Wight (In)	1,575
Isle of Wight (Out)	1,825
Leith	1,225
Liverpool	1,550
London	1,850
Londonderry	950
Manchester	1,450
Methil	1,050
Newport	1,300
Plymouth	1,100
Port Talbot	1,200
Preston	1,200
Seaham	1,000
Sunderland	1,150
Swansea	1,550
Tees	1,500
Tyne	1,150

In this table there are set out thirty-two pilotage districts (or stations within districts) in the United Kingdom and the recommended net earnings for the first class or equivalent status of pilots. Retainers paid to choice pilots have been exluded but otherwise the figures include the various sources of income brought into account in assessing the net earnings for the particular district or station.

To avoid recurring examination of the pilotage rates whenever earnings are rather more or rather less than the recommended level I have agreed that, in the districts included in the list, there should be a margin within which net earnings should be allowed to fluctuate and that this margin should be ten percent.

A revision of these rates will be considered or made in the following circumstances.

1) A general increase or decrease in the National Maritime Board scales of pay for navigating officers.
2) A substantial change in the character of the trade. If a port is developed as an oil terminal or if a significant trade ceases at the port.
3) A fundamental change in the sources from which the pilots derive their earnings.

The committee suggest that the arrangements contained in this report should be allowed to continue until 31st December 1959, whereafter it would be open to the ship owners or pilots associations subscribing to this report to request a general review. This document was signed by:

Chamber of Shipping of the United Kingdom
Liverpool Steam Ship Owners Association
Transport and General Workers Association
United Kingdom Pilots Association

LETCH COMMITTEE REPORT
GRADUATED TABLE OF RECOMMENDED EARNINGS

POSITION EARNINGS*	DISTRICT	RECOMMENDED	
		May 1957	October 1962
		£	£
1	London	1850	2411
2	I O Wight (out)	1825	2378
3	Clyde	1650	2150
4	*Liverpool	1600	2085
5	I O Wight (in)	1575	2052
6	Swansea	1550	2020
7	Bristol, Falmouth, Tees	1500	1955
10	Manchester	1450	1889
11	Hull	1400	1824
12	Belfast, Goole, Newport	1300	1694
15	Barrow	1250	-
16	Grangemouth, Leith	1225	-
18	Barry, Cardiff, Port Talbot, Preston	1200	-
22	Sunderland, Tyne	1150	-
24	Blyth, Ipswich, Plymouth	1100	-
27	Aberdeen, Dundee, Hartlepool, Methil	1050	-
31	Seaham	1000	-
31	Londonderry	950	-

* Liverpool: The figure originally in the Report was £1550. It was subsequently agreed by the signatories to the Report that this figure had taken into account too high a figure for earnings outside the District. It was therefore amended to £1600.

APPENDIX VII

AGREEMENT ON THE EARNINGS OF PILOTS

1. It is recognised by the General Council of British Shipping, the United Kingdom Pilots' Association and the Transport and General Workers' Union that the re-organisation of pilotage under the provisions of the Merchant Shipping Act, 1979 will lead to greater efficiency, the benefits of which should be shared both by shipowners as users of the pilotage service and the pilots who provide it.

2. As a result of negotiations commenced before the Merchant Shipping Bill was introduced into Parliament and concluded following its enactment, this Agreement has been reached on the recommended earnings of pilots, their pensions and other matters relating to their working arrangements and conditions of service.

3. In the following table are set out thirty-five pilotage districts in the United Kingdom, the groups to which they have been allocated and the recommended net earnings in each group for the first class or equivalent status of pilots. The figures shown embrace all the pooled income of pilots from pilotage within the limits of the districts as established under re-organisation.

GROUP	Recommended Level of Earnings on Annual Review of Rates Basis £	DISTRICTS
1.	16,000	LONDON, ISLE OF WIGHT, CLYDE, FORTH, HUMBER, LIVERPOOL, MILFORD HAVEN, TEES.
2.	14,500	MANCHESTER, SOUTH EAST WALES.
3.	13,000	BELFAST, BRISTOL, FALMOUTH, PORT TALBOT, SWANSEA, TYNE.
4.	11,500	BARROW AND FLEETWOOD, DUNDEE, GLOUCESTER, GOOLE, IPSWICH, *KINGS LYNN, PRESTON, *SHOREHAM, *TRENT, *YARMOUTH AND SOUTHWOLD.
5.	10,000	ABERDEEN, BLYTH, *BOSTON AND SPALDING, HARTLEPOOL, LONDONDERRY, PLYMOUTH, *POOLE, SEAHAM, SUNDERLAND.

*Non-Letch Scheme Districts with five or more actual pilots.

---

15. At 1st July, 1983, the recommended earnings in paragraph 3 above will become:—

GROUP	Recommended Level of Earnings on Annual Review of Rates Basis £
1.	17,000
2.	15,500
3.	14,000
4.	12,500
5.	11,000

Like the recommended earnings in paragraph 3 these are figures appropriate at the date of the Agreement. Over the period up to 1st July, 1983 they will attract the same proportional increases as the figures in paragraph 3.

16. At 1st July, 1983 and every three years thereafter, the scale of recommended earnings as determined under paragraph 15 will be subject to re-assessment.

APPENDIX VIII

MANCHESTER PILOTAGE COMMITTEE

SHIP CANAL HOUSE - KING STREET - MANCHESTER M2 4WX

Secretary's Office

Telegrams: "CANAL MANCHESTER"
Telephone: 061-832 2244

April 26, 1976

Dear Mr Clulow,

PILOTAGE SERVICE

I have this morning received your very interesting document setting out in detail your views on Manchester pilotage, and I shall, of course, give copies to the Pilot Manager and to the representatives whom I am meeting for a further discussion this afternoon. I have not yet had a chance to study the document properly but I am sure that it will be very helpful and I am most grateful to you for going to so much trouble.

Yours sincerely,

P I W MAYNE

D A Clulow Esq.,
"Bowman",
Lever Causeway,
Storeton,
Wirral,
Merseyside

EAM

Mr P I W Mayne,
Secretary,
Pilotage Committee,
April 4th, 1976,

Dear Sir,

Reorganisation of the Pilot Service

In order to start a reorganisation of the Service (the word 'service' is meant to include Helmsmen) bold and imaginative steps must be taken and a complete new appraisal of the service in general, taking into consideration three important points.

1 An Early Retirement Scheme
2 New Working Arrangements
3 New Recruitment Scheme for Pilots
4 New Recruitment Scheme for Helmsmen

On all the above points each one must be dependent on the other, otherwise none will really work to one's entire satisfaction. I think of all the above points the one of paramount importance is the Early Retirement Scheme: this, I feel, is the foundation that any future Service must be built upon and unless this is discussed first and settled, none of the other schemes could possibly be implemented. If we are to have any semblance of success in a solution to our present day and future problems an Early Retirement Scheme is a must. The following pages I have written are my ideas and suggestions and are not meant to be critical of the Pilotage Committee. I only hope you may be able to find some information within this report that may be able to help you in your marathon deliberations in the many months ahead.

Yours very sincerely,
D A CLULOW, PILOT

EARLY RETIREMENT SCHEME

The ER Scheme will be open to all Pilots who have held a First Class Licence for a minimum of 15 years.

SCHEME 1

ALL PILOTS OVER 60 YEARS OF AGE

Because these Pilots have obviously planned for their retirement at 65, the last few remaining years of earning are of paramount importance and therefore every consideration must be given to them. I am not sure but I think there are 8 Pilots who will be over 60 on 1 January 1977. On their retirement they will receive:

1 A reduced Pension from the Pension Fund
2 A subsidy from the savings made within the service to bring their annual income to £6,500
3 Full Pension from Fund on attaining 65

The figure £6,500 is arrived at taking into consideration that they will no longer have to buy Insurance Stamps (£260 this year) or have the expense of having to go to work.

SCHEME 2

ALL PILOTS OVER 55 YEARS AND NOT REACHED 60

This scheme to run in conjunction with Scheme 1. They shall receive:

1 A reduced Pension from the Pension Fund
2 A subsidy from the savings made within the service to bring their annual income to £6,000
3 The annual income will increase to £6,500 on attaining the age of 60
4 A full Pension at 65

SCHEME 3

ALL OTHER PILOTS WHO HAVE HELD A LICENCE FOR 15 YEARS

This Scheme to be run in conjunction with 1 and 2, with preference given in order of seniority in age. They will receive:

1 A reduced Pension from the Pension Fund
2 A subsidy from the savings made within the service to bring their annual income to £4,500
3 Annual income to increase as they reach each age-level

It is very difficult for me to arrive at the cost of subsidising of the Pensions, having no figures for the amount of Pension a Pilot would recive from the fund at a reduced scale, but in trying to reach a figure I have calculated thus.

Scheme 1	Reduced Pension £2,000
Scheme 2	Reduced Pension £1,500
Scheme 3	Reduced Pension £ 750

On this basis if all Pilots (8) took advantage of the 60 and over, six Pilots from 55 and over, the total cost would be £63,000. I cannot imagine many Pilots accepting Scheme 3, but just for the record if another 6 accepted this offer the total cost would be £85,000. This is well within the figure I quote for savings from the service. In bearing with their increases one should allow an inflation factor each year until they reach 65.

All Pilots who take early retirement will be expected to continue to contribute to the Pilots' Pension Fund in order to claim a full Pension at the end of their early retirement. Any monies in excess of the subsidising at the end of each year will be invested and used as an inflation barrier.

SUBSIDISING THE EARLY RETIREMENT SCHEME

If the manning procedure was put into operation (Page 2 Helmsmen's Service) it would need only twelve Helmsmen to give an efficient service. I would need access to Canal Co. records for past years to gain a more accurate figure, but I do feel my estimation of Helmsmen required would be within two or three of a more accurate figure. Therefore, a sum of £188,000 already being paid by the Shipowner would go towards the ER Scheme. It naturally follows a savings of travelling expenses of the Helmsman - an estimated figure of £6,000. Under the heading of Travelling Expenses a more efficient system could save the Shipowner a further £10,000. - a total saving of £116,000.

NEW RECRUITMENT SCHEME FOR PILOTS

QUALIFICATIONS

Master Mariner Foreign Going. Not over 35 years, having sailed at least as a First Officer.

TRAINING

A man seeking the position as a Pilot and holding the above qualification must be a competent, intelligent and highly desirable individual to have in the Pilot Service. He will have already had some experience in ship handling and certainly have a wide knowledge of the effect of wind and tides on a vessel. He may also have been in command and with these qualifications behind him and let us not underestimate the degree of mental awareness required to pass a Master's certificate, the transition to a Pilot in the Manchester District is far from being the long-drawn out process it is today. With very few exceptions every port in the UK and in the Suez, Kiel and Panama Canals, Pilots are appointed directly from sea with master qualifications. The quaint and totally unrealistic view held, that Pilotage in the Port of Manchester is something unique, is as out of date as a gold sovereign. This view may well have seemed so when the only qualification a Pilot had years ago was that he had stood behind the wheel of a ship for ten years or more. There is nothing more soul destroying, mentally destroying or vocationally destroying than to ask a highly intelligent man holding a Master's certificate to stand behind a wheel for ten years under the guise of learning to become a Pilot. Evidence of this can be seen today that very few of the new Helmsmen with Master's Certificates have remained in the service on learning of the time that could be spent behind a wheel.

Therefore I propose when a new Pilot is appointed he will serve a probationary period of one month under the instruction of another Pilot on vessels not exceeding 2,000 GRT. He will be expected to perform at least 20 passages - half of which will be full transits and half during the hours of darkness - on completion of which he will be granted a week's leave to study for his Third Class Licence, and, if successful, shall be paid for his probationary period. After one year he will be examined for a Second Class Licence and allowed to pilot larger and deeper vessels. After a further one year he will be examined for his First Class Licence. NOTE Prior to his examination for a First Class Licence he must perform the duty as a second Pilot (NOT A HELMSMAN) under the instruction of a First Class Pilot on First Class Vessels. He will be expected to perform at least 20 passages: 4 of which will be into or out of the

Q E II Oil dock, the remaining services between Eastham and Latchford or vice-versa, and half the passages by night. The size of vessels to be Piloted under each Licence can easily be categorised at a later date.

THE HELMSMEN'S SERVICE

In this day and age the recruiting and training Helmsmen to be Licensed Pilots is archaic to say the least. Long gone are the days when men were and I quote "Taken from behind a plough and put behind a wheel", or putting it another way: "From Tillman to Tillerman". In those days the training to be a Pilot from behind the wheel was indeed the most suitable way, but not in these times. I think that the Pilots and the Port Authority have a moral obligation to ensure all the present Helmsmen eventually gain a Pilot's Licence, and this can be achieved if the Early Retirement Scheme is implemented and then an entirely new Helmsmen's Service could be initiated. The new Helmsmen's Service would recruit seafarers to be Helmsmen - only never becoming Licensed Pilots as in the Kiel Canal and London River. It may be beneficial if the Authority wrote to the PLA and the Kiel Canal for information on the working system, pay scale and qualifications of those Helmsmen.

QUALIFICATIONS FOR NEW SERVICE

a Second Mate FG or First Mate HT
b Senior AB holding EDH and having at least 7 years' experience on deck FG or HT
c No candidate to be over 30 years of age when commencing steering

REMUNERATION

A rate of pay slightly above the earnings between a 3rd Officer and Second Officer of a large Foreign-Going Vessel. They would be employees of the Port Authority and therefore be eligible to join the company's Pension Scheme and sickness scheme. Travelling allowances as per canal schedule. They would receive any increase in pay equal to the awards given by the NMB to their officers, as well as locally negotiated increases. They would not receive any increases granted to Pilots either nationally or locally. They would organise their own leave rota either on the lines of today or with discussions with the Port Authority. These are but a few subjects to be worked out, but a genuine effort must be made to make the Helmsmen's Service attractive to the seagoer mainly to bring men into the service quickly. This is why the accent must be placed on Pay and Leave especially if it is closely related to their pay and leave at sea. NOTE: In order that a fixed monthly income can be achieved the rates charged for the new service would be pitched higher than required in order that a reserve could be built up to cover for any fall, due to trade, as does happen from time to time.

MANNING SCALE

The number of Helmsmen required can and should be greatly reduced and a careful study should be conducted along the following lines.

DISTANCE

a) Vessels moving between points from Eastham to Ince, irrespective of size shall proceed without a Helmsman.

EXCEPTIONS

1 Vessels carrying dangerous cargoes.
2 Vessels with restricted visibility.

b) Vessels moving between points from Eastham to Runcorn irrespective of size will proceed without a Pilot. Exceptions as in last para.
c) Vessels moving between points from Barton Top Dolphins and Manchester Docks will proceed without a Helmsman. Exceptions as in previous para.
d) Any vessel found to be undermanned in the above paras., a Pilot may request a Helmsman.
e) A new length X breadth formula to exempt certain vessels from employing Helmsmen who already do, but careful consideration must be given to specialised vessels.

If all these points were instituted one would virtually have a full tonnage service, greatly reducing the Helmsmen's Service yet still giving adequate cover from the safety angle of Piloting. Other deeper discussions will have to be conducted on other points not mentioned here but basically the main issues are printed here.

THE TRANSITIONAL PERIOD

This will be a difficult period but not insurmountable if all parties - especially the Pilots - are willing to accept that if radical changes are to be made some suffering must be borne, and that many of the great benefits they will receive in the future totally outweigh the few months of possible discomfort in the beginning. Pilots will not be setting a precedent in taking Helmsmen on Full tonnage ships with less than one year's experience. In 1954 many Pilots accepted Helmsmen of 2 and 3 months experience on Full tonnage vessels at a draught of 26 feet all the way to Manchester not once but many times; also tankers to Stanlow with no ill effects to trade or Pilot. At present 23 Helmsmen have 10 years or more experience and it is logical to state they are all capable of Piloting vessels after a successful examination for a Licence. The majority of Pilots at present served far less a time behind the wheel and (dare I say it?) proved quite capable of Piloting vessels of all sizes. You will appreciate that this system depends entirely on the ER Scheme. Assuming on 1st January 1977 (an earlier date I cannot foresee to implement all the changes) 10 First Class Pilots take advantage of the ER Scheme, having intimated their desire three months prior to that date or at the commencement of the Pilotage year. The 10 senior Helmsmen will be promoted to Pilots being allowed to Pilot vessels larger than the present limitations for a Second Class licence, possible up to the size envisaged going without a Helmsman. The 5 senior Helmsmen promoted will be allowed to shift vessels of any size at Eastham and in the Manchester Docks in the normal Rota fashion, but not in the QE II Oil Dock. After 6 months they will be promoted, after examination, to First Class, and the second 5 Helmsmen proceed as the first 5 had done: thus in 12 months you will have replaced the 10 Pilots who retired and be back at full strength. As further Pilots retire Helmsmen will be promoted accordingly in the same manner.

The new Helmsmen's Service would for a time have to operate alongside the old Service working on one Rota but earnings calculated separately. I am sure this would not be insurmountable in this computerised era. The new Helmsmen entering the service will be expected to do a one month probationary period. During this one month period he will be expected to attend a Full tonnage vessel every day with the exception of Saturday and Sunday. An equal number of passages must be made between Eastham and Manchester and vice-versa, and at least 14 passages during the hours of darkness. A private report will be made by the Pilot and Helmsman as to his ability, conduct and progress on each passage. This incentive period would quickly build up a good cross-section of work and give the new Helmsman quick experience and general knowledge of the intricacies of getting to and from various berths on the Canal at all times of day and night. On successful completion of his probationary period he shall be paid for that month in accordance with the scale set.

TRAINING OF FIRST CLASS PILOTS FROM PROMOTED HELMSMEN

I had first considered promoting the first 10 senior Helmsmen directly to First Class Pilots, for the hardest transition was not from Helsman to Second Class Pilot but Second Class Pilot to First Class Pilot. To clarify this point, the Helmsmen today are on board more First class vessels than a Rota Pilot First Class and probably know more how a deep draughted vessel handles. The hardship comes when they have to serve three years Second Class, never boarding a Full tonnage vessel. It can be an enormous strain the first six months or more of First Class Piloting. The examinations for the two licences are identical. Some Helmsmen have steered for 16 years and know every inch of the Canal by day and by night from the bridge of a Full tonnage vessel. The only difference between them and a First Class Pilot, other than the examination for a licence, is that they lack experience of giving direct orders, being in command of a vessel and being totally assured of their ability to Pilot. One must agree the present Helmsmen's Service has more sea-going qualifications than any other past Helmsmen's Service with a far greater proportion of Masters and 1st Mates than ever before. With this intelligence they have brought with them a deeper sense of responsibility for a job well done, and a greater desire to become a Pilot. In this atmosphere I can hardly see these men taking their duties as Pilots and their responsibilities lightly, and it is for this reason I proposed they should be promoted to First Class after six months. I make one further addition to their first six months as a Pilot. The final two months of their new Piloting life they must Pilot a minimum of 12 Full tonnage vessels, 4 of which must be in or out of the QE II Oil Dock under the supervision of a Senior First Class Pilot. All these services to be performed outside his normal Rota Duties. During this period of six months provision must be made on the Rota to ensure that these Pilots do have priority for Dock Shifting, shifting in the Canal and at least Eastham Shifting once a week on all class of vessels. I am sure with youth on their side they will grasp this opportunity with both hands and show they can and will become Pilots that the Port of Manchester can be proud of. I must point out once more that a precedent is not being set. In 1954 Helmsmen were promoted to Pilots after 4 years - in one case less than 4 years' steering - and the older and unenlightened Pilots howled and poured scorn and derision on their heads. They were referred to as the four-year wonders and they would wreck the Canal and the ships within a year. The new boys never did, and they now carry the burden of the work on most Full tonnage vessels. I feel equally certain that the future Pilots will also commit themselves to Piloting in the same professional manner as their predecessors.

TRAVELLINGARRANGEMENTS

The present system of paying expenses (£2.20) for attending certain vessels will cease.

A 24-hour taxi system will operate on the following basis.

FOR ALL PILOTS BASED AT EASTHAM

1 Transport will be available from Eastham Pilot Station to any point within the Pilotage District IF THAT SAID VESSEL IS COMPLETING HER PASSAGE AT EASTHAM.
2 Transport will be available FROM any point within the Pilotage District to take a Pilot to his vessel IF THAT SAID VESSEL IS COMPLETING HER PASSAGE AT THAT POINT, eg Partington to Ince. Transport from Ince Manchester to Latchford, transport from Latchford.
3 Transport will be available from any point within the Pilotage District TO EASTHAM IF THE SAID VESSEL COMMENCED HER PASSAGE FROM THAT POINT.
4 Transport will be available to return to any point within the Pilotage District from whence the vessel sailed, eg Stanlow to Barton Oil Wharf. Transport return to Stanlow. Runcorn to Partington. Transport return to Runcorn.

Point 1

In order to still qualify for an Income Tax allowance for the use of a car in carrying out the duties of a Pilot, the Pilots will use their own cars to arrive at the various ports of sailing. The vessel or transport will return them to their cars.

Point 2

The distinction of living at either Manchester or Eastham will no longer apply. All Pilots will be based as working from Eastham Pilot Station. No other Port has this rather quaint ruling or allowance as to say where you live.

Point 3

For any vessel requiring to be shifted only eg Manchester Docks, Runcorn docks, Stanlow, Eastham Shifting, QE II Oil dock etc, etc. A Pilot will use his own transport.

Point 4

For a Pilot who does not own a car (2 at present), special arrangements will have to be made at ordering time.

Point 5

There must be complete co-operation between Pilots and Helmsmen. Two forms of Transport will not be allowed for one vessel.

I consider that this system will save up to £10,000 or even more, but it does have one more factor in its favour. If the Pilots are to work at a greater tempo transporting a Pilot to a ship swiftly and comfortably and returning him to base or car swiftly and comfortably, is of paramount importance in running a healthy and efficient service. It will pay handsome dividends in the increased efficiency in moving vessels from A to B, with Pilots suffering far less fatigue. Nothing is more stamina sapping than to have to travel back to Eastham or Manchester by public transport having been on passage all night, and as a Pilot gets older it takes him longer to recover from night work.

CONCLUSIONS

I would again repeat and emphasise that an Early Retirement Scheme must be implemented before any other discussions take place, top priority should be given to this subject at all future Pilotage Committee meetings. If this opportunity is not grasped to make bold, sweeping and revolutionary changes, if this moment is allowed to slip by within 5 years and form of radical change will be too late and too expensive to implement. The ER Scheme and other proposals linked with it are unique from the point that for once, for a very small increase to shipowners at its inception, in later years the Pilot's Service will cost them less. The Shipowners would be investing monies in a scheme now to reap big rewards later: surely this must be a very big attraction to today's modern approach to business. An ER Scheme made compulsory would be very desirable for many reasons mainly.

1 A younger and more efficient service, efficient to mean less liable to illness and fatigue.
2 Increase in work tempo could be achieved thus reducing number of Pilots required and therefore reducing the number of Pilots required and safeguarding overmanning if trade decreases in later years.
3 Retirement after a minimum of 25 years' service, if a new Pilot joins the service at maximum age of 35. This would be an excellent attraction to the service for new recruits.

In pilotage abroad in extreme climates eg Red Sea, Far East and India, retirement is set at 50 to 55 to compensate for the climate's toll on Pilots. This formula could be applied in Manchester for Pilots accepting extra work. I feel that a younger service would be prepared to accept working harder in order to retire sooner, coupled with the ability to earn more during their working life, thus being able to plan ahead much easier for their retirement. I earnestly ask you to take a long hard look at the system of recruiting Helmsmen, to consider the psychological implications I have pointed out. This is no figment of my imagination but a genuine appraisal of fact seen at first hand and one that would be supported by any medical board. The Helmsmen's Service is already hard put to keep new recruits, even to attracting new men with the qualifications required; the daunting prospect of 10 to 15 years behind a wheel must be the greatest obstacle. If you persist in recruiting Helmsmen in this manner and asking for the same high qualifications you will not have an efficient or reliable service, as we know today, in 5 years' time. The time has come in your deliberations to think big, act big and reap big rewards. I thank you for your patience in reading this rather long report.

D A CLULOW
21 April 1976

It is strange that so many of these proposals and statements regarding the future of the service have been implemented and have come to pass - but not until 1990, far too late. Why, I have often wondered, was this report never considered in 1976 or even acknowledged by the Pilot's Association of that day????

APPENDIX IX

CONTRACT FOR PILOTS TO PROVIDE SERVICES AS SELF-EMPLOYED CONTRACTORS, 1ST OCTOBER 1988

1 RECITALS

A MSC is the competent harbour authority within the meaning of S.1 (1) of the Pilotage Act 1987 for the Manchester harbour area and will provide pilotage services for the harbour area as defined in the Pilotage Direction dated 15 December 1987.

B Under Heads of Agreement dated 29 February 1988 MSC has agreed conditions with the Manchester Pilots' Association whereby the 33 pilots remaining for the time being will each contract with MSC to provide pilotage services for shipping on a self-employed basis within the Manchester harbour area.

C The said 33 Pilots by a majority have released MSC from its obligation to employ within the meaning of Section 4 (2) of the Pilotage Act 1987.

D Each contracting Pilot will subscribe equally to Manchester Pilots Limited (hereinafter called "MPL") a Cooperative registered under the Industrial and Provident Societies Acts 1965-1978 which will establish and administer a fund to which all agreed payments will be made by MSC for pilotage services rendered (hereinafter called the "Pilot Pool").

E Pilotage services shall mean the piloting of vessels within the harbour area at such times and places as MSC through the Harbour Master shall direct.

2 AGREEMENT

A This contract will commence on the 1st day of October 1988 and will be for a period of one year until the 30th day of September 1989 unless earlier agreement is reached between MSC and Mersey Docks and Harbour Company to amalgamate pilotage in the River Mersey and the Ship Canal, or the Secretary of State for Transport makes a direction under Section 12 (2) of the Pilotage Act 1987, whereupon this contract will terminate on the earlier of either the agreement of fresh terms of engagement for the Pilot between MSC and MPL or the award of an arbitration panel under Section 5 of the Pilotage Act 1987.

b If the PILOT is in breach of any of the conditions of this contract, his authorisation may be suspended or revoked by MSC as Competent Harbour Authority.

c In consideration of the Pilots supplying pilotage services to MSC, MSC shall on behalf of the agreed number of pilots' pay per pilot the sum of £1,750 per month plus a further sum of £250 per month for productivity to the Pilot Pool or such other sums as may be agreed within the Contract period.

d The PILOT shall be a member of Manchester Pilots Limited in accordance with the Memorandum and Articles of Association thereof, and on an equal basis with other like contracted Pilots.

e The PILOT shall share in the work with other contracting Pilots and shall provide cover as necessary for Pilots absent due to sickness, holiday or other causes.

f The PILOT undertakes to participate with other contracting Pilots in a system to give a continuous pilotage service for the Manchester Harbour Area 24 hours per day throughout the whole year.

g The agreed number of contracting pilots for the Manchester Harbour Area shall be determined on the basis referred to in the Heads of Agreement.

h Every PILOT shall at all times comply with the DUTIES OF PILOTS as detailed in the Schedule annexed hereto.

i The PILOT undertakes at all times to obey the lawful directions of the Harbour Master as to the allocation of berths, priority and rotation of ships to be handled, and as to movement within the harbour.

j MSC will not intercede between the PILOT and the MASTER of any vessel under pilotage without just cause and in general the PILOT will be responsible for the handling of the vessel whilst under pilotage subject to the vessel remaining under the overall direction of the Harbour Master.

k MSC shall appoint a Pilotage Liaison Committee on which MCL will be represented, which shall meet at such intervals as may be appropriate, in order to discuss matters of mutual concern including:

Conditions of Service
Operation of the Pilot Service
Changes in navigation aids
Accidents

and such other matters as may be mutually agreed.

l In case of any dispute which cannot be resolved by the Harbour Master alone, the matter may be referred to the Pilotage Liaison Committee.

m MSC undertake to provide suitable accommodation for and to defray all reasonable heating, lighting, telephone and subsistence costs of the pilots, when on duty.

n The PILOT shall be responsible with other Pilots for the cost of personal radio equipment, lifejackets, protective clothing and telephones as and when required.

o The PILOT undertakes to work at all times in conformity with the Company's Bye-Laws and current legislation in force, and in conformity with Sections 3 and 8 of the Health and Safety at Work Etc Act 1974.

SCHEDULE
DUTIES OF PILOTS

A The Pilots shall give ready obedience to all lawful orders and directions of the Harbour Master or his assistants and in every case where such orders or directions are not obeyed he shall immediately inform MSC.

B The Pilots shall give proper attention to all vessels requiring their assistance entering, leaving and moving in the Harbour Area. Every endeavour shall be made by the Pilots to supply pilotage services to ships requiring their services.

C A Pilot shall throughout the time he is in charge of a vessel use his utmost care and diligence for her safety and the safety of her crew, other vessels and property.

D If a Pilot becomes unfit through defective sight, hearing or other physical defect for the efficient performance of his duties he shall report the fact to MSC. A Pilot who becomes incapable by illness of taking his turn for duty shall if required by MSC produce medical evidence of his incapacity.

E A Pilot when on duty shall be uniformly dressed to a standard agreed with Manchester Pilots Limited - ie dark blue suit, white shirt, Pilot tie, dark socks, black shoes, overgarments: approved flotation coat - and shall have with him his Pilot's Authorisation, a reliable watch and Tide Tables.

F A Pilot shall report to MSC without undue delay on completion of a pilotage service the name of the vessel piloted, the nature of the service, the vessel's tonnages, size and draught and the time of arrival at, and departure from, the vessel. On completion of a pilotage service, the Officer in charge of the piloted vessel shall be required to sign a certificate for the services performed.

G A Pilot shall not undertake pilotage services outside the Harbour Area for which he is authorised.

H Whenever any accident shall have happened to or have been caused by any vessel while attended by a Pilot, such Pilot shall, as soon as practicable, report the facts of such accident, so far as he knows them, to the Harbour Master, or other authorised officer, and forward a written report to MSC. Such written report shall be made on the form provided for the purpose and be forwarded within five days of such accident.

I A Pilot on boarding a vessel in the Harbour Area shall, (as soon as possible), require the Master to give his name, the nature of the cargo, the draughts of the vessel and to declare any known defects or condition which may affect the safe navigation of the vessel in the harbour.

J Whenever any Pilot shall observe any alteration in any of the banks or in the depth of water in the Harbour Area, or shall observe that any buoys, beacons, or lights have been driven away, broken down or damaged, or are out of place, or shall observe any circumstances affecting safe navigation within the harbour Area, he shall report the facts forthwith and confirm them in writing to the Harbour Master.

K A Pilot shall at all times keep himself duly informed as to navigational aids, channel depths, and all other pertinent port data necessary to the execution of his duties as a Pilot.

APPENDIX X

CHANGE IN PILOT NUMBERS
As at May 1989

EMPLOYED STATUS

	1987	1989
Aberdeen	9	9
Belfast	12	12
Berwick	2	1
Bridgwater	1	1
Clyde	26	13
Coleraine	3	3
Crouch	6	2
Dover	New	4
Falmouth	6	6
Harwich	New	38
Heysham	4	2
Inverness	2	2
Kings Lynn	9	9
Liverpool	130	55
London		
North	103	32
Medway	31	29
South	64	26
West	61	28
Lowestoft	3	3
Milford Haven	17	13
Montrose	4	2
Orkney	11	12
Peterhead	3	3

Total reduction 159 Pilots (London North, Medway, South, West)

	1987	1989
Plymouth	3	3
Portsmouth	New	3
Ramsgate	New	3
Seaham	3	3
Shoreham	8	7
Southampton	40	31
Sullom Voe	11	8
Sunderland	5	6
Swansea incl Port Talbot	11	9
S E Wales	29	20
Gt Yarmouth	11	6
Totals	680	441

SELF-EMPLOYED STATUS

	1987	1989
Blyth	3	1
Boston	2	7
Bristol	24	12
Brixham	1	1
Dundee	9	8
Europilots	43	44
Forth	49	41
Londonderry	5	4
Fowey	7	4
Gloucester	12	8
Penzance	1	1
Holyhead	1	1
Lancaster	1	1
Manchester	60	33
Mostyn	2	3
Poole	7	4
Humber Goole & Trent		
Tees & Hartlepool	53	44
Teignmouth	2	3
Tyne	27	12
Weymouth	1	1
Whitehaven	7	3
Totals	491	400

THE JEWISH JOKE

DEVORAH BAUM is the author of *On Marriage* (Hamish Hamilton, 2023) and *Feeling Jewish (a Book for Just About Anyone)* (Yale, 2017), and co-director of the documentary feature films *The New Man* (2016) and *Husband* (2022). She is Associate Professor in English Literature at the University of Southampton.

ALSO BY DEVORAH BAUM

Feeling Jewish (a Book for Just About Anyone)

On Marriage

THE JEWISH JOKE

An essay with examples
(less essay, more examples)

DEVORAH BAUM

P

PROFILE BOOKS

For Josh, Manny and Isaiah

This paperback edition first published in 2023
First published in Great Britain in 2017 by
Profile Books Ltd
29 Cloth Fair
London
EC1A 7JQ

www.profilebooks.com

10 9 8 7 6 5 4 3 2 1

Designed and typeset by Jade Design
Printed and bound in Great Britain by
CPI Group (UK) Ltd, Croydon, CR0 4YY

A CIP catalogue record for this book is available from the British Library.

ISBN 978 1 80081 9115
eISBN 978 1 78283 193 8

Contents

INTRODUCTION

LESS ESSAY, MORE EXAMPLES

AND FINALLY . . .

Introduction

HOW DO YOU TELL THE DIFFERENCE BETWEEN A SHLEMIEL AND A SHLIMAZEL?

The Jewish joke is as old as Abraham. Like the Jews themselves, it has wandered over the world, learned various languages, worked with a range of different materials, and performed in front of some pretty hostile crowds. That it's been able, for the most part, to adapt and survive in ever-new pastures and among ever-new company is no mean feat. Jokes don't tend to travel all that well. And a lot of things that once seemed funny no longer are. Yet Jewish jokes, or a fair few of them, have had astonishing staying power. The popularity of a recent TV show, *Old Jews Telling Jokes*, plays up to this: the jokes and the jokers may be old, the show suggests, but they've still 'got it'. But *why* have they still got it? Is there no last laugh to be had? How old, really, can a joke get?

'There's an old joke,' Woody Allen's character Alvy says in the opening monologue of *Annie Hall* (1977):

> Uh, two elderly women are at a Catskills mountain resort, and one of 'em says, 'Boy, the food at this place is really terrible.' The other one says, 'Yeah, I know, and such ... small portions.' Well, that's essentially how I feel about life. Full of loneliness and misery and suffering and unhappiness, and it's all over much too quickly.

But what exactly *is* the old joke here? Is it the still-good punchline about 'such small portions'? Or is it the way of telling the joke so hesitantly that its punchline gets overwhelmed by the joker's neurosis? Are we laughing along with this comedian, or are we laughing at him? Are we laughing at the funny ha ha or at the funny peculiar? Or could it be something sadder we're finding funny? Might we be laughing, for instance, at how seriously the joke gets taken by a joker who has no sooner uttered it than he adds a commentary detailing an existential view of the world – one with a distinctly melancholic undertone?

'The-the other important joke for me,' Alvy falters on:

> ... is one that's, uh, usually attributed to Groucho Marx, but I think it appears originally in Freud's wit and its relation to the unconscious.* And it goes like this – I'm paraphrasing: Uh ... 'I would never wanna belong to any club that would have someone like me for a member.' That's the key joke of my adult life in terms of my relationships with women. Tsch, you know, lately the strangest things have been going through my mind, 'cause I turned forty, tsch, and I guess I'm going through a life crisis or something, I don't know. I, uh ... and I'm not worried about ageing. I'm not one o' those characters, you know. Although I'm balding slightly on top, that's about the worst you can say about me. I, uh, I think I'm gonna get better as I get older, you know? I think I'm gonna be the-the balding virile type, you know, as opposed to say the, uh, distinguished grey, for instance, you know? 'Less I'm neither o' those two. Unless I'm one o' those guys with saliva dribbling out of his mouth who wanders into a cafeteria with a shopping bag, screaming about socialism.

* Sigmund Freud's *Jokes and Their Relation to the Unconscious* (1905) is a sober study of the psychoanalysis of jokes and other uses of humour. Most of the jokes Freud offers by way of example are Jewish jokes.

That's some shtick: digressive, interpretative, remonstrative. And it's got a long memory too, treating an 'important joke' as if it were a piece of scripture to be traced back, first to its earlier comic source (Groucho), and then to an even earlier scholarly source (Freud – although I haven't spotted it there). But who on earth wants to hear shtick like that? Doesn't everyone know that jokes are best left at their punchlines? Nobody wants their jokes *explained,* do they? ... Unless explaining the joke is part of the joke – or part of the *Jewish* joke?

Alvy, above, makes no mention of Jewishness. Still, it's hard not to detect it in, for instance, the joke about belonging to clubs. For to get why this joker tells this joke in this particular way, by placing it within its Jewish heritage – Freud and (Groucho) Marx – you surely need an ironic sense of Jews as quintessentially members of a club to which they only really belong to the extent that they resist their membership. It's no accident, for example, that Alvy's life crisis has ensued because he can't make it work with a Jewish woman *or* with a shiksa (non-Jewish woman). Although if the shtick feels Jewish, then so too does the comedian himself, whose bespectacled face looms large and centre screen, eyes direct to camera, as if this were a joke on the cinema-going audience, who find themselves addressed by a less than obviously cinematic figure busily assuring them that he is a man in his prime, now and for ever the 'balding virile type'. Ha!

Of course, in 1977 Woody Allen was indeed a man in his prime, and he was taking the little respected art of comedy and turning it into something smart, serious and sublime. This he did with the comedian's gift for great timing. Just when the traditional frameworks and religious institutions of Jewish life were losing appeal for an upcoming generation determined to throw off the shackles of the old and substitute the new liberal order in all its lustre and complexity, Allen showed audiences that he knew and understood the critical value of time-keeping:

> I'm very proud of my gold pocket watch. My grandfather, on his deathbed, sold me this watch.*

> You look so beautiful I can hardly keep my eyes on the meter.**

> More than any other time in history, mankind faces a crossroads. One path leads to despair and utter

* *Stand Up Comic: 1964–1968.*
** *Manhattan* (1979).

> hopelessness. The other, to total extinction. Let us pray we have the wisdom to choose correctly.*

He showed, in other words, that he had his finger on the pulse of not only the present moment but the historical one. Because it isn't *really* the gold watch or ticking meter that tells the value of time for the comedian. It's a feel for the audience's narrative expectations and the ability to confound these with a sudden reversal or change of direction: what's known in the gag trade as a switcheroo. So where we're expecting a gift we get a sale, where we're expecting romance we get realism, where we're expecting a positive we get a second negative. To wit, the comedian is the person who reveals this to us, reveals that things can change when you least expect them to.

And the times they *do* keep on changing. Thus, in the words of the young American comedian Lena Dunham:

> Over time, my belief in many things has wavered: marriage, the afterlife, Woody Allen.**

* *New York Times*, 'My Speech to the Graduates' (1979).
** *Not That Kind of Girl: A Young Woman Tells You What She's 'Learned'* (2014).

Dunham's dismay at the clay feet of her comedy hero is palpable. Yet in saying so she also offers us a great line – a line reminiscent *of* Woody Allen, whose comic cadence it resembles while reminding us of Allen's main preoccupations: marriage, the afterlife, himself. So could this mean that – irony of ironies! – Allen *does* have an afterlife? Could all that Woodyish comedy – the sexual angst, the existential angst, the navel-gazing – have a young, hipster, *female* future?

When things reach crisis point, as they often do in Jewish history, it is Jewish custom to return to traditional sources for inspiration. According to the foundational text of Jewish mysticism, the Zohar, the biggest joke in the Hebrew Bible is the one when God tells Abraham to sacrifice his 'only son' Isaac. Isaac, whose name in Hebrew means 'laughter' on account of his mother Sarah's laughter upon learning at the age of ninety that she was about to become a parent for the first time – funny! – wasn't actually Abraham's 'only son'. He also had a son called Ishmael. Yet three times in the biblical story God insists that Isaac is the 'only one' to be sacrificed. Then, at the last moment, an angel stays Abraham's hand and recommends he sacrifices a ram in Isaac's place. So, a classic switcheroo. And boy oh boy, Abraham really fell for that one. The God of the Jews is clearly a prankster of the highest order. He's the God who laughs hard when, as the old joke goes, you tell Him your plans.

The darkly funny writer Franz Kafka detected in the same story a sort of blueprint for Jewish comedy. Once again, the joke is on Abraham, who now appears as less of a 'knight of faith' – as in the (also darkly funny) Protestant philosopher Søren Kierkegaard's sobriquet for him* – and more of a schlemiel. As Kafka tells it:

> It is as if, at the end of the year, when the best student was solemnly about to receive a prize, the worst student rose in the expectant stillness and came forward from his dirty desk in the last row because he had made a mistake of hearing, and the whole class burst out laughing. And perhaps he had made no mistake at all, his name really was called, it having been the teacher's intention to make the rewarding of the best student at the same time a punishment for the worst one.**

* Though in claiming that one arrives at Abrahamic faith 'by virtue of the absurd', Kierkegaard's *Fear and Trembling* (1843) clearly sees some humour in the escapade too.

** This can be found in Kafka's *Parables and Paradoxes in German and English* (Schocken Books, 1961).

Kafka's Abe has been singled out not for praise but for derision. He's the total shlemiel who, as he proudly walks to the front of the class to accept his 'prize', doesn't yet realise that the other kids are already laughing at the 'kick me' sign stuck to his back.

So is *that* – a sort of 'Bathos 101' – what explains the miraculous longevity of the Jewish joke? Does the full pantheon of Jewish comedy with all its parading fools – its shmucks, shlemiels, shlimazels, shnorrers, shmendricks, (sh)mothers (Yiddish has as many terms for fool as there are Inuit words for snow) – ramp up these various differences simply in order to disguise the overarching fact that any and every Jew answering to the name is not only 'in' on the joke, but the butt of it?

Or to put it slightly differently:

> Q: How *do* you tell the difference between a shlemiel and a shlimazel?
>
> A: The shlemiel is the one who slips up and spills his soup *over* the shlimazel.*

* From the Yiddish *shlim* (bad, wrong) and *mazl* (luck). While in America the use of the Yiddish word *shlimazel* nearly always alludes to a born loser, in Britain you'll just as often find it referring to a messy situation. In June 2004 *shlimazel* was voted one of the ten hardest-to-translate non-English words by a British translation company.

And in a joke, a little slip can make all the difference. Not that you can put limits on slipperiness. For as different as we may well be from each other, we're all, surely, alike in this: our identities are not so much fixed, as a matter of where it is we happen to be standing in relation to everyone else at any given time. Hence if, as Kafka has it, Jews are history's greatest schlemiels, then that doesn't make them *so* different. What it makes them is one half of an eternally returning comedy double act in which, as we'll see, all other Jews, Gentiles, the Chinese and *even* God can't help getting a little soupy.

The Chinese?

Yes. Jews distinguish Chinese people from all other Gentiles on account of a) China being a very long way away from where most Jews find themselves standing, and b) the privileged position of Chinese cuisine within the Jewish *Weltanschauung* (Jews may abandon Jewish dietary laws when inside Chinese restaurants alone):

> A Jewish man and a Chinese man were conversing. The Jewish man commented upon what a wise people the Chinese are.

'Yes,' replied the Chinese man, 'our culture is over four thousand years old. But you Jews are a very wise people, too.'

The Jewish man replied, 'Yes, our culture is over five thousand years old.'

The Chinese man was incredulous. 'That's impossible,' he replied. 'Where did your people eat for a thousand years?'

More recently, however, the Chinese have also been introduced to Jewish cuisine:

Upon leaving a kosher restaurant, one Chinese diner says to another: 'The problem with Jewish food is that two days later you're hungry again.'*

* The jokes I've included in this book belong to two categories: those that illustrate the arguments of the essay and those, like this one, that have no obvious place in the essay but were too good to leave out.

Less Essay,
More Examples

HOW DO YOU TELL THE DIFFERENCE BETWEEN ONE JEW AND ANOTHER JEW?

You'll have heard it said that wherever you can find two Jews, you'll find at least three opinions. It's because Jews don't only disagree with Gentiles, or with each other, they don't even agree with themselves:

> A Jew is shipwrecked on a desert island. Years later, a passing ship notices his campfire and stops to rescue him. When the captain comes ashore, the castaway thanks him profusely and offers to give him a tour of the little island. He shows off the weapons he made for hunting, the fire pit where he cooks his food, the synagogue he built for praying in, the hammock

> where he sleeps. On their way back to the ship, however, the captain notices a second synagogue. 'I don't understand,' the captain asks; 'why build two synagogues?' 'This,' says the Jew, motioning to one, 'is the synagogue I pray in, and this,' he motions at the other, 'is the synagogue I wouldn't be seen dead in.'

What is quintessentially Jewish? It's being at odds with oneself. It's taking pride in one's difference *and* feeling ashamed of it at the same time. Hence, perhaps, why self-deprecation plays such a key role in Jewish joking – so much so, in fact, that Freud could ponder 'whether there are many other instances of a people making fun to such a degree of its own character'.

And yet the funniest thing about Jewish self-deprecation is the pride that Jews are wont to take in it:

> It is the Yom Kippur service and the cantor suddenly stops mid-prayer and declares, 'Forgive me, God! I can't say this! I'm just a nothing!' Later the rabbi, mid-sermon, stops and cries, 'Forgive *me*, God! *I* am not worthy! *I'm* only a nothing!' Seeing this, the synagogue's caretaker charges from the back of the synagogue. 'If you two great men are unworthy to

> beseech God, then what right have I, as someone so ordinary? I'm a complete nothing! Oy vey, am I a nothing!' At which point the rabbi taps the cantor on the shoulder: '*Look* who thinks he's nothing.'

No two nothings are ever quite the same. Thus the joker's modest pose is assumed, the better to distance the joker from the real butt of her joke – always those *other* Jews whom she doesn't resemble in the least:

> A woman is riding a bus in the Midwest, when a man gets on the bus and sits down next to her. He's wearing a black hat, long black coat, black trousers and shoes, and he has a long curly dark beard.
>
> The woman looks at him with disgust. 'Jews like you,' she hisses at him.
>
> He looks up at her, puzzled, and says, 'I beg your pardon, madam?'
>
> She says, 'Look at you. All in black, a beard, never take off your hat! It's Jews like you that give the rest of us a bad name.'

> 'I beg your pardon, madam, but I am not Jewish. I'm Amish.'
>
> The woman suddenly smiles, 'Oh, how *darling*! You've kept your customs.'

It's a Jewish joke, in effect, *about* the Jewish joke – about the types of jokes that assimilated Western Jews have historically told to denigrate and thus distance themselves from their poorer relatives, the so-called *Ostjuden* (Jews from the East). Indeed, given how often Jewish jokes seem to turn on such divisions and doublings within Jewish identity, one wonders if Jewishness itself mightn't be structured like a joke.

Of what such a suggestion might mean, there's more in the rest of the book. But for now let's simply note that, *like* jokes, Jews love nothing more than telling the difference between things – and especially each other:

> Q: How do you tell the difference between one Jew and another Jew?
>
> A: Wait, wait. They'll tell *you*.

HOW DO YOU TELL THE DIFFERENCE BETWEEN A JEW AND A GENTILE?

There are occasions, though, when Jews *do* form a collective identity:

> Back in the day, two Jews, Moishe and Itzik, are walking in the Ukrainian forest. In the distance, they see two local guys walking towards them. Moishe turns to Itzik, panics, and says, 'Itzik, what should we do? There's two of them, and we're all alone!'

There are a great many candidates for the world's most Jewish joke, but this one, for me, tops the list. Because there they are, those proverbial 'two Jews' – all alone in a big bad world, feeling weak and outnumbered (regardless of their strength or numbers), as two non-Jews (brute simpletons, obviously) approach them ... Ahhhh! Danger! Help! What are two all-alone Jews expected to do in such a dastardly situation? Tell jokes?

Well, yes, as it happens. Here, for example, are those same two Jews encountering difficulties again:

> Two Jews, driving a wagon along a narrow road, come to a place where boulders are blocking their path. They sit, considering what to do, discussing each of their options in great detail. Suddenly two Gentiles come along in another wagon, jump out of their seat, roll up their sleeves and push the boulders off the road.
>
> 'There, that's goyish thinking for you,' says one of the Jews, 'always with the might.'

Here, on the other hand, is Jewish thinking for you:

> A Jewish woman in a hospital tells the doctor she wants to be transferred to a different hospital.
>
> The doctor says, 'What's wrong? Is it the food?'
>
> 'No, the food is fine. I can't kvetch [complain].'

'Is it the room?'

'No, the room is fine. I can't kvetch.'

'Is it the staff?'

'No, everyone on the staff is fine. I can't kvetch.'

'Then why do you want to be transferred?'

'I can't kvetch!'

Kvetching is that special type of pleasure to be elicited from complaining even when things go right – because if there's one thing Jews can be sure of, it's that there's *always* a negative.

And, as we'll discover, there are reasons for that. For it's not only that Jews love to kvetch, they also take a pretty dim view of the world:

Q: How many Jewish mothers does it take to change a lightbulb?

A: That's OK, don't trouble yourself, we'll sit in the dark.

Given the ordeal that characterises so much of Jewish history, it's hardly surprising if Jews *do* tend to see things darkly (not to mention the expense to be spared when the lights are turned off*). But what jokes like these also show is that, while an intolerable heaviness has been the burden of Jewish history, it's a heaviness accompanied by an irreverent levity whose aim it is to make that intolerable heaviness a little more, well, tolerable:

> Two Jews sat in a coffeehouse, discussing the fate of their people.
>
> 'How miserable is our history,' said one. 'Pogroms, plagues, discrimination, Hitler, neo-Nazis ... Sometimes I think we'd be better off if we'd never been born.'
>
> 'Sure,' said his friend. 'But who has that much luck, maybe one in ten thousand?'

So it's not for nothing that the waiter must ask of the Jewish diners, 'Is *anything* all right?' Though the waiter's question is best considered alongside the

* Hard to resist, though precisely the kind of borderline anti-Semitic joke that only Jews can reasonably expect to get away with.

jokes Jews sometimes like to tell about their comedy counterparts – those peculiarly unflappable creatures known as 'Gentiles' ...

Two Gentiles run into one another in the street.

'Hi, John. How are you?'

'Oh, hello, Freddie. I'm fine, thanks.'

Jews find that one side-splittingly funny. And this one ...

A Gentile calls his mother.

'Hello, Mum.'

'Hi, darling.'

'I can't come over for dinner tonight after all.'

'OK. See you soon.'

Hilarious!

As for the mothers of *Jews*, still sitting there, lightbulb-less, in the dark ('Honestly, we're fine like this, you go ahead and enjoy yourself ...'), well, at least they have each other to kvetch with:

'Oy,' says one.

'Oy vey,' sighs a second.

'Nu,' shrugs the third.

At this, the fourth gets up from her chair, glowering. 'I thought we'd agreed *not* to talk about our children!'

HOW DO YOU TELL THE DIFFERENCE BETWEEN A JEWISH PERSON AND A COMEDIAN?

Remember that episode of *Seinfeld* when Jerry's dentist converts to Judaism?* Jerry is seated in his dentist's chair, and his dentist tells him a (not very good) Jewish joke about matzo balls:

> Jerry: 'Do you think you should be making jokes like that?'
>
> Dentist: 'Why not, I'm Jewish, remember? Jerry, it's our sense of humour that sustained us as a people for three thousand years.'

* 'The Yada Yada' (TV episode, 1997).

Jerry: 'Five thousand.'

Dentist: 'Five thousand – even better.'

His dentist, Jerry figures, shouldn't get to tell Jewish jokes – you need millennia of persecution to have a sense of humour like that (though, you have to admit, 'Five thousand – even better' *is* a pretty good Jewish joke). But does Jerry really have the right to kvetch? For while having badly-told Jewish jokes visited upon you while supine in your dentist's chair is no picnic, Jerry hasn't *personally* suffered so much of that history of persecution. Yet there's something about his dentist's conversion to Judaism that troubles him. What, he suspects, his dentist may *really* be after is the holy grail of comedy: 'total joke-telling immunity'. Getting to tell any joke he likes. Which is such chutzpah, it's enough to lead Jerry to a confession box to grass on the dentist to his former priest:

Jerry: 'I have a suspicion that he converted to Judaism only for the jokes.'

Father: 'And this offends you as a Jewish person?'

Jerry: 'No, it offends me as a comedian!'

And if you remain unsure *how* exactly to tell the difference between a Jewish person and a comedian, then you're probably getting what I take to be the point of the whole episode: it isn't so easy to tell.

In fact, when his dentist first announces his conversion, Jerry's response – 'Welcome aboard!' – is less offended, or delighted, than bemused. If, indeed, *anything* tells the difference between Judaism and the major monotheisms to which it's most often compared, this could well be it: while Christians and Muslims tend to regard converts to their faith as serious people of good sense, Jews harbour a sneaking suspicion that the would-be Jewish convert must be joking.

Although if Jews often have a hard time accepting why anyone would want to convert *to* Judaism, they're usually even less accepting of those who attempt to convert *out* of it:

Two Jews are strolling down the street one day in the Pale of Settlement, when they happen to walk past a church. Above the door of the church they see a big sign that says 'Convert and get ten rubles'. Moishe stops, stares at the sign and turns to his friend:

> 'Avreleh, I'm thinking of doing it.' With that, he strides purposefully into the church. Twenty minutes later he comes out with his head bowed.
>
> 'So', asks Avreleh, 'did you get your ten rubles?'
>
> Moishe looks at him contemptuously: 'Is that *all* you people think about?'

Which is surely one of the best jokes, let alone Jewish jokes, of all time, because it demonstrates so neatly how power really works.

And such jokes also help to explain why Jews, historically, have often viewed conversion as a sociopolitical rather than authentically religious phenomenon:

> Four converts trade stories about why they converted. The first claims he was a victim of a false accusation and converted to escape the harsh sentence he would otherwise have had to serve. The second confesses that her parents drove her wild with complaints about her lax observance, so she converted to spite them. The third gives a rambling account of falling in love with a Christian boy: she converted in order to marry him. The fourth pipes up: 'Unlike the

> rest of you, I converted out of a firm conviction that Christianity is a religion of a higher order.'
>
> 'Oh, PLEASE!' the others interrupt him. 'Save that for your goyishe friends!'

Which suspicion of conversion has lingered even when Jews have turned to other religions during more liberal times:

> My best friend is a Jewish Buddhist. Believes you should renounce all material possessions but still keep the receipts. *David Baddiel*

So you think you can cease to be Jewish, huh? Well then, the joke's on you:

> Mr Dropkin was on a business trip in a small town and was giving his major presentation on the stage when he bent over and gave the loudest fart anyone had ever heard. He never showed up in that small town again. But many, many, many years later he was invited back. Undecided whether or not he could yet show his face, he tried to coax himself: 'I'm so old now,' he thought. 'Surely no one will remember me from all those years ago. I don't even look as I did

then.' So he decided to return. All the same, when checking into the hotel he took the precaution of changing his name.

'Have you ever visited our pretty town before?' the hotel receptionist asked him, genially.

'Only once,' said Mr Dropkin. 'But it was a long time ago and between you and me I haven't returned until now because I've always been so embarrassed about a very painful experience that happened to me when I was here, and have feared that people might still remember it.'

'Oh, what a shame!' said the receptionist, before reassuring him, 'you know, people have such short memories and they're really only focused on their own lives – things are never quite so bad as you think. So I'm sure you're being paranoid. I mean, how long ago *was* this incident?'

Dropkin said he didn't exactly remember.

'Well, was it before or after the Dropkin fart?'

HOW DO YOU TELL THE DIFFERENCE BETWEEN A JEW AND A PARROT?

We can think of the Dropkin fart as a metaphor for Jewish history: however much Jews try to repress their origins, they've learned the hard way that what they thought was past always returns to embarrass them by slipping out one way or the other:

> A Jew converts and becomes a priest. He gives his first Mass in front of a number of high-ranking priests who came for the occasion. At the end of the new priest's sermon a cardinal goes to congratulate him. 'Father Goldberg,' he says, 'that was very well done, you were just perfect. Just one little thing. Next time, try not to start your sermon with 'My fellow goyim ...'

It can happen anywhere:

> James and Gracie Carter put on their finest clothes and head out to one of London's swankiest restaurants for their anniversary dinner. The waiter hands them the menu. James looks it over as if a habitué.
>
> 'And what would sir like for his main?' the waiter asks.
>
> 'Whatever you recommend,' says James dismissively, 'just so long as it's treyf [non-kosher].'
>
> 'Oy vey!' exclaims a nearby diner … 'Whatever *that* means.'

It's a problem that Jews have even had to contend with in the *new* world – the reason, for example, why the Cohens of Boston decided to name their newborn son Luke Lincoln Cohen because *Abraham* Lincoln sounded too Jewish.

What such jokes – and there are many of them – seem to suggest is that there's something unshakeable about Jewishness. 'When you wake up,' the American comedian Judy Gold was once asked, 'do you feel more Jewish or more lesbian?'

> I always feel Jewish. I get up and my back hurts, I've got to go to the bathroom, I've got to have a coffee. I'm a Jew. I don't wake up and go, 'Oh, my God, that girl's hot.' It's 'I gotta put some beans in the coffee thing. Should I make oatmeal? I need to go to the gym – no, I don't feel like going.' I wake up like an elderly Jew in assisted living.*

A new day it may be, but still there's the same old tsores (troubles, sufferings, oy oy oys) – and it's *that* (plus the vague distrust of the coffee 'thing') that feels Jewish.

Which isn't, of course, to deny that other people have their tsores too:

> A formerly religious young man is attending Oxford University. When his father, with a long beard, skullcap and side curls, comes to visit him, he is filled with shame and tells his father in no uncertain terms that he feels all his success at fitting in at one of Britain's elite institutions will be undone by this spectacle of difference. Wanting to aid his son, his father heads for a barber and has his side curls removed, his beard shaved off, and he even takes off his skullcap. At that

* Interview for *Out Magazine* (2016).

> point his father bursts into tears. Profoundly moved, his son says, 'But, Father, I never meant for you to lose your identity entirely. I just wanted you to minimise your difference, not obliterate it. I'm so sorry for the pain I've caused you.'
>
> 'No, no, it's not that,' says his father, 'I'm crying because we lost India.'

Oy oy oy indeed.

But even when a Jew, such as the man weeping openly for the loss not of his side curls, but of India, does genuinely appear to have recalibrated his identity, the lesson of the Dropkin fart may still apply. Thus, if we say, for the sake of argument, that a Jew wakes up, goes to the bathroom, has coffee and oatmeal, and is looking and acting much like anyone else by the time they're on the street, even then there's usually some other Jew threatening to expose them. As Freud tells it:

> A Galician Jew was travelling in a train. He had made himself very comfortable, had unbuttoned his coat and put his feet up on the seat. Just then a gentleman in modern dress entered the compartment. The Jew promptly pulled himself together and took up a

proper pose. The stranger fingered through the pages in a notebook, made some calculations, reflected for a moment and then suddenly asked the Jew, 'Excuse me, when is Yom Kippur [the Day of Atonement]?'

'Oho!' said the Jew, relaxing entirely, and put his feet up before answering.

But, who is the butt of the joke here? Is it the old-world Jew as seen through the eyes of his assimilated cousin, or isn't the Galician Jew just another shlemiel making a shlimazel out of the straight guy?

A woman on a train leans over to another passenger. 'Excuse me,' she says, 'but are you Jewish?'

'No,' replies the man.

A few minutes later she asks again. 'Excuse me,' she says, 'are you sure you're not Jewish?'

'I'm sure,' says the man.

But the woman's unconvinced, and a few minutes later she inquires a third time. 'Are you absolutely sure you're not Jewish?'

> 'All right, all right,' the man says. 'You win. I'm Jewish.'
>
> 'That's funny,' says the woman.' You don't look Jewish.'

For who but a Jew would dream of showing so little sign of it?

Then again, Jews are liable to find equally suspect the Jew who appears *not* to be hiding:

> Two rivals meet in the Warsaw train station. 'Where are you going?' says the first.
>
> 'To Minsk,' says the second.
>
> 'To Minsk, eh? What a nerve! I know you're telling me you're going to Minsk because you want me to think that you're really going to Pinsk. But it so happens that I know you really *are* going to Minsk. So ... why are you lying to me?'

So you're telling the truth? Well, isn't *that* a good disguise!

Jokes about Jews on a train are jokes about Jews as passengers – as people who are always attempting to pass ... go along with ... assimilate ... parody ... *parrot* ...

Meyer, a lonely widower, was walking home one night when he passed a pet store and heard a squawking voice shouting out in Yiddish, 'Quawwwwk ... vus machst du ... yeah, du ... outside, standing like a shlemiel ... eh?'

Meyer rubbed his eyes and ears. He couldn't believe it. The proprietor sprang out of the door and grabbed Meyer by the sleeve. 'Come in here, fella, and check out this parrot.'

Meyer stood in front of an African Grey that cocked his little head and said, 'Vus? Ir kent reddin Yiddish?'

Meyer turned excitedly to the store owner. 'He speaks Yiddish?'

In a matter of moments, Meyer had placed five hundred dollars down on the counter and carried the parrot in his cage away with him. All night he talked with the parrot in Yiddish. He told the parrot about his father's adventures coming to America, about how beautiful his mother was when she was a young bride, about his family, about his years of working in the garment centre, about Florida. The parrot listened and commented. They shared some walnuts.

The parrot told him of living in the pet store, how he hated the weekends. Finally, they both went to sleep.

Next morning, Meyer began to put on his tefillin [phylacteries], all the while saying his prayers. The parrot demanded to know what he was doing, and when Meyer explained, the parrot wanted to do it too. Meyer went out and made a miniature set of tefillin for the parrot. The parrot wanted to learn to daven [pray], so Meyer taught him how to read Hebrew, and taught him every prayer in the Siddur with the appropriate nusach [version] for the daily services. Meyer spent weeks and months sitting and teaching the parrot the Torah, Mishnah and Gemara. In time, Meyer came to love and count on the parrot as a friend and a Jew.

On the morning of Rosh Hashanah, Meyer rose, got dressed and was about to leave when the parrot demanded to go with him. Meyer explained that shul [synagogue] was not a place for a bird, but the parrot made a terrific argument and was carried to shul on Meyer's shoulder. Needless to say, they made quite a sight when they arrived at the shul, and Meyer was questioned by everyone, including the rabbi and cantor, who refused to allow a bird into the building on the High Holy Days. However, Meyer convinced them to let him in this one time, swearing that the parrot could daven.

Wagers were made with Meyer. Thousands of dollars were bet that the parrot could NOT daven, could not speak Yiddish or Hebrew, and so on. All eyes were on the African Grey during services. The parrot perched on Meyer's shoulder as each prayer and song passed – Meyer heard not a peep from the bird. He began to become annoyed, slapping at his shoulder and mumbling under his breath, 'Daven!'

Nothing.

'Daven ... Feigelleh, please! You can daven, so daven ... come on, everybody's looking at you!'

Nothing.

After Rosh Hashanah services were concluded, Meyer found that he owed his shul buddies and the rabbi several thousand dollars. He marched home quite upset, saying nothing. Finally, several blocks from the shul, the bird, happy as a lark, began to sing an old Yiddish song. Meyer stopped and looked at him.

> 'You miserable bird, you cost me over four thousand dollars. Why? After I made your tefillin, taught you the morning prayers and taught you to read Hebrew and the Torah. And after you begged me to bring you to shul on Rosh Hashanah, why? Why did you do this to me?'
>
> 'Don't be a shlemiel,' the parrot replied. 'You know what odds we'll get at Yom Kippur?'

What kind of Jewishness is the parrot parroting? Not, it seems, the official text – the liturgy, the language and the law – but the subtext – the ghetto, street-smart survival instinct and adaptability. *Convert and get ten rubles!* Or, as Groucho Marx had it:

> These are my principles! If you don't like them, I have others.

Hard not to laugh at such a luminous line. Still, there is, undeniably, a problem here: the problem as to why so many Jewish jokes and jokers depict Jews as charlatans or liars – so sneaky that even the honest ones are condemned as duplicitous. For if even Jews don't trust each other, what are non-Jews meant to make of them? Aren't Jewish jokes then guilty of *stoking* anti-Semitism?

In some cases, perhaps they are. But we can equally hear these same jokes, alongside Groucho's quips, as engaged in something more subtle: by joking about the slipperiness of the Jew, what such jokes also describe is the inherent slipperiness of the outsider's position. For in order to fit in with the dominant social group, the parrot will try to imitate the language of its hosts so as to get noticed, establish lines of communication and have its needs met. So if even for the *parrot* parroting is essentially a survival strategy, then the same, surely, may be assumed of the parroting Jew.

Do jokes about the slipperiness of Jewish identities appear less damning, then, if considered in such terms? The line to be drawn here is nothing if not blurry. Because it's true: when jokes about Jews attempting to pass are told by non-Jews, they *do* sound suspiciously similar to anti-Semitic ones. And actually, come to think of it ...

HOW DO YOU TELL THE DIFFERENCE BETWEEN A JEW AND AN ANTI-SEMITE?

> The anti-Semite thinks the Jews are a despicable race, but Cohen? He's not too bad actually. Kushner? A stand-up guy. The Jew, on the other hand, believes his people are a light unto the nations, but Cohen? What a shmuck! Kushner? Don't get me started!

So when it comes to telling the difference, even here we're in the realm of the slippery. And thus the same may be said of the difference between a Jewish joke and an anti-Semitic one. For while some Jewish jokes seem to manifest an internalised anti-Semitism, others poke fun at the anti-Semitism they parrot:

Rabbi Altmann and his secretary were sitting in a coffeehouse in Berlin in 1935. 'Herr Altmann,' said his secretary, 'I notice you're reading *Der Stürmer*! I can't understand why. A Nazi libel sheet! Are you some kind of masochist, or, God forbid, a self-hating Jew?'

'On the contrary, Frau Epstein. When I used to read the Jewish papers, all I learned about were pogroms, riots in Palestine, and people leaving the faith in America. But now that I read *Der Stürmer*, I see so much more: that the Jews control all the banks, dominate in the arts and are on the verge of taking over the entire world. You know – it makes me feel a whole lot better.'

Jews have got rather used to hearing that they're responsible for all the world's problems. And not only the man-made ones, the natural ones too:

'Did you hear that Jews sunk the *Titanic*?'

'The Jews? I thought it was an iceberg.'

'Iceberg, Goldberg, Rosenberg, they're all the same.'

But even during the worst of times they've found ways to joke:

> Cohen lives in Berlin in 1933. He's walking along the street when Hitler drives up in a Volkswagen and leaps out with a Luger pistol in his hand. 'Get down in the gutter and eat the filth like the dog you are, Jew!' he snarls.
>
> Cohen has no choice. He obeys and eats the filth. Hitler starts laughing at the sight so hard that he drops the gun. Cohen snatches it up. 'Your turn, mein Führer,' he says, and points to the gutter.
>
> Later that night, Cohen comes home. His wife asks how his day went.
>
> 'Oh, so-so ... But you'll never guess who I had lunch with today ...'

Although, as we find in the following dialogue from Woody Allen's film *Deconstructing Harry* (1997), one can't always tell if the joker *is* even joking:

> Burt: 'Do you care even about the Holocaust, or do you think it never happened?'

Harry: 'Not only do I know that we lost six million, but the scary thing is that records are made to be broken.'

HOW DO YOU TELL THE DIFFERENCE BETWEEN JOKING AND NOT JOKING?

When Jerry's dentist proclaims, with the zeal of the newly converted, that 'it's our sense of humour that sustained us', he may make *us* laugh, but he isn't joking. Though to truly appreciate his formula for funniness – the more suffering you've had, the funnier you get to be – you'd need to look not to the minor irritations that rankle the cast of *Seinfeld*, but to Jewish life in the kind of pogrom-prone place where it's not always that easy to tell the difference between what *is* and isn't a joke:

> 'Good news! Good news! The child that got killed in the forest yesterday? He's Jewish!'

The 'joke'? That one murdered Jewish child in the forest may be counted 'good news' when contrasted with the pogrom liable to follow the discovery of a murdered Christian child. Sometimes we laugh, in other words, when we recognise a (terrible) truth. Or when we realise that what we're hearing *should* be a joke, but isn't.

We tend to think of wit as a form of levity, but as even the joke's own vocabulary attests, there are darker, more aggressive sides to humour. Consider the word *punchline*, for instance, with its suggestion that someone, by the end of the joke, is guaranteed to get knocked out. How should we understand such a 'technical' term? Do jokes necessarily require victims?

In the annals of Jewish joking we can see why punchlines might make sense:

> Mendel the butcher is walking to his store one morning when a stranger runs up, punches him in the face and says, 'That's for you, Yossel.'
>
> Mendel is surprised, but quickly starts to laugh.
>
> The stranger says, 'Why are you laughing? Do you want me to punch you again?'

> Mendel says, 'No, it's just that the joke's on you – I'm not Yossel!'

For when life's bound to beat you one way or another, you get your laughs however you can.

Though 'having a laugh' clearly isn't the only thing going on here. In Israeli author David Grossman's novel, *A Horse Walks into a Bar* (2017), set in a comedy club in which a stand-up comedian intersperses stock-in-trade gags within a much more disquieting monologue, it's the propensity to self-harm that first sets his audience on edge: 'He gives his forehead a loud, unfathomably powerful smack ... It was an awful blow, that slap. An outburst of unexpected violence, a leakage of murky information'. And as the comedy swerves towards the painfully testimonial, our narrator, watching him, begins to understand what that murky information is: 'he is uniting with his abuser. Beating himself with another man's hands.' Thus what we see in the novel, rather like its pictured audience of repelled but fascinated spectators, is a sort of disrobing of the entire comedic project: instead of a comedian telling 'cracks' and the audience 'cracking up', his 'cracks' reveal deeper cracks as roles are reversed and it's the man on stage who cracks up.

Joking has always been a good cover for not joking. When speaking 'only in jest', one may speak of unspeakable things. The Holocaust survivor and novelist Aharon Appelfeld has written of how immediately after the war the victims of the camps were unable to talk about their experiences with each other directly *other* than through grotesque comic performances. Rather than thinking of comedy as tragedy plus time,* he found that comedy was the language that instinctively came first – possibly because it was the only genre that acknowledged the sheer impossibility of representing what the victims had lived through…

> A Holocaust survivor gets up to heaven, meets God.
>
> He tells God a Holocaust joke: God doesn't laugh.
>
> He shrugs: I guess you had to be there.

The child of a Holocaust survivor, David Schneider has long since been interested in the curious compulsion of so many jokers to find the laughs in

* A popular definition of comedy that has been attributed to various people but was most probably coined in the 1950s by Steve Allen, an American TV personality.

those things that clearly aren't in any straightforward sense 'funny':

> As a comedian, I've always been fascinated by whether you can do comedy about such a difficult and taboo subject.
>
> I used to compere Jewish comedy gigs and I remember once getting a note passed to me backstage saying: 'We are a coach party of Auschwitz survivors come to see you. Please can you say hello to us during the gig?'
>
> And I just thought, what am I meant to do? Go on and shout: 'Hi, is there anybody from Auschwitz in the place tonight?'

Thus, while it's understandable when people prefer not to laugh at such horrors, or feel shocked when others do, it would be a mistake to assume too much about anyone's laughter. Laughter, after all, frequently assails its subjects unbidden, implying that there may be things folded into it that aren't always known or recognised by the one who laughs. What's more, by paying attention to the alternative ways there always are of viewing even the darkest things, seeing the funny side is a skill worth having – not only for its ability to leaven our bleakest moments, but because joking is what occasionally allows otherwise unspeakable truths to come out. And should there be any doubt about the gravity of the situations to which comedy can sometimes rise, note that Volodymyr Zelenskyy, the former Jewish comedian turned President of Ukraine leading the resistance against the military invasion of his country, hasn't found that war leader and joker are altogether incompatible roles – in October 2022, for instance, when interviewed by David Letterman for the Netflix series 'My Next Guest Needs No Introduction', he told this joke:

> Two Jewish guys from Odessa meet up. One asks the other: 'So what's the situation? What are people saying?'
>
> 'What are people saying? They are saying it's a war.'
>
> 'What kind of war?'
>
> 'Russia is fighting NATO.'
>
> 'Are you serious?'

> 'Yes, yes! Russia is fighting NATO.'
>
> 'So how's it going?'
>
> 'Well, 70,000 Russian soldiers are dead. The missile stockpile has almost been depleted. A lot of equipment is damaged, blown up.'
>
> 'And what about NATO?'
>
> 'What about NATO? NATO hasn't even arrived yet.'

So why, in the midst of such darkness, see the funny side? Because to do so can admit of hard-to-grasp realities, just as it can identify blind spots, multiply perspectives, and even create new possibilities. For which reason, there's little to wonder at in the thought that Jews, wishing to expand the often narrowest of horizons, have so frequently *depended* on the funny. After all, there's nothing so bad that it can't get worse:

> Two Jews are in front of a firing squad awaiting their execution. As they stand there, the leader of the firing squad asks them, 'Do either of you have any last requests?'

The first Jew says, 'There's been a terrible mistake!'

The second Jew turns to him and whispers, 'Morris, don't make trouble.'

Nor anything so innocuous that it won't prove malign:

An Englishman, a Scotsman and a Jew are sitting on a park bench.

The Englishman says, 'I am so tired and thirsty, I must have beer.'

The Scotsman says, 'I am so tired and thirsty, I must have whisky.'

The Jew says, 'I am so tired and thirsty, I must have diabetes.'

Nor any response so enthusiastic that it doesn't reveal a criticism:

A Jewish mother gives her son two neckties for his birthday. The boy hurries into his bedroom, rips off the tie he's wearing, puts on one of the ties his mother

> has brought him, and hurries back.
>
> 'Look, Mama! Isn't it gorgeous?'
>
> His mother responds, 'What's the matter? You don't like the other one?'

Which is a bit of a mood-killer admittedly, and yet it's in precisely this nit-picking response that we can identify the lesson of Jewish history, along with that of the joke: there's always a flipside.

HOW DO YOU TELL THE DIFFERENCE BETWEEN A BLESSING AND A CURSE?

That the Jews who can spot the cheerier side of bad news can also spot the gloomier side of good news explains the deliciously contrarian spite to be found in typical Yiddish curses:

> 'May you become so rich that you're the richest person in your whole family!'

> 'May you become so rich that your wife's second husband never has to work a day in his life!'

Indeed, the standard response of today's average teenager upon hearing anything positive – 'good luck with *that*' – has long since been the standard Jewish blessing: 'Mazel tov!' (literally 'good luck' rather than, as is more commonly translated, 'congratulations'). And certainly nothing gets a Jew down like 'positive thinking':

A group of Jews are discussing the state of the world:

'The economy is crashing and you know who they'll blame for it, don't you?'

'Have you *seen* the things they've been saying about us on social media?'

'Everyone's an anti-Semite. Trust nobody.'

'They always claim it's our fault.'

'Or Israel's fault.'

'What's *wrong* with you people? Why can't you be a bit more positive? Me, I'm an optimist!'

'You look pretty anxious for an optimist.'

'You think it's *easy* being an optimist?'

For most of their long history in the Diaspora, Jews have not had the resources to become warriors for their cause. As such, they've become worriers for their cause:

> The citizens of Chelm [fantasy shtetl of Jewish joking lore] used to spend a good deal of time worrying – so much time, in fact, that they soon began to worry about how much they worried.
>
> The Grand Council of Wise Men convened a meeting to discuss all this worrying, and to find a solution for it. For seven days and seven nights the wise men of Chelm discussed the problem, until finally the chairman announced a solution: Yossel, the chimney sweep, would be the official Chelm Worrier. In return for one ruble a week, he would do the worrying for everybody in Chelm. The Grand Council members all agreed that this was the ideal solution, but just before the vote was taken, one of the sages rose to speak against the proposal.
>
> 'Wait a minute,' he announced. 'If Yossel were to be paid one ruble a week, then what would he have to worry about?'

Still, Jews try not to worry until the optimal moment:

> The astronomer was concluding a lecture: 'Some believe the sun will die out within about four or five billion years.'
>
> '*How* many years did you say?' asked Mrs Shindler.
>
> 'Four or five billion.'
>
> 'Phew!' she replied, 'I thought you said *million*!'

And they can usually spot when the tides are turning and the signs are looking good:

> Two Jewish POWs are about to be shot. Suddenly the order comes to hang them instead. One smiles to the other: 'You see? They're running out of bullets.'

Telling the blessing from the curse, in other words, is really a matter of where you lay the emphasis – just as, no matter how good the joke you're about to utter may be, it'll fall flat on its face if you don't intone it right.

But while such jokes are obviously funny, they do more than merely amuse. For the laughter that hinges on surprise – for example, at the sudden reversal of meaning when a hanging becomes evidence of a bullet shortage – reminds whoever hears it that it's possible to *be* surprised. And that, interestingly, is something the joke shares with the messianic structure of the story that Jews tell of their own history. Indeed, what both Jewish history and Jewish jokes reveal is not dissimilar: there's always another way of seeing things, always another place to lay the emphasis, and always another future to look towards – so expect the unexpected!

HOW DO YOU TELL THE DIFFERENCE BETWEEN A GOOD DEAL AND A BAD DEAL?

In the domain of the Jewish joke, you can find beneficiaries of this 'double vision' everywhere:

> Mr and Mrs Horowitz are in a restaurant, having soup. Across the room an elegant young woman grins and waves at Mr Horowitz. He tries to shrug it off.
>
> Mrs Horowitz: 'Manny! Who is dat voman?'
>
> Mr Horowitz: 'Dat's ... I'm afraid dat's mine paramour.'

Mrs Horowitz is shocked. After a moment, she asks, 'And who is da other voman vith her?'

Mr Horowitz: 'Dat? Dat's Klein's paramour.'

Mrs Horowitz thinks for a moment: '*Ours* is better.'

While the same historical forces that have taught Mrs Horowitz how to make the best out of a raw deal have also taught Moshe how to query the deal's terms:

Moshe walks into a post office to send a package, but the package is too heavy.

'You'll need another stamp.'

'And *that* should make it lighter?'

Since some things are non-negotiable, however ('money is better than poverty, if only for financial reasons' – Woody Allen), it's fortunate that Jews should happen to be so awfully good at business:

A young Jewish boy starts attending public school in a small town. On day one the teacher asks the class, 'Who was the greatest man that ever lived?'

A girl raises her hand and says, 'Was it Winston Churchill?'

'A good answer,' says the teacher, 'but not the answer I'm looking for.'

Another young student raises her hand and says, 'Was it Shakespeare?'

'Still not the answer I had in mind,' says the teacher.

Then the new Jewish boy raises his hand and says, 'I think Jesus Christ was the greatest man that ever lived.'

The teacher is astonished. 'Yes!' she says. 'That's the answer I was looking for.' She invites him to the front of the class and gives him a lollipop.

Later another Jewish pupil asks him, 'Why did you say "Jesus Christ"?'

The boy replies, 'Look, I know it's Moses, and YOU know it's Moses, but business is business.'

Meanwhile, in the Jewish school, the Hebrew teacher used to boast:

> 'If I were Rothschild I would be richer than Rothschild.'
>
> 'Why?'
>
> 'Because *I* would teach Hebrew on the side.'

Not everyone, however, is so easily impressed:

> 'Mummy I saved money today!'
>
> 'How?'
>
> 'Instead of buying a ticket to take the bus home, I ran after it all the way!'
>
> 'You couldn't have run after a taxi?'

A good deal is just a case of being in the right place at the right time with the right equipment:

> Two members of a congregation are talking.

'Our cantor is magnificent,' says the first.

'What's the big deal?' says the second. 'If I had his voice, I'd sing just as well.'

And sometimes *without* the right equipment:

'How much is this pickle?'

'A nickel.'

'But the stall down the street sells them for just three cents!'

'So why don't you buy there?'

'Cos he's run out of pickles.'

'When I run out of pickles, I also sell them for three cents.'

Still, everyone feels there's one deal that escaped them:

Maurice, a young Jew, comes to north London and applies for a job as caretaker at the Edgware

> Synagogue. The synagogue committee are just about to offer him the job when they discover that he is illiterate. They decide for many reasons that it would be inappropriate to have an illiterate caretaker. So Maurice leaves and decides to forge a career in another business. He chooses to sell plastic goods door to door. He does well and soon is able to buy a car and, later, to open a store, and then a second and a third. Finally he is ready to open a vast chain of stores and so applies to the underwriter for insurance. But when the underwriter asks him to sign the contract it becomes obvious he cannot write. Shocked to discover that such a successful man has no education, the bank manager says, 'Just think what you could have been if you had learned to read and write.'
>
> 'Yes,' says Maurice regretfully, 'caretaker at Edgware synagogue.'

But if Mrs Horowitz and the chain-store owner have learned how to succeed by adopting bourgeois values under capitalist conditions, Jews have also had to manage the art of the deal under communist ones:

> One winter in Soviet Moscow, the rumour went around that a meat delivery had arrived from the

collective farm. Real sausage! Within minutes, a vast queue wound around Peshkov the butcher's, like an anaconda around a cow. But after an hour, the manager came out and announced, 'Comrades, there is less meat than we thought. Can all the Jews leave.'

Out go the Jews. Two hours later, the manager faces the crowd again: 'I'm afraid there's even less than we thought – only enough for Party members.'

Half the crowd shuffles off. An hour later: 'There really is very little meat. Anyone who didn't fight in the October Revolution must go.'

Now just two old men are left. Three hours later, as darkness falls, the manager emerges: 'Comrades, there will be no sausage after all today.'

'You see,' says one old man to the other, 'The Jews get the best deal.'

(No wonder Jews have a reputation for double-dealing.)

HOW DO YOU TELL THE DIFFERENCE BETWEEN A TAILOR AND A PSYCHIATRIST?

A deal is a deal is a deal, and you have to deal with whatever hand you're dealt. That means, in the first place, being adaptable. And one advantage to Jews of having learned to expect the unexpected is that they've acquired just that skill: the ability to change just enough to meet the latest terms and conditions.*

As too have their jokes. Thus whether it's Capitalist America or Soviet Russia, the same old jokes should always be framed in terms of the current polity:

* According to the historian Yuri Slezkine, it's their talent for adapting that rendered Jews modern people *avant la lettre*: 'Modernisation is about everyone becoming urban, mobile, literate, articulate, intellectually intricate, physically fastidious and occupationally flexible.' (Not to mention witty.)

> Back in the shtetl, Moishe got a job looking out for signs of the coming of the Messiah: 'It's a boring job, and the pay's terrible – but at least it's steady work.'

While in the Soviet era his job changed: Moishe now found himself looking out for signs of world revolution. The job proved equally steady.

Which I guess you could say is the *other* message we get from both the Jewish joke and Jewish history: expect the unexpected for sure, but also – expect more of the same. For as earnestly as they may long for the Messiah, Jews are also a people who've learned to pray: 'Lord, don't let this war last as long as we're able to survive it.' And so, since they've grown a bit weary of big-time historical promises, what you often find in Jewish jokes is a capacity for looking past the popular ideology of the moment towards the brute material reality running beneath:

> 'By the year 2000 Russians will be able to get a rocket to Mars,' declared Brezhnev.
>
> 'And when,' asks Mendel, 'will we be able to get to Vienna?'

Mendel's real wish, though, is to travel overseas – to America:

> He goes to get a visa. 'There's a long, long queue for those,' he's told by the official, 'you'd best come back in another ten years.'
>
> 'Fine,' says Mendel, 'in the morning or the afternoon?'

Mendel's patience, in fact, is not unlike that of the Jewish joke, whose very endurance is a testament to its critical powers. For if the joke's *still got it,* then the new ideology, no matter how different or how radical, can't be quite so transformative as advertised. So while some of the best Jewish jokes *have* been put out of action by recent transformations – email, for example, has called time on the traditional Jewish telegram:

> Start worrying. Details to follow.

Still, the sentiment remains the same: if you start worrying now, history will be sure to prove you right.

But never forget the flipside, that what goes around comes around:

> A Jewish couple are wheeling their baby boy in a pram. A woman peeks in and says, 'What a sweet child! What's his name?' 'Shloyme.' 'Shloyme! What kind of name is that?' 'We named him after his grandfather, Scott.'*

Thus, lots of Jewish jokes have kept pace with modernity not only because Jews have been sceptical about historical change, but because they've also been so very good at it:

> Q: What's the difference between a tailor and a psychiatrist?
>
> A: A generation.

* This one's very much an insiders' joke alluding to changing fashions in Jewish assimilation: whereas early generations of Jewish immigrants tended to Americanize their names by translating Yiddish or Hebrew names into English near equivalents, in recent years there has been a trend for young hipster Jews to select the sort of names their great-grandparents might have had.

HOW DO YOU TELL THE DIFFERENCE BETWEEN MORALITY AND NEUROSIS?*

Here, on the other hand, is what distinguishes a *physician* from a psychiatrist:

> A psychiatrist is a Jewish physician who can't stand the sight of blood.

Jewish history, after all, has not only seen a lot of blood, it's also seen a lot of psychology.

And for Freud, of course, jokes, alongside dreams and verbal slips, are a way *in* to the unofficial part of oneself he called the unconscious. So do Jewish jokes

* If only I knew. Freud's entire life's work was arguably an attempt to tell this difference.

provide evidence of the *Jewish* unconscious? If so, the Jewish joke might then be supposed to remember what other archives of Jewish life have sought to forget. Starting with this joke:

> What's the definition of Jewish Alzheimer's? You forget everything but the guilt.

Oh boy, the guilt! What a Gordian knot of an emotion that is. Jews might *well* forget everything but the guilt – because guilt attests to a history that you can deny all you like, but it's still got its hands around your neck.

But while our guilt likes to remind us that there's something in our past that needs dealing with, it tends not to be too straightforward about what that something is. Guilt is a feeling that hides as much as it reveals, and it's a feeling that works to repress other feelings: aggressive feelings, for example, or incestuous ones. So you could say that guilt, too, is a bit of a joke. Hence why Maureen Lipman's revision of the joke – 'Jewish Alzheimer's is forgetting everything except a grudge' – is just as funny and equally revealing. For both guilt *and* jokes are socially sanctioned ways of masking our unconscious intentions towards those we feel guilty about, or feel inclined to joke about (albeit by finding an outward outlet for its forbidden feelings, joking is generally the healthier of the two). Might that, then, explain why there are so many Jewish jokes *about* Jewish guilt?

We're back to those Jewish mothers sitting in the dark. And when it comes to pinning guilt on the Jewish mother, Jewish jokes can get *very* dark. See for instance the most lightbulb-less example of a Jewish mother joke in Philip Roth's novel-length send-up of the Jewish mother, *Portnoy's Complaint* (1969). It features a neighbourhood kid whose suicide note reads:

> Mrs Blumenthal called. Please bring your mah-jongg rules to the game tonight.
>
> Ronald

No matter the fallout, though, you should know that the Jewish mother does have a method to her madness:

> Let your son hear you sigh every day. If you don't know what he's done to make you sigh, *he* will.

And, to be fair to her, guilt is a symptom from which she too suffers:

> When the Jewish mother was called up for jury service, they had to send her home because she kept on insisting *she* was guilty.

So it's only reasonable if she passes it on to her friends:

> The afternoon is drawing to a close, and the guests are getting ready to leave.
>
> 'Mrs Goldberg,' says one of the ladies. 'I just wanted to tell you that your cookies were so delicious I ate four of them.'
>
> 'You ate five,' replies Mrs Goldberg. 'But who's counting?'

And to her family:

> The Jewish mother, upon receiving a phone call from her adult daughter, announces: 'I'm very weak, I'm starving, I haven't eaten for two weeks'

'Why ever not, Mother?!'

'Because I didn't want that I should have my mouth full when you rang.'

HOW DO YOU TELL THE DIFFERENCE BETWEEN A JEWISH WOMAN AND A SHIKSA?

Of course, the Jewish mother also has plenty to say when it's someone else who's starving:

> Once, a homeless woman accosted her on the street:
>
> 'Miss, I haven't eaten in three days.'
>
> 'Force yourself', she replied.

If 'let them eat cake' is the mistake that too much money can make, 'force yourself' is an error of too much analysis:

Sadie Goldberg wants to expand her intellectual horizons, so she goes to a lecture on 'Human Sexuality' by the eminent psychoanalyst Dr Feigenbaum.

She is so entranced that at the end of the lecture she decides to approach him.

'Dr Feigenbaum,' she says, 'I want you to know I found your lecture fascinating. There was just one thing I didn't quite get. You kept referring to "bestiality". What is that?'

'OK,' Feigenbaum says, 'so bestiality is the practice of a human being having relations with an animal. For example, you may wanna have sex with a dog.'

'A dog?!'

'Yeah, a dog. Or you may wanna have sex with ... a horse.'

'A *horse*?!?!'

'Yeah, a horse. Or you may wanna have sex with a bull.'

'A BULL???!!!!?!!'

'Yeah, a bull, or maybe you wanna have sex with a chicken?'

'A chicken? Feh ...'

But though Sadie Goldberg may fancy a bull, the husband of a Jewish woman will get no action if he compares her to a cow:

An impoverished couple in a poor shtetl in Poland couldn't make a living on their farm so they asked their neighbour what to to. 'You must buy a cow, feed it up, and then when it is ready take it to a bull. When she mates, you will have a calf, the calf will grow up and then you have two cows.' This is the way to riches. So they saved and saved and saved until they could afford to buy a cow. Then they fattened her up and took her to the bull. However, whenever the bull came close to the cow, the cow would move away.

The couple were frantic; they decided to ask the rabbi what to do. They told the rabbi what was happening: 'Whenever the bull approaches our cow, she moves away. If he approaches from the back, she moves forward. When he approaches her from the front, she backs off. An approach from the side and she just walks away to the other side.'

The rabbi thought about this for a minute and asked, 'Did you buy this cow from Minsk?'

The people were dumbfounded. 'You are truly a wise rabbi,' they said. 'How did you know we got the cow from Minsk?'

The rabbi answered sadly, 'My vife, she is from Minsk.'

Winning the heart of a Jewish woman is thus a complex and subtle art:

Heschel was in awe of his friend Abe. Abe could get any woman he wanted – and he did. 'Teach me how you do it,' Heschel begged him.

'It's easy,' said Abe, 'the trick with attracting Jewish women is that you have to show them you care about three things: food, family and philosophy. Food, because that means you care about their physical well-being. Family, because that means your intentions are serious. Philosophy, because that means you respect their intelligence.'

Heschel was thankful for the advice and asked a woman he fancied on a date. 'Tell me,' he opened, 'do you like to eat kugel [baked noodle pudding]?'

'I can't stand kugel,' his date replied.

'Hmm, so does your brother eat kugel?' he tried again.

'I don't have a brother,' she retorted.

'I see,' Heschel pressed on, 'And tell me, if you *did* have a brother, do you think he would like kugel?'

But philosophy isn't only useful when dating – it has its place in the bedroom too:

Shmuley returns home to find clothes strewn everywhere, and his wife undressed in bed, tying up her hair. Feeling suspicious, he starts frantically searching around until at last he finds his old foe Itzhik hiding in the cupboard.

'Vhat,' Shmuley splutters, 'are *you* doing here?'

'Everyone,' Itzhik replies, 'has got to be somewhere.'

He's got a point. Though Itzhik's philosophical defence might at root be considered an historical one if we recall all those out-of-place Jews who were forced, under somewhat different circumstances, to use much the same defence when faced by interrogators far more fearsome than Shmuley.

But never mind Abe and Heschel or Shmuley and Itzhik. We're talking here of the Jewish woman, and of what Jewish jokes tell us about *her*. And what they tell us, for one thing, is that she adheres to neither side of patriarchy's most enduring binary – the virgin/the whore – but admits instead of another stereotype: a stereotype that's still sexist, but at least she makes it her own.

Because you *can* get a Jewish woman into bed, it's just that she doesn't make it easy for you. And besides, she's always dealing with a million other things at the same time:

Three old men are discussing their sex lives.

> The Italian says, 'Last week, my wife and I had great sex. I rubbed her body all over with olive oil, we made passionate love, and she screamed for five minutes at the end.'
>
> The Frenchman boasts, 'Last week when my wife and I had sex, I rubbed her body all over with butter. We then made passionate love and she screamed for fifteen minutes.'
>
> The Jewish man says, 'Last week, my wife and I had sex. I rubbed her body all over with chicken fat, we made love, and she screamed for six hours.'
>
> The others are stunned and ask, 'What could you have possibly done to make your wife scream for six hours?'
>
> 'I wiped my hands on the curtains.'

Since sex in Jewish law *is* considered a mitzvah (good deed), however, even a very orthodox Jewish woman can find reasons to enjoy it:

> A nineteen-year-old religious boy marries an eighteen-year-old religious girl. Both are sexual innocents

before their wedding. After the wedding ceremony and celebration is over they go home and do the mitzvah. On the second night after they're married, he says to her, 'You know, I had a grandmother, of blessed memory, who raised me like a son. She couldn't be at our wedding. In memory of her soul we should do the mitzvah again.' Third night he says to her, 'I had a cousin, we were like brothers. He died too young. In his memory we should do the mitzvah again.' And they do. On the fourth night he mentions another cousin. On the fifth night an uncle, then an aunt, and a great-uncle.

Come Shabbat, she gets herself to synagogue. All her friends surround her: 'Nu, what's he like?'

'He's a fool, but I get nachas [pleasure] from the family.'

To find this joke as funny as I do – I find it very funny – you'd need to understand the context: the importance, in orthodox circles, of marrying into a respectable family. For only then can you expect to find yourself laughing aloud at what I take to be the joke's key revelation: that however hard you may try to hide what gets you going under the cover of respectability – such as within the sanctity of a marriage, for instance – still, there's no such thing as an 'innocent pleasure'.

How so?*

To recap, two young, religious and sexually inexperienced people are rather more capable than they might have us believe of following the logic of their own desires. Although, throughout the joke, we're made aware of the groom's use of pious rhetoric to serve his own pleasurable ends, it's the punchline revelation of the bride's polymorphously perverse satisfactions – i.e. the pleasure identified in the joke as 'nachas' is that huge turn-on enjoyed by a Jewish woman who senses she's 'married well' – that really gives the game away. Because, my goodness, here we have a Jewish woman who, no less than the Jewish man, no less than anyone in fact, is her own brand of pervert! She gets her pleasure, that is, from the feeling that there's something more to be enjoyed, something beyond or beside what she's been officially given. Thus her sexual pleasure is not unlike the pleasure *we* get from the joke: the pleasure of secrecy, of doubleness, of a double entendre. So

* One benefit of including an abstruse joke fewer readers are liable to get is that the po-faced business of then explaining and interpreting the joke should feel a bit less ruinous.

it's a joke, in other words, whose comic disturbance of its protagonists' presumed innocence perfectly illustrates what delights and disturbs us all in that everyday form of taboo-breaking we try to pass off as nothing really, as an innocent pleasure – as only joking.

What's critical, then, is that, no matter how she gets her kicks, this young woman's piety remains unimpeachable. She does nothing overtly transgressive. On the contrary, she's doing her duty – her conjugal duty. As such, she's hard put to explain the sex – or the pleasure – that *isn't* a mitzvah:

> Becky returns home and finds her husband in bed with her best friend. Shocked, she rounds on her friend: 'Me – I have to, but *you*?'

Truly, the bedroom is full of philosophy.

But if the Jewish woman typically needs to be talked into bed, shiksas, we're assured, are always up for it:

> A rabbi and a beautiful model get stuck in a lift. The model turns to the rabbi and says, 'Before we press the alarm ... I have to confess, I, I, I ... always

fantasised about having sex with a rabbi. Why don't we take this opportunity?'

The rabbi thinks about it for a moment and then asks, 'What's in it for me?'

And they're endlessly obliging:

A congregation honours a rabbi for twenty-five years of service by sending him on holiday to Hawaii, all expenses paid.

When the rabbi walks into his room, there's a gorgeous woman lying naked on the bed. She tells the rabbi that she is here for him at any time during his trip. Naturally, the rabbi is shocked and extremely embarrassed. Who has dared to imagine that he would even *want* such a thing?

The woman tells him who is paying for her services. He picks up the phone, calls the synagogue, and asks for the president of the congregation: 'Where is your respect, how could you do something like this? Have I ever done anything to suggest that I'm the type of person to appreciate this sort of "gift"? As your rabbi, I am very hurt, and very angry.'

> As he continues to berate the president, the woman gets up and starts to get dressed, not wanting to embarrass the rabbi any more than necessary.
>
> The rabbi turns to her and says, 'Where are you going? I'm not angry at *you*.'

I love that joke, but who is it a joke 'on' exactly? Am I laughing along with an anti-Semitic slur – an essentially racist joke about hypocritical Jews? Or is the joke a subtler but still rather anti-Semitic indictment of the sophistry of *religious* Jews specifically? Or maybe it's a joke about not Jews so much as men – as in *all* men, including rabbis? Unless, that is, it's a joke on each and every one of us – a joke about the self-justifying manoeuvres that one can always discern between the lines of just about *any* system of public morality. (Though that it's a rabbi who teaches us this moral lesson – a moral lesson about the immorality of morality – does make it that bit funnier):

> A rabbi who's been leading a congregation for many years is upset by the fact that he's never been able to eat pork. So he devises a plan whereby he flies to a remote tropical island and checks into a hotel. He

immediately gets himself a table at the finest restaurant and orders the most expensive pork dish on the menu, a whole suckling pig.

As he's eagerly waiting for it to be served, he hears his name called from across the restaurant. He looks up to see ten of his loyal congregants approaching. His luck, they'd chosen the same time to visit the same remote location!

Just at that moment, the waiter comes out with a huge silver tray carrying a whole roasted pig complete with an apple in its mouth. The rabbi looks up sheepishly at his congregants and says, 'Wow – you order an apple in this place and look how it's served!'

Well, at least it makes a change from man's standard calumny of blaming his *own* hankering for forbidden apples on a woman.

And not just any woman ...

HOW DO YOU TELL THE DIFFERENCE BETWEEN A JEWISH MOTHER AND A JEWISH MOTHER-IN-LAW?

Here's how:

> Goldie and Frieda were chatting. Goldie says, 'So nu, how's your daughter?'
>
> Frieda responds, 'Oh, just fine. My daughter is married to the most wonderful man. She never has to cook, he always takes her out. She never has to clean, he got her a housekeeper. She never has to work, he's got such a good job. She never has to worry about the children, he got her a nanny.'
>
> Then Goldie asks, 'And how is your son these days?'

> Frieda says, 'Just awful. He is married to such a witch of a woman. She makes him take her out to dinner every night, she never cooks a dish. She made him get her a housekeeper, God forbid she should vacuum a carpet! He has to work like a dog because she won't get a job, and she never takes care of their children, because she made him get her a nanny!'

Ouch.

But let's deal with the mother-in-law first:

> A Jewish town had a shortage of men for wedding purposes, so they tried to import men from other towns. Finally a groom-to-be arrived on a train, and two mothers-in-law-to-be awaited him, each claiming true ownership.
>
> A rabbi was called to solve the problem. After a few minutes of thought, he said, 'If this is the situation, you both claim the groom, we'll cut him in half and give each one of you half of him.'
>
> To this replied one woman, 'If that's the case, fine, give him to the other woman.'

> The rabbi intoned wisely, 'So be it. The one willing to cut him in half, *that* has to be the real mother-in-law!'

Thus, while a father-in-law can sometimes disguise his true feelings ...

> A girl brings her new boyfriend, a serious young scholar studying Torah, home to meet her father. The father takes the boy into his study and begins to ask him questions.
>
> 'So,' says the father, 'you're a Torah scholar. How do you plan to support my daughter?'
>
> 'Don't worry,' says the boy, 'God will provide.'
>
> 'And where will the two of you live?' asks the father.
>
> 'Don't worry, God will provide.'
>
> 'And how will you support your children?'
>
> 'Don't worry,' says the boy, 'God will provide.'

The father finishes his discussion and the young man leaves. The daughter then comes in and asks her father, 'So, what did you think of him?'

'I like him,' says the father. 'He thinks I'm God.'

... a mother-in-law will always let you know what she thinks:

Jake visited his parents. He said, 'Finally, I've found my true love. Just for fun, I'm going to bring over three women and you can guess which one she is.'

The next day he brought three beautiful women, who sat on the sofa and chatted with his parents over a little cake. After they left, he challenged, 'OK, guess which one I'm going to marry?'

'The one in the middle with the red hair,' his mother replied instantly.

'Right! But ... how did you know?' asked Jake, amazed.

'Simple,' his mother said. '*Her,* we don't like.'

Which doesn't mean she won't get as good as she gives:

> Sadie is dying. As she lies on her deathbed, she says to her husband, 'Shlomo, I want you to promise me one thing.'
>
> 'Anything darling,' says Shlomo.
>
> 'On the day of my funeral I want you to look after my mother. And you and she must travel there together in the same car,' says Sadie.
>
> Shlomo squirms. He struggles. At last he says, 'For you, on your funeral, I will do this. But let me tell you right now – it will *completely* ruin the day for me.'

When it comes to his *own* mother, though, a Jewish man sees things rather differently:

> Hymie is beside himself – his wife is in bed and it's clear she's dying. Nothing will revive her – not water, not whisky, not food of any kind. 'Is there *anything* I can do to bring you joy in your last moments?' he pleads.

'Well, there is one thing,' she replies, 'I'd like to have intercourse with you, Hymie, one last time.'

Hymie obliges. Miraculously, his wife is completely revivified by their coupling. She's not only better, she's better than ever. She leaps out of bed, ready for anything. Hymie, seeing this, bursts into tears.

'Whatever's wrong, my Hymie?' she asks. 'Aren't you pleased to see me so well? We'll have many more happy years together.'

'It's not that,' sobs Hymie, 'it's just got me thinking – *I could have saved Mother*!'

So the Jewish joke, then, has a theory of neurotic guilt that both extends and revises the one we've inherited from Freud; for, as we find it here, what the Jewish son feels most guilty about is precisely his *failure* to be incestuous (which theory, personally, I think has some mileage).

Ah, but Oedipus Shmedipus, as long as he loves his mother:

Mother 1: My son loves me so much – he constantly buys me gifts.

> Mother 2: My son loves me so much – he always takes me on holiday.
>
> Jewish Mother: That's nothing. My son loves me so much, he goes to see a special doctor five times a week to talk exclusively about me.

So we must pity the Jewish mother! Sometimes it seems as if the entire Jewish joking industry exists only in order to poke fun at her: narcissistic, self-martyring, smothering, guilt-inducing, hysterical, paranoid, overweening, complaining, castrating – honestly, is there any sin she *hasn't* been accused of by her ungrateful children?

Her daughter certainly expects the world of her:

> Mitzy springs to the telephone when it rings and listens with relief to the kindly voice in her ear.
>
> 'How are you, darling?' it asks. 'What kind of a day are you having?'
>
> 'Oh, Mother,' she says, breaking into bitter tears, 'I've had such a bad day. The baby won't eat and the washing machine broke down. I haven't had a chance to go shopping, and besides, I've just sprained my

ankle and I have to hobble around. On top of that, the house is a mess and I'm supposed to have two couples to dinner tonight.'

The mother is shocked and is at once all sympathy. 'Oh, darling,' she says, 'sit down, relax and close your eyes. I'll be over in half an hour. I'll do your shopping, clean up the house and cook your dinner for you. I'll feed the baby and I'll call a repairman to fix the washing machine. Now stop crying. I'll do everything. In fact, I'll even call Simon at the office and tell him he ought to come home and help out for once.'

'Simon?' says Mitzy. 'Who's Simon?'

'Why, Simon! Your husband!'

'No it isn't. I'm married to Shlomo.'

'Oh, I'm sorry. I guess I have the wrong number.'

There's a short pause before Mitzy says, 'Does this mean you're *not* coming over?'

But when it comes to mother-blaming, it's really the Jewish mother's ultimate victim, her poor emasculated son, who is the first to point the finger and cry '*J'accuse*'. He, after all, is famously the object of such mountainous maternal pride that she can't even stop herself boasting about him when he's in mortal danger:

> 'Help! Help! My son – a doctor! – is drowning!'

Though her maternal narcissism took root much earlier, of course:

> Mrs Cohen is pleased to announce the birth of her son, Dr David Cohen.

The announcement may *sound* premature, but you have to remember at which moment life is said to begin in Jewish tradition:

> In Jewish tradition the foetus is not considered a viable human being until after graduation from medical school.

And actually Mrs Cohen predicted Instagram too:

> When pushing David along in his buggy one day, she bumps into Mrs Shindler.

'Oh, what a beautiful baby!' Mrs Shindler coos.

'Meh, that's nothing,' replies Mrs Cohen, 'you should see his photos.'

But that's what you get in a culture that puts family first:

Ninety-one-year-old Morris and Sophie, his eighty-nine-year-old wife of sixty-six years, go to their lawyer to get a divorce. Puzzled, the lawyer asks, 'Why did you wait all this time if you were both so miserable for so long?'

Sophie replies, 'We were waiting for the children to die.'

And a culture that will do whatever it takes to keep loved ones close:

Goldie Cohen, an elderly Jewish lady from New York, goes to her travel agent. 'I vont to go to India.'

'Mrs Cohen, why India? It's filthy, and much hotter than New York.'

'I vont to go to India.'

'But it's a long journey, and those trains, how will you manage? What will you eat? The food is too hot and spicy for you. You can't drink the water. You must not eat fresh fruit and vegetables. You'll get sick: the plague, hepatitis, cholera, typhoid, malaria, God only knows. What will you do? Can you imagine the hospital, no Jewish doctors? Why torture yourself?'

'I vont to go to India.'

The necessary arrangements are made, and off she goes. She arrives in India and, undeterred by the noise, smell and crowds, makes her way to an ashram. There she joins the seemingly never-ending queue of people waiting for an audience with the guru. An aide tells her that it will take at least three days of standing in line to see the guru.

'Dat's OK.'

Eventually she reaches the hallowed portals. There she is told firmly that she can only say three words.

'Fine.'

She is ushered into the inner sanctum, where the wise guru is seated, ready to bestow spiritual blessings upon eager initiates. Just before she reaches the holy of holies she is once again reminded: 'Remember, just three words.'

Unlike the other devotees, she does not prostrate herself at his feet. She stands directly in front of him, crosses her arms over her chest, fixes her gaze on his and says: 'Sheldon, come home.'*

So while the Jewish mother can be overprotective:

What's a Jewish sweater? The woollen garment worn by a child when his mother is cold.

That's only because she doesn't like to see him sitting around like a guru all day doing nothing useful.

On the contrary, she's ambitious for him:

* Whenever I hear that joke it's always with the name Sheldon in the punchline, which dates the joke (taking it back to the countercultural trends in America in the 1950s and 1960s), but also makes the joke impossible to update: no other name seems as funny or works as well.

> A little Jewish boy is telling his mother about how he's won a part in a play at school. His mother asks, 'What is the part you will play, Saul?' Saul responds, 'I shall play the Jewish husband,' to which the mother replies, 'Pah! Well, you go right back to that teacher and tell her that you want a SPEAKING part!'

Hang on! Is it *really* the woman who gets such a great speaking part in all these Jewish jokes? Or aren't these jokes mostly told by men precisely in order to pin the blame for their own guilt – or their own Jewishness – on a woman? And, as we know, it was Adam, the first man, who paved the way here, by blaming his own tsores on Eve, the first woman.

Adam started a trend. For who, in any man's life, *is* the first woman if not his mother: a woman so spectacularly powerful that he entered the world wholly on her account, and then relied on her for his own survival? So it's having a mother at all that's emasculating. And that goes double for Jewish men – and especially Jewish men from first-generation immigrant families who tended to wield less power in the world than Gentile men, rendering them subject to more domesticity and more mothering. Hence, though to some extent *all* the jokes Jewish men tell about Jewish women seem really to be jokes about the overwhelming influence of their mothers, the merciless mother-bashing of the male Jewish stand-up act during its 1950s and 1960s heyday should be seen in the context of a distinct historical backdrop.

That said, the most notorious comic creation of the Jewish mother stereotype belongs to neither biblical patriarch nor secular stand-up, but comes to us instead from a novelist. It's Philip Roth's 'most unforgettable character', Sophie Portnoy, who is the guilt-inducing Jewish mother par excellence.* As Alex, her long-suffering son, complains:

> The legend engraved on the face of the Jewish nickel – on the body of every Jewish child! – not IN GOD WE TRUST, but SOMEDAY YOU'LL BE A PARENT AND YOU'LL KNOW WHAT IT'S LIKE.

And the novel comprises exclusively Alex's monologue as he lies on his back on a psychiatrist's couch, tirelessly complaining about the damage inflicted on him by his mother's fantasised omnipotence:

* Roth entitles the first section of the novel, about Sophie, 'The Most Unforgettable Character I've Met'.

> It's a family joke that when I was a tiny child I turned from the window out of which I was watching a snowstorm, and hopefully asked, 'Momma, do we believe in winter?'

If a Freudian slip is when you say one thing but mean your mother, then every joke is a 'family joke'.

HOW DO YOU TELL THE DIFFERENCE BETWEEN A MALE JEWISH COMEDIAN AND A FEMALE JEWISH COMEDIAN?

Alexander Portnoy complains that 'I am the son in the Jewish joke – only it ain't no joke!' But it's Sophie – the target not only of the Jewish joke's internalised anti-Semitism, but of a large dose of misogyny as well – who can really be found drowning in the Jewish joke. So who will rescue *her*, another writer, Grace Paley, asks, from 'her son the doctor and her son the novelist'?

Why, the female joker, of course!*

Yet there's a nasty rumour abroad, you hear it again and again: women just aren't as funny as men. To which you always want to reply: well, they try not to laugh in your face maybe. For women in public *are* much more bound by the conventions of civility – of having to please everyone all the time – that can make poking fun a riskier business for them. This was something that the late Joan Rivers, perhaps the most caustic of female comics, understood only too well. 'One of the most rebellious things a woman can do,' she once said, 'is allow people to think she's mean.' The mere fact, in other words, of a woman going public with her funniness can throw a certain light on the degree to which a misogynist culture has turned comedy – including Jewish comedy – into an ultra-defensive boys' club.

Not that it's so hard sending up the boys:

> My ancestors wandered lost in the wilderness for forty years because even in biblical times, men would not stop to ask for directions. *Elayne Boosler*

* At least, when she isn't self-harming or being taken to task for doing so. Alluding to fellow Jewish 'funny girl' Fanny Brice's rhinoplasty in 1923, Dorothy Parker quipped that Brice had 'cut off her nose to spite her race.'

> Most men are secretly still mad at their mothers for throwing away their comic books. They would be valuable now. *Rita Rudner*

> My mother always said don't marry for money. Divorce for money. *Wendy Liebman*

> I don't have any kids. Well, at least none I know about. *Cathy Ladman*

But female comedians do more than simply deliver low blows where they know it hurts. They also use their acts to critique the stratagems of male-centric comedy. When, that is, we hear men's jokes told *by* women, we cannot but hear them differently – hence why that line from Cathy Ladman, which word for word parrots a stereotypically male comedy brag, is about as deft a moment of comic outwitting as you could wish for.

And the same logic goes doubly when women tell jokes about areas of female experience that no male comic should reasonably expect to get away with. Here, for instance, is Sarah Silverman:

> I was raped by a doctor, which is so bittersweet for a Jewish girl.

To my ears, there's a world of difference between this and a male-authored 'rape joke', but not everyone believes that gender does anything to justify such a gag. And that, in a nutshell, is the trouble for the comedian – and especially the female comedian, whose use of obscenity or brashness always sparks greater outrage – there are those who will be scandalised by pretty much every joke she tells. Hence the advice of Joan Rivers: 'We don't apologise for a joke. We are comics. We are here to make you laugh. If you don't get it, then don't watch us.'

Such advice can only be inspirational for Sarah Silverman. Because it's true, Silverman's Jewish jokes *have* upset certain Jews, and her rape jokes *have* upset certain women – including certain Jewish women* – and it's true too that Silverman has stood accused, as Philip Roth was in the 1960s, of self-hatred. So with an act like Silverman's we can find, once again, the same old questions getting asked: is such comedy needlessly offensive? Is it, all told, even witty? And is it, ultimately, defensible or indefensible?

And, as ever, context is everything: it always depends on who is telling the joke, who is hearing it, and to what end. Roth, for instance, has assured

* 'Put me up against Sarah Silverman and I could take her' *Joan Rivers.*

us that he has yet to receive a letter of thanks from an anti-Semitic organisation. And so far as I'm aware, misogynists haven't written to thank Silverman for her great services to their cause either. So while it's important to be mindful of sensitivities, it's just as important to remain wary of the humour police, those punchline vigilantes who so often wind up silencing the very people they're claiming to defend. For though, in the majority of situations, humour is seldom the only answer, and by no means always the best one, what humourlessness always fails to recognise is just how *useful* a sense of humour can be for confronting what one finds offensive, including offensive jokes – as can be seen from the long tradition of comedians wrong-footing their abusers by making the mud slung their way a valuable commodity: material they can *work* with.

Take, for example, another young Jewish American comedian, Amy Schumer, who sparked the predictable yowls of outrage after tweeting this image of herself:

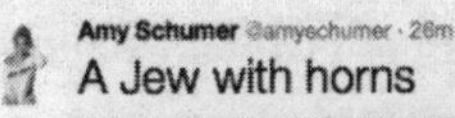

51 520

And who then doubled the 'offence' by parodying the demand for an apology in her follow-up tweet:

.@amyschumer my bad. I meant to say "A Jew with 2 horns"

1:32 PM - 2 Mar 2016

Some allege that such quips see Schumer reinforcing the ugly stereotyping of Jews throughout their history. But can't we regard them instead as an intervention *into* that history? Because what we find with playfulness like Schumer's is not anti-Semitism, surely, but quite the opposite: a seriously funny Jewish woman taking on history *by* the horns.

HOW DO YOU TELL THE DIFFERENCE BETWEEN A KING AND A BEGGAR?

Ever since the first ape slipped on the first banana skin, a sense of humour has assumed a sense of the slippery: a sense with which one can not only find the funny *in* the joke, but one can transform what's funny *about* the joke.

The Jewish joke is a case in point. The debate over whether Jewish jokes are battling anti-Semitism or are in fact forms of it isn't anything so new. Back in the bad old days, for example, there was clearly an anti-Semitic way of interpreting the joke about the Jew who, upon finding his fellow passenger is also Jewish, instantly puts his feet up on the seat in front of him ('You see! Jews among themselves reveal who they *really* are ... dirty and uncivilised!'). And yet precisely here is where that most famous promoter of the slip – Sigmund Freud – identified something else: the democratic spirit of a people who will brook no hierarchy, because all, ultimately, are members of the same human family. (Especially if you're from a Sephardi family and have been told that pretty much everyone you meet is related to you – you're just never quite sure how.)*

We see this no better than in the typical Jewish beggar/shnorrer joke. In the oral storytelling of the Hasidim, the shnorrer in the parable invariably turns out to be a king (or an angel) in disguise. But in the Jewish joke it's the other way around, as *now* it's the nobleman who winds up exasperatedly begging:

> A shnorrer tries without success to get an appointment with Rothschild. Finally he stands outside the family mansion and shouts, 'My family is starving to death and the baron refuses to see me!'

> Rothschild acquiesces and gives the shnorrer thirty rubles. 'Here you are,' he says. 'And let me tell you

* Like Freud's own examples of Jewish jokes, the examples given in this book are overwhelmingly rooted in the Ashkenazi tradition as the tradition I know best – there's surely another book to be written about the specific sensibility that marks the Sephardi Jewish joke as the closest of relatives in the same human family.

that if you hadn't caused such a scene, I would have given you sixty rubles.'

'My dear Baron,' replies the shnorrer, 'I don't tell you how to conduct your business, so you don't tell me how to conduct mine.'

* * *

In Rome, two beggars are sitting on the ground, a few feet apart. One wears a large cross. The other, a Star of David. Needless to say, the plate of the former fills up quickly, with almost nothing in the plate of the latter.

After some time, a kindly priest passes and sizes up the situation. He turns to the Jewish beggar: 'My son, you should put away that Star of David. You will never make enough money wearing that.'

After he leaves, the Jewish beggar turns to the other with an annoyed look: 'Could you believe that guy, telling the Goldberg brothers how to run their business?'

* * *

The shnorrer begged the baron for some money for a journey to Ostend; his doctor had recommended sea-bathing for his troubles. The baron thought Ostend was a particularly expensive resort; wouldn't a cheaper one do equally well? The shnorrer disagreed. 'Herr Baron,' he said, 'I consider nothing too expensive for my health.'

* * *

A poor and desperate man borrowed £100 from a rich acquaintance. The very same day his benefactor met him again in a restaurant with a plate of caviar in front of him.

'What? You borrow money from me and then order yourself caviar? Is that what you've used my money for?'

'I don't understand you,' replied the poor man. 'If I haven't any money I can't eat caviar, and if I have some money then I mustn't eat caviar. Then, when can I eat caviar?'

* * *

A shnorrer, allowed as a needy guest into a wealthy man's house every Sabbath, one day brings an unknown young man with him and sits down to eat.

'Who is this?' asked the householder.

'He's my new son-in-law,' the shnorrer replied. 'I've promised him his board for the first year.'

* * *

Chernov, the shnorrer of Petrograd, had a very wealthy patron who, for some obscure reason, had taken a liking to the nervy little beggar. Each year he would give Chernov a handsome stipend – never less than five hundred rubles. One year, however, the rich man gave him only two hundred and fifty rubles.

'What is the meaning of this?' demanded the insolent shnorrer. 'This is only half of what you have been giving me!'

'I'm sorry, Chernov, but I must cut my expenses this year,' apologised the wealthy man. 'My son married an actress and I am paying all the bills.'

'Well, of all the chutzpah!' roared Chernov, hopping mad. 'If your son wants to support an actress, that's his business. But how dare he do it with my money!'

Thinking of the Jewish concept of tzedakah – a form of charity that equates to social justice – Freud says: 'The truth that lies behind is that the shnorrer, who in his thoughts treats the rich man's money as his own, has actually, according to the sacred ordinances of the Jews, almost a right to make this confusion.' So the very same jokes that denigrate Jews in the eyes of some appear as powerful lessons in Jewish ethics in the eyes of others. Though there are of course limits:

A baron, deeply moved by a shnorrer's tale of woe, rang for his servants. 'Throw him out!' he said. 'He's breaking my heart!'

HOW DO YOU TELL THE DIFFERENCE BETWEEN JEWS AND ISRAELIS?

If two Jews alone with each other on the same train feel free to make themselves at home by flouting the rules, then what can we expect of the Jewish State? Can a whole country run on chutzpah?

By the looks of things, yes. In Israel it does appear as if those same overfamiliar manners have prevailed:

> As the plane set down at Ben Gurion airport, the voice of the captain came on: 'Please remain seated with your seat belt fastened until this plane is at a complete standstill and the seat-belt signs have been turned off.
>
> 'To those who are seated, we wish you a merry Christmas, and hope that you enjoy your stay in Israel ... and to those of you standing in the aisles

> and pushing towards the doors, we wish you a happy Hanukkah, and welcome back home.'

Yet there are those who maintain a big difference between diasporic and nationalist personalities. Israelis, says a character in the film *The Infidel* (2010), are 'Jews without angst, without guilt, therefore not really Jews at all'. Or, in other words, what makes Jews recognisably Jewish is their self-consciousness before an audience, which brings them a constant nagging sense of how they might be seen from the outside:

> On a bus in Tel Aviv, a mother is talking to her small child in Yiddish. But he keeps answering her in Hebrew. Each time, his mother corrects him: 'No, no, talk Yiddish.'
>
> An increasingly exasperated Israeli, overhearing all of this, demands to know, 'Why do you insist your son speaks Yiddish instead of Hebrew?'
>
> 'Because,' the boy's mother replies, 'I don't want him to forget he's a Jew.'

She gets the problem, in other words – if diasporic Jewishness has become a byword for difference, then how can Jewishness be sustained in Israel? The stereotypical splits and tensions to be found within diasporic jokes can hardly be expected to work in a place where the majority are Jews:

> A classical musician was performing a solo recital in Israel. As he concluded his performance he was astounded by the cries from the audience: 'Play it again!' He was incredibly moved by this response, and gladly did so. As he finished a second time, he was astonished to hear their demands once more: 'Play it again!'
>
> He bowed to the audience, wiped a tear from his eye, and said, 'I have never felt more humbled. Truly it is the greatest wish of any musician to have such an appreciative audience. And I would dearly love to play it for you again, but, sadly, I must away to Tel Aviv, where I am due to give another concert this evening.'
>
> At this point a voice from the crowd was heard: 'You must stay here and play it again until you get it right.'

The refined classical musician turns out to be just another shlemiel who, not unlike Kafka's Abraham, imagines applause where there's only derision – only now the mockers are his fellow Jews. (It's why Israelis, despite their rep for bad manners, will never engage in sexual intercourse on the street for fear that a passer-by may stop to point out they're doing it wrong.)

Clearly, then, Israelis are no longer quite the same as those meek and terrified back-of-the-queue Jews we find in jokes about Soviet Russia ...

> A journalist asks a Pole, a Russian, an American and an Israeli the same question.
>
> He asks the Pole, 'Excuse me, sir, what is your opinion on the meat shortage?'
>
> The Pole replies, 'What is meat?'
>
> He asks the Russian, 'Excuse me, sir, what is your opinion on the meat shortage?'
>
> The Russian replies, 'What is an opinion?'

> He asks the American, 'Excuse me, sir, what is your opinion on the meat shortage?'
>
> The American replies, 'What is a shortage?'
>
> He then asks the Israeli, 'Excuse me, sir, what is your opinion on the meat shortage?'
>
> And the Israeli replies, 'What is "excuse me"?'

But still, there are some things you can't leave behind, and in Israel the Jewish propensity for a gallows sense of humour has not only been sustained, it's if anything intensified:

> Anat in Jerusalem hears on the news about a bombing in a popular cafe near the home of relatives in Tel Aviv. She calls in a panic and reaches her cousin, who assures her that the family's OK.
>
> 'And Yael?' Anat asks after the teenager who frequents that cafe.
>
> 'Oh, Yael,' says her mother reassuringly, 'Yael's fine. She's in Auschwitz.'

… Auschwitz being the fail-safe destination of Israeli school trips.

And the furrowed brow of the optimist hasn't gone away in Israel either:

> Things are going badly for Israel. The occupation, social unrest, the extreme right attacking the extreme left, the economy in a tailspin, inflation getting higher and immigrants flooding in from all over. Problems, problems, problems, but what to do? So the Knesset holds a special session to come up with a solution. After several hours of talk without progress, one member stands up and says, 'Quiet, everyone, I've got it, the solution to all our problems.'
>
> 'What?'
>
> 'We'll declare war on the United States.'
>
> Everyone is shouting at once: 'You're nuts! That's crazy!'
>
> 'Hear me out!' says the minister. 'We declare war. We lose. The United States does what she always does when she defeats a country. She rebuilds everything – our highways, airports, shipping ports, schools,

> hospitals, factories – and loans us money, and sends us food aid. Our problems would be over.'
>
> 'Sure,' says another member, '*if* we lose.'

So the punchlines haven't died, they've merely relocated:

> Four Israelis have arranged to meet in a cafe. For a long time, nobody says anything. Then, one man groans, 'Oy.'
>
> 'Oy vey,' says a second man.
>
> 'Nu,' says the third.
>
> At this, the fourth man gets up from his chair and says, 'If you guys don't stop talking politics, I'm leaving!'

Thus, even in 'Zion' Jews are still kvetching, and still sitting in the dark telling each other the lightbulb-less jokes that remain the most bearable form available for transmitting a traumatic history. Though it's a traumatic transmission that, sadly, doesn't stop there. For just as Diaspora Jews have passed their gallows sense of humour on to Jewish

Israelis, Jewish Israelis appear to have passed it on to … Palestinian Israelis.

No one conveys the tragic absurdity of that situation better than the very funny Palestinian-Israeli writer Sayed Kashua, whose novels remind one of Kafka and whose Israeli sitcom, *Arab Labour,* is partly inspired by *Seinfeld*. 'I use a lot of humour,' Kashua remarks, 'and I follow the saying that if you want to tell people the truth, you better make them laugh first, otherwise they will shoot you.' Tragically, he isn't joking. What he *is* doing is knowingly focusing attention on the way in which Palestinians have been inveigled into not only the traumatic aspects of Jewish history, but the mordant wit required to survive it. Thus the uncannily familiar tenor of Kashua's quintessentially outsider comic sensibility turns 'getting' his jokes into an implicit mode of acceptance of the very form of historical recognition that has so far, for Palestinians, been politically denied.

That said, the primary thing Jewish humour seems to have given Kashua is someone to blame for his people's sufferings:

> I couldn't lie any more to my kids, telling them that they are equal citizens in the state of Israel. They

> cannot be equal because in order to fit in and to be accepted and to be a citizen in Israel, you need a Jewish mother. So basically what I'm trying to tell my kids is just, it's their mother's fault and it's not my fault.*

A line that's both funny and, potentially, hopeful, if we recall Freud's remark that 'laughing at the same jokes is evidence of far-reaching psychic conformity.' For if two people or peoples can share a laugh, then mightn't it be possible for them to share other things as well?**

* From an interview with American NPR in 2016.

** That's the dream, but current reality does not reflect it. Thus in 2014 Kashua lost faith that he could change attitudes in Israel and so uprooted his family to the US – a despairing move reflected in his increasingly sober weekly columns for the Israeli newspaper *Haaretz*. 'To have humour,' he explained, 'you have to have hope.' And here we might again consider David Grossman's rendering of an Israeli comedian whose stand-up act is one of such unmitigated desperation that the Jewish joke, while still being pressed into the service of defence and attack, seems, in this novel, to have finally run out of gas. In an admiring review of the book in the *NYRB*, literary critic Stephen Greenblatt describes it as 'one of the least funny novels I have ever read'.

HOW DO YOU TELL THE DIFFERENCE BETWEEN LIFE AND DEATH?

'They tried to kill us, we survived, let's eat' is the mantra of a people whose history has required them to take crises in their stride. But even then, someone still needs to prepare the food:

> The dutiful Jewish son is sitting at his father's bedside. His father is near death.
>
> Father: 'Son.'
>
> Son: 'Yes, Dad.'
>
> Father (weakly): 'Son. That smell. Is your mother making my favourite cheesecake?'

Son: 'Yes, Dad.'

Father (even weaker): 'Ah, if I could just have one more piece of your mum's cheesecake. Would you get me a piece?'

Son: 'OK, Dad.'

(Son leaves and walks towards the kitchen. After a while the son returns and sits down next to his father again.)

Father: 'Is that you, son?'

Son: 'Yes, Dad.'

Father: 'Did you bring the cheesecake?'

Son: 'No, Dad.'

Father: 'Why? It's my dying wish!'

Son: 'Mum says the cake is for after the funeral.'

And someone still needs to pay for it:

> Moshe was on his deathbed and raised his head gently. 'Mendel, are you there?'
>
> 'Yes, Moshe, I am here.'
>
> A moment later Moshe said, 'Izzi, are you there?'
>
> His son, Izzi, assured him he was by his side.
>
> 'Jessica,' said the ailing Moshe, 'are you there?'
>
> 'I'm here, Poppa,' said Jessica, taking his hand.
>
> Moshe raised himself on his elbow. 'Then who the hell is minding the shop?'

Practicality rather than loftiness is the gutsy ghetto answer to life's ultimate situations:

> A Jewish grandmother is watching her grandchild playing on the beach when a huge wave comes and takes him out to sea. She pleads, 'Please, God, save my only grandson. I beg of you, bring him back.'
>
> A big wave comes and washes the boy back on to the beach, good as new.

> She looks up to heaven and says, 'He had a hat!'

It's about keeping your eye on the ball:

> An elderly Jewish man is sideswiped by a bicycle as he is trying to cross the street. After a long five or ten minutes, the ambulance comes and the paramedics put him on a stretcher and lift him into the ambulance, bumping him a bit. As they speed off to the hospital, one of the paramedics puts his hand on the old man's shoulder and asks, 'Are you comfortable?'
>
> The old man shrugs: 'I make a living.'

Without losing your critical powers:

> An old Jew gets run over by a car and lies down on the ground, bleeding. A priest happens to pass by and rushes over. As he sees the condition of the man, he says, 'Do you believe in the Father, the Son and the Holy Spirit?'
>
> Says the Jew: 'I'm dying and he's asking me riddles?'

(He's still got it.)

If the suggestion in that joke is that Judaism and Christianity draw a subtly different line between life and death, we can find a similar idea in an anecdote told by the author of the new constitution of post-apartheid South Africa, Justice Albie Sachs. During his time as an anti-apartheid campaigner, Sachs was the victim of a bomb that had been planted to kill him. When, after awaking in hospital, he realised he'd survived the blast, he was reminded of a Jewish joke:

> Hymie Cohen falls off a bike and as he gets up he makes the four motions of crossing himself and someone says, 'Hymie, I didn't know you were Catholic,' and he says, 'What do you mean, Catholic? Spectacles, testicles, wallet and watch.'

'The first thing Comrade Albie did,' the ANC declared afterwards, 'was reach for his balls!'*

And it's this unswervingly unspiritual response to catastrophe ('still got my testicles, now where's my hat?') that also gave Sachs hope for the future of his country: 'This is how we'll get our new South Africa, the Jewish joke, appealing to the African sense of storytelling.'

* Extracted from a talk given by Justice Albie Sachs in the University of Toronto, 2010.

And speaking of an unswervingly unspiritual response to catastrophe, here's a joke that got widely shared during the early days of the COVID-19 pandemic:

What do you want people to say at your funeral?

Imam: I hope they say I put the needs of others above my own.

Priest: I hope they say I extended my ministry beyond the walls of my church.

Rabbi: I hope they say, 'Look! He's moving!'

So for Jews, you could say, life is where it's at, death not so much ...

Cohen is on his deathbed and tells his kids to call a priest.

'But, but, but, Dad ...'

'Call the priest,' I said.

Wanting to honour his wishes, they call the priest. Cohen insists on converting. Then he gets better. Months go by, a year. He is back on form, going to synagogue, keeping kosher, observing the festivals. They muster the courage and ask him, 'That time on your deathbed, Dad, the conversion – what was that all about?'

'I just figured,' says Cohen, 'better one of them than one of us.'

HOW DO YOU TELL THE DIFFERENCE BETWEEN THE TRINITY AND THE ALMIGHTY?

If Christianity has had an ambivalent relationship to Judaism as both the generator and betrayer of its own creed, Judaism has been no less ambivalent about Christianity:

> Three proofs that Jesus was Jewish:
>
> 1. He went into his father's business.
>
> 2. He lived at home until the age of thirty-three.
>
> 3. He was sure his mother was a virgin, and his mother was convinced he was God.

Rendering it a source of pride on the one hand:

> A rabbi once asked his old friend, a priest, 'Could you ever be promoted within your Church?'
>
> The priest says, thoughtfully, 'Well, I could become a bishop.'
>
> The rabbi persists, 'And after that?'
>
> With a pause for consideration, the priest replies, 'Maybe I could be a cardinal, even.'
>
> 'And then?'
>
> After thinking for some time, the priest responds, 'Some day I may even rise to be the Pope.'
>
> But the rabbi is still not satisfied. 'And *then*?'
>
> With an air of incredulity, the priest cries, 'What more could I become? God Himself?'
>
> The rabbi says quietly, 'One of *our* boys made it.'

And a source of perplexity on the other:

A Jewish father was troubled by the way his son had turned out, and went to see his rabbi about it.

'I brought him up in the faith, gave him a very expensive bar mitzvah. Cost me a fortune to educate him. Then he tells me last week he has decided to become a Christian! Rabbi, where did I go wrong?'

'Funny you should come to me,' said the rabbi. 'Like you, I too brought my boy up in the faith, put him through university. Cost me a fortune, then one day he too tells me he has decided to become a Christian.'

'What did you do?' asked the father.

'I turned to God for the answer,' replied the rabbi.

'And what did he say?' pressed the father.

'God said, 'Funny you should come to *me* ...'

Although it's always nice when the two sides can come together:

About a century or two ago, the Pope decided that all the Jews had to leave Rome. Naturally there was a big uproar from the Jewish community. So the Pope made a deal. He would have a religious debate with a member of the Jewish community. If the Jew won, the Jews could stay. If the Pope won, the Jews would leave.

The Jews realised that they had no choice. They looked around for a champion who could defend their faith, but no one wanted to volunteer. It was too risky.

So they finally picked an old man named Moishe, who spent his life sweeping up after people, to represent them. Being old and poor, he had less to lose, so he agreed. He asked only for one addition to the debate. Not being used to saying very much as he cleaned up around the settlement, he asked that neither side be allowed to talk. The Pope agreed.

The day of the great debate came. Moishe and the Pope sat opposite each other for a full minute before the Pope raised his hand and showed three fingers. Moishe looked back at him and raised one finger. The Pope waved his fingers in a circle around his head. Moishe pointed to the ground where he sat. The Pope pulled out a wafer and a glass of wine. Moishe pulled out an apple. The Pope stood up and said, 'I give up. This man is too good. The Jews can stay.'

An hour later, the cardinals were all around the Pope asking him what had happened. The Pope said, 'First I held up three fingers to represent the Trinity. He responded by holding up one finger to remind me that there was still one God common to both our religions. Then I waved my finger around me to show him that God was all around us. He responded by pointing to the ground, showing that God was also right here with us. I pulled out the wine and the wafer to show that God absolves us from our sins. He pulled out an apple to remind me of original sin. He had an answer for everything. 'What could I do?'

Meanwhile, the Jewish community had crowded around Moishe, amazed that this old, almost feeble-minded man had done what all their scholars had insisted was impossible. 'What happened?' they asked.

'Well,' said Moishe, 'first he said to me that the Jews had three days to get out of here. I told him that not one of us was leaving. Then he told me that this whole city would be cleared of Jews. I let him know that we were staying right here.'

'And then?' asked a woman.

Moishe shrugged. 'We broke for lunch.'

Not that one should ever get blindsided by religion:

A priest, an imam and a rabbi are waiting one morning for a particularly slow group of golfers.

The rabbi fumes, 'What's with those guys? We must have been waiting for fifteen minutes!'

The imam chimes in, 'I've never seen such inept golf!'

The priest spies the green-keeper and calls him over. 'Hello, George. Do you have any idea what's wrong with that group ahead of us? They're rather slow, aren't they?'

The green-keeper replies, 'Oh, yes. That's a group of blind firemen. They lost their sight saving our clubhouse from a fire last year, so we always let them play whenever they like for free.'

> The group fall silent for a moment.
>
> The priest says, 'That's so sad. I will say a special prayer for them tonight.'
>
> The imam says, 'Good idea. I'm going to collect charity for them.'
>
> The rabbi says, 'They couldn't play at night?'

Though this is a joke in which Judaism retains its reputation as a worldly religion with an emphasis on practical (win-win) solutions, Jewish charity doesn't look too worthy when contrasted with the other religions out there on the golf course. Were you to hear this joke told by a non-Jew, therefore, you might find yourself worrying about the teller's motive – inviting the question: *is* it ever possible for someone who isn't Jewish to tell that kind of joke with a clear conscience ... *just* for a laugh?

And funnily enough, the blind golfers joke *is* related in a recent American novel, *To Rise Again at a Decent Hour* (2014), by the non-Jewish writer Joshua Ferris. The joke is told by the protagonist, a dentist who, like the dentist in *Seinfeld,* is hoping to convert to a version of what he understands to be Judaism primarily by means of telling Jewish jokes. And as in *Seinfeld* also, the dentist in the novel tells the joke poorly, with comically bad timing. He's accused of this by his unsmiling Jewish girlfriend:

> 'Why,' I said, 'is it anti-Semitic? It's not anti-Semitic, is it?'
>
> I was always paranoid that I might be saying something anti-Semitic.

Always paranoid? *That* sounds (Jewishly) familiar.

HOW DO YOU TELL THE DIFFERENCE BETWEEN MAN AND GOD?

While Jews don't accept the Christian belief that a man can also be a divinity, they're generally pretty good at spotting the human side of the godly:

> Moshe and Abe were partners in a very successful clothing factory. It had been in operation for many years and there wasn't much they didn't know about the shmatta business [rag trade]. One day, Moshe decided to take a trip to Rome.
>
> As Abe had many Catholic friends, he surprised Moshe by getting him an audience with none other than the Pope.

On Moshe's first day back at work after his Rome trip, Abe asked him, 'So, Moshe! What kind of a man is the Pope?'

'Hmm,' said Moshe, 'I would say he's a 44 regular.'

And when it comes to the Almighty, Jews tend to take things pretty personally too. As Sholom Aleichem's character Tevye complains to God:

'*You help complete strangers* – why *not me*?'

But then, when you know someone *that* long and still they turn a cold shoulder, it's hard to keep up the pretence that it *isn't* personal:

A journalist heard about a very old Jewish man who had been going to the Western Wall to pray twice a day, every day, for a long, long time, so she went to check it out. She went to the Western Wall and there he was, walking slowly up to the holy site. She watched him pray and after about forty-five minutes, when he turned to leave, using a cane and moving very slowly, she approached him for an interview.

'Pardon me, sir. What's your name?

'Morris Feinberg,' he replied.

'Sir, how long have you been coming to the Western Wall and praying?'

'For about sixty years.'

'Sixty years! That's amazing! What do you pray for?'

'I pray for peace between the Christians, Jews and the Muslims. I pray for all the wars and all the hatred to stop. I pray for all our children to grow up safely as responsible adults, and to love their fellow man.'

'How do you feel after doing this for sixty years?'

'Like I'm talking to a bloody wall.'

Jews have long since realised that God can be something of a let-down:

Moses is walking in the hills. He slips. Finding himself hanging between heaven and earth, he calls out: 'Is there anyone there?'

> A voice responds from above: 'Yes, I'm here. It's God. Don't worry, I'll save you.'
>
> Pause.
>
> Moses: 'Is there anyone else there?'

Which doesn't mean God is a bad guy. Rather, as Woody Allen has it, 'You know, if it turns out that there *is* a *God,* I don't think that *He's* evil. I think that the worst *you can say* about Him is that, basically, *He's an underachiever'**:

> A man brings some very fine material to a tailor and asks him to make a pair of trousers. When he comes back a week later, the trousers are not ready. Two weeks later, they are still not ready. Finally, after six weeks, the trousers are ready. The man tries them on. They fit perfectly. Nonetheless, when it comes time to pay, he can't resist a jibe at the tailor.
>
> 'You know,' he says, 'it took God only six days to make the world. And it took you six weeks to make just one pair of trousers.'

* From *Love and Death* (1975).

'Ah,' the tailor says. 'But look at this pair of trousers, and look at the world ...'

So the world was a bit of a rushed job. And if that explains the state of the world, then it also explains why man, as the product of just one day's work, isn't exactly an overachiever either:

Moishe is driving in Jerusalem. He's late for a meeting and he's looking and failing to find a parking place. In desperation, he turns towards heaven and says, 'Lord, if you find me a parking place, I promise that I'll eat only kosher, respect Shabbos and all the holidays.' Miraculously, a place opens up just in front of him. He turns his face up to heaven and says, 'Never mind, I just found one!'

Because when you get a shlemiel people, you're bound to get a shlimazel God:

There is this very pious Jew named Goldberg who always dreamed of winning the lottery. Every Sabbath, he'd go to synagogue and pray, 'God, I have been such a pious Jew all my life. What would be so bad if I won the lottery?'

But the lottery would come and Goldberg wouldn't win. Week after week, Goldberg would pray to win the lottery, but the lottery would come and Goldberg wouldn't win.

Finally, one Sabbath, Goldberg wails to the heavens and says, 'God, I have been so pious for so long, what do I have to do to win the lottery?'

And the heavens parted and the voice of God came down: 'Goldberg, meet me halfway. At least buy a ticket.'

Though never say the people don't at least *try*:

God: And remember, Moses, in the laws of keeping kosher, never cook a calf in its mother's milk. It is cruel.

Moses: Ohhhhhh! So you are saying we should never eat milk and meat together.

God: No, what I'm saying is, never cook a calf in its mother's milk.

Moses: Oh, Lord, forgive my ignorance! What you are really saying is we should wait six hours after eating meat to eat milk so the two are not in our stomachs.

God: No, Moses, what I'm saying is, don't cook a calf in its mother's milk!

Moses: Oh, Lord! Please don't strike me down for my stupidity! What you mean is we should have a separate set of dishes for milk and a separate set for meat and if we make a mistake we have to bury that dish outside ...

God: Ach, do whatever you want ...

Thus, just because the Jewish joke tends to be more logistical than spiritual, doesn't mean it's not serious – *even* about God. We might see it instead as an extension of the Jewish covenantal tradition that sees man in a partnership with God. Albeit a partnership that gives him, just as it gives God, the right to kvetch.

HOW DO YOU TELL THE DIFFERENCE BETWEEN A GOOD JOKE AND A BAD JOKE?

Jews get a lot of laughs out of God. But how godly is the joke?

In the Jewish joke, sometimes godliness is a source of wisdom:

> A Hasid comes to see his rabbi.
>
> 'Rabbi, I have had a dream in which I am the leader of three hundred Hasidim.'
>
> The rabbi replies: 'Come back when three hundred Hasidim have had a dream that you are their leader.'

Yet at other times it's a mockery of wisdom:

> A man was boasting about his rabbi: 'My rabbi is so modest about his piety. If he eats, it is only to hide from others the fact that he is fasting.'

Believers in comedy will often invoke the subversive power of joking to keep us honest by ridiculing the pretensions of the powerful. Yet we know, of course, that the joke is just as often a tool *of* the powerful to make laughing stocks of the weak. And that, as positions and perspectives constantly slip, slide and change, the identity of who is powerful and who weak is seldom set in stone. Thus, while we might be perfectly within our rights to send someone up one day, we may be abusing an unfair advantage if we do so the next. There are few utterances more flush with unchecked privilege, after all, than the sneering sound of someone insisting, in the face of another's hurt, that they really ought to be able to 'take a joke'.

It's the job of the comedian, therefore, to gauge what is and isn't 'fair game', which is another way of saying that a comic requires a sense of that other slippery concept: justice.* And they require it not least because by being as clear-eyed and non-prejudicial as possible about the times in which they're living, comedians can hone their sense of timing to make their acts that bit funnier:

> Every incredible achievement in human history was done with slaves. Every single thing where you go, 'How did they build those pyramids?' They just threw human death and suffering at them until they were finished ... Even today, how do we have this amazing micro-technology? Because the factory where they make them, they jump off the fucking roof because it's a nightmare in there. You really have a choice: you can have candles and horses and be a little kinder to each other, or let someone far away suffer immeasurably so you can leave a mean comment on YouTube.
> *Louis C.K.***

Of course, the (good) comedian doesn't imagine he's any better than the time he's telling. (The fact, for example, that Louis C.K. has tended to make self-

* Interpreting a verse from Ecclesiastes, 'And God will seek the pursued', the rabbis of the Talmud suggest that God is always shifting positions to take the side of the pursued over that of the pursuer, regardless of each figure's moral character or social identity.

** From his HBO stand-up special *Oh My God* (2013).

admonishments at his own moral failings a constant theme of his comedy was brutally revealed to be no laughing matter.*) But what the comedian possibly does get better than most is that no one can claim to be entirely innocent when they're laughing:

> A Nazi sees a Jew walking towards him.
>
> As the Jew passes by, the Nazi says 'Swine!'
>
> The Jew tips his hat and says, 'Cohen.'

Or:

> An old Jew was refused service in a restaurant.
>
> 'We don't serve Jews here,' said the waiter.
>
> 'Don't let that bother you,' replied the old man. 'I don't eat Jews.'

Neither of these jokes strikes me as laugh-out-loud funny. But if we see the punchline as mocking by

* On Nov 10 2017, in a letter in *The New York Times* responding to allegations by a number of female comics that he had sexually harassed them, C.K. confessed that 'these stories are true.'

resembling the original attempt at a put-down, we can see the joke as a means of showing how a lousy sense of humour can always get its comeuppance.

What typifies a lousy sense of humour? I'd say it's a failure to understand the material it's working with. And by material I mean *words,* as slippery as any banana skin:

> I had dinner with my father last night, and I made a classic Freudian slip. I meant to say, 'Please pass the salt,' but it came out, 'You putz, you ruined my childhood!' *Jonathan Katz*

Words have a funny habit of turning their sense around to make the teller of the joke the butt of the joke. It's the reason why most jokes in circulation appear un-authored, as if they'd erupted autonomously out of our everyday language, laying waste to common sense. Indeed, it's precisely because jokes appear disparaging of anything so proprietorial as authorship or beard-stroking authority that they're broadly untroubled by issues of copyright (hence why I can raid other people's joke-book collections for favourite examples in my own). So are our jokes then evidence that our words may be laughing *at* us? In which case, language would be just like the God who laughs when you tell Him your plans – the God who, as Heinrich Heine intimated, is nothing if not an ironist.*

Perhaps the difference between a bad and a good joke, then, is not unlike the difference between sarcasm and irony. Sarcasm pokes fun without any notion that there may be something misunderstood or unrecognised about the object of its derision (I'm so *obviously* right about this).** Irony, though, gestures towards the unknown and unknowable, getting laughs precisely at the point where other, more direct, forms of representation have reached their limits. Hence if sarcasm suggests a know-it-all attitude, irony, *pace* Socrates,*** finds the funniness where it *knows it knows nothing*:

> Moskowitz and Finkelstein were in a cafeteria, drinking tea.

* The German romantic poet Heinrich Heine (1797–1856), who was born into a Jewish family but later converted to Lutheranism (which didn't prevent his becoming the target of anti-Semitic attacks and subsequently Nazi demonisation), attested to 'God's irony' and 'the irony of the great poet of the world stage up there'.

** Though I align it for the sake of argument with nominally 'bad' humour here, I don't deny that sarcasm is often merited, nor that it can be extremely funny.

*** The Greek philosopher identified by Kierkegaard as the world's greatest ironist.

Moskowitz studied his cup and said with a sigh, 'Ah, my friend, life is like a cup of tea.'

Finkelstein considered that for a moment and then said, 'But why is life like a cup of tea?'

Moskowitz replied, 'How should I know? Am I a philosopher?'

HOW DO YOU TELL THE DIFFERENCE BETWEEN COMEDY AND THEOLOGY?

One common rendering of today's typically religious person is someone with so many sacred cows that they're constantly taking offence. A comedian, on the other hand, in the popular imagination, is someone for whom nothing is sacred – it's someone who gives offence rather than taking it. And yet if there's one thing that *can* be guaranteed to offend comedians, it's sacred cows. Be they religious pieties, social snobberies or political correctnesses, sacred cows are like red flags to the comedian's bull. In fact, they attack them with such missionary zeal, it's almost as if some sacred cow of their own was driving their iconoclasm. So what, we might ask, is the comedian's sacred cow?

Back in the shtetl, Moishe was in his bed, dying. They brought him fresh milk from the cow to help him feel less parched, but he was too weak to get out any words. Maybe, his daughter thought, some spirits could help revive him. She put a little whisky in with the milk and gave it to him. Moishe shot bolt upright in bed and said his immortal last words: 'Don't sell the cow!'

Okay, okay, so that's not the comedian's sacred cow ...

A rabbinical student is about to set off on his first job in a far-flung community away from everyone he knows. He asks his own rabbi, a famous scholar of the Talmud, for some final words of wisdom before he leaves.

'Life is a fountain,' his teacher tells him. The young rabbi is moved by the profundity of those words as he embarks on a hugely successful career.

Many years later, hearing his teacher is dying, he visits him one last time. 'Rabbi,' he says, 'I have one question for you. For so many years now, whenever I've been sad or confused, I've told myself that "life

> is a fountain" – your words of precious wisdom – and that thought has always helped me get through even the worst of times, and yet truth be told I have never really understood what that adage means. Please can you tell me: *why* is life a fountain?'
>
> 'All right,' says his rabbi wearily, 'so life *isn't* a fountain.'

Sometimes, that is, a joke is just a joke. And not only that: the acceptance of chance, accident and contingency ought to even be considered a condition of possibility of the joke. For while theologians are tempted to see everything as part of a divine plan, comics find their freedom in the right to be *un*serious – and in the distinctly profane enjoyment to be had in the spectacle of a serious man, a man in a business suit, who is walking determinedly to work when, for no apparent reason, he slips and finds himself flat out on the ground.

In admitting that, however, can we ever be *entirely* sure when a slip is just a slip, a joke just a joke, a kiss just a kiss, or even a cigar just a cigar? It was Søren Kierkegaard, after all, one of the greatest modern theologians, who, when faced with the hapless man in a business suit, could not but detect the divine comedy at work: '[When] a tile from the roof falls down and strikes him dead, then I laugh heartily.'* And whether or not you're tempted to join him in that confounding laughter, you can hardly fail to notice the irony or self-contradiction of an essay strung together by jokes attempting to make a case for the joke as that which radically refuses the kind of meaning or determination that it might expect to receive in an essayistic interpretation.

Thus, while there's some truth to the idea that a comedian is someone prepared to transgress laws, rules and reasons – or do *anything* for a laugh – there are nonetheless limits to the liberties any such comedian will likely take. Most comedians, for example, *do* have lines they won't cross or things they feel they can't say without doing damage to the funny. As Jerry Seinfeld tells the priest, he's offended by his dentist's conversion, not as a Jewish person but as a *comedian*. Because not everyone gets to tell the same jokes as well as each other. His dentist, Jerry thinks, is acquiring 'joke-telling immunity' by underhand means – he's converting to Judaism not as a creed, but as a sense of humour. And you can't convert to a sense of humour, can you? I mean, much as he'd love to, Jerry doesn't get to tell all of Richard Pryor's jokes.

* *Either/Or, Part 1* (1843).

You can't *convert* to blackness, no more than you can to whiteness:

> People are always introducing me as 'Sarah Silverman, Jewish comedienne'. I *hate* that! I wish people would see me for who I really am – I'm *white*!

Or can you?

HOW DO YOU TELL THE DIFFERENCE BETWEEN JEWISH AND GOYISH?

Here's how Lenny Bruce tells it:

> Dig: I'm Jewish. Count Basie's Jewish. Ray Charles is Jewish. Eddie Cantor's goyish. B'nai B'rith is goyish; Hadassah, Jewish. If you live in New York or any other big city, you are Jewish. It doesn't matter even if you're Catholic; if you live in New York, you're Jewish. If you live in Butte, Montana, you're going to be goyish even if you're Jewish.
>
> Kool-Aid is goyish. Evaporated milk is goyish, even if the Jews invented it. Chocolate is Jewish and fudge is goyish. Fruit salad is Jewish. Lime jello is goyish. Lime soda is very goyish.

> All Drake's Cakes are goyish. Pumpernickel is Jewish and, as you know, white bread is very goyish. Instant potatoes, goyish. Black cherry soda's very Jewish, macaroons are very Jewish.
>
> Negroes are all Jews. Italians are all Jews. Irishmen who have rejected their religion are Jews. Mouths are very Jewish. And bosoms. Baton-twirling is very goyish.
>
> Underwear is definitely goyish. Balls are goyish. Titties are Jewish.
>
> *Celebrate* is a goyish word. *Observe* is a Jewish word. Mr and Mrs Walsh are celebrating Christmas with Major Thomas Moreland, USAF (ret.), while Mr and Mrs Bromberg observed Hanukkah with Goldie and Arthur Schindler from Kiamesha, New York.

Bruce, one suspects, almost *could* have got away with telling Richard Pryor's jokes.* For what he's suggesting in this sketch is a whole new way of telling the difference. Neither Jewish nor goyish are

* And vice versa. Richard Pryor once claimed to owe his career to Lenny Bruce: 'I played his record over and over, every night. It was him who said comedy wasn't about telling jokes – it was about telling the truth.'

absolute categories – everyone is who they are-*ish* – hence you can count yourself among the Jew-*ish* set of differences if you like Bruce's shtick and you laugh along with his jokes.

And it's on the same basis, presumably, that you can convert to blackness. Or to whiteness. Or to a sense of humour. In fact, why not go further still? Maybe converting to a sense of humour *is* the most authentic means of conversion. Because isn't it the moment when someone *gets* our jokes or finds the same things funny as we do that we *do*, implicitly, recognise them as one of our own kind? (Note that, before it found its way into the annals of Jewish joking, the whisky-mixing cow started out on an Irish dairy farm in a joke about a dying Mother Superior surrounded by nuns who were already showing their talent for serving more than one order of high spirits.)

And Bruce's sense of his own Jew-*ish* kind was the nervous kind, the vulnerable kind, the willing to show you're flawed, human and mortal kind. So he'd have likely agreed with Jerry's dentist about the sustaining power of humour. If, that is, Bruce *could* spot his own peeps everywhere, it's because he recognised something critical about the funny – how it's always got a hidden history of suffering buried somewhere inside it:

> A black man was reading a Yiddish newspaper on the New York subway.
>
> Someone stops and asks, 'Are you Jewish?'
>
> 'Oy gevalt,' he replies, 'that's the *last* thing I need.'

Since a sense of humour surely *is* what he needs, however, he's a man who makes perfect sense in the Jewish joke.

'Every black man,' the narrator of Paul Beatty's extremely funny novel *The Sellout* (2015) confesses, secretly thinks he can 'tell jokes' better than anyone else in the world. And we get from the novel why that is: because of the suffering, pain, powerlessness and diverted aggression and anger that goes into it. It's this, in fact, that comes into sharp focus at the conclusion of the novel, which winds up at a stand-up gig in which a black comedian admonishes the white couple in the front row for laughing at his jokes. In a reverse heckle that's completely serious, although the couple at first assume he must be joking, he tells them to 'get the fuck out!' because 'This is our thing!' The problem, this comedian implies, with the white people laughing along with his act, is that they don't really *get* what they're laughing at. And the same, naturally, may be true for the white people laughing along with Beatty's novel. Although the narrator's subsequent question – 'So what exactly is *our thing*?' – sounds a little more dubious than is the comedian about the rules of belonging. Which, arguably, was also Bruce's point: that just as joking is slippery, so must its recipients be. For while it's true that no joke can be for everyone – and the joke will always depend on someone being 'in' on it, and someone left out – stand-up, being very much a 'live' act, can have no guarantees in advance as to who, if anyone, will find it funny.

Not, it's important to add, that comedy is the *only* creative outlet for historical suffering:

> We've come from the same history – two thousand years of persecution – we've just expressed our sufferings differently. Blacks developed the blues. Jews complained – we just never thought of putting it to music. *Jon Stewart*

HOW DO YOU TELL THE DIFFERENCE BETWEEN SPORTING AND JOKING?

So let's return to the analogy we've spoken of between religious persons and comedians, which is starting now to make some sense – for if the religious person appears as one kind of extremist, the comedian appears as another. It was Lenny Bruce who led the way here by turning stand-up into something of an extreme sport. And thank heavens for that, because Jews, on the whole, aren't too good at sports:

> Yeshiva University decided to field a crew in the rowing race. Unfortunately, they lost race after race. They practised for hours every day, but never managed to come in any better than dead last.

> The chief rabbi finally decided to send Yankel to spy on the Harvard team. So Yankel goes to Cambridge and hid in the bullrushes off the Charles River, from where he carefully watched the Harvard team as they practised.
>
> Yankel finally returned to Yeshiva. 'I have figured out their secret,' he announced. 'They have eight guys rowing and only one guy shouting.'

Extreme talking, you could say, is the *aim* of the Jewish athlete:

> The rabbi was an avid golfer and played at every opportunity. He was so addicted to the game that if he didn't play he would get withdrawal symptoms. One Yom Kippur the rabbi thought to himself, 'What's it going to hurt if I go out during the recess and play a few rounds? Nobody will be the wiser, and I'll be back in time for services.'
>
> Sure enough, at the conclusion of the morning service, the rabbi snuck out of the synagogue and headed straight for the golf course. Looking down upon the scene were Moses and God.

> Moses said, 'Look how terrible – a Jew on Yom Kippur. And a rabbi besides!'
>
> God replied, 'Watch. I'm going to teach him a lesson.'
>
> Out on the course, the rabbi stepped up to the first tee. When he hit the ball, it careened off a tree, struck a rock, skipped across a pond and landed in the hole for a HOLE IN ONE!
>
> Seeing all this, Moses protested, 'God, this is how you're going to teach him a lesson? He got a hole in one!'
>
> 'Sure,' said God, 'but who's he going to tell?'

But if not being able to tell is the cruellest punishment for a Jew who's indulged his guilty pleasure, telling the things you *can't* tell is a guilty pleasure all of its own – as in the joke about the guy who goes to confession and tells the priest that after a lifetime of respectability he suddenly finds himself having an affair with two young married women half his age. When the priest urges him to seek Jesus' forgiveness he replies that he can't do that because he's Jewish. 'Then why on earth are you telling me?' 'I'm telling *everyone*.'

Or you need only consider the taboo-breaking excitement of a Lenny Bruce gig. In his major novel *Underworld* (1997), the American author Don DeLillo captures that atmosphere by imagining a scene in which Bruce is performing a set in California during the Cuban Missile Crisis. The set has just one 'joke', but it's one he tells over and over again to evermore nervous laughter:

'We're all gonna die!'

Hahahahahahahahahahahahahaha.

Darkness, death, war, the unknown, the unknowable – that's where the nervous laughter comes from. And both the Jewish person and the comedian are familiars here. Both know what it is to perform in front of hostile crowds, always with the aim of trying to get the audience on side. Both have felt the need to constantly adapt their acts and find a quick-fire response for the latest hecklers. And both also recognise the fatal consequences of not being approved of. Jews know this in their (funny) bones. And a bad night for a comedian is one when nobody finds their shtick funny. When that happens, the comedian will tell you, they 'died'.

And Finally …

HOW DO YOU TELL THE DIFFERENCE?

On Passover, Jews ask the question 'Why is this night different from all other nights?' But *is* it so different? Not in one respect, at least: asking why anything is different from anything else *isn't* especially unusual for Jews.

If Jews love anything, it's telling the difference. What's kosher or unkosher? Milky or meaty? Circumcised or uncircumcised? Thirst or diabetes? In yeshivas (religious schools), Jews study the Talmud and the law, always with an eye on how to tell the minutest distinctions between seemingly similar things. Sometimes the difference simply comes down to how you ask the question:

> Two yeshiva students, Yankel and Moshe, discuss whether it is permitted to smoke while learning Torah. They disagree. Yankel says, 'I will go and ask the rabbi.'
>
> Yankel: 'Rabbi, is it permitted to smoke while learning Torah?'
>
> Rabbi states in a severe tone: 'No!'
>
> Moshe: 'Rabbi, let me ask you another question. May we learn Torah while we smoke?'
>
> Rabbi, benign: 'Yes, of course!'

But at other times differences are maintained far more strictly:

> A modern, orthodox Jewish couple, preparing for a religious wedding, meet with their rabbi. The rabbi asks if they have any last questions before they leave.
>
> The man asks, 'Rabbi, we realise it's tradition for men to dance with men, and women to dance with women, at the reception. But we'd like your permission to dance together.'

'Absolutely not,' says the rabbi. 'It's immodest. Men and women always dance separately.'

'So after the ceremony I can't even dance with my own wife?'

'No,' answered the rabbi. 'It's forbidden.'

'Well, OK,' says the man, 'what about sex? Can we finally have sex?'

'Of course!' replies the rabbi. 'Sex is a mitzvah within marriage.'

'What about different positions?' asks the man.

'No problem,' says the rabbi. 'It's a mitzvah!'

'Woman on top?' the man asks.

'Sure,' says the rabbi. 'Go for it!'

'Doggy style?'

'Sure! Another mitzvah!'

'On the kitchen table?'

'Yes, yes! A mitzvah!'

'Can we do it standing up?'

'No,' says the rabbi.

'Why not?' asks the man.

'It could lead to dancing!'

This obsession with telling the difference forms a big part of Alexander Portnoy's complaint about a family endlessly invested in keeping up with the Cohens and telling their difference from the Joneses – not to mention their effort to keep up with the Joneses and tell their difference from the Cohens. And it was precisely this kind of point-scoring that Freud also identified and called 'the narcissism of small differences' (show-off). Lenny Bruce, meanwhile, tells the difference between Jewish and goyish differently – but still, the point is he *tells* it.

However if 'How do you tell the difference?' is the Jewish question par excellence, it's also, as we've seen, the standard question of any number of classical jokes. So isn't *that* telling? The joke we told earlier, for example, about how to tell the difference between a Jew and an anti-Semite ...

> The anti-Semite thinks the Jews are a despicable race, but Cohen? He's not too bad actually. Kushner? A stand-up guy. The Jew, on the other hand, believes his people are a light unto the nations, but Cohen? What a shmuck! Kushner? Don't get me started!

... is a joke that gains its humour from the fact that this difference turns out to be a surprisingly subtle one. Yet it's precisely the seeming smallness of the difference that shows us why the joke is Jewish rather than anti-Semitic. For while the anti-Semite may imagine that categories and people are so completely opposed that they have nothing whatsoever to do with each other, the Jewish joke understands that every self is fractured and run through with otherness. Everyone is split by something unassimilable or strange: the sense of difference within that puts each of us in an eternal double act with all others, including those others posing as ourselves. Consider, for instance, the words of Groucho Marx's Captain Spaulding in the film *Animal Crackers* (1930):

> Spaulding: Say, I used to know a fellow looked exactly like you, by the name of ... ah ... Emanuel Ravelli. Are you his brother?
>
> Ravelli: I'm Emanuel Ravelli.
>
> Spaulding: You're Emanuel Ravelli?
>
> Ravelli: I'm Emanuel Ravelli.
>
> Spaulding: Well, no wonder you look like him ... But I still insist, there is a resemblance.

What Jewish jokes consistently reveal is much the same: there's always some sort of doubleness at play in Jewish identity, just as there is in joking itself, or in language itself. And it's this doubleness that makes even the truth a kind of lie ('You say you're going to Minsk and I happen to know you really *are* going to Minsk, so why are you lying to me?'), which is probably what's so funny about the truth – the reason why it tickles us.

So what, then, *is* the difference between a Jewish person and a comedian? Is it simply a question of distinguishing the funny peculiar from the funny ha ha? Or might it be that those two types of funny are as inseparable from each other as are Laurel and Hardy, Laverne and Shirley,* or any other shlemiel/shlimazel comedy double act? Besides, can we even *tell* if it's the fall guy or the straight guy who we're laughing at? What if the funny ha ha of the shlemiel's various pratfalls is really just a cover story for exposing how funny peculiar the supposedly 'straight guy' is?

Even Emanuel Ravelli is only *passing* as Emanuel Ravelli, after all. And even those things we would most dearly like to believe are unquestionable, universal, and completely unmarked by differences, have a tendency to mislead us:

> A non-Jewish maths teacher gets a job in a Jewish primary school.
>
> 'Are you concerned at all, since you're not Jewish yourself, about what it might be like teaching Jewish children?' the head teacher asks him.
>
> 'Not remotely,' says the teacher. 'I teach mathematics, and maths knows neither creed nor colour nor age

* Laverne and Shirley were the female co-stars of an American sitcom in the late 1970s to early 1980s, whose theme song opened, 'One, two, three, four, five, six, seven, eight, shlemiel, shlimazel ...'

nor gender – it's a universal language, and that's what makes it beautiful.'

Next day, the teacher teaches his first class. He draws a diagram on the blackboard and asks, 'What's two per cent?'

At which point a small boy in the front row opens out his palms, shrugs his shoulders and admits, 'You're right.'*

There are a great many things one could find to say about a young boy for whom mathematics is just another vernacular – a set of rules more practical than Platonic, a language of compromise, of give and take – but this joke is no more about mathematics than the joke about conversion is about Christianity, or the joke about queuing about communism. Rather, what all these Jewish jokes have in common is the conviction that universal claims, whether made in the name of religion, politics, science or even golf, always leave someone on the outside – someone who sees or hears things differently:

* Most jokes are best heard aloud, but this one especially.

> At Columbia University [this one's meant to be a true anecdote] the great linguist J. L. Austin once gave a lecture about language in which he explained how many languages employ the double negative to denote a positive – 'he is not unlike his sister', for example. 'But there exists no language in which the equivalent is true,' said Austin. 'There is no language that employs a double positive to make a negative.' At this point the philosopher Sidney Morgenbesser, sitting at the back of the lecture theatre, could be heard audibly scoffing, 'Yeah, yeah.'

Telling the difference, in other words, is a way of telling the truth *about* language – about how language is nothing *but* difference:

> Before the war, there was a great international Esperanto convention in Geneva. Esperanto scholars came from all over the world to give papers about, and to praise the idea of, an international language. Every country on earth was represented at the convention, and all the papers were given in Esperanto. After the long meeting was finally concluded, the great scholars wandered amiably along the corridors, and at last they felt free to talk casually among themselves in their international language: 'Nu, vos macht a yid?'

That, for those in the know, is a Yiddish 'how do you do'. Indeed Esperanto, another modern utopian dream of a universal system – in this case the dream of a universal language – was invented by a Polish Jew, L. L. Zamenhof.* So what are we to make of this? That only those who've been forced to *feel* their differences would dream up such hare-brained schemes for overcoming them ... ?

Possibly. And yet another Jewish philosopher, Jacques Derrida, doesn't think differences *can* be overcome. In fact, for Derrida, *all* language tells of difference (and even the word *difference* is one he inflects with a subtle semantic difference, spelling it 'différ*a*nce'). Here, accordingly, is his take on another classic Jewish joke:

> There are three people isolated on an island: a German citizen, a French citizen and a Jew, totally alone on this island. They don't know when they will leave the island, and it is boring.
>
> One of them says, 'Well, we should do something. We should do something, the three of us. Why don't we write something on the elephants?' There were a

* He was also responsible for writing the first published grammar of Yiddish.

number of elephants on the island. 'Everyone should write something on the elephants and then we could compare the styles and the national idioms,' and so on and so forth.

So the week after, the French one came, with a short, brilliant, witty essay on the sexual drive, or sexual appetite, of the elephants; very short, bright and brilliant essay, very, very superficial but very brilliant. Three months or three years after that, the German came with a heavy book on the ... let's say a very positive scientific book on the comparison between two kinds of species, with a very scientific title, endless title for a very positive scientific book on the elephants and the ecology of the elephants on the island. And the two of them asked the Jew, 'Well, when will you give us your book?'

'Wait, it's a very serious question. I need more time. I need more time.'

And they came again every year asking him for his book. Finally, after ten years, he came back with a book called 'The Elephant and the Jewish Question'.

Faced with the Jewish question, the question of difference itself, you always need to defer the answer (Derrida's 'différ*a*nce' is a composite of *difference* and *deferral*). You always need more time – so much time, in fact, that the Jewish question has made something of a shaggy dog story out of Jewish history:

> A young Jewish Frenchman brought his trousers to a tailor to have them altered. But by the next day France was occupied and it was too dangerous for Jews to appear in public. He hid underground. Soon enough he got involved in the Resistance. He eventually found his way to a boat and managed to escape the death camps of Europe. He settled in Israel. Ten years later he returned to France. While dressing, he reached into his jacket pocket and found the tailor's receipt for his trousers. He went to look for the tailor's shop and, amazingly, it was still there. He handed the tailor the receipt and asked, 'Are my trousers here?'
>
> 'Yes, of course,' said the tailor. 'Be ready next Tuesday.'

And yet the fact that the Jewish question, like the Jewish joke, endures, finding itself constantly repeated and recycled, as if no change in time or place or polity could make the blindest bit of difference, is also cause for a very Jewish kind of optimism:

> On the eve of the Day of Atonement, when all Jews are asked to seek forgiveness, two Jews who hate one another see each other in shul.
>
> One approaches the other and says, 'I wish for you everything that you wish for me.'
>
> The other replies, '*Already*, you're starting again?'

Never forget the Dropkin fart! For it's a joke to imagine the slate can be so easily wiped clean, just as it's a folly to presume that hostilities can be easily upended or differences simply overcome. And Jewish jokes all pay homage to such a world: a world that's complicated, non-homogeneous and full of irreconcilable differences.* But yeah, yeah, who says repetition *doesn't* make a difference? For though he may well have given up all hope of reconciliation because he finds his rival *un*bearable, each man in the Yom Kippur joke *does* briefly bear with the other

* Which is why the mainstreaming of Jewish humour in America especially should not be read as a trend towards universalising the joke, but should rather be understood the other way round: as a sign that more and more people may be feeling themselves outsiders.

man. And isn't it precisely that bearable/unbearable coming together in an intimate space, where one doesn't deny one's contradictions, confusions and differences, the dynamic that's at play in every good joke?

Just as tickling isn't stroking, laughter has something of aggression in it. But given the capacity of the funny to sustain differences, contradictions and uncertainties rather than seeking their obliteration, it's generally a better way of dealing with aggression than the alternatives. Thus, if Jews have, at certain points in their history, developed a particular appreciation for the funny side, it's likely because they've needed to mitigate the terrors of a world in which differences are no longer tolerated.* One

* Of course, there are plenty of Jews who neither joke nor get tickled by jokes. Such humourlessness merits its own historical explanation. It's not my purpose here to suggest one, but I will briefly draw attention to two different types of humourlessness hinted at in David Grossman's unfunny book about a comedian. One of these is fair game for the caustic stand-up: 'Have you ever seen a lefty laugh? ... they just can't see the humour in the situation.' You can poke fun at lefties, in other words, for their sententiousness, for their political correctness and for their implicit bad faith. But the novel also features a less partisan example: a disturbingly child-like looking older member of the audience who is always in earnest and who functions as a kind of conscience for the stand-up who will show no mercy to anyone *except* for this 'tiny woman' whom he dimly recalls from his own childhood as the other troubled kid on the block to become an object of derision and general punch-bag, but who never learned, as he did, to take on that sadism and use it as a tool of survival in a harsh and pitiless world.

need only look at the fate of 'the Jewish question' for example. The questions faced by post-Enlightenment Jews – 'What is the nature of your identity? What unites you as a group? What makes you different?' – would prove so incredibly dangerous because Jews were unable to answer them in a manner that could satisfy their interrogators. *What,* their interrogators wanted to know, were they hiding? After all, nothing provokes aggression like the feeling that those one finds funny (peculiar) must be sharing some sort of secret joke with each other (ha ha). And there's little worse than the thought that other people may be secretly or not so secretly laughing *at* us.

So it is that Jewish comedians have tended to cover their own backs with self-deprecation – because they *get* how nervous laughter is. Indeed, if Don DeLillo's Lenny Bruce inspires increasingly nervous laughs by saying 'We're all gonna die!' over and over again, the rabbi turned stand-up comedian Jackie Mason has been able to elicit equally manic laughter from his audiences by saying just one word over and over again:

> Jew. Jew. Jew. Jew. Jew.

Clearly there isn't, for Mason, all that much of a difference between a Jew and a joke. Not when it's possible to pare down his act to this one lonely word, saying it over and over until the whole room is in hysterics. Or, rather, all the Jews are laughing, and all the non-Jews are wondering what the hell the Jews are laughing about ('Hmmm, I always *knew* there was something funny about those peculiar people').

But why is the word *Jew* sometimes funny? For if the same 'joke' were told by a non-Jew, wouldn't a very different kind of audience be cracking up at it? The word or the joke would be exactly the same, but wouldn't that comedy now be a kind of hate speech? So who gets to decide that the word *Jew* is or isn't a joke? And how can you tell the difference between this joke when it's told by a Jewish comedian or an anti-Semitic one?

It's a version of the Jewish question that's been more or less asked by another (partly Jewish, though mostly lapsed Catholic) comedian, Louis C.K. 'Jew,' he notes, is 'the only word that is the polite thing to call a group of people and the slur for the same group ... It's the same word, just with a little stank on it, and it becomes a terrible thing to call a person.' So not unlike Mason, and to similarly irrepressible laughter,

C.K. has also tried out the good and the bad 'Jew' on audiences:

> Jew. *Jew.* Jew. *Jew.* Jew.

Though it's precisely because he enunciates it both ways that we needn't fear his Jewish joke is an anti-Semitic one.

However for me the most perfect illustration of this same Jewish 'joke' comes to us via the Twitter account of a British comedian, David Baddiel, whose profile identifies him quite simply:

And that seeming banality has the odd effect of functioning like a kind of Rorschach test for the online hoards: at once literal and confounding, it manages somehow to troll the trolls even before they've arrived at the scene. Indeed, Twitter profiles don't get much funnier. Thus, in his stand-up show *My Family: Not the Sitcom* (2016), Baddiel elicits roars of appreciative laughter from his audience when he projects an image of his Twitter by-line onto a large screen. No need, in other words, to follow convention and name his profession as a 'comedian' – by naming himself 'Jew' we can already tell he's a comedian. So it is that Jews, as another British comic, Sacha Baron Cohen, confirms, 'have a tendency to *become* comedians.'

To help us decipher this brainteaser, whereby the same word is both a joke and not a joke, both a cordiality and a slur, we might try telling the difference between the Jewish 'Jew' and the anti-Semitic 'Jew' this way: whereas an anti-Semite purports to know exactly what they mean when they say the word *Jew*, always with the intention of provoking derision or laughter, Jews couldn't tell you what *Jew* means, they just know it's funny. And what Jews find particularly funny about it is linked to the assumption that they must have some sort of insider's knowledge as to *why* it's funny. It's the notion that *they* know what the difference is that gets them rolling in the aisles. Because they haven't a clue! Thus knowing that you *don't* know what Jewish means is what makes you Jew-ish, just as the repeated discovery of what you consistently fail to know – especially when it's something you technically *do*: 'We're all gonna die!' – is unfailing fodder for the enduring joke. The ha ha may make us laugh, in other words, but it's the peculiar that makes us hysterical. Or, as the novelist Saul Bellow once put it:

> In Jewish stories laughter and trembling are so curiously intermingled that it is not easy to determine the relation of the two.*

Such a curious intermingling is bound to make for a lot of nervous laughs, lol. But that's not the whole of it. Failing to tell the difference between laughter and trembling also makes for something else: the shuddering sound of a laughter that, at certain points in life and history, does not quite tell its difference from a prayer.

PUNCHLINE
Oy vey! *Look* who thinks she knows she knows nothing.

* Quoted by Irving Howe in his introduction to *Jewish American Stories* (1977).

Index

Y

Z